CW01261213

Learning Morality, Inequalities, and Faith

Christian and Muslim schools have become important targets in families' and pupils' quests for new study opportunities and for securing a 'good life' in Tanzania. These schools combine secular education with the moral (self-)formation of young people, triggering new realignments of the field of education with interreligious coexistence and class formation in the country's urban centres. Hansjörg Dilger explores the emerging entanglements of faith, morality, and the educational market in Dar es Salaam, thereby shedding light on processes of religious institutionalisation and their individual and collective embodiment. By contextualising these dynamics through an analysis of the politics of Christian–Muslim relations in postcolonial Tanzania, this book shows how the field of education has shaped the positions of these highly diverse religious communities in diverging ways. In doing so, Dilger suggests that students' and teachers' religious experience and practice in faith-oriented schools are shaped by the search for socio-moral belonging as well as by the power relations and inequalities of an interconnected world.

HANSJÖRG DILGER is Professor of Social and Cultural Anthropology at Freie Universität Berlin. His research interests include the anthropology of religion and religious diversity, critical medical anthropology, and the study of global and transnational processes. He is co-editor of *Affective Trajectories: Religion and Emotion in African Cityscapes* (2020).

THE INTERNATIONAL AFRICAN LIBRARY

General editors

LESLIE BANK, *Human Sciences Research Council, South Africa*
HARRI ENGLUND, *University of Cambridge*
DEBORAH JAMES, *London School of Economics and Political Science*
ADELINE MASQUELIER, *Tulane University, Louisiana*
BENJAMIN SOARES, *University of Florida, Gainesville*

The International African Library is a major monograph series from the International African Institute. Theoretically informed ethnographies, and studies of social relations 'on the ground' which are sensitive to local cultural forms, have long been central to the Institute's publications programme. The IAL maintains this strength and extends it into new areas of contemporary concern, both practical and intellectual. It includes works focused on the linkages between local, national, and global levels of society; writings on political economy and power; studies at the interface of the socio-cultural and the environmental; analyses of the roles of religion, cosmology, and ritual in social organisation; and historical studies, especially those of a social, cultural, or interdisciplinary character.

For a list of titles published in the series, please see the end of the book.

Learning Morality, Inequalities, and Faith

Christian and Muslim Schools in Tanzania

Hansjörg Dilger
Freie Universität Berlin

International African Institute, London
and

CAMBRIDGE
UNIVERSITY PRESS

CAMBRIDGE
UNIVERSITY PRESS

University Printing House, Cambridge CB2 8BS, United Kingdom

One Liberty Plaza, 20th Floor, New York, NY 10006, USA

477 Williamstown Road, Port Melbourne, VIC 3207, Australia

314–321, 3rd Floor, Plot 3, Splendor Forum, Jasola District Centre, New Delhi – 110025, India

103 Penang Road, #05-06/07, Visioncrest Commercial, Singapore 238467

Cambridge University Press is part of the University of Cambridge.

It furthers the University's mission by disseminating knowledge in the pursuit of education, learning, and research at the highest international levels of excellence.

www.cambridge.org
Information on this title: www.cambridge.org/9781316514221
DOI: 10.1017/9781009082808

© Hansjörg Dilger 2022

This publication is in copyright. Subject to statutory exception and to the provisions of relevant collective licensing agreements, no reproduction of any part may take place without the written permission of Cambridge University Press.

First published 2022

A catalogue record for this publication is available from the British Library.

ISBN 978-1-316-51422-1 Hardback

Cambridge University Press has no responsibility for the persistence or accuracy of URLs for external or third-party internet websites referred to in this publication and does not guarantee that any content on such websites is, or will remain, accurate or appropriate.

Contents

List of Figures		*page* vi
Acknowledgements		viii
Note on Language Use		xii
1	Introduction: The Quest for a Good Life in Faith-Oriented Schools	1

Part I (Post)Colonial Politics of Religious Difference and Education

2	Entangled Histories of Religious Pluralism and Schooling	35
3	Staging and Governing Religious Difference in the Haven of Peace	64

Part II Moral Becoming and Educational Inequalities in Dar es Salaam

4	Market Orientation and Belonging in Neo-Pentecostal Schools	99
5	Marginality and Religious Difference in Islamic Seminaries	137
6	Privilege and Prayer in Catholic Schools	177
7	Conclusion: Politics, Inequalities, and Power in Religiously Diverse Fields	218
	References	236
	Index	259

Figures

2.1 Schools listed as CSSC schools in 2008 were concentrated in those regions (Arusha, Kilimanjaro, Mbeya, etc.) that were also 'favoured in colonial times'. *page* 56
3.1 Registration of Christian and Muslim entities at the MoHA (1980–2009). 79
3.2 Open files of Christian and Muslim entities at the MoHA (1980–2009). 80
3.3 Rejection or revocation of Christian and Muslim entities at the MoHA (1980–2009). 81
3.4 Refusal notification for the Life Bible church in Tanzania (Mbeya), dated 29 August 2000 ('This church is not desired in Tanzania'). 82
3.5 Christian and Muslim applications to the MoHA and RITA (1980–2009). 84
3.6 Photographs of (a) the cover of the EAMWS file at RITA and (b) the letter by A. S. Fundikira dated 4 April 1968. 91
4.1 'Make a true decision: keep your education in mind!' Mural in Dar es Salaam, 2010. 104
4.2 School buses and pupils in St Mary's International Primary School's inner yard, Dar es Salaam, 2009. 110
4.3 Pupils performing in Maasai and in national costumes at the morning assembly of St Mary's International Primary School, Dar es Salaam, 2009. 121
4.4 'Forward ever, backward never.' Mural on the perimeter wall of Kenton High School, 2010. 128
5.1 'Avoid bad groups [of people]!' Mural in Dar es Salaam, 2010. 152
5.2 Learning about ethical and unethical behaviours in class (class notes in English on the right). 153
5.3 Courtyard of the Al-Farouq Islamic Seminary for Boys as seen from one of the classrooms. 160

5.4	The location of the interview room in the Kipata Seminary for Girls (third floor, Kipata mosque).	169
6.1	The CSSC, government, and (international) partners fighting 'poverty', 'diseases', and 'illiteracy' in a CSSC leaflet.	180
6.2	The distribution of gifts to 'the orphans' during the St Joseph's school's charity trip.	194
6.3	A primary school pupil's drawing of the morning assembly grounds.	199

Acknowledgements

This book is the result of a long journey. Its completion has been possible only due to the generous support of multiple individuals, institutions, and organisations.

First and foremost, I would like to thank the six schools in Dar es Salaam that granted me permission to conduct fieldwork in their everyday learning and teaching environments. I express my heartfelt thanks to the students and teachers of the schools for sharing their experiences with me, and to the administrators and management for providing me with insights into the challenges and opportunities of their everyday work. The voices of these many individuals are rendered through pseudonyms in this book in order to protect their privacy. Thus, while I am not able to thank them by name, I hope that they will know how much I appreciated their assistance and our instructive conversations throughout my fieldwork.

Many individuals at different institutions and organisations in Dar es Salaam provided me with information and materials for my research. I thank especially the following persons (in the order in which I encountered them during my fieldwork): Sheik Issa Othman (chairman of the Mwinyi Baraka Islamic Foundation); Auxiliary Bishop Method Kilaini (Catholic Church in Tanzania; at the time, the auxiliary bishop of the Diocese of Dar es Salaam); Father Mauro (Embassy of the Vatican in Tanzania); Archbishop Dimitrios and Father Frumentius (Orthodox Church Diocese of Dar es Salaam, Tanzania); Dr Frederick C. Kigadye (Tanzania Episcopal Conference); Father Richard Kamenya (Anglican Church of Tanzania); Senior Pastor Abel Majaliwa and Pastor James Mlali (Dar es Salaam Pentecostal Church); Sheikh Suleiman Lolila and Mr Magubika (Baraza Kuu la Waislamu Tanzania); Sheikh Hassan Chizenga (Islamic Social Services Development); Mr Mwaisela (Christian Council of Tanzania); Bishop David Mwasota (Council of Pentecostal Churches of Tanzania); Dr Godwin Ndamugoba and Ms Anastasia Martin (Christian Social Services Commission, Tanzania); Yussuf (whose last name I unfortunately never asked for; Muslim Students Association,

University of Dar es Salaam); Sheikh Yahya, Mr Mohsen Ahmed, and Mr Khalid Sinani (Africa Muslims Agency, Tanzania); Mr Pazi Semili (Tanzania Muslim Professionals Organization; now Tanzania Muslim Professionals Association); Mr Godson Lema (Tanzania National Institute of Education); and the late Sister Sandra Stich (Baldegger Schwestern).

I am very grateful to Dr Gertrude Rwakatare, the late owner of the St Mary's schools network and late bishop of the Mikocheni B Assemblies of God, for granting me access to two of her schools and her church. Dr Rwakatare died in April 2020, when the Covid-19 pandemic started to spread across the world. I express my deep gratitude to the late Professor Mohabe Nyirabu from the Department of Political Science and Public Administration, University of Dar es Salaam. He assisted me generously with the process of obtaining research clearance through the university that allowed me to conduct fieldwork in Dar es Salaam. Last but not least, numerous employees of the Registration Insolvency and Trusteeship Agency, the Ministry of Home Affairs, the former Ministry of Education and Vocational Training (now the Ministry of Education, Science, Technology and Vocational Training), and the former Ministry of Health and Social Welfare (now the Ministry of Health, Community Development, Gender, Elders and Children) provided me with access to relevant information and documents. I want to thank all of them collectively.

My various stays in Dar es Salaam were not only professionally instructive but also personally enriching and fulfilling. Ouru Abuya and Monica Abuya (Mama Eddie) and their family have always welcomed me with open arms since my first field stay in Tanzania in 1995. Their children, whom I first met more than 25 years ago, have extended the same care for me as adults. Connecting with all of them regularly, on the phone or in person, made me feel that I belonged during my stay in Tanzania – and beyond. They also taught me much about how individual families have navigated Tanzania's highly stratified education system over the past decades, and how young people's educational trajectories are inseparably intertwined with whole families' and kinship networks' quests for a good life.

During my multiple stays in Dar es Salaam, Perisi Hamka's (Mama Jenny's) continued friendship and support were invaluable. Her brothers Charle, Philippo, and Jeremy Hamka became equally good friends, and Charle and Jeremy introduced me to the two Muslim schools of my study. Conny Becker and Christian Torkler invited me to stay with them in their house during my fieldwork in 2008. I thank them for wonderful dinners and conversations.

Many colleagues have provided inspiring feedback on previous presentations on my research or have shared their stimulating thoughts at discussions that were closely related to the topic of my book. Among them are Kelly Askew, Felicitas Becker, Daan Beekers, Marian Burchardt, Joel Cabrita, Fungai Chirongoma, Daniel Nilsson DeHanas, Deborah James, Marloes Janson, Omar Kasmani, Kai Kresse, Roman Loimeier, Kristina Mashimi, Dominik Mattes, Birgit Meyer, Mussa Muhoja, Jacob Olupoa, Dorothea Schulz, Nasima Selim, Anthony Simpson, Eva Spies, Amy Stambach, Noelle Sullivan, Abdulkader Tayob, Felician Tungaraza, Peter van der Veer, and Rijk van Dijk. I also want to thank the anonymous reviewers of the International African Library series, published by the International African Institute (IAI) and Cambridge University Press, for their insightful and constructive comments on an earlier draft of the manuscript.

The completion of this book would have been impossible without the writing residency at the Centro Incontri Umani in Ascona in 2015. I am deeply grateful to Angela Hobart for inviting me to write a first partial draft of the manuscript at the Centro and to David Napier for introducing me to the programme. While the beautiful scenery of Lake Maggiore contrasted starkly with the experiences of everyday life in urban Tanzania, it was exactly this contrast that helped me to think about how to write about socio-religious inequalities in a context that seems so removed from, yet is still closely connected to, people's everyday life in north-west Europe. The multiple conversations with Angela Hobart, Barbara Gerke, Thomas Shor, Ying Li, and Hideko Mitsui – whose sites of work and research are all located in the Asian context – made me think about how learning morality was unique in a religiously diverse city such as Dar es Salaam, where members of different faiths coexist largely peacefully despite long-standing historical divisions. In 2018, I was able to join Marisa Maza during her artist's residency funded by the DAAD (German Academic Exchange Service) at the Fundación Más Arte más Acción in Bogotá. I want to express my gratitude to Fernando Arias and Jonathan Colin for welcoming me into their home and for giving me the opportunity to write the first full draft of this book during our stay in Colombia.

I am grateful to Stephanie Kitchen at the IAI for guiding me graciously and efficiently through the editorial process. Harri Englund provided helpful feedback on earlier versions of the manuscript and gave important advice on how to address the readers' comments in my revisions. I thank Maria Marsh and Atifa Jiwa at Cambridge University Press for their interest in my work, and Judith Forshaw for the excellent copyediting of the final manuscript. Erin Martineau was a wonderful proofreader with a sharp eye for analytical and ethnographic details. Marisa Maza edited the photographs appearing in this book. Miles Irving redrew Figures 2.1, 3.1, 3.2, 3.3, and 3.5. I thank my former student assistants Karoline Buchner, Manuel Robert, Max Schnepf, and Jenny Rosenberg for literature reviews, formatting, and the preparation of graphs.

In all the years of becoming and remaining an anthropologist, my parents have been a constant source of encouragement, affection, and care. Their intellectual curiosity about other cultures and societies, our regular travels during my youth, and our life in Greece during my early childhood taught me not to take my own socialisation for granted. I am deeply grateful to them for supporting me to become the person I am today.

Marisa Maza, my life companion, has accompanied me through the multiple sites of this journey. In January 2021, when writing these acknowledgements, her mother, Josepha Maza, had just passed away. She and her family have always welcomed me during our stays in Madrid; they have included me in their laughter and joy as well as in their sorrow and mourning. I am grateful to Marisa for our shared life, her love and humour, and her continued faith in me.

Note on Language Use

While Kiswahili is Tanzania's national language and thus omnipresent in everyday interactions, the use of English is mandatory in secondary and tertiary education – and even at the primary level at English-medium private schools. Consequently, most of the interviews and more formalised conversations undertaken for this research were conducted and transcribed in English. However, numerous conversations and several interviews were also conducted in Kiswahili, not only in the Islamic seminaries, where English is taught less consistently, but also in informal conversations within and outside both Christian and Muslim schools where the use of Kiswahili expressed a certain level of trust and where it would have been awkward to communicate in English. Thus, the use of English versus Kiswahili mirrors not only the structural position of specific schools in Tanzania's stratified educational market, but also the social and cultural logics of language use in urban Tanzania. Quotes from interviews and conversations that were originally conducted in Kiswahili are translated into English, but terms that were originally used in English are set in italics. On the other hand, in some of the English translations I provide select original Kiswahili terms in order to illustrate the lexicological and metaphorical richness of the Kiswahili language when speaking about different nuances of learning and teaching values in urban Tanzania.

1 Introduction
The Quest for a Good Life in Faith-Oriented Schools

At the turn of the twenty-first century, families in rural and urban Tanzania began looking for new educational opportunities in faith-oriented schools. From 1969[1] until the (partial) privatisation of the educational sector in the mid-1990s, attending a government school had been perceived as foundational for securing a 'good life' (*maisha mazuri*), and potentially a job, in the East African country. But by the early 2000s, Christian private schools in particular had become a new destination in the quest for 'good education' and a means to the good life, for both individuals and the collective.

Tanzanian families' quest for a good life through faith-oriented education coincided with the emergence of a new market for Christian and Muslim[2] schools in the country's urban centres from the mid-1990s onwards. Thus, as in other parts of Africa, the number of often very expensive private (especially Christian) schools grew quickly, and these schools became increasingly opposed to the even larger number of 'poor-quality free schools' (Hunter 2019: 199) provided by the state.

In Tanzania, the newly established Christian schools became especially attractive for the growing urban middle classes from both Christian and Muslim backgrounds, as these groups increasingly turned their backs on government schooling in times of mass education and due to the widely perceived 'failure' of public schools. The Muslim schools, in contrast, most of which were weaker performing, catered to families from mainly poorer socio-economic – and exclusively Muslim – backgrounds. For these people, Muslim schools were often the only chance

---

[1] Tanzania's socialist Ujamaa period lasted from the late 1960s to the mid-1980s and included the nationalisation of all private and faith-oriented schools in 1969.
[2] I use the term 'Muslim schools' due to my analytical focus on students' and teachers' lived experiences and practices of their faith in educational settings. The terms 'Islamic schools' and 'Islamic seminaries' are used when I focus on the theological-normative frameworks of these schools. The Muslim schools of my study have a Sunni orientation and are different from the Shi'a- or Gülen-oriented schools in Dar es Salaam (see Dohrn 2014; 2017).

for their children to get a higher education. *All* these groups sought a moral and ethical orientation for their children in the changing urban economy, which they perceived as ambiguous and risky. Many families also invested significant amounts of money to secure a good life for their children through the best possible education (Phillips and Stambach 2008: 157ff.; for South Africa, see Hunter 2019: 13).

How have these transformations in Tanzania's educational sector, and in students' and teachers' quests for a good life, affected their school and professional trajectories? *Learning Morality, Inequalities, and Faith* sheds light on how 'new'[3] Christian and Muslim schools – established in the wake of privatisation – are sought by families and students due to their promise to combine high-quality education with the moral (self-) formation of young people. It also shows that the deregulation of Tanzania's educational sector in the early 1990s and the impact of transnational reform programmes addressing access to primary and secondary education since the early 2000s led to a realignment of faith-oriented schooling,[4] the embodiment of values, and social stratification in the neoliberal market economy. While these processes extend far beyond Tanzania's urban centres, cities such as Dar es Salaam have become a stage for a particular kind of 'assemblage' (cf. Ong and Collier 2004) in which postcolonial articulations of faith, class formation, the market, transnational educational policies, changing urban infrastructure, bodies, moralities, and subjectivities are being configured and reconfigured in relation to each other in unprecedented ways.

Dar es Salaam is a particularly compelling place for exploring all these dynamics. After the partial privatisation of the education sector in 1995, a wide range of Christian and Muslim actors became reinvolved in education in the city, and their schools reflect Dar es Salaam's enormous religious diversity and its multiple entanglements with historical and global processes. These schools include newly established educational

---

[3] In Tanzania, and in other parts of Africa, religious organisations have a long history of providing social services (Quarles van Ufford and Schoffeleers 1988; Comaroff and Comaroff 1991; 1997; Kaiser 1996; Hunt 1999), often in close collaboration with colonial governments (on the field of schooling, see Leurs et al. 2011: 14; Dilger 2013a: 460). Thus, the more recent engagements of Christian and Muslim actors with education have to be understood against the background of these historical precursors (see Chapter 2).

[4] I use the term 'faith-oriented' in order to emphasise the fact that the schools in my study often have only an implicit grounding in religious and/or denominational values and practices. Furthermore, the designation sets these schools apart from the field of 'faith-based development', to which most of them are only loosely linked beyond wider processes of urbanisation, privatisation, and class formation. At the same time, 'faith' is a distinguishing feature of these schools and plays an important role in the learning and teaching of values in their students' and teachers' everyday lives.

institutions of the former Catholic and Protestant mission churches, as well as former mission schools that were returned to the churches by the government in the wake of privatisation. They also comprise the educational projects of mosques and individuals from revivalist and/or transnationally promoted strands of Sunni Islam, whose position has been affected in the wake of 9/11 and the terrorist attacks in Tanzania and Kenya in 1998 (Dilger 2013a; 2017), and recently by the shifting power relations in Turkey (Dohrn 2014; 2017). Finally, some schools were established by individuals from the Evangelical spectrum, partly with connections to North America and Europe (see Stambach 2010a); these are often run like businesses, without an immediately recognisable denominational orientation. However, while some of these individually owned Christian schools were open to students from all religious backgrounds, their symbolism was often related to the neo-Pentecostal spectrum. One of the schools where I conducted research was run by a well-known Pentecostal leader and offered little religious content in its teaching. At the same time, the school used the pastor's religious title in its advertising and its slogan was widely recognised as a Pentecostal message of delivery and hope: *Acha kuteseka, K. High School ni jibu lako* (Stop suffering, K. High School is your answer). In an increasingly competitive urban educational landscape of public and private institutions, how faith-oriented schools categorised themselves was a matter of strategic self-positioning to attract new clients.

My analysis of students' and teachers' quests for a good life in this diverse landscape of Christian and Muslim schools in Dar es Salaam is shaped by three interrelated arguments. First, quests for a good life in faith-oriented schools include the search for 'moral meanings' (Fischer 2014: 5) with regard to strong academic performance and material success, but also as they relate to all other aspects of life involving questions 'about value, worth, virtue, what is good or bad, right or wrong' (Fischer 2014: 4–5). These 'ordinary ethics' (Lambek 2010) are made 'explicit' (Bochow et al. 2017: 451) in the formal value frameworks of Christian and Muslim schools and position such schools in relation to each other – but also in relation to government schools – in Tanzania's educational market. These values also become embodied – and modified or challenged – in the everyday interactions (Mattingly 2013) between and among students and teachers, who often perceive themselves as studying and working in 'morally superior' schools.

Second, notions of and aspirations for a good life in Tanzania's faith-oriented schools are 'imagined' (Weiss 2004) and embodied by students and teachers in relation to large-scale historical and political-economic forces. These forces include colonial and postcolonial histories of education and Christian–Muslim relations, alongside more recent histories of privatisation and faith-based development (Stambach 2010a), all of which have shaped the structural positions of Tanzania's Christian and Muslim schools in highly specific ways (Dilger 2013a). These various dynamics highlight the fact that faith-oriented schools – which are embedded in state-structured systems of education and learning, and are thus both state projects and religious projects in the context of transnational governance – mould everyday practices of moral becoming among Tanzania's young citizens in relation to religious belonging and marginalisation (see Loimeier 2007), social stratification, and larger urban and global transformations (Dilger 2017).

Third, this book provides a unique perspective on how the politics of Christian–Muslim difference and the formation of socio-economic inequalities in contemporary Tanzania have become deeply entrenched in students' and teachers' quests for a good life in faith-oriented schools. In particular, the book provides an understanding of the 'common' (Larkin and Meyer 2006: 286) – and simultaneously highly unequal – grounds on which the individual and collective quests for a good life in the country's Christian and Muslim schools are based. It demonstrates that 'faith', 'religion', and 'values', while being central to moral becoming in these schools, acquire their place in specific educational settings and individual lives only in their entwining with larger colonial and postcolonial histories of religious difference and education. The comparative angle shows that the articulation and rearticulation of moral and religious belonging in Christian and Muslim schools always 'involve broader interactional and institutional configurations of social power' (Altglas and Wood 2018: 3) and thus have implications for the study of religiously diverse settings more widely (Soares 2016: 679).

Let me introduce these various aspects through the vignette of Teresa King,[5] who visited different Christian seminaries during her education. While Teresa's schools were all located outside Dar es Salaam, her story is emblematic of the experiences of many other young people attending faith-oriented schools in the city.

Zooming in: Young People's Moral Agency and Striving

When I asked Teresa King for an interview about her schooling experiences, she had just enrolled in a Lutheran seminary in Moshi that

---

[5] In this book, all names of students, teachers, and school administrative staff are pseudonyms, except in those cases when they held a particularly prominent position or office and can therefore be understood as public figures.

typically admitted only pupils from the Lutheran church[6] and that charged comparatively high school fees. In 2010, Teresa's parents – who came from a relatively modest rural background – paid around 1.25 million Tanzanian shillings (TZH; about €600 at the time) in order to keep their daughter in school; this added significantly to their annual expenses, which also included the education fees for their other three children and some of their relatives' offspring.[7]

Teresa explained that the Lutheran seminary for girls had been the right choice for her. She was particularly positive about the 'systematic' approach that the school used in its teaching and management, as well as the way in which 'good morals' (*maadili mazuri*) were inculcated in the minds and bodies of both pupils and teachers. She also enjoyed the daily church attendance that had become an integral part of her rigid schedule, which started with the student-led morning prayers at 7 a.m. and ended with the (equally student-led) night prayers at 9.30 p.m. When I asked Teresa what she perceived to be the main difference between a government school and her Lutheran school, she claimed that her seminary's Christian framework ensured that its graduates would not go on to become involved in 'corrupt practices'. She also emphasised that the boarding school had a strong impact on her own life, which she described as having been lifted beyond the state of 'pure existence' (*kukaa tu*):

> I can say that the church school has helped me a lot in my faith. Every day you are told that you are not supposed to commit sin; you are given examples [of] how people get healed, those who were [mute] begin to speak, [and] this is how you know that God exists. [In a government school] I would be very different. I would go to school and when I return home I would attend the church service just like everyone else. But in [my] school there are young people like me; we organise meetings around issues of the church. These meetings build [you] [*zinakujenga*] – different from the government schools where I would just sit.

The language that Teresa employed reflects how other pupils in my study compared the education in a government school with that of a faith-oriented school. Thus, the verb '*kukaa*' means sitting, living, or dwelling in English and is reduced to the meaning of 'existence' by adding the adverb '*tu*' (just, only). The use of the verb '*kujenga*', in turn, emphasises the widely described capacity of faith-oriented schools to

---

[6] Teresa was an exception in this regard as she had been baptised in a Mennonite church.
[7] In 2009, the state limited tuition fees for government boarding schools to 70,000 TZH per year but allowed private schools to charge boarders up to TZH 700,000 per year. This amount could be increased even further for extra services such as special food or transportation. In 2014, the tuition fees for state-run secondary schools were abolished. However, parents have to 'purchase uniforms for school and sports activities, exercise books and pens and pay for the medical expenses of their children' (Godda 2018: 3).

'build' or 'make grow' (although it is usually left open what exactly is built in a particular context – for example, a person's individual faith, a community of people, or a sense of belonging).

In Teresa's case, her reference to her school's capacity to 'build' was related to her strong desire to find meaning in life, something that she had experienced since childhood. Her father especially was not interested in faith-oriented activities or church attendance of any sort. He particularly disliked those churches that, Teresa reported, employed '*kelele*' (yelling) or divisive speech in their services (for instance, the neo-Pentecostal churches). However, although Teresa's father tried to regulate his family's church attendance, his wife and his daughter were persistent in finding their own position within the denominational spectrum that was available to them in their rural area, and Teresa was baptised in the local Mennonite church in 2005.

At the time of our conversation in 2010, she was still happy to belong to the Mennonite church, stating that it had prepared her to pray in other Protestant churches. In fact, during our conversation, she told me that she had been 'saved' in the previous year, a sign of the ongoing Charismatic renewal of the former mission churches in the country (Smith McKinnon 2017: 94ff.). She ascribed this change not least to the influence of her school, although she simultaneously emphasised that her state of salvation was 'still weak' when compared with some of her fellow students. When I asked her what she meant by being 'saved' (*kuokoka*), she replied:

TK I love Jesus [*nampenda Yesu*]. If you want to be saved, you pray the prayer of confession [*sala ya toba*]; then you do the things God likes. I have been saved, but I do not pray for other people [when they are possessed]. I have been saved with my own self [*binafsi yangu*]. Those who pray for other people have *extraordinary power*, they can *drive [the] devil away*.
HD[8] How did you become saved?
TK Almost everybody at my school is saved, but to varying degrees. There are those who were born with God, they are *so close*, everything they say is God. *I am close to him*, but others [are closer]. This means that at school everybody is saved, everybody is a *good Christian* but to a differing *degree*. There are those with *extraordinary power*.

Teresa King's story shows how the religious context of her seminary shaped her stance towards faith and religion – and her understanding of 'good morals' – in particular ways. Like the students of Simpson's research in a Catholic boarding school in Zambia, whose quest for upward social mobility became connected to their conversion to fundamentalist Christianity (Simpson 1998), she became 'saved' upon entering her

---

[8] In all dialogue, 'HD' is the author, Hansjörg Dilger.

Lutheran seminary. At the same time, her narrative highlights that there is no *automatic* relationship between attending a faith-oriented school and the deepening of a person's existing faith or their conversion to another. The reorientation of Teresa's faith depended as much on the communicative 'co-presence' (Pels 2013 [1999]: 25ff.) of students and teachers in her Lutheran school as on her personal and family background and her continued commitment to the Mennonite faith.

Furthermore, Teresa King's story reflects the interrelatedness of moral becoming with the political-economic dimensions of faith-oriented schooling in Tanzania. Like many other families in the country since the mid- to late 1990s, her family has expended great effort to gather together the always rising school fees necessary to attend well-performing private (often Christian) schools. In a context where the constantly increasing expectations of the labour market have changed the value of educational degrees all over East Africa (Brown and Prince 2015: 31), students and their families struggle hard to find the best possible education. In Tanzania, while a diploma from one of the better-ranked secondary government schools (ordinary level or Form IV) was assumed to be sufficient for securing a job in the late 1990s, that qualification was perceived to be insufficient for finding employment, not to mention a 'good' job, in the 2010s. That the search for the best educational opportunities was often closely connected to the perceived moral framework of a school was emphasised by Teresa, who compared the academic success of church and government schools:

> These days, even government boarding schools allow their students to pray. But the church schools promote morals more strongly. If you look at the *performance* of all schools in Tanzania – the *top one hundred* are church schools, the next one hundred are government schools. This is why church schools teach morals [*maadili*] better than non-church schools [*shule ambazo sio za kanisa*].

Navigating the Educational Market: School Rankings and Socio-Religious Inequalities

The attraction of a specific school in Tanzania's educational market was reflected in, and at the same time produced by, the annual rankings published by the government, based on schools' performance in the national exams. As Teresa King's concluding statement made clear, these rankings were particularly important for the way in which people positioned 'government' (*serikali*) and 'church' (*kanisa*) schools in relation to each other. Even though these categories – or that of 'Islamic' (*kiislamu*) schools – are not officially used by the government in the statistical classification of schools (see Chapter 2), they shape public discourse on the educational landscape, and individual quests for a good school, to a significant extent. These rankings have therefore become a significant part of Tanzania's governance – and people's navigation – of the education sector, which is guided by the goals of efficiency, quality, and transparency and shapes both institutional practices and individual subjectivities and desires in comprehensive ways (see Shore and Wright 2015: 22).[9]

The 'life-orienting' capacities of these rankings in relation to the attractiveness of different types of schools became especially apparent in my conversation with Ms Martin, one of the officials of the Christian Social Services Commission of Tanzania (CSSC) in 2008.[10] The official provided me with the 2004–5 list of the country's 200 best-performing secondary schools, which contained only the name of the school and its rank. I asked her to identify, on the basis of the name of the school, to which category (government, church, or Islamic) each of them belonged.[11] The CSSC official's categorisation confirmed what has been claimed by the media and the public for several years: 'church' schools figured disproportionately highly in the rankings, with 41.5 per cent of the 200 top-performing secondary schools (a total of 83 schools). They were followed by 'government' schools, which comprised 20 per cent,

---

[9] What struck me during my study was that even very young children followed the national school rankings that were published annually by the National Examination Council of Tanzania (NECTA); they were also highly aware of the shifting positions of individual schools in the list of top-performing schools in the country. How quickly a school's position could change was illustrated by the St Joseph's Millennium Secondary School (Chapter 6), which was ranked number 3 and number 14 in 2011 and 2012, respectively, but fell to number 34 in 2013 (NECTA 2012; 2013). The Feza Boys' Secondary School, which was renowned among both Muslim and Christian students and teachers I encountered as one of the 'top schools' in Tanzania, fell from number 3 in 2012 to number 28 in 2013 (NECTA 2012; 2013). All these ups and downs affected the reputations of the schools and were carefully noted by my interlocutors and affected their educational choices.

[10] Interview with Anastasia Martin, Dar es Salaam, 10 August 2008. On the CSSC, see Chapter 2.

[11] My request was motivated by the fact that it is difficult to state exactly the number of faith-oriented schools in Tanzania as statistics do not count them separately (except for denominational schools that are categorised as 'seminaries'). In 2001, Lassibille and Tan (2001: 148) claimed that 'Christian schools run by the Catholic Church and the Evangelical [probably Evangelical-Lutheran] Church of Tanzania … make up about 16% of the country's secondary schools'. In contrast, Leurs et al. (2011: 3) refer to Tanzanian government figures that 'show that in 2003, of the 42 per cent of secondary schools that were privately run, 45 per cent were run by Christian and 12 per cent by Muslim organizations'. My own study found that, depending on the mode of counting, Tanzania's faith-oriented schools comprise 9–20 per cent of all secondary schools, with significantly fewer Muslim than Christian schools. See Chapter 3 for the challenges of grasping the classificatory and statistical aspects of faith-oriented schooling in Tanzania.

and other 'private for profit' schools (a category that may also include schools with religious orientation) at 13.5 per cent. 'Islamic' or 'Muslim' schools comprised only 3.5 per cent, while the remaining 21.5 per cent could not be placed in any of these categories by the CSSC official.

Reading this ranking against the three types of schools made salient a set of claims with which I had confronted the CSSC official and that I had heard voiced by various Christian actors – and by students such as Teresa King – in conversations about the quality of the *shule za kanisa* (also labelled *shule za dini*, or 'religious schools'). These included assertions of the alleged moral superiority and strong performance of Christian schools, the importance of good management and leadership for educating the future leaders of Tanzania (as allegedly practised in Christian schools), and the overall significance of Christian schools for a successful education sector. These assertions were coupled with statements about the alleged weakness and 'decline' of government schools, and Christian (and generally private) schools' struggles to attract more affluent students in order to sustain themselves through the payment of school fees. Most notably, there was a striking silence about 'Islamic' or 'Muslim' schools in all these comparative statements.

However, among revivalist Muslims, claims about the superiority of Christian education – which were widely shared by the mainstream media – were countered by a discourse that pointed to Muslims' historical marginalisation. According to scholars such as Said (nd[a]; nd[b]), both the poor performance of Muslim schools and the underrepresentation of Muslims in higher education and public employment in Tanzania (Ishumi 2006; Musoke 2006) are tied to: the historical marginalisation of Muslims and their education institutions in colonial Tanganyika, the politics of excluding Muslims in Tanzania's post-independence governments, an alleged conspiracy within government circles and ministries to bar Muslims from entering higher education or leading positions in the public sector, and an overarching alliance between the government and the (international) Christian churches that has allegedly ensured the dominance of Christians in all central areas of politics and society for more than a century. According to this discourse (see Chapters 2 and 3), the specific moral positions of students and teachers in faith-oriented schools – and their quests for a good life in the hierarchical educational system – are tied up with long-standing processes of social and economic (re)production that have perpetuated religious inequalities from colonial times.

In this book, I argue that the specifics of moral becoming in Dar es Salaam's faith-oriented schools gain meaning only when they consider how historical and political forces – and their continued interweaving with socio-religious and educational inequalities – are experienced and interpreted by students and teachers 'as complex multiscalar place-making projects' (Gille and Ó Riain 2002: 279) in specific schools. I also aim to explore how 'the negotiation of interconnected social actors across multiple scales' shapes moral becoming in both foreseeable and unexpected ways (ibid.: 279). In particular, during my research I was often struck by the way in which the relationship between processes of power and individual trajectories in the quest for a good life was not necessarily one-sided – and by the fact that many families sought every possible means to overcome structural hurdles in their quest for education. This also applied to Muslim families' struggles to improve their position in the educational market by scraping together school fees, often beyond their means, with the support of relatives, friends, or organisations within their reach.[12]

Ramadan Hamid provided one example of how even socio-economically deprived Muslim students actively navigate the educational market in their quest for a good life. Ramadan was 22 years old when I met him at an Islamic secondary school in Dar es Salaam in 2009. He was born on Mafia, an island south of Dar es Salaam; despite the fact that it has become a popular location for upmarket scuba-diving tourism, the island remains one of Tanzania's poorest districts. Due to the poor state of Mafia's educational system in the 1990s, when Ramadan was five years old his father, an employee at the national power company TANESCO, sent him to Zanzibar. There, Ramadan lived with his maternal aunt and completed public primary school and the first two levels of a government secondary school. In 2006, Ramadan's father moved him to Dar es Salaam. As Ramadan recalls, his chances of completing higher education in Zanzibar were slim and the academic achievements of the other children living with his aunt were comparatively poor. In Dar es Salaam, Ramadan was sent to the secondary school of the Africa Muslims Agency (see Chapter 5), and in 2009 he was about to complete Form III. Ramadan saw clear advantages in attending 'a private Islamic school', as he termed it. Along with the alleged better quality of private Islamic schools compared with public secondary schools, he referred to the teaching of moral religious values:

As Muslims we have to know the values and proper conduct of Islam [*maadili ya waislamu*]. Even if we learn secular things [*mambo ya secular*] in this school too, we must also receive guidance [*uongozi*] [for our lives]. Our friends, the Christians, are taught by other Christians too.

---

[12] However, the dynamics of upward social mobility in faith-oriented schools were certainly limited (see Chapters 4–6).

Overall, however, children and young people from the Christian field in particular were often able to adopt a proactive role in the educational market; this highlighted these pupils' often more privileged position in their quest for a good life as they navigated educational hierarchies. Tellingly, the CSSC official whom I have quoted above emphasised not only the choice available to middle- and upper-class parents and families in opting for a certain school – which in turn shaped the mindset of teachers and employees whose jobs and existence depended on these choices – but also the active role of young children in moulding their parents' and families' decisions, often to the benefit of the top-performing 'church' schools. Ms Martin said:

In church schools, teachers are responsible for their work. If you don't perform well, no parent will take their children to this school. It is like a business for attracting students so that your school can work. Government schools have a fixed budget and don't have to worry about the money. Even my own children have the vision of going to a church school because they will score a high division there.

Learning Values: An Embodied, Fluid, and Affective Process

How, then, are moral becoming and the embodiment of values defined in the context of faith-oriented schooling? Mattingly argues that the anthropology of moral self-formation has been defined by two different approaches. On the one hand, 'first-person' accounts of moral becoming foreground 'humans as "self-interpreting" moral beings whose perceptions, interpretations and actions help shape moral subjectivities in the singular as well as the collective' (Mattingly 2012: 171). On the other hand, 'post-structural' accounts of moral self-formation assume that the telos of ethical striving is predefined by 'powerful pre-existing moral codes and practices' (ibid.: 175) that become part of people's everyday lives through processes of institutional governance. While post-structural – and especially Foucauldian – approaches have the ability to analytically dissect institutional moral frameworks and the way in which people embody them through technologies of the self, the focus on the 'moral ordinary' highlights how individual subjects become capable of 'acting upon' these frameworks and inducing social change (ibid.: 179, 177; see also Mattingly 2014: 27).

With regard to the moral becoming of students and teachers in Dar es Salaam's faith-oriented schools, the focus on the 'moral ordinary' helps us understand how institutional value frameworks translate into the everyday experiences, reflections, and practices of students and teachers.

It also explains how students' and teachers' quests for a good life are located 'in the conjunction or movement between explicit local pronouncements and implicit local practices and circumstances' (Lambek 2010: 7). Thus, similar to a wide range of institutions in other African countries, Christian and Muslim schools in the city have become engaged in 'propagating ideas on how people should achieve or lead a good, prosperous, healthy and just life' (Bochow et al. 2017: 451). They aim at the explicit formulation of the ethical values they promote, which thus 'become "extraordinary" in their potential and significance' (Bochow et al. 2017: 451). They also engage in practices of teaching morals in order to instil their locally, nationally, and transnationally embedded value frameworks in the lives of both students and staff (Stambach 2010a; Dilger 2013a; 2017; Dohrn 2014; 2017).

In Dar es Salaam's faith-oriented schools, the explicitness of moral (self-) formation was most visible in the ways in which they positioned themselves – towards the wider public as well as the families and students they (intend to) serve – as unique providers of both secular and moral-ethical training. All of the schools in my research claimed to provide avenues for the cultivation of values among children and youths, and that, as a consequence, they were different from Tanzania's government schools, which – according to them – focused primarily on the teaching of secular subjects.[13] Furthermore, these schools formulated – and actively established – specific value frameworks for their students and staff that distinguished them from other faith-oriented educational institutions. For instance, Christian and Muslim schools made their ethical orientations explicit in mission statements, in public advertisements, in lessons on religion and/or morality, and in morning assemblies or in church or mosque services attached to the schools. In so doing, they positioned themselves as distinct moral and ethical spaces and as sites for instilling 'order and discipline' among young people (Simpson 2003: 37) within the wider cityscape of Dar es Salaam (Dilger 2013a; 2017; Dohrn 2014; 2017).

However, the dynamics of moral becoming in Dar es Salaam's faith-oriented schools involved 'ordinarisation', too: that is, the process of making 'ethical commitments' habitual 'in people's everyday lives' (Bochow et al. 2017: 451). Thus, the teaching and appropriation of values also happened implicitly at the schools I studied, for instance in

---

[13] These self-representations of Christian and Muslim schools do not imply that moral values are *not* taught in Tanzania's government schools. However, this aspect is not highlighted in public educational discourse, which associates faith-oriented schools with the teaching of 'good morals'. In contrast, government schools often have the reputation of teaching 'bad morals' to their students.

the more informal interactions between and among teachers and students during class breaks, in the schools' boarding sections, and during leisure time. Furthermore, children and young people enacted – and sometimes engaged with – multiple value frameworks to which they were exposed in their lives: of their school, the nation, the family, the urban environment, their peers at school, their friends at home, and so on. Thus, this book aims to uncover the various ways in which 'children actually behave in moral situations' (Woods 2013: 9) and how they were actively involved in making values ordinary through a wide range of verbal and non-verbal practices (see Rydstrøm 2001; 2003). It explores the agency of children and young people in the formation of their own local moral worlds (Hirschfeld 2002) and their active involvement in 'trying to live a life that one deems worthy, becoming the sort of person that one desires' (Fischer 2014: 2).

While both explicit (mostly discursive)[14] and implicit (embodied) aspects are seminal for understanding students' and teachers' moral becoming in Dar es Salaam's faith-oriented schools, the boundaries between these domains were porous and often dissolved altogether in the lifeworlds of students and teachers. Moreover, the pupils and staff of faith-oriented schools themselves rarely made an analytical or terminological distinction between explicit (or objectified) ethical frameworks and implicit (or embodied) moral practices. They referred instead to 'morality' or 'morals' (and often also to Kiswahili equivalents such as '*maadili*') as a marketing feature that distinguished their educational setting and the way of life actually practised by its staff and students. Similarly, the 'good life' (*maisha mazuri*) denoted a moral and affective orientation in their quest for a better future as well as the social reality in which they were already living. In this book, I therefore differentiate heuristically between the explicit (largely discursive) ethical frameworks of religiously oriented schools, on the one hand, and the way in which they become embodied in the implicit moral practices of students and teachers, on the other. At the same time, however, if not indicated otherwise, and in line with my interlocutors' own preferences, the terms 'morality' and 'moral values' refer both to institutional discourses on

---

[14] The explicitness and implicitness of moral becoming in faith-oriented schools correspond with Bourdieu's theory of cultural capital formation in institutional settings. According to Bourdieu (1986), cultural capital exists in the embodied state, in the objectified state, and in the institutionalised state. While I use the categories 'explicit/objectified' and 'implicit/embodied' interchangeably in this book, I am most interested in the way in which the boundaries between these categories become dissolved in students' and teachers' everyday quests for a good life and their embeddedness in larger historical contexts (see the following section).

ethical and moral values – and their manifestations in educational materials and didactic practices – and to their embodiment in the everyday practices and interactions at particular schools.

In particular, I argue that the everyday quests for a good life in Dar es Salaam's Christian and Muslim schools are shaped by three dimensions. First, the learning – and teaching – of values is an embodied process (Rydstrøm 2003; Swain 2003) that (re)orients students and teachers in relation to their schools and the wider world they inhabit. These values concern: consciousness of the self and others; body and dress; social status and difference; the presence of, and ways of engaging with, religious difference; notions of doing good and bad; the goals of learning and work; and relationships of affect and belonging. By reflecting on and embodying these values, students and teachers negotiate their moral becoming as the result of an intersubjective process that connects and cuts across the bodies and minds of the actors involved (Csordas 2008: 119). Furthermore, the process of learning values (re)orients students and teachers in specific ways to their socio-religious and socio-economic environments (a particular school, a certain discourse on the religious and moral self, a group or class of people, including their families, or the Tanzanian history and nation at large). At the same time, their embodiment of values contributes to the active building of socio-moral environments that are both locally 'emplaced' (Faubion 2011: 144) and simultaneously interwoven with national and transnational development, urban stratification, and class formation (cf. Fitzgerald 2017: 230–1; see also the following section).

Second, the embodiment of 'moral selfhood' (Winchester 2008: 1756) in Christian and Muslim schools is a situated process that includes both the non-conscious performance and the intentional – often pragmatic – enactment of values in everyday encounters. It is also a highly fluid process, one that is often fragmented and partly conflicted. In all these regards, the embodiment of values in faith-oriented schools is 'discontinuous' and 'partial', because moral and ethical commitments can shift over time (Lambek 2015: 309) and/or are performed for specific purposes. As Turner (2015: 59) argues, embodiment can refer to both a 'transitory, temporary, and partial experience' and 'a psychophysical transformation that generates a level of cognitive understanding and bodily knowing derived from intense experience that constitutes embodied knowledge'. The learning and embodiment of values in the schools of my study are therefore to be understood as practices that are characterised by ethical convictions, aspirations, and certainties as much as by 'contradictions, juxtapositions and impossible equations' (Schielke 2009: 178). Furthermore, moral becoming in religious settings can entail the ethical desire to establish 'continuity' in one's life (Mahmood 2001: 212) as well as the 'preparedness to reflect on the ambiguity of selfhood' (Janson 2015: 38).

Finally, I show how the learning and embodiment of values in Christian and Muslim schools involve an affective orientation that guides and shapes the intensity of students' and teachers' moral ways of being in the world. Throop (2012) explains that 'moral sentiments' refers to how people embody certain affective sensibilities and values in relation to their wider social and political environments. In contrast to short-term emotional sensations – which are felt in relation to specific situations in a person's life – moral sentiments can be conceived as 'affective dispositions' that 'refer to an individual's conscious anticipation of an event and justify the appearance of a corresponding response' (Reihling 2013: 31). Furthermore, such affective dynamics not only are relevant in the immediate context of the schools but also involve 'highly diversified forms of sensation, which point to the dissolution and opening of human experience … into its surrounding (urban) forms' (Dilger et al. 2020: 14). In the context of the schools of my study, it is important to highlight that moral sentiments have an ambiguous dimension: they not only cultivate attitudes and practices towards a 'good life' (cf. Robbins 2013), but also include instances of resentment – sensations of anger and frustration, for example – that may become central to students' and teachers' perceptions of situations of injustice and injury (Fassin 2013). This becomes relevant, for instance, in the context of some of the Islamic seminaries, where grievances about socio-religious inequalities in Tanzania – and their entwinement with the history of the colonial and postcolonial states – are particularly relevant (see Chapter 5).

Politics, History, and Inequalities: Moral Becoming in the Educational Market

While the moral becoming of individual actors always takes place in specific socio-historical and institutional settings (Mattingly 2012: 164), research on 'ordinary ethics' – or the 'moral ordinary' – says surprisingly little on how everyday moral experiences and practices are interlinked with larger processes of power and inequality. In his call on anthropologists to do more research on people's everyday struggles 'to do what they consider right or good', Lambek criticises the fact that the discipline has largely overlooked 'all this in favor of analyses that emphasize structure, power, and interest' (Lambek 2010: 1). Similarly, Mattingly argues that 'explanatory frameworks that emphasize the social and structural' have 'insufficient conceptual resources to reveal how individuals struggle to judge how to realize "best goods" in the singular circumstances that ordinary life presents them with' (Mattingly 2012: 179). According to this line of reasoning, power is reduced largely to a Foucauldian perspective on 'oppressive social structures' and the disciplining – and life-shaping – capacities of *institutional* forces (ibid.: 175, emphasis added).

In *Learning, Inequalities, and Faith*, I aim to show how students' and teachers' quests for a good life in Dar es Salaam's faith-oriented schools are both individual and political affairs. As Didier Fassin has argued, morality and ethics 'are often intimately linked with economic and political dimensions', while '[t]he ethical grounds on which agents justify their conduct are influenced by the moral climate of the time' (Fassin 2015: 2, 21). Consequently, anthropological investigations need to explore how specific ethical and moral issues have become 'at stake' under particular social and historical circumstances and how 'the boundaries between these two forms of life, ordinary and public, tend to be empirically blurred' (ibid.: 3). It is only in this way that anthropologists will be able to grasp how large-scale historical forces intersect in the bodies and moral becoming of individual actors in the specific places of their research.

In the faith-oriented schools of my study, students' and teachers' quests for a good life were inseparably entwined with the urban, national, and transnational settings in which the country's educational market has flourished since the mid-1990s. These political-economic contexts define these schools' structural and curricular frameworks, for instance through the implementation of global and national policies and reform agendas; they also implicate the schools in nation building (Coe 2005; Fumanti 2006; Phillips 2011), the governance and politics of religious diversity and difference, and the production and reproduction of the socio-political and socio-moral order at large (for example, through processes of urbanisation and class formation; see Lentz 2015). Furthermore, the mere existence of these faith-oriented schools – and their position in Tanzania's educational market today – is deeply entrenched in wider reconfigurations of the relationships between state, society, and the neoliberal economy in African countries over the last decades (Comaroff and Comaroff 2000; Mbembe 2001; Ferguson 2006). The (partial) withdrawal of postcolonial African states from the provision of social services to their citizens has triggered the entrance of a wide range of non-governmental – both secular and religious – actors into the field of education, all of which play a role in moulding children into 'good moral citizens'.

In order to understand how all these large-scale dynamics shape the quests for a good life in faith-oriented schools, it is important to turn to the anthropology of education and the study of religion and development in (and beyond) African settings. Since the early 2000s, anthropologists have adopted an increasingly experience- and practice-centred perspective, one that focuses on individual actors' voices and actions within the context of schooling and power (Bettie 2003).[15] In particular, they have explored the multiple ways in which power relations are implemented and enacted in specific schools on both the micro- and the macro-level (Collins 2009: 43) and increasingly also in transnational and global settings (Stambach 2014; Stambach and Ngwane 2011; Fichtner 2012). They have also analysed how the formation and reproduction of gender, class, and race identities in educational settings are connected to large-scale socio-economic transformations and inequalities (Stambach 2000; Hunter 2019). Furthermore, schools have been examined as sites of disciplinary power where dense webs of surveillance and counter-surveillance are established, and where norms and values that are central for the functioning of the surrounding society are inscribed in the bodies of pupils and teachers (Baumann 2004: 2; Chicharro-Saito 2008; Blum 2011: 132).

While the anthropology of schooling has flourished as a field in Africanist anthropology, fewer studies have focused on subject formation or the dynamics of moral becoming in faith-oriented schools,[16] although there is a growing number of ethnographies of Christian and Muslim education and learning in African settings. Many of these more recent studies draw attention to the divergent ambitions, strategies, and resources mobilised by individual religious schools and actors in implementing – as well as challenging, modifying, or subverting – official educational policies with regard to the standards and meanings of 'good' education and learning in a particular political context (Strayer 1973: 329–30). They also emphasise the need to analyse the generation

---

[15] These works differed from anthropological and sociological research on schooling during the 1960s and 1970s, which pursued a predominantly Marxist approach and established connections among political economy, class-based inequalities, and the articulation of cultural consciousness in schools. According to these studies, different forms of cultural, economic, and social capital reinforce differences in the socio-cultural order that are 'reflected in the conduct and organization of classrooms and curricula and assigned a causal role in perpetuating linguistic, cultural, and economic inequalities' (Willis 1977; Collins 2009: 34).

[16] According to Stambach (2006), anthropologists of schooling have subscribed largely to a secularisation paradigm that assumes education is governed by predominantly secular states. Within this framework, religion has been analysed, if not as a private affair, then as a challenge to state-led projects of subject formation through the provision of public education. This paradigm, and the public/private, religious/secular dichotomies that it presumes (Casanova 1992), may have prevented scholars from studying the relationship between religion and education systematically.

and transmission of religiously inflected knowledge and practice in faith-oriented educational settings as being closely intertwined with transnational religious networks of knowledge production, as well as with the political-economic agendas and bureaucratic processes of colonial and postcolonial states (Brenner 2001; Loimeier 2009). Finally, they shed light on these schools' cultural projects of 'civilization' and 'modernity' (Simpson 1998; 2003), 'enlightenment' and 'reform' (cf. Masquelier 1999: 235ff.), and the ways in which these projects have been embodied in many parts of Africa from the late nineteenth century to the present day.[17]

In this book, I argue that students' and teachers' moral becoming in faith-oriented schools in Dar es Salaam is closely intertwined with the specific religious and ideological – local and transnational – networks of individual schools that, to a large extent, shape their ethical frameworks and approaches to learning and teaching values (Stambach 2010a; Dohrn 2014; Dilger and Janson forthcoming 2022). Furthermore, their quests for a good life have been shaped by the partial withdrawal of the government from the provision of educational services; this has coincided with a new political role for and visibility of religious organisations in facilitating access to mass education among the country's citizens. The former mission churches in particular have thereby assumed a seat at the high table of public policy (Stambach 2006: 4), and they use educational projects as a means to intervene in the global apparatus of development and to lobby for the implementation of 'faith-friendly' policies and educational initiatives (ibid.: 3). And although the Muslim organisations that I discuss in this book operate on a significantly lower scale than their Christian counterparts – and struggle with a lack of resources as well as adversarial political forces in establishing their educational projects – revivalist Islamic actors approach education as a means for socio-political interventions too, and for launching heated moral debates about the marginal status of Muslims in Tanzanian society (Loimeier 2007: 139, 147; Dilger 2013a: 462ff.; Becker 2015: 118). These large-scale contexts and debates had a significant impact on the social and moral status of the schools of my study and became deeply engrained in their students' and teachers' quests for a good life and in the embodiment of their institutions' ethical frameworks.

---

[17] In particular, work on Qur'anic schools in West Africa has shown how religious knowledge becomes embodied in the lives of young Muslims through specific forms of discipline, ritual, and training (Ware 2014; Hoechner 2018). Such bodily formations may aim both at the preservation of indigenous knowledge and communal life and at the accommodation of societal change (Boyle 2004).

Towards a Comparative Study of Religiously Diverse Institutional Fields

Last but not least, the moral becoming of students and teachers in Dar es Salaam's Christian and Muslim schools has to be understood in the context of the highly unequal positions that these schools hold in the educational market and in Tanzanian society more widely. Thus, the overall privileged status of Christian schools and the structurally weak position of Muslim educational institutions are closely entwined with educational policies and the governance of religious difference during colonial and postcolonial times (see Chapters 2 and 3). More recently, Christian and Muslim schools have established relations with, and have secured resources from, religious bodies in Europe, North America and the Arab world. This had implications for the way in which the government attempted to regulate especially the activities of Muslim revivalist organisations in the public domain after the 1998 bombings in Dar es Salaam and Nairobi and after the events of 11 September 2001 (Ahmed 2009: 427; Dilger 2013a: 464). In all these regards, the educational engagements of Muslim and Christian actors cannot be separated from the growing pluralisation and politicisation of the religious field from the early 1990s onwards, with a broad range of actors being able to propagate their moral positions publicly via different media channels and new institutional interventions with local and transnational publics.[18]

Scholars of religion in Africa have long studied either diverse articulations of Christian ideas, practices, and organisations (Gifford 1998; 2004; Spear and Kimambo 1999; Meyer 2004; Maxwell 2006; Kirsch 2008; Marshall 2009) or the ways in which Muslims in Africa experience, perform, and navigate their social, cultural, and political environments (Loimeier 1997; 2013; Levtzion and Pouwels 2000; Schulz 2011; Kresse 2018).[19] Contact zones between the two religious fields – or between indigenous or 'traditional' religions and Christianity or Islam – have been studied primarily with regard to conversion, thereby highlighting not only biographical narratives and experiences of conversion from one religion to another (Langewiesche 2007; Scharrer 2007) but also the

---

[18] Public debates on the involvement of religion in politics have been articulated historically, too, for instance with regard to the banning of the East African Muslim Welfare Society by the postcolonial state (Heilman and Kaiser 2002: 701–2; Loimeier 2007: 141; see also Chapter 3).

[19] Even in edited collections that analytically compared the social and/or cultural position of different religious actors in postcolonial settings, individual contributions usually focused on Christianity, Islam, *or* 'traditional' or 'indigenous' religion (e.g. Hansen and Twaddle 1995; Schulz and Dilger 2013).

wider religious, political, and economic settings of individual experiences of cross- or intra-religious transitions (Comaroff and Comaroff 1986; 1991; Meyer 1999; Engelke 2004; Becker 2008; Scharrer 2013; Janson 2014; Leichtman 2015; Saurer 2018).[20]

Especially since the early 2000s, a new strand of scholarship has focused on the field of Christian–Muslim relations in Africa. Scholars of religious studies and theology have argued that Christians and Muslims have coexisted peacefully in large parts of the continent for a very long time (Ammah 2007: 152). According to these scholars, these generally good relations have been disturbed particularly by colonialism and the growth of both Islamic and Christian fundamentalist groups after independence (Ojo 2007; Rukyaa 2007; Frederiks 2010: 266–7). The 'offensive' preaching of some Christian leaders (Magesa 2007: 172), the mutual 'stereotyping' among both Christian and Muslim groups (Mwakimako 2007: 288), and global events such as 9/11 and other terrorist attacks are said to have caused a turn to 'fundamentalist religiosity ... which [is] characterised by an exclusivist and often antagonistic stance towards both more liberal representations of their own traditions and towards people of other religious persuasions' (Frederiks 2010: 267). Such tensions and conflicts – and the mutual intolerance that fosters them (Mwakimako 2007: 295–6) – can be overcome, according to these scholars, as religious teachings and scriptures contain opportunities for dialogue and ecumenical engagement that need to be built on in the face of poverty and conflict (Ammah 2007: 148–50; Frederiks 2010: 270).

Anthropologists and other scholars of religion have challenged such a narrative. They argue that both Christianity and Islam are inherently diverse religions that are shaped not only by the dynamics of internal differentiation but also by internal politics, discontinuities, moral ambivalence, and competition (Meyer 1998a; Engelke 2004; Schielke 2009; Janson 2014; 2015). Because religion is only one facet of social and cultural identities (Soares 2006: 3), the diversity and discontinuity within and across religious debates and practices are complicated further by political and economic processes and interests (Becker 2006; Obadare 2006; 2007). Similarly, the circulation and appropriation of new media technologies have led to the public contestation of religious 'authority' and 'truth', including transnationally (Eickelman and Piscatori 2004; see also Schulz 2006). Against this background, it is hard to imagine that Christian–Muslim relations in (and beyond) Africa will not *always*

---

[20] Processes of conversion also often remain partial or syncretic in that, for instance, adherents of Yoruba religion in Nigeria incorporate Islam or Christianity in their religious identities (Olupona 2011).

include contestation as well as appropriation and mutual learning (Soares 2006: 13) in the inherently messy entanglements of a globalising world.

Learning Morality, Inequalities, and Faith builds on Soares (2006) and Larkin and Meyer (2006), who all call for the study of Christian and Muslim ideas, practices, and organisations in sub-Saharan Africa as part of overarching historical configurations and within a single analytical framework. It contributes to the still comparatively small corpus of anthropological studies that try to understand how 'encounters' (Soares 2006) between Christians and Muslims – symbolic, discursive, or imagined, as well as physical, institutional, or spatial – are enacted and embodied.[21] As Larkin and Meyer (2006: 286) have remarked, Christian and Muslim revivalist organisations – and, I would add, other religious actors such as the Catholic church – 'share a great deal of common ground' in contemporary sub-Saharan Africa; while they often position themselves as competitors or opponents, they 'overlap strikingly in the procedures in which they have come to prominence, the practices on which they depend, and the social processes they set in motion' (ibid.: 286).

In this book, I analyse comparatively how Christian and Muslim actors' contemporary engagements with schooling in Dar es Salaam have led to, and were triggered by, the repositioning of 'faith' and 'religion' through wider societal and political-economic transformations. I focus on how these educational initiatives are experienced and enacted by students and teachers through the lens of 'learning values' in order to shed light on both the ethical frameworks of these schools and their everyday embodiments. In all these aspects, it is important to note that the 'common ground' (Larkin and Meyer 2006: 286) of Christian and Muslim interventions in the field of schooling in urban Tanzania refers not so much to the direct encounters between students and teachers of these faiths, although these do occur, especially in Christian schools where Muslim students and teachers are admitted and employed. Rather, the common, and highly unequal, ground of these schools is constituted through their mutually entangled positions in the histories of education and religious difference in colonial and postcolonial Tanganyika/Tanzania, and how these histories have shaped their shared

---

[21] Recent social scientific work that has explored Christian–Muslim encounters focuses especially on West Africa (Peel 2015; Janson 2016; Nolte et al. 2017; Obadare 2018). In Tanzania, there are few empirical studies that have explored Christians and Muslims in a joint analytical framework, but see Omari (1984), Ndaluka and Wijsen (2014), and Dilger (2013a; 2014a; 2014b; 2017).

project of 'learning values' under conditions of state regulation and the free market economy.

Against this background, a comparative focus on moral becoming in Christian and Muslim schools allows for a new understanding of the multiple practices of power that have shaped – and continue to shape – religiously diverse urban settings in East Africa, both in transnational contexts and through the local educational engagements of particular actors. In the conclusion to this book, I argue therefore that 'the similarities and differences, the overlaps and tensions, between Christian and Muslim actors and organizations in Africa' (Janson and Meyer 2016: 618) need to be understood in relation to the larger contexts of politics, inequalities, and power that have shaped the quests for a good life in religiously diverse fields in urban Africa over the last decades (Soares 2016: 679). This entails not only a broadening of perspectives with regard to exploring the long-standing histories of Christian and Muslim encounters in particular local contexts, but also the opening up of different methodological approaches, including the critical use of quantitative methods and of relevant statistical figures in our field sites (see Nolte et al. 2016), for analysing these mutual entanglements.

Studying Moral Becoming in Dar es Salaam's Christian and Muslim Schools

The ethnographic research on which this book is based was conducted in six faith-oriented schools in Dar es Salaam between 2008 and 2010 (ten months of fieldwork in total). Baumann and Sunier (2004) emphasise the importance of doing comparative fieldwork in educational settings in order to understand how schools become *distinct* cultural places where overarching values of a society or nation state are taught and embodied in specific ways. They argue that it is only through comparative field research that 'pointed contrasts and surprising internal consistencies' (ibid.: 21) become visible.

In a similar vein, the questions of my research evolved and were refined as I moved from one field site to the next, understanding that each of the schools in my sample had its particular narratives, routines, and practices that set it apart from – and simultaneously connected it to – the others. In some cases, specific topics became especially relevant during the time of my stay: for instance, class debates on the conduct of a charity event before Easter 2010 in the Catholic schools (Chapter 6). In other cases, these different thematic foci were representative of students' and teachers' long-standing concerns at a school and depended especially on the students' age and gender as well as on the socio-economic status of their school. Thus, while the Christian primary schools struggled with the playfulness of their pupils, both the Muslim and Christian secondary schools became a space for the negotiation of love relationships and individual styles of dress. Furthermore, the strict emphasis on speaking English was particularly prominent in the affluent Christian and Muslim schools whose students and teachers were usually fluent in the language. This differed from the structurally weaker Muslim seminary, where most informal conversations and part of the teaching were conducted in Kiswahili.

My selection of the six schools aimed to reflect this diversity by considering the following aspects.[22] First, the sample tried to represent the most prominent types of religious involvement in Dar es Salaam's educational sector from the mid-1990s onwards, while acknowledging the dominance of Christians in both education and the overall population.[23] Second, it points to different educational levels and socio-economic backgrounds in the city's educational market. Thus, four of the schools operated on the secondary level (two Muslim, two Christian) and two on the primary level (both Christian). One of the secondary Muslim schools was run by the Africa Muslims Agency (AMA), the other by a reformist[24] mosque; both were gender-segregated schools (for boys and girls respectively). Two of the Christian schools (one primary, one secondary) were established privately by a neo-Pentecostal pastor, while the other two (one primary, one secondary) were originally Catholic missionary schools that had been nationalised during the Ujamaa period and then transferred back to the Catholic church in the early 2000s. The four Christian schools and the mosque-owned school catered to the upper middle classes and the lower middle classes respectively; the Catholic schools ranked highest socially. The AMA-owned school attracted mostly students from poorer families.

All these schools followed the same secular state curriculum and were subject to state standards for examination procedures. At the same time,

---

[22] However, the selection was also partly based on the mere accessibility of individual schools (see below).

[23] The Pew Forum estimates that the majority of Tanzania's population is Christian (60 per cent), 36 per cent are Muslim, and 2 per cent practise 'traditional religion' (US Department of State 2014; see also Chapter 3). These statistics are hotly contested in Tanzania (see Chapter 3).

[24] Many of the new Islamic organisations and mosques differentiated themselves – religiously and politically – from the national Muslim organisation BAKWATA, which was established in 1968 and is widely perceived as a government body (Loimeier 2009: 73). I refer to these organisations, as well as to the new generation of Christian (especially neo-Pentecostal) churches, as 'reformist' (or, alternatively, 'revivalist' or 'activist'), although they would not necessarily call themselves this (Dilger 2014b).

they were dedicated to teaching moral values and, in part, religious content, which was typically connected to an explicitly Christian or Muslim (though not necessarily denominational) framework. At the Muslim secondary schools, for example, religious knowledge was taught during Islamic Knowledge and Arabic classes, and there was an obligatory midday prayer in the on-site mosque. In the Catholic schools, religious knowledge was taught in Bible Knowledge or Divinity Studies classes and church attendance was mandatory; the Pentecostal schools had classes in *dini* ('religion') and/or 'Pastoral Programme Instruction'.

In each of these schools I conducted participant observation for three to four weeks,[25] focusing on one classroom per school, and held more than 70 interviews as well as numerous informal conversations with students, teachers, and administrators. The research also included a questionnaire on the socio-demographic profiles of students and their families and the students' expectations for the future, as well as a drawing project in one of the Catholic schools. To understand the schools in their wider contexts, I studied the six schools' institutional histories and their connections with various religious and non-religious actors (government ministries, faith-oriented development organisations, religious leaders) within and outside Dar es Salaam. Finally, I reviewed literature from secondary sources and archives, including articles in Kiswahili and English newspapers, statistical data, registration and policy documents, and aerial photographs documenting the transformation of urban space in the immediate neighbourhoods of the schools. The close attention to these larger socio-political contexts helped me understand how my study sites' position – or their mere existence – in the educational market has been shaped by often long-standing histories (Gille and Ó Riain 2002: 288).

Doing Research in a Setting of Politicised Religion

During my stay at the schools, my positionality as an ethnographic researcher was challenged in multiple ways. Power differentials were established by my position as a white, advanced researcher from a German university, and also by my age (see Barker and Smith 2001; Punch 2002). My daily presence in the classrooms – seated in the back rows, without actively contributing to teaching activities – helped

---

[25] Students and teachers in faith-oriented schools spend sometimes eight to ten hours per day in the schools, and in boarding sections even longer. The fieldwork therefore delivered substantial insights, even though it lasted 'only' several weeks in each institution.

establish rapport with the students. At the same time, it was important to build a relationship with the 'adult gatekeepers' (Punch 2002: 329),[26] and I complied with my expected social status by staying with the teachers during breaks and occasionally spending time with them outside school. Furthermore, my positionality as a middle-aged male researcher became relevant during my research at the Muslim girls' school, where staff paid careful attention to how I conducted one-on-one interviews with the students (see Chapter 5); it was also important in how male and female students responded differently about the subject of sexual relations in the Catholic and Muslim boys' secondary schools (see Chapters 5 and 6).

On another level, however, my positionality as a researcher was also shaped by the strong politicisation of religious differences in Dar es Salaam – and beyond. Thus, when I inquired at the Ministry of Education and Vocational Training about information concerning the status of religious instruction in public schooling, the employee – a self-declared Roman Catholic – asked me whether I was not 'afraid' of doing research in Muslim schools. If she were doing this research, she added, she would be concerned about 'taking sides'. Similarly, at a workshop on faith-based organisations (FBOs) in Germany in 2019, a (Christian) FBO practitioner asked me 'how I could compare these [Muslim] schools with Christian schools'. He insinuated that the Muslim schools of my study – which he obviously confused with Qur'anic schools that he associated with 'an anti-educational stance' – could not be compared with the successful Christian schools in Tanzania. Such questions prompted me to reflect on my status of doing research in the context of religiously diverse settings broadly, and specifically of anti-Muslim sentiments and the perception among Muslim revivalists in Tanzania that the state – and the international development community – were discriminating against them (Ndaluka 2014a: 82ff.).

Anthropologists have raised questions about how a researcher's religious commitments – or, alternatively, an agnostic or atheist stance – affect their understanding of religious practices and feelings and shape their position/positionality in the field. Is the non-religious researcher unable 'to take the religious part of the religion seriously' (van der Geest 1990: 596)? Does 'confessing' to being an atheist lead to reduced trust, or even outright rejection by a religious community (Blanes 2006: 228; Wiegele 2013)? Does an ethnographer's faith make them more

---

[26] In the neo-Pentecostal schools, some of the teachers were initially suspicious of my everyday presence in the classroom, which they associated with the visits of school inspectors (see Chapter 4). Notions of suspicion and mistrust in one of the Muslim seminaries are discussed later in this chapter.

sympathetic to 'the dilemmas, or visions, expressed in another' (Clough 2006: 278)? And can their religious commitment help reduce any emotional and intellectual distance with their interlocutors (McClutcheon 2006: 746)? Researchers need to understand how their multiple positionalities shape social relations and communication during ethnographic research on religion and religious difference (Blanes 2006: 223–5; DiCarlo 2013: 76; Mattes et al. 2019a; Mattes 2020).

During my research, I attended church services of various Christian communities associated with the schools I was studying. My Protestant upbringing in Germany, and my largely agnostic stance during my youth and adult years, had not prepared me for praying the 'Way of the Cross' in a Roman Catholic church or for participating in the highly emotional services of the neo-Pentecostal churches in Dar es Salaam.[27] Participating to a certain degree in some religious practices in these settings was a way to show respect for the faith and the feelings of my hosts (Blanes 2006: 229–30) – and it was also connected to my desire not to stand out in the crowd more than I already did due to my skin colour. However, sensations of discomfort or uncertainty are experienced not only by agnostic anthropologists but often also by church members themselves (DiCarlo 2013: 79; Mattes et al. 2019a). Religious or moral feelings may also vary among church attendees, and they are not necessarily judged for this (Blanes 2006: 229–30).

Doing research in a context of religious difference was therefore even more challenging for me at the Muslim schools and when engaging with interlocutors on the revivalist Muslim spectrum. Such troubles were only partly related to the often strongly moralistic world views that my interlocutors held with regard to gender, sexuality, and family life. I faced similar challenges in Catholic and neo-Pentecostal settings (see Van Klinken 2019: 67). Furthermore, I experienced some gatekeepers' 'delaying tactics', not only in Muslim contexts but also in Christian or government settings, when trying to gain access to information (see van de Bruinhorst 2007: 52). These delays were sometimes not even strategic, but rather connected to people's reluctance to accept the idea that an anthropologist might be curious about the (personal, political, financial) context of a certain research finding. However, I encountered particularly strong mistrust on the part of some of my Muslim interlocutors, not necessarily with regard to me as a person but often to other actors in society or in relation to 'life at large', which also included widespread perceptions of the West as 'anti-Muslim' (see Becker 2006: 596).

---

[27] However, I was more prepared for the latter due to my previous research in a neo-Pentecostal church in the city (Dilger 2007).

At the beginning of my fieldwork, notions of suspicion became visible when I attempted to establish access to several Muslim schools as field sites. I was aware that the research permit from the University of Dar es Salaam and the letter of introduction from the district officer were not sufficient for establishing trust in a context of potentially strong reservations towards state institutions. Thus, when I visited schools, I was always introduced by someone who was personally acquainted with some of the teachers or the headmaster – and my good knowledge of Kiswahili certainly helped open many doors in the field. But while I was generally well received by the schools I visited, not all of them wanted me to conduct research at their particular site. In one of the Islamic seminaries that I visited as a potential field site, I was quickly drawn into a conversation with two teachers who told me that the educational activities of Muslims were often suspected of leading to 'terrorism' (*ugaidi*). The teachers emphasised that they did not think that I personally held such views but that they 'just wanted to prepare me' for the questions that others with a certain 'bitterness' (*uchungu*) might have towards my project. Despite their reassuring words, however, a few days later I received a short text message from one of the teachers stating that the headmaster had declined my request to do research there.

During my fieldwork, I carefully avoided being drawn into – or starting – conversations about religion and politics in Tanzania. However, especially in the AMA boys' school, named Al-Farouq, I was repeatedly asked to adopt a position on the marginalisation and suppression of Muslims in Tanzania. On one occasion, I presented my research questions and methods to a group of teachers who listened carefully to my speech before raising questions about my deeper motivations for this study. One teacher in particular – who was known in the school for his committed demonstration of faith – asked about my position on the lumping together of Islam and terrorism in public discourse, and about my stance towards Islam 'in general'. I responded that I was hoping to show with my research that, as well as the widely known, highly ranked Christian schools, Muslim schools also played an important role in education in Tanzania. While the teacher was satisfied with my answer, he was keen to follow up on my subsequent point that a mutual understanding between Christians and Muslims required a deeper understanding of the viewpoints of Muslim students and teachers themselves. Before I could answer his question about what I – 'a researcher with an MA and PhD degree' – thought personally about Islam and Muslims, the other teachers in the room, who were seemingly embarrassed by his insistence, told their colleague that I 'had already responded'.

The students of Al-Farouq were also curious about my views on Islam and politics, even after I had completed my research. When I returned for a visit to the school several months later, I was received warmly by the students. One of them was quick to ask what had happened to the questionnaires that they had filled in the year before. Another student asked: 'How do you feel when you return to a school like Al-Farouq?' In that moment, I realised (again) that such questions were never asked by the pupils and teachers of Christian schools. The students' reaction also reiterated how strongly a public discourse that labelled Muslims as 'hostile' (*wabishi*) and 'violent' (*wajeuri*) shaped the young men's perceptions of themselves[28] – and simultaneously their perception of me as a white researcher from Germany, an earlier colonial power. I responded that I had 'locked away' the questionnaires in a place where they could be accessed only by me (as I had promised them) and that I felt 'welcomed' (*karibishwa*) by the students, 'as had also been the case in the preceding year'. The students did not persist with further questions about the research; instead, one of them asked whether I had ever eaten *ugali* or *makande*.[29] When I affirmed that I had, the young men seemed pleased and some of them laughed.

Back at my desk – struggling to bring my diverse research materials into a coherent narrative – I aimed to do justice to the feelings of injustice and inequality I had encountered in the field and that often went hand in hand with my interlocutors' individual quests and hopes for a good life. I attempted to achieve a balanced representation of Christian and Muslim engagements with education in a historical context, where especially the interventions of the latter were discussed as being highly controversial in public discourse. I also made an effort to provide a thorough analytical contextualisation of the dynamics of privilege and marginality at the schools of my study, dynamics that are rooted in long-standing colonial and postcolonial histories of religious difference, education, and social stratification. Finally, I intend to promote a stronger focus on processes of politics and power in anthropological studies of the entangled dynamics of institutionalisation and moral becoming in the highly varied Christian and Muslim contexts of global Africa (see Chapter 7).

---

[28] In fact, many of my Christian interlocutors expressed strong reservations about certain cultural traits that they linked to Islam and that they found fundamentally different from their own religious background. One employee of a Christian NGO argued that Muslims had a problem with being governed by a Christian leader, as, 'for them', all Christians were 'unclean'. Others emphasised the alleged 'aggressiveness' of Muslims, which they linked to the idea that Islam was a 'religion of war' (*dini ya vita*).

[29] *Ugali* (porridge-like meal made from maize or millet) and *makande* (a dish made from kidney beans and corn) are staple foods in Tanzania.

Outline of the Book

The first part of this book explores the common – and yet unequal – historical background to the emergence of the new generation of Christian and Muslim schools in Dar es Salaam. Chapter 2 describes how Christian and Muslim encounters in the city have been shaped by colonial and postcolonial histories and by related memories of religious and educational differences. I argue that the 'past-oriented narratives' of Islamic activists and media actors in particular have become emblematic of the ways in which Muslims perceive their position and status in the wake of globalisation and the market economy. I show that a focus on specific historical events has sustained the moral sensation among Muslims that they are systematically denied access to education and positions of power in contemporary Tanzania. Furthermore, the 'language gap' that resulted from Tanzania's post-independence language policy in education[30] has reinforced the growing popularity of church-run schools in the stratified educational landscape, where a good command of English becomes a condition for success.

Chapter 3 describes the historical development of the educational system in Tanganyika/Tanzania and how it has become entangled with growing socio-religious inequalities since the mid-1990s. I argue that the various moral, political, and epistemological uncertainties that the increasingly diffuse religious landscape of Dar es Salaam presents to its inhabitants are all closely intertwined. Religious competition and the desire to claim spiritual, moral, and geographical territory in Dar es Salaam impel the state to intervene and establish order (for example, by vetting new religious organisations). But they also present a moral challenge for students and teachers at faith-oriented schools, who are often highly aware of public perceptions of their institutions' religious networks and their efforts to sustain and further expand their claims. In order to understand the politicisation of religious differences over the last decades, I explore the dynamics of inter- and intra-religious competition and polemics in Dar es Salaam, as well as experiences and memories of the state's attempts to govern religious difference and conflict in the postcolonial context; the latter became particularly emblematic in the dissolution of the East African Muslims Welfare Society in 1968.

The second part of the book focuses on the multiple experiences, practices, and politics of moral becoming in six Christian and Muslim schools in Dar es Salaam. Chapter 4 describes the establishment of two

---

[30] In Tanzania, the language of instruction in primary schools is Kiswahili, whereas the use of English is mandatory in secondary and tertiary education.

schools by the pastor of one of the largest neo-Pentecostal churches in the city against a background of processes of social segregation as well as spiritual insecurity in the context of perceived urban ambiguity. The two schools, which cater to students from different socio-economic backgrounds, foster class formation among students and staff as well as the ethos of a 'caring discipline' among the teachers. At the same time, there are significant tensions among the staff that result from concerns about national and ethnic favouritism and from a rigid system of performance monitoring. The two schools also establish networks of local, national, and international belonging, which are particularly valued among teachers hired from abroad. Furthermore, an essential part of the two schools' reputation derives from the fact that they are perceived as faith-oriented schools providing 'moral education'. However, articulations of faith and morality play a rather implicit role in the everyday practices of the schools, with regard to not only the learning of values but also the (informal) healing prayers that are conducted for (exclusively female Muslim) students who are believed to have been exposed to evil spirits and witchcraft attacks.

Muslim schools hold a specific status in Dar es Salaam's educational landscape. While many activist organisations have worked to overcome the historical marginalisation of Muslims in Tanzania, Islamic schools remain largely hidden in the public discourse on education. Chapter 5 provides insight into the histories and practices of two gender-segregated Islamic seminaries in Dar es Salaam. It argues that educational practices and experiences in these schools have been shaped by networks of revivalist Islamic thought within and beyond the city of Dar es Salaam, as well as by perceptions of marginality, especially in the boys' school. In particular, the students and staff of the boys' seminary share a discourse on religious difference that is closely tied to their experiences of underprivileged educational and living situations, and their perceptions of poor future prospects overall. At the same time, the sensation of being religiously different gives rise to practices of Islamic self-cultivation that extend, in both seminaries, to gender-specific notions of gender, dress, and the body and, in the girls' school, the sense of belonging to an aspiring urban Muslim middle class. In contrast, in the boys' seminary, striving to become 'good Muslim men' was tied to a rigid discipline for meeting the challenges of an 'unclean' and 'depriving' world.

In contrast to the Muslim revivalist organisations and neo-Pentecostal actors, both relative newcomers, the former mission churches have been at the forefront of educational service provision during large parts of Tanganyika's/Tanzania's history. Chapter 6 examines a Catholic primary school – established by a German order of nuns in the early twentieth century, nationalised in 1969, and then returned to the Catholic church in the early 2000s – and its corresponding high school, which was opened in 2010. The owner of the schools, the Catholic Archdiocese of Dar es Salaam, emphasises that it collaborates closely with the Tanzanian government to provide social services for the socially underprivileged. However, the two schools operate on the basis of comparatively high school fees and have the reputation of being 'top schools' that attract families and students from the middle and upper classes. The chapter argues that the Catholic schools are aware of the discrepancies between these diverging ethical orientations and their work to forge an affective commitment to the workplace among their teachers, who feel somewhat inferior to their pupils due to differences in social status and the parents' condescending attitudes. It also shows that pupils are trained to embody the values of the Catholic middle-class environment through particular forms of bodily discipline and regular attendance at church events. Finally, students engage in cultivating an ethos of helping and caring for 'the needy' in Dar es Salaam, for example by participating in a charitable trip to a local orphanage.

The conclusion compares the diverse educational engagements of Christian and Muslim actors in Dar es Salaam, highlighting the convergences and divergences in the quest for a good life across these two religious educational fields. I argue that anthropological research is particularly well suited to producing new empirical insights into the coexistence of Christian and Muslim actors and lives – and their entangled struggles for moral becoming – in urban Africa. The ethnographic research of this book makes clear that, in contemporary Tanzania, faith-oriented schools have become – in highly varied ways – a public force in the wake of urbanisation and its unequal articulations. I argue that comparative studies of religiously diverse urban landscapes in Africa need to adopt a stronger focus on processes of institutionalisation, as well as on configurations of inequality and power (Soares 2016: 679; Altglas and Wood 2018), in order to understand the close entanglement of moral becoming, social stratification, and religious differences in the highly volatile contexts of the globalising market economy.

Part I

(Post)Colonial Politics of Religious Difference and Education

2 Entangled Histories of Religious Pluralism and Schooling

> Muslims suffer religious discrimination and humiliation in their contact with vertical institutional power, in schools and government offices. Muslims do not experience religious discrimination horizontally in their social relationship with Christians at the market place, or as neighbours and friends. *Hamza M. Njozi*, Mwembechai Killings, and the Political Future of Tanzania *(2002)*

> [We] have seen that there are intentional efforts of some government leaders, members of parliament, as well as Islamic leaders ... to introduce the kadhi court in the constitution and the joining of Tanzania with the 'Organization of Islamic Conference' (OIC) ... While the Muslims claim that Christians won't be affected, we have to warn our fellow believers to beware of political parties with such a dangerous agenda. *Statement of the bishops and pastors of the Pentecostal Churches of Tanzania*

In Dar es Salaam, religious diversity and the encounters between actors of different denominations and faiths are a largely uncontested part of everyday life. The cityscape's public sphere is shaped by a breathtaking multitude of different places of religious worship, remembrance and social intervention (Dilger 2014a: 53). Whenever I walked and rode through the city during my fieldwork, I was impressed by the close proximity of different religious buildings and architecture, which were mirrored by the striking coexistence of the muezzins' calls to prayer and the omnipresence of religiously diverse objects and Christian songs in public transportation and institutions. The multiple, often equally audible and visible, Muslim and Hindu festivals and celebrations throughout the year – as well as the numerous advertisements for religious educational sites[1] and other social services – all added to Dar es Salaam's

---

[1] Such schools included Islamic seminaries, such as the Al-Farouq Islamic Seminary (see Chapter 5), that accepted only students of their own faith. Others with a Christian denominational affiliation (such as the Catholic St Joseph Millennium Secondary School; see Chapter 6) were also open to students with other religious or

highly 'affective cityscape' in the context of seemingly harmonious religious pluralism (Dilger et al. 2020: 17; see also Ibrahim 2020).

Thus, despite the growing presence since the 1990s of neo-Pentecostal crusades (Ludwig 1996: 221ff.; Hasu 2006: 681–2; Wilkens 2009: 23–4) and Muslim revivalist preachers in the city (Ludwig 1996: 226ff.; Ndaluka et al. 2014: 65–6) – who all aggressively recruit new followers (Ahmed 2008) and include references to politics in their proselytisation efforts (Hasu 2006: 685) – the inhabitants of Dar es Salaam are pragmatic in their approach to the articulation of religious diversity in everyday life (Njozi 2002: 47–8). As has been described for other parts of Africa (Soares 2006; Peel 2015; Nolte et al. 2017), people change their religious or denominational affiliation due to marriage or other circumstances without this necessarily inducing discord in their social relationships.[2] They also attend various churches and mosques over their lifetime and consult traditional healers in times of sickness – even if they vehemently reject them at other times (Dilger 2005: 261ff.). And people of divergent faiths respect each other's holidays and join their neighbours and friends in celebrating Eid al-Fitr, Christmas, or Diwali. In short, many such everyday interreligious encounters speak to the often repeated claim that Dar es Salaam has been a literal 'haven of peace' for a very long time when it comes to everyday religious coexistence (Ndaluka 2014a: 82).

However, Christian and Muslim encounters in Dar es Salaam are not defined solely by fluidity, hybridity, and mutual tolerance but also by their potential for conflict, especially at the institutional and political level, where the relationships between religions are a delicate matter (Ludwig 1996; Wijsen and Mfumbusa 2004). In particular, the inclusion of both Christian and Islamic symbols and representation in political processes has been negotiated carefully at least since the transition to multiparty democracy in the early 1990s, and representatives from both religions are usually present at government social occasions (Rukyaa 2007: 192) and other official events.[3] Furthermore, an unwritten policy of alternating Christian and Muslim presidents has been observed since the retirement of President Nyerere in 1985. During the time of my research, President Kikwete, a Muslim, paid careful attention to creating

---

denominational backgrounds. The Christian seminaries were located mostly in regions outside Dar es Salaam.

[2] However, occasionally such decisions may also give rise to tensions within families (Scharrer 2013: 269ff.).

[3] Wijsen (2014: 202) notes that 'members of parliament swear an oath on the Bible or the Qur'an' on entering office, an act he defines, with reference to Westerlund (1980a), as a form of 'civil religion'.

a balanced media presence by attending both Christian and Muslim public events.[4]

In fact, sometimes this orchestrated public acknowledgement of Tanzania's religious pluralism for the sake of 'national cohesion' (Ng'atigwa 2013: 2) hints at the fact that Christian–Muslim relations are embedded in historically produced power relations that mirror both global tensions and religious differentiation within the country. In Dar es Salaam, such frictions were expressed in public debates on the country's religious demography[5] – but also on the introduction of sharia law and Tanzania joining the Organisation of the Islamic Countries in the late 2000s, something that has been contested fervently by neo-Pentecostal groups.[6] On the other hand, some Muslim revivalists claim that Tanzania is gradually turning into a 'Christian state', tracing this shift not only to colonialism and Christian missions but to recent development politics and Tanzania's transition to democracy (see Chapter 3). Activists' and (some) religious and political leaders' narratives of the country's history and politics diverge along religious lines, and continued allegations of religious favouritism and the abuse of faith have resulted in instances of violence on both sides, starting in the early 1990s and reported ever since by the English- and Kiswahili-language media.[7]

In this chapter, I explore how encounters between Christian and Muslim parts of the population in Tanganyika/Tanzania have been shaped by the entangled histories of religious difference and education in precolonial, colonial, and postcolonial settings. I argue that Christians'

---

[4] See, for example, 'Kikwete advises envoys not to politicise religion', JamiiForums, 8 October 2014, www.jamiiforums.com/threads/kikwete-advises-envoys-not-to-politicise-religion.738112/ (accessed 8 October 2014); 'JK pays tribute to late bishop', *The Citizen*, 27 August 2009, on President Kikwete paying tribute to the late Bishop Mayalla; and *Majira*, 2 October 2008, for a picture of Kikwete attending Dar es Salaam's Eid prayers. In 2015, John Pombe Magufuli, a Catholic, was elected the fifth president of Tanzania. President Magufuli died in March 2021; he was followed in office by Samia Suluhu Hassan, Tanzania's previous vice president.

[5] Conforming with the Tanzanian government, the US Department of State claimed in 2007 that Muslims and Christians in Tanzania each constituted 30–40 per cent of the population, with the 'remainder consisting of practitioners of other faiths and indigenous religions, and atheists' (US Department of State 2007). More recently, the Pew Forum on Religion and Public Life stated that the majority of the population is Christian (60 per cent), 36 per cent are Muslim, and 2 per cent practise 'traditional religion' (US Department of State 2014). In the absence of a national census on, and a clear definition of, religious affiliation, all these figures are hotly contested by religious activists from both religions and all denominations (see Chapter 3).

[6] On the historical precursors of this debate in Zanzibar, see Lodhi (1994: 92ff.).

[7] For an overview of religiously motivated violence in Tanzania since the 1990s, see Heilman and Kaiser (2002), Wijsen and Mfumbusa (2004), and Maghimbi (2014: 185ff.).

and Muslims' diverging access to education – and thus to social and cultural capital (Bourdieu 1974) – has been particularly important in shaping notions of socio-religious inequality and difference during the colonial and post-independence eras. Combined with more recent educational shifts caused by global (especially World Bank) policies and government decisions, these histories have sustained the belief, especially among revivalist Muslims, that they are systematically denied access to education and positions of power in contemporary Tanzania (Ndaluka 2014a). It is therefore mostly Muslim activists and organisations that have drawn on these past-oriented narratives, in order to make sense of their current socio-political position.[8] Furthermore, the 'language gap' that has resulted from Tanzania's language policy, which is hotly debated in terms of both educational failures and the core values of national belonging, has become closely entwined with the unequal structural positions of Christian and Muslim schools in Dar es Salaam's educational market. But before I elaborate on these various issues, let me first turn to the question of how these entangled histories can be written anthropologically, given the overall scarcity of comparative scholarship on socio-religious difference and educational inequalities in colonial Tanganyika and postcolonial Tanzania.

How to Write Entangled Histories? A Reflection on (Absent) Sources

Memory and history play a central role in shaping identity – individually as well as collectively – and in constructing consciousness in postcolonial societies (Comaroff and Comaroff 1992; Cole 1998; Fabian 1999). As Nora (1989) remarked, it is quite impossible today to draw a clear line between officially authorised 'objective' history and the 'subjective' memories of individuals or groups. With the growing 'movement toward democratization and mass culture on a global scale' (ibid.: 7), marginalised groups in particular are 'haunted by the need to recover their buried past' (ibid.: 15) and have become invested in the 'revitalization of their history' (ibid.: 15).

In this and the following chapter, I aim to explore how history (as written or orally transmitted 'authoritative' sources) and memory (as the

---

[8] However, interreligious competition and contestation have also been driven by Christian individuals and organisations from neo-Pentecostal groups and by representatives of the former Catholic and Lutheran mission churches. As will be shown, such political interventions also include statements and speeches by Christian leaders in the public domain. For a discussion of this aspect, see Ludwig (1997; 1999).

lived interpretation of these sources and the past; see Berliner 2005: 201) are mobilised by a wide range of religious, academic, and political actors within and beyond the city of Dar es Salaam. I show how they construct entangled historical trajectories of religious coexistence and the politics of education in colonial and postcolonial settings. I also discuss how these various versions of history and memory have an impact on the positionalities of Christian and Muslim political actors today, continuing to shape their understandings of the effects of religious difference on educational achievement and socio-economic status and guiding their interventions in the field of faith-oriented schooling in contemporary Dar es Salaam.

One challenge in writing about these entangled histories and memories of religion, politics, and schooling in Dar es Salaam arises from the fact that few sources cover both the colonial and postcolonial eras (but see Von Sicard 1978; Rasmussen 1993; Mbogoni 2005) or concern the city specifically.[9] Furthermore, there is a dearth of reliable statistical and empirical data concerning the way in which religious pluralism has become entangled with urbanisation and globalisation processes in urban Tanzania over the last decades.[10] A few historical studies on Christian–Muslim encounters in the country provide valuable insights into how relationships between the two religions have been shaped by growing tensions and conflicts over the past few decades (Ludwig 1996; 1999; Wijsen and Mfumbusa 2004; Ndaluka and Wijsen 2014), but some of them tend to assume that Muslims and Christians largely coexisted harmoniously during colonial and postcolonial times, and that this peace was disturbed primarily by revivalist movements, both Christian and Muslim, from the 1980s onwards (Wijsen and Mfumbusa 2004: 16ff.).

With regard to the histories of Christians and Muslims in Tanzania – still largely written separately – a further challenge arises in relation to the sources on which they are based (cf. Masebo 2014). Colonial administrators and Christian missionaries authored many of the more 'authoritative' historical sources that both scholars and religious actors in Tanzania rely on for understanding the 'past–present–future relation' (Munn 1992: 115) of religion and politics in the country; these must be read carefully with regard to the ideological contexts in which they were produced (Masebo 2014: 9). Moreover, there is only a limited body of sources on the subject of religion in the first decades of the

---

[9] The book by Brennan et al. (2007) is an exception in this regard. However, while it provides a fascinating insight into the social history of Dar es Salaam, issues of religion and schooling remain curiously absent.

[10] An exception is the book by Wilkens (2009), which provides a good summary of the history of religious pluralism in (urban) Tanzania in the context of issues of healing and medicine (especially 20ff.).

postcolonial nation-state (ibid.: 9–10).[11] In line with the socialist visions of Tanzania's first president, Julius Nyerere, religious and ethnic affiliation were never included in the national census or official statistics, as doing so was feared to harm national unity (Ndaluka 2014d: 2). Also, as scholars from the humanities and social sciences were strongly committed to the idea of nation building in these years, they rarely made religion a topic of critical academic research. Masebo writes:

> As part of nation building nationalist scholars paid attention to unity, not to destabilising themes like tribalism, religion, regionalism and racism. The predominance of nationalist history, whose orientation was nation building and consolidation, dealt with issues that in most cases legitimised the nation-state. So long as religions did not threaten the smooth functioning of the state, they did not feature on the agenda of these contemporary scholars. (Masebo 2014: 17)

This and Chapter 3 are linked: first, in this chapter, I provide a 'linear chronology' (Caplan 1999: 287) of the history of Christian–Muslim encounters in precolonial and colonial Tanganyika, and their successive entwinement with the growing focus of mission churches and the German and British colonial states on schooling. I aim to establish a coherent conversation among a range of heterogeneous scholarly, missionary, activist, and government sources on the histories of Christianity, Islam, and education that have remained largely unconnected thus far. Because such a sweeping account of Christian–Muslim encounters cannot reflect the *diverse* articulations within or between each of the religious fields, I then take up the single issue of schooling after independence, discussing how socio-religious inequalities were tackled through Nyerere's socialist (and egalitarian) policies on education. Still, school-related socio-economic inequalities remain closely interlinked with religious difference, as I show with regard to 'new' Christian schools in contemporary Tanzania. Their overall position of privilege, I argue, is maintained not only through their support from the government and international development organisations but also as a result of the continued language gap in the country.

Chapter 3 then highlights how certain historical events have become issues of contestation among Christian and Muslim actors in Dar es Salaam today and touchstones for the government's attempts to regulate the increasingly diffuse terrain of religious pluralism. I argue that an ethnographic approach can provide a unique insight into the highly politicised dynamics of religious difference and faith-oriented schooling in the city, and thus contribute a nuanced perspective to a growing body

---

[11] But see, for instance, Westerlund (1980a; 1980b; 1982) and Omari (1984).

of scholarly works on religion and politics in the urban African context. Of note with regard to the Tanzanian setting is recent work on religion, development, and the post-independence state (Wijsen and Mfumbusa 2004; Mbogoni 2005; Mukandala et al. 2006; Ndaluka and Wijsen 2014), as well as the recently established interdisciplinary Society and Religion Research Centre at the University of Dar es Salaam (Ndaluka 2014b).

Muslim–Christian Encounters on the East African Coast until 1885

Historians and Africanist scholars of Islam date the presence of Muslims in Tanzania to the first millennium AD, when merchants from Ḥaḍramawt and Persia – some arriving via Somalia – established trading centres along the East African coast, the most famous of them being Kilwa and Mombasa (cf. Loimeier 2013: 211–12). The first written mention of Muslims in the region was made by the traveller Ibn Batūta, who visited Kilwa and Mombasa in 1331, where he 'was welcomed by Muslim rulers he described as sheikhs or sultans' (Becker 2018; see also Trimingham 1964: 67; Lodhi 1994: 88–9).[12] However, these commercial centres on the coast – which relied significantly on the black 'Zanj' population on the mainland for their trade of slaves, ivory, mangrove poles, and grains across the Indian Ocean (Loimeier 2013: 212) – were never really 'interested in establishing (costly) political domination over the hinterland' (ibid.: 211). Thus, it was only in the nineteenth century that the Muslim traders of the coast started to establish closer relations with the 'bush people' (Kiswahili: *wanyika*) of the mainland who had 'remained anchored in the African religious traditions' (ibid.: 211).

According to Sahlberg (1986: 12) – a former missionary and theologian at the Makumira Lutheran Theological College in north Tanzania – the Islamic influence on the East African coast was interrupted during the fifteenth and sixteenth century with the establishment of Portuguese rule and the arrival of Catholic missionaries accompanying Vasco da Gama. Later on, some of these missionaries travelled far into the interior of the African continent and were in some cases quite successful in their

---

[12] In some translations and interpretations of Batūta's travel reports, he is said to have referred to the region as 'Sawahil' (Tolmacheva 1976: 30; Horton and Middleton 2000: 16). However, Loimeier (2013: 212) writes that 'the term Swahili (Arab. sawāḥīla) became current only in the nineteenth century, and originally was a derogatory Arabic term for "de-tribalized Africans" living on the coast, often of slave descent'. In his published writing, Ibn Batūta refers to the region as the 'country of the Zanūj' and its inhabitants as belonging to 'the sect of Shāfia' (Ibn Batūta 1829: 57).

proselytising endeavours. However, Sahlberg also writes that the early influence of Christianity in East Africa remained limited. Not only did the Portuguese focus more on commerce than on mission but the 'extremely tyrannical' rule of the early colonisers gained little support among the population (ibid.: 13). There were also internal conflicts among the Europe-based missions, and most of them made little effort to integrate 'local cultural' elements into their work (ibid.: 13). In the early 1650s, the Portuguese were expelled from Malindi (Kenya); the newly won Christians either converted back to Islam or were killed or sold as slaves to Mecca (ibid.: 14).

During Omani rule in the seventeenth century, Islam began to flourish again and was transported by Arab and Indian merchants along the trading routes into the interior of East Africa (Nimtz 1980: 5–6; Lodhi 1994: 89). The Omani rulers consolidated their territorial claims not only by moving the sultanate from Muscat to Zanzibar in 1832 but also through trade. The sultanate gained power and influence through the circulation of slaves, ivory, and cloves, establishing a dense social, cultural, and economic nexus between the populations of the interior and Zanzibar's rulers and merchants and their trading partners in the Indian Ocean (Sheriff 1987). While the Arab traders seem to have been mostly concerned with establishing commercial ties, their mere presence in the communities – and the appeal of Islam as a 'vehicle of modernization' – often sufficed to attract local men and women to the 'new' religion (Nimtz 1980: 7ff.).[13]

The Omani rulers seem to have been so confident of their newly established political and economic position that they welcomed newly arriving Christian missions into their territory and granted them permission to pursue their work on the mainland. Sahlberg (1986) writes that Protestant and Catholic missionaries sought entry via the sultan of Zanzibar and started to establish stations along the coast and in the interior. During the first half of the nineteenth century, the proselytising efforts of these missionaries – among them Johann Ludwig Krapf, the German missionary who allegedly 'brought dawn to East Africa' (cf. ibid.: 23ff.) – seem to have encountered little resistance from the Muslim rulers and converts. A missionary report from the Tanga region in north-east Tanganyika, written in the late 1870s, claims:

---

[13] The assumption that conversion to Islam in East Africa was driven mostly by material interests may be a result of the bias of primary sources (missionaries' diaries and letters, colonial reports, etc.) from the time. For a more detailed discussion of this aspect, see Singleton (1977) and Becker (2008).

On that last evening ... [t]he interest was intense ... for we had announced the subject 'A contrast between the life of Mohammed and the life of Jesus Christ.' While the evil and impure life of Mohammed was contrasted with the holy and blessed life of Jesus, not a sound was heard. When we had finished, a man stepped forward and said: 'We became Mohammedans because we had no religion, and the coast people came and taught us theirs; but we don't like them, for they cheat us, and if Christianity is better than Islam, we will follow it.' (quoted in Sahlberg 1986: 39)

The reportedly relatively harmonious relationship between Muslims and Christians changed with the establishment of German colonial rule in Tanganyika in 1885. Relationships between the two religions – and the response of local populations towards both Christianity and Islam – became increasingly embedded in oscillating alliances between colonial state authorities and different Christian and Muslim groups and institutions.

Interreligious Relations in the Context of German Colonial Rule

Historians and theologians agree that, at the beginning of German colonial rule, Muslims – who had learned to read and write in Qur'anic schools[14] – were the preferred employees for tax collection, cash crop supervision, and the implementation of new colonial decrees (Von Sicard 1978: 61; Rasmussen 1993: 21; Mushi 2009: 55). Sudanese Muslims in particular were recruited into the military and became instrumental in defeating revolts and outbreaks of violence among the local population. Kiswahili became the official administrative language of the colonial state (Nimtz 1980: 12). Thus, while there were several violent encounters between the colonial administration and 'hostile' Muslims (for example, the Bushiri revolt in 1888–9; Moffett 1958: 382–3), overall there were strong pro-Islam tendencies among the colonial authorities.[15] They assumed that Muslims were 'easier to rule' than Christians (Singleton

---

[14] Especially in coastal Tanzania, Qur'anic schools (madrasa) remain important for the transmission of Islamic knowledge and values, and for the learning of Arabic. In Tanga, some of them even 'offer a full 12-year course of religious education' (van de Bruinhorst 2007: 106–7). In Dar es Salaam, some students in my study attended a madrasa after school, but their (mostly secular) Christian and Muslim schools or seminaries were more important for their educational or preferred future school trajectories. Similarly, Van de Bruinhorst (ibid.: 106) writes that, in Tanga, 'future prospects for graduated madrasa students' are mostly as religious teachers or leaders (see also Chande 1998: 208–9).

[15] A distinction was made by the colonial state between newly converted 'local' or 'African' Muslims and the 'Omani and Swahili Muslim elites' on whom German colonial rule was built (Haustein 2017). This focus on the political utility of Islam also superseded earlier, critical sentiments among the colonisers against slavery as an 'Arab' institution to be ended through 'Christian civilization' (ibid.: 499ff.).

1977: 281) and that they were 'the economically more suitable alternative for "civilising" and disciplining Africans' (Haustein 2017: 503). There was also a perception that the newly converted Christians were 'too servile' (*kriecherisch*) (Singleton 1977: 281) and that Christian missionaries (especially Catholics) were pushing their own agenda of establishing 'a state within a state' (ibid.: 282).

The generally good relationship between the colonial state and the Muslim population was met with a growing use of polemics by Christian missionaries, who started to engage in 'theological controversy' and the public denouncement of Islamic teachings (Von Sicard 1978: 62). It also became strained by the Maji Maji rebellion of 1905–7, which, in the eyes of the colonial authorities, was connected to the growing popularity of Islam among the local population.[16] Together with other pre-existing concerns about an alleged 'Islamic danger' in the territory (Haustein 2017: 506ff.),[17] this led the colonial government to offer support to Christian missionaries and their activities, especially with regard to establishing mission schools, which had previously been restricted in favour of 'erecting state or secular schools' (Nimtz 1980: 12). This shift in policy was reflected explicitly in the 1912 circular of the German district officer in Tabora, Mr Hermann:

Henceforth it is forbidden to take part in Muslim feasts. Christians must be given preference in jobs, allowed freedom to practice their faith and build schools; anyone who mocks them (which indirectly suggests many did [annotation by Singleton]) should be severely punished. (quoted in Singleton 1977: 286)

While there had been mission schools before 1905–6, their numbers grew rapidly with the German colonial government's new policy, as did the numbers of Christian converts (Sahlberg 1986: 90–1). The importance of education for proselytising was grasped readily by the missions, especially the Catholics. In 1911, the German Benedictine Bishop Thomas Spreiter proclaimed: 'Whoever wins the youth will win the future' (Sahlberg 1986: 91). Other missions also welcomed the opportunity to use schools for proselytisation, and many saw it as a response to their growing concerns about the 'threat of Islam' (Iliffe 1979: 223; Sanders 2011: 16). In the final years of German colonial rule, in the

---

[16] While the Maji Maji rebellion was driven by many different factors and also included 'attacking Muslim intermediaries of colonial rule', it was simultaneously connected to 'mass conversions to Islam' in south-east Tanzania and the rebels' hope 'to acquire a new status ... as Muslim freemen' (Becker 2004: 20–1).

[17] Concerns about the potentially undermining impact of Islam were also raised by the 'so-called "Mecca letter affair" of 1908, when letters were discovered all over the colony, containing an alleged admonition by the Sharif of Mecca to all Muslims not to collaborate with unbelievers' (Haustein 2017: 509).

schools of the Church Missionary Society alone the number of pupils increased from 3,989 in 1910 to 17,202 in 1913 (Iliffe 1979: 224).[18]

However, with the outbreak of World War One, the situation shifted again; 1914–18 can be described as 'a time of great Islamic expansion' (Iliffe 1979: 256) in Tanganyika. According to Nimtz (1980), the Muslim population grew from around 3 per cent in 1916 to 25 per cent in 1924. This development has been attributed to several factors: the newly established alliance between the Germans and the Turks against the British, the weak presence of the colonial state during the war years, the interruption of missionary work due to the insecurity of the war and political persecution,[19] and the millenarian tendencies triggered by the 1918 influenza epidemic (Nimtz 1980: 14–15; on the popularity of Muslim millennialism in this larger context, see also Singleton 1977: 294–5).

Christians and Muslims under British Colonial Rule

After World War One, control over Tanganyika was transferred from the Germans to the British by mandate of the League of Nations in 1920. In its first years, the British colonial government was concerned primarily with consolidating the new regime and restructuring the military and the police, as well as with post-war reconstruction, such as the building of railways. It was only after 1924 that the colonial government started to focus on the provision of education and health services, both of which would come to rely strongly on the contribution of Christian missions in subsequent decades.[20] This also implied a general repositioning of the Christian mission churches in colonial Tanganyika, which 'were becoming increasingly integrated with colonial society' (Iliffe 1979: 358).

The integration of Christian missions into the provision of social services was promoted primarily by the Phelps Stokes Commission from

---

[18] While Muslim students and families continued to have strong reservations about missionary activities, the mission schools were often their only option to receive the education they desired. Von Sicard (1978: 58) writes that 'Muslims were quite happy for their children to attend and to learn English and Mathematics', although their 'reaction to Religious Instruction was unequivocal, to the extent that the missionaries described the parents as "bigoted Mohammedans."'

[19] Iliffe (1979: 255–6) states that the war was a 'catastrophe' for Christian missions. While British missionaries and teachers were interned or persecuted by the Germans during the war, after the war German missionaries were expelled by the new colonial rulers 'remorselessly'.

[20] While German missionaries did not return to Tanganyika before 1925, some of their work 'was taken over temporarily by British societies' (Iliffe 1979: 256). In other cases, they were replaced by Tanzanian Christians, some of whom 'took charge of the missions and parishes after Europeans left the field' (Hölzl 2016: 415; see also Iliffe 1979: 256ff.).

the USA, which visited East Africa in 1924 and stayed in Tanganyika from 15 to 29 April.[21] The commission consisted of eight members from the USA and Great Britain, including someone who was a 'Native of the Gold Coast' and a former Livingstone College professor, as well as several representatives of Christian missions, among them the 'official' representative of the Church Missionary Society and several 'non-officials' (in Tanganyika from the Bielefeld, Berlin, and Leipzig missions).[22] The commission's stated main purpose was to 'investigate the educational needs of the [East African] people in the light of the religious, social, hygienic and economic conditions' and to 'assist in the formulation of plans designed to meet the educational needs of the Native races' (Jones 1924: xiii).[23]

In particular, the commission emphasised that current education funding was insufficient. Thus, while the colonial government allocated 6.7 per cent of its total budget to health services in Tanganyika in the years 1923–4, it invested 'less than 1%' in education (ibid.: 176). Against this background, the commission recommended the systematic involvement of Christian schools in order to achieve the goal of educating 800,000 boys and girls in the territory (see also Iliffe 1979: 338). It stated:

It is difficult to understand the failures of the Government to cooperate with the numerous missions, who, even if their work in Tanganyika itself be on simple lines, are famous for their really great achievements in education in different parts of Africa ... [T]hey are the pioneers of the land. (Jones 1924: 189)[24]

Over the following decades, the Christian missions became indispensable to the educational system of the colonial state in Tanganyika, even

---

[21] See www.empire.amdigital.co.uk/Documents/Details/Phelps-Stokes-Commission-to-East-Africa/Phelps%20Stokes%20Commission%20to%20East%20Africa%2019231925 (accessed 8 May 2019).

[22] Ibid.

[23] The commission also made several observations about the state of health in the colonies, including that, compared with the field of education, health services were 'on the whole good' and received relatively strong support from the colonial government (Jones 1924: 177). Furthermore, the commission highlighted the need to integrate missionary schools with the promotion of health and sanitation (ibid.). On the development of the Christian missions' medical work in the subsequent decades, see Dilger (2014a: 57).

[24] As indicated above, the colonial governments in East Africa were in some cases rather reluctant to allocate too much power to the Christian missions. The recommendations of the Phelps Stokes Commission were therefore also an outcome of missionaries' lobbying, as they feared becoming marginalised by the British government's aim to bring (secular) education under its direct (and sole) influence. In Kenya, the government's post-war preference for secular education was also supported by Kenyans themselves, who became increasingly critical of missionary influence via education (King 1971: 103ff., 112).

though some missions were initially reluctant to seize this opportunity to exert societal influence. A 1952 text by historian Roland Oliver (Oliver 1952, quoted in Pels 2013 [1999]: 201) describes how Cardinal Hinsley – a delegate from the Vatican – admonished his missionaries in Dar es Salaam in 1928: 'Where it is impossible for you to carry on both the immediate task of evangelization and your educational work, neglect your churches in order to perfect your schools.' This seemed to confirm the suspicions of other missionaries, who were worried that 'when teachers were going to be paid by government, they would ... neglect their religious duties' (Pels 2013 [1999]: 202).

In the subsequent years, a 'golden chain' of mutual dependency was forged between the colonial state and the missions (Pels 2013 [1999]: 202) and both government and mission schools increased in number. Between 1923 and 1960, government schools in Tanganyika rose from a total of 65 (Jones 1924: 179) to 753 primary standard (Forms I–IV), 149 middle standard (V–VIII), and 12 secondary standard schools (IX–XII) (HMSO 1961: 105). In addition, there were a further 1,929 primary standard, 212 middle standard, and 16 secondary standard schools that were mostly run by Christian missions (ibid.: 105).[25] While these mission schools received financial and personnel assistance from their headquarters abroad, they were largely supported by the colonial government through subsidies. In 1960, the British government paid a total of £1,703,055 to 'voluntary agencies engaged in educational work' (HMSO 1961: 131). Only 0.86 per cent of this was allocated to Muslim associations and agencies (HMSO 1961: 131). In the process, the character of the mission churches changed considerably in the interwar years, as they became 'modern organisations', not only with regard to issues such as 'authoritarianism, bureaucracy, impersonality, specialization' (Iliffe 1979: 358) but also with the integration of mission teachers into 'the growing income differentials of colonial society' (ibid.: 359).

The British colonial government's favouring of Christian mission churches in the provision of social services – and in the building of the colonial state more broadly – was regarded critically by the Muslim population (Von Sicard 1978: 58; see also Pels 2013 [1999]: 226). Not only was education in mission schools perceived as a medium for transmitting colonial ideologies and for moulding employees for colonial service but many students were also converted to Christianity and trained in trades and agricultural work, which further served the expansion of the

---

[25] On the exponential growth of mission schools in south-east Tanzania from the 1920s onwards, see Hölzl (2016: 408–9).

missions (Mushi 2009: 82). According to Von Sicard, 'the stumbling block' of mission education for Muslims was:

> the so-called Conscience Clause [of the Memorandum, Education Policy in British Tropical Africa], which allowed freedom of Religious Instruction to each faith, but which was interpreted to mean that mission schools were not prevented from giving religious instruction to Muslim children unless the parents or guardians objected. The fact that nearly the whole educational system was in the hands of the missions placed the Muslims in a difficult position if, as they did, they desired an acceptable education for their children. (Von Sicard 1978: 64)

Given the adverse reactions of many Muslims, including Muslim teachers, who called on Muslim parents 'to stay away from the missionaries' schools, or to neglect the study of catechism' (Pels 2013 [1999]: 226), the expansion of Christian schools was concentrated in predominantly non-Muslim regions, including in the economically profitable regions of Kilimanjaro, Mbeya, and Bukoba (see also Mushi 2009: 62; Leurs et al. 2011: 20–1).

However, there were also proactive efforts by Muslims to counteract the marginalisation – or potential conversion – of their fellow believers in the colonial setting. As the German government policy excluded 'Asians'[26] from the provision of social services, the (Shi'a) Ismaili communities started to build their own schools and clinics in 1905. In many instances these facilities were exclusively for Ismailis, but they sometimes also catered to the educational and health needs of 'other Asians' (Kaiser 1996: 62–3).[27] In contrast to the 'Christian', 'Indian', or other (Sunni) 'Muslim' schools,[28] however, the Ismaili schools and medical centres were often not eligible for government grants, as most of them were located in cities and town centres (where most of the 'Asian' communities lived); the government grants primarily targeted rural areas, where educational and health services were largely absent (ibid.: 24).

---

[26] In the context of British colonial rule, 'political and legal rights [were tied] to the racial categories of European, Asian, Arab, and African', and the majorities of the 'Arabs' and 'Europeans' were Muslims and Christians respectively (Heilman and Kaiser 2002: 699). Most members of the 'Asian' community (many of whom were of Indian origin) were Shi'a Ismaili Muslims; a minority were Hindus.

[27] One of the first hospitals in Dar es Salaam was a result of the charitable activities of Sewa Haji, an Indian businessman who donated land to the Fathers of the Holy Ghost Mission for the purpose of building a hospital for sick porters. The hospital was completed in 1893 (Matson 1966: 93–4).

[28] The British colonial state organised education according to the subcategories 'African education', 'European education', 'Indian education', and 'other non-native education' (Moffett 1958: 365ff.). For grants, schools were classified according to denomination (in the case of Christian missions) or the category 'Muslim' (including 'Muslim associations and agencies') (HMSO 1961: 131). The Ismaili schools belonged to the category of 'Indian education' (Moffett 1958: 368).

Despite this lack of state support, the Ismailis continued to build their own schools, hospitals, and dispensaries. By 1942, they had established 43 schools that served 3,062 students; these operated 'alongside thirty-one grants-in-aid Indian schools with 2,688 students, and also three completely government-funded Indian schools, which served 1,250 students' (Kaiser 1996: 24–5). From the mid-1940s onwards, the Ismaili communities were supported in their endeavours by the East African Muslim Welfare Society (EAMWS), after it was established in 1945 by the Aga Khan (the imam of the Ismaili Muslims) in Mombasa. (It was dissolved again under Nyerere's post-independence government in 1968; see Chapter 3.) Shortly before independence, the *Tanganyika Report for the Year 1960* (HMSO 1961: 118) counted 37 primary Muslim schools (standards I–IV), 106 aided, and five government-run Indian schools; in 1966, 86 schools were supported by the EAMWS alone (Ludwig 1999: 97).

On another level, the Muslim community reacted to the firmly established alliance between the colonial government and Christian missions by retreating into nationalist movements. This development also related to significant cleavages within the Muslim community itself that were based on race and class. In 1934, 'African (Sunni) Muslims' founded the Muslim Association of Tanganyika (Nimtz 1980: 86–7), as they felt increasingly misrepresented within the East African Muslims Association that had been established previously to include all coastal Muslims irrespective of ethnicity.[29] This feeling of exclusion became particularly strong when the 'Indian' Muslims started to build their own schools that 'did not admit African children' (ibid.: 86–7).

The founders of the Muslim Association of Tanganyika also helped establish the Tanganyika African Association, the predecessor of the Tanganyika National Union, which was later guided by President Nyerere. However, their seminal contribution to the struggle for independence in Tanganyika was not well acknowledged in the postcolonial state, where Muslims were again marginalised and high-ranking government positions were mainly given to the better-educated Christian leaders, many of them Catholics (Heilman and Kaiser 2002: 701). Furthermore, despite the EAMWS' interventions to improve Muslim schools' educational standards, the independent state's educational system was considerably unequal with regard to religion, region, and gender. According to educational scientist Mushi (2009: 83–4), the ratio of Muslim to Christian pupils was 1:3 at the beginning of the 1960s, even

---

[29] Nimtz (1980) mentions both the East African Muslims Association and the EAMWS in his book, without distinguishing them clearly from each other.

though the ratio of Muslims to Christians in the total population was estimated to be 3:2.[30] Mushi concludes that, 'at the time of independence, most of the educated people in the country were Christians who later became dominant in politics and government' (ibid.: 84). This lack of parity has been discussed in several academic and activist publications for many decades (for example, Said 1998) and has featured prominently in Muslim revivalists' discourse about the allegedly deliberate marginalisation and exclusion of Muslims in contemporary Tanzania (Heilman and Kaiser 2002: 701–2).[31]

After Independence: Egalitarian Ideologies versus Continued Inequalities

Although, overall, Muslims were marginalised in the assignment of leadership positions in the new government, President Nyerere made active efforts to eliminate existing differences based on religion, class, and regional or ethnic origin in his socialist visions for postcolonial society. In one of his early speeches from 1961, quoted by Kaniki in Ruhumbika's book *Toward Ujamaa: twenty years of TANU leadership* (Kaniki 1974), Nyerere emphasised that neither religious nor ethnic difference was to play a role in the new social and political order, and that all Tanzanian citizens were to benefit:

[O]ur nation shall be a nation of free and equal citizens, each person having an equal right and opportunity to develop himself [sic], and to contribute to the maximum of his capabilities to the development of our society. We have said that neither race nor tribe, nor religion or cleverness, nor anything else, could take away from a man his own rights as an equal member of society. This is what we have now to put into practice. (quoted in Heilman and Kaiser 2002: 700)

With regard to education, during the 1960s and 1970s Tanzania's socialist government developed numerous programmes for the reduction of inequalities, which in the context of the politics of self-reliance focused primarily on adult education and training and educating the peasantry (Stambach 2000: 41ff.). In 1969, the government addressed inequalities in secondary and tertiary education by introducing a quota system for all regions of the country and nationalising mission schools. In addition, the

---

[30] On the contestation of religious demographic statistics in Tanzania by religious activists from all denominations, see Chapter 3.
[31] This does not mean that Muslims did not have any political power in postcolonial Tanzania. Nimtz (1980: 87–8) highlights the important role of Sufi orders in the nationalist struggle and emphasises that many of their leaders advanced to influential positions in national and local governments.

goal of national, social, and cultural unity motivated Tanzania's 1968 choice of Kiswahili as the national language of instruction (Stites and Semali 1991: 53); Kiswahili was strongly associated with the Arab influence of the urban Swahili coast but was also the lingua franca during German (and partly British) colonial rule.[32]

Until the late 1970s, Tanzania's educational reforms – which focused on mass education and universal primary education – were regarded both domestically and internationally as modestly successful (Cooksey et al. 1994: 229). The illiteracy rate dropped from 69 per cent at the time of independence to 27 per cent in 1977, according to one study (Stites and Semali 1991: 53–5). At the same time, however, the post-independence government's policy of self-reliance through education had weaknesses, especially in rural areas (Buchert 1994: 123–4). To remedy this, the community school movement was established in 1971 with the main aim of connecting education to the country's larger development efforts, and specifically to the mobilisation of village populations (ibid.: 125). The movement was introduced in select rural regions of the mainland and included not only the participation of village members on school committees but also 'the active participation of the school[s] in village affairs', for example by involving students in farming lessons and adult literacy classes (ibid.: 128).

Despite these various efforts, however, the goal of reaching social equality through education continued to face challenges. In the early 1980s, the shortcomings of Tanzania's educational system – among them its failure to facilitate the transition from primary to secondary and then to higher education (Cooksey et al. 1994: 218) – became increasingly linked to the country's growing economic and political problems, which were partially due to the international oil crisis of the early 1970s and the parallel decline in the price of cash crop products on the world market. These problems were deepened by the Tanzanian government's increasing inability to sustain the full financing of its social services, as well as the war with neighbouring Uganda in 1978–9. Furthermore, many of the social and religious cleavages that had begun during colonialism continued to have an impact during the Ujamaa years. While Muslim students benefited especially from primary education, Chande (1998: 196ff.) writes that the 'Muslim percentage' at secondary school level and in institutions of higher learning in coastal Tanzania was

---

[32] The shaping of Kiswahili through various colonial influences has also raised concerns about its status as a national language as there were both 'Christian reservations about the Islamicity of Swahili [and] Muslim fears about its seeming dis-Islamization in the hands of Europeans' (Mazrui 2017: 59–60).

disproportionately low in the late 1970s. In 1994, Cooksey et al. (1994: 229) stated: 'The high degree of overlap between class, religious, ethnic, regional, and gender inequalities makes education a potential minefield for future politicians and policymakers.'

As a result of the growing economic crisis – and international pressure from the World Bank and the International Monetary Fund (IMF), which 'have played a rising role during the past half century as purveyors of policy solutions to national educational (as well as economic) problems' (Mundy et al. 2016: 6) – Tanzania embarked on an economic recovery programme in 1986 that was tied to a series of structural reforms. From 1982 onwards, the public education system was gradually released from being solely the government's responsibility, and, in 1995, it adopted an *Education and Training Policy*. Programmes based on self-reliance, such as the community school movement, were abandoned because community schools did not improve their graduates' transition to the secondary level (Buchert 1994: 130ff.). Furthermore, the quota system was abolished (Cooksey et al. 1994: 229) and replaced with a free market economy approach, which was assumed to create equal chances for all in accessing education.

The Privatisation of Education and Its Impact on Christian Schooling

Private or 'non-governmental'[33] schools had begun to be established in Tanzania as early as the mid-1980s. But in 2001, a report by Lassibille and Tan (2001: 166), based on a survey 'conducted in 1994–1996 by the Bureau of Educational Research and Evaluation at the University of Dar es Salaam in collaboration with the World Bank', expressed concern about the rather low level of competitiveness of these market-dependent schools. On the one hand, the study claimed that deregulation and privatisation had caused 'a spectacular growth in enrolment, suggesting that an increased role for the private sector had indeed helped to counteract the adverse effects of the country's tight public budget situation on sector development' (ibid.: 146). Despite this overall optimistic assessment, however, the authors found that educational standards in many of these newly established private institutions were poor. In their estimation, these schools were lagging behind the public sector with regard to efficiency and had little chance of becoming financially sustainable.

---

[33] According to the Tanzanian government, the category 'non-governmental schools' covers both Christian and Muslim schools (including their seminaries) as well as other schools run by NGOs, private individuals, or international organisations.

Consequently, the authors called on the Tanzanian government to review its 'policy of benign neglect toward the private sector' and to make private education sustainable through further deregulation (ibid.: 147).

In the mid-2000s, private schools in Tanzania received a significant boost when the national government and the World Bank started a joint programme to increase enrolment rates at the secondary level, especially by strengthening community schools. In 2004, a credit-cum-grant of US $150 million was approved by the World Bank's International Development Association (IDA) in support of Tanzania's Secondary Education Development Plan (SEDP I) (Tanzania 2004; World Bank 2004).[34] The SEDP I was launched the same year and aimed not only to triple secondary school enrolment rates within a period of six years but also to improve the overall quality of higher education for the benefit of the 'development of society as a whole' (Tanzania 2004: i). As Joseph J. Mungai, the minister for education and culture at the time, put it: 'Without the expansion in access stipulated in SEDP, the transition from primary to public secondary schools would drop dramatically. This would clearly be unacceptable, not only to the Government, but also to the parents. It certainly would have acted as a disincentive to primary school enrolment, retention and completion' (ibid.: i).

The idea to rely on the earlier (Ujamaa) model of community schools in order to increase access to education – schools that were constructed by communities and whose recurrent costs (especially teachers' salaries) were financed by the government – was in line with the World Bank's preference for participatory development and community ownership at the time. Furthermore, Lassibille and Tan (2001: 152) found that community schools performed relatively strongly, especially when compared with the poorly performing Christian and *wazazi*[35] schools. In this regard, they surpassed their predecessors of the 1970s, which had been abandoned in the wake of structural reforms because of their alleged failure 'to be understood as a concept by rural populations' (Buchert 1994: 141).

In 2010, the Tanzanian Education Sector Development Programme (Tanzania 2010: 7) stated that the SEDP I had been successful in

---

[34] The SEDP I was a direct successor to the Primary Education Development Plan (PEDP), which was launched in 2001 and doubled enrolment rates by 2004 (compared with the level before the PEDP). One of the measures of the PEDP was the introduction of 'free' primary education, which released families from paying school fees; however, families still had to pay for school books and uniforms.
[35] *Wazazi* schools are managed by a parents' branch of the ruling party Chama Cha Mapinduzi. In 2001, they represented 10 per cent of the secondary schools in the country and depended almost exclusively on school fees, as did the Christian schools (Lassibille and Tan 2001: 148).

reaching its main goal: to significantly expand access to secondary education. Between 2004 and 2009, enrolment rates showed a 249 per cent increase in Forms I to IV and a 109 per cent increase in Forms V and VI. Furthermore, the transition rate from primary to secondary education had improved by 51.6 per cent during the same period. But, according to the Education Sector Development Programme, the SEDP I had failed to reach its goal to improve the quality of public secondary education, and it confirmed some of the concerns raised by the World Bank in 2004, which hinted at the 'moderate risks' posed by the SEDP I:

> One risk is that the government will be unable to deliver on promises to allocate more funds to education in general, and secondary education in particular in view of competing priorities ... A further risk is that the government may be unable to produce or hire sufficient numbers of teachers for the expansion of enrollments, or attract them to underserved areas. (World Bank 2004: i)

In 2010, the Tanzanian Ministry of Education and Vocational Training launched the SEDP II, emphasising that the new programme would address these shortcomings. In particular, the SEDP II contained strategies to overcome not only the 'poor performance in secondary examinations' but also the 'asymmetrical deployment of teachers of required qualifications ... whereby urban areas [are] having an advantage in recruiting more and better teachers compared to rural community secondary schools' (Tanzania 2010: 15). Furthermore, the SEDP II aimed to tackle the problem of 'insufficient infrastructure', including the high number of incomplete school construction projects and the lack or non-use of laboratories, as well as the issue of 'poor teaching approaches in the classroom' (ibid.: 15).

Despite the efforts of the SEDP I and SEDP II, however, both government and community schools continued to suffer from the rapid expansion of the public education sector, which was unable to provide the human and material resources necessary for such an ambitious undertaking. Between 2001 and 2008, the number of government secondary schools in Tanzania rose exponentially from 527 to 2,893, of which 2,802 were community schools. During the same period, the number of 'non-governmental' (i.e. mostly private) schools at the secondary level increased from just over 400 to 755. In the late 2000s, a wide range of Tanzanian sources in both print and visual media discussed the general decay of the public education system, including its low rates of recruitment and retention of teachers in the newly created positions and its generally poor infrastructure.[36]

---

[36] 'Has our education system gone to the dogs?', *The Citizen*, 15 October 2009.

The widely shared perception of a 'learning crisis' in Tanzania (Sumra and Katabaro 2014: v) triggered a dramatic change in the relationship between the non-governmental and the public educational sectors, making non-governmental schools significantly more attractive to students and their families. In particular, these massive shifts strongly enhanced the reputation of the Christian schools, which, in the early 2000s, had still been lagging behind government schools in the core curriculum subjects: mathematics, English, and Kiswahili (Lassibille and Tan 2001: 164). In subsequent years, many of these Christian schools were able to capitalise on their long-standing contribution to the educational field as well as on a range of ties with international organisations; this was highly beneficial for their position in the competition over resources, clients, and teachers.[37] Furthermore, after a number of critical internal assessments of church-run schools (CSSC 2001; 2005a), improvement measures were implemented, including teacher training and the development of training manuals in the sciences (CSSC 2005b). In the national Form IV results for 2004–5, 'Christian schools' improved their performance in all science subjects (except mathematics) and figured prominently among the top-ranked schools in the country (Martin nd; see also Chapter 1). As a consequence, the attractiveness of church-run schools in the increasingly stratified educational market grew significantly, and, during my research in 2008–10, Christian schools had become the preferred option for a good education, especially for rural and urban middle-class families (for the number and location of CSSC schools in Tanzania in 2008, see Figure 2.1).

Students' and families' quest for a good school has become particularly pertinent for secondary education because attending a 'good' secondary school is decisive for young people's future and the public education sector has significant weaknesses. Whether a school is judged 'good' or 'bad' is based not only on the performance of the school in the annual rankings but also on the quality and reliability of teaching. Language instruction is especially important: while English is the official medium of

---

[37] This is not to say that Muslim schools were marginalised intentionally by the Tanzanian government or by World Bank policies or that they have not profited from transnational ties. As elsewhere in Africa (Kaag 2018), investments from the Gulf and other Islamic countries have strengthened Islamic charities in Tanzania. However, as will be shown in Chapter 3, global events such as 9/11 combined with the structural arrangements of Muslim schools placed them in a weaker position overall when compared with their Christian counterparts (cf. Kaag and Sahla 2020). A significant exception are the Ismaili schools, which do not have an explicitly religious orientation. Equally, the Feza schools, which are run by the Gülen movement but do not position themselves publicly as 'Muslim schools', are ranked among the best-performing educational institutions in the country (Dohrn 2014; 2017).

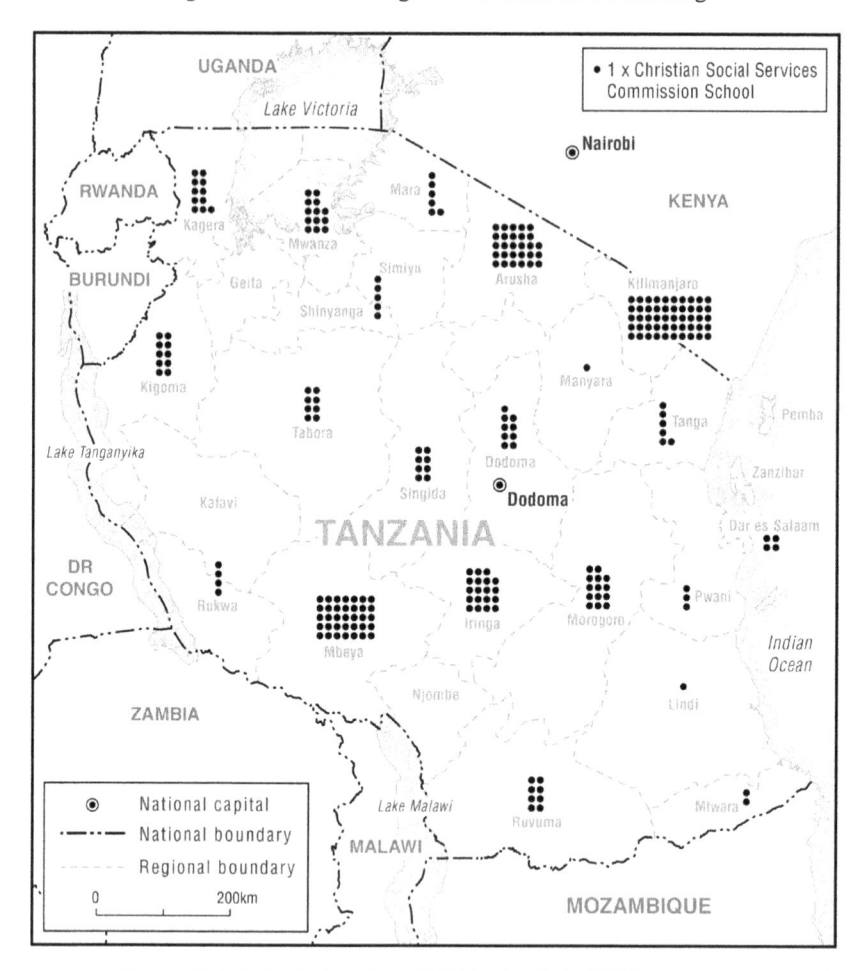

56   Entangled Histories of Religious Pluralism and Schooling

Figure 2.1 Schools listed as CSSC schools in 2008 were concentrated in those regions (Arusha, Kilimanjaro, Mbeya, etc.) that were also 'favoured in colonial times' (Mushi 2009: 62; Leurs et al. 2011: 20).

instruction in Tanzania, from the secondary level onwards, few state-run schools or higher learning institutions consistently employ English in their everyday teaching and learning. This in turn has a significant impact on students' performance and futures, since all national exams are conducted in English (Brock-Utne and Holmarsdottir 2004: 75ff.). As it is especially the private Christian schools that teach consistently in English – and as Tanzania's policy on the language of instruction has strengthened these schools' position considerably in recent years – the subsequent two sections discuss this aspect in detail.

Privatisation, Class Formation, and the 'Language Paradox'

It is remarkable that neither the SEDP I/II nor the evaluations of these programmes ever mentioned the 'language paradox' (cf. Mazrui 2004b) that has been responsible for some of the shortcomings of Tanzania's educational system – and its perceived 'crisis' – over many decades.[38] Thus, the situation in most government secondary schools in Dar es Salaam in 2009–10 mirrored the conclusion reached by Brock-Utne and Holmarsdottir (2004: 81) after studying the language policies and practices in primary and secondary schools in Tanzania and South Africa: '[L]earners are unable to benefit from educational opportunities if these are provided through a foreign medium of instruction that the learners do not understand.' They quote from a 1998 consultancy report commissioned for the Tanzania Ministry of Education and Culture:

> At secondary level the data reveals that teachers and students fail to learn effectively through the sole medium of English. Kiswahili is used in class for teachers to express themselves effectively and for students to understand their teachers. Kiswahili is the de facto medium of instruction in many classrooms. Those teachers who were seen using only English in class were often found to be misleading their students. Code-switching is not the solution for a bilingual education system. (quoted in Brock-Utne and Holmarsdottir 2004: 74)

Furthermore, no mention is made in the SEDP II of the connection between the issue of language and the dynamics of privatisation and social stratification. Brock-Utne and Holmarsdottir remark that language policy is also 'a class issue and ... the private schools find they can charge higher fees when they advertise with English medium schools, thus making it impossible for the children of the poor to attend these schools' (2004: 71). In this regard, the architects of the SEDP II could have learned from neighbouring Kenya, where a parallel development of class formation in relation to language use had been observed in the early 1990s. While English in Kenya had already been introduced from Standard 1 during British colonial rule, in the early 1990s it was found that the children who benefited from this policy were those who had access to the English language 'in their homes and community' (Bunyi 1997: 37). Furthermore, Abdulaziz stated that during this time in Kenya there was an increasing:

---

[38] While the SEDP II does not address the language challenge explicitly, it has included a strategy to 'improve English language competency to teacher trainees by making the language a compulsory subject at all Teachers College [sic] by 2012' (Tanzania 2010: 36).

number of high cost private and international schools where many of the teachers are expatriate native speakers of English. Children who go to these expensive schools come from the rich, Western educated élite, normally with both wife and husband possessing high competence in the English language ... The children live in exclusive and expensive multiracial and multinational suburbs where the primary language of the playground, shopping centres, schools, places of entertainment, churches and hospitals is English. (Abdulaziz 1991: 397)

In Tanzania, the use of Kiswahili in primary education dates back to the German colonial government, which introduced Kiswahili not only as the language of administration but also as Tanganyika's lingua franca and as the medium of instruction in primary schools. Kiswahili was then maintained for instruction at the primary level by the British government, but the new colonial power also changed the overall language of administration to English and introduced the latter as the medium of instruction in the newly established secondary education sector.

After independence, and in the context of Ujamaa politics, the decision to use English as the language of instruction in secondary and higher education was hotly contested. Kiswahili was introduced as the country's national language in 1962, and Nyerere's government launched several efforts to establish Kiswahili as the medium of instruction at the secondary level, too.[39] In 1980, Nyerere established a Presidential Commission on Education 'to review the entire educational systems' (Brock-Utne 2002: 26) and to examine the status of language as a medium of instruction.[40] The commission presented its findings in 1982 with the explicit recommendation to change from English to Kiswahili in higher education. It even set a date for the transition; it was to become operational at the secondary level in 1985 and at the university level in 1991 (Brock-Utne 2002: 26). However, the movement towards Kiswahili was abruptly stopped in 1983: the then minister of education, J. Makweta – who had chaired the Presidential Commission on Education – published an official press release saying that the 'expected change of medium' in education had been abandoned (ibid.: 27). The recommendation itself was never included in the published version of the report in 1984 (ibid.: 26).[41]

---

[39] On the history of language policies and politics in Tanzania's education system, see Roy-Campbell (1992), Brock-Utne (2002), and Gran (2007).

[40] Previously, a study commissioned by the National Kiswahili Council had identified the use of English in secondary education as a significant barrier to successful learning (Brock-Utne 2002: 26).

[41] Mazrui (2004a: 47–8) emphasises that Tanzania's sudden decision to maintain English as the medium of instruction at the post-primary level occurred at the same time 'as the country capitulated to the IMF and its draconic conditionalities, which forced it to reduce its subsidies in education and other social spheres'. While the World Bank officially encouraged the use of African indigenous languages at the primary level at

The decision to maintain Kiswahili as the medium of instruction at the primary level – and, concurrently, to mandate the use of English in secondary and higher education – is still reflected in Tanzania's educational policies today. The continued use of Kiswahili in primary education touches on the language's – historically not uncontested (Mazrui 2017) – symbolism of core values of national belonging and attachment in the country, and Tanzania's *Education and Training Policy* states that primary education should 'enable every child to acquire, appreciate and effectively use Kiswahili and to respect the language as a symbol of national unity, identity and pride' (Tanzania 1995: 5). In contrast, the teaching of English after primary level is addressed in a much more sober tone:

[A]t the end of seven years of primary education, pupils will have acquired and developed adequate mastery of this language, both spoken and written, to cope with the English language proficiency demands at secondary, post-secondary levels and the world of work ... The medium of instruction for secondary education shall continue to be English except for the teaching of other approved languages and Kiswahili shall be a compulsory subject up to Ordinary Level. (Tanzania 1995: 45)[42]

The consequences of the language gap between the different levels of Tanzania's educational system continue to be hotly debated (Stambach 2004: 97). The participants in this debate share the conviction that the current situation makes it more difficult for Tanzanian pupils and students to develop their full potential, although they disagree profoundly with regard to the conclusion that they draw from this predicament. In a telling exchange in the Tanzanian parliament (Kiswahili: *bunge*) in 2009, Dr Gertrude Rwakatare – a prominent neo-Pentecostal pastor, a Special Seats Member of Parliament from 2007 until her death in 2020, and the late owner of the St Mary's schools network in the country – referred to a (then) recent international university competition in which the Tanzanian participants had not scored highly. According to Dr Rwakatare, the main

---

the time – not only for the benefit of children's cognitive development but also to avoid interfering with national sovereignty (ibid.: 45–6) – it never provided the resources to make such efforts sustainable and, with its structural adjustment programmes, it contributed to 'the consolidation in the use of imperial languages in education' (ibid.: 46). In support of this policy, the British Overseas Development Agency launched a 'multi-million dollars English Language Teaching Support Project' in Tanzania in 1987 (ibid.: 49).

[42] Interestingly, Arabic – which was seminal for shaping the Kiswahili language through loanwords – does not play any role in these national debates. Arabic is seen today mostly as a language for the transmission of the Qur'an; even in the madrasa, it is often only 'passively acquired' (van de Bruinhorst 2007: 108). At the Islamic seminaries I studied, where lessons in Arabic were taught, mosque services were held mostly in Kiswahili, with the repeated infusion of Arabic words and phrases.

reason for the Tanzanian students' weak performance was the fact that 'many were unable to express themselves in the English language and ... that they lack confidence [*kujiamini*][43] and cleverness [*ujanja*] to respond as quickly as their competitors'.[44] Encouraged by the applause of the other members of parliament, Dr Rwakatare claimed that Tanzanian graduates were often unsuccessful in competing for 'international posts' and that this was due to the fact that they were not able to express themselves properly.[45] She continued:

> Even in [this competition], the young man couldn't explain *global warming*, but he could explain it in Kiswahili. Therefore, it is important now that we join our friends from Rwanda, who are *Franco-phone* [sic] and who are now changing to *Anglo-phone* because [the East African Community] is coming, how are we going to compete with them? Which *posts* are we going to get, if we cannot prepare our people so that they know English? If we ignore English [*tukipuuzia Kiingereza*] which is the language spoken by the whole world.[46]

The prime minister, who responded to Dr Rwakatare, was a passionate defender of the use of Kiswahili and insisted that the poor performance of the Tanzanian students in the competition could not possibly be related to the issue of language: Tanzanians were used to the 'daily switching between English and Kiswahili', he argued, so the competitors had probably been some odd students who 'hadn't prepared well' for the competition. He made an eloquent plea for the continued use of Kiswahili in the country:

> To tell the truth, I think that we need to try to strengthen the Kiswahili language, to build respect for it [*tuijengee heshima yake*], so that even if we go there [to this competition], they know that ... English is only our second language, our official language is Kiswahili. Let us go there and, if necessary, use a translation service in the same way as other countries are doing it.[47]

As Dr Rwakatare became even more insistent on her point in a follow-up statement, the prime minister switched to polemics, addressing 'Mama Rwakatare' directly in his response:

> [I]s it really true that the Nigerians know English better than the Tanzanians? If this is the argument [*hoja*], I do not believe it. I just say that there are Tanzanians in international organisations and they are doing well. Tanzanians join competitions and they *perform* very well. Aah! Mama Rwakatare, I believe that

---

[43] Debates in the Tanzanian *mbunge* are conducted in Kiswahili. However, participants often use English terms and phrases in order to highlight certain points.
[44] 'Majadiliano ya Bunge. Mkutano wa Kumi na Sita. Kikao cha Kumi na Tisa – Tarehe 2 Julai, 2009', National Assembly of Tanzania, 2 July 2009, p. 19, www.bunge.go.tz/polis/uploads/documents/1464197307-HS-16-19-2009.pdf (accessed 14 October 2019).
[45] Ibid., p. 20.   [46] Ibid., p. 21.   [47] Ibid., p. 21.

even you, if you go to England, you will speak English just fine.[48] ... *Jamani*, listen to the Kenyans speaking English, and then listen to me as a Tanzanian speaking English, Tanzania *is much better off if I may put it in English* than even [the Kenyans]. [Applause][49]

Getting by through 'Claiming'

While debates about the use of English versus Kiswahili in Tanzania's educational system have been ongoing for decades now – and while no solution to the resulting dilemmas is in sight – students and families adopt a rather pragmatic approach to dealing with the situation.[50] Thus, many families are investing a lot of money in order to secure a place for their children in a well-performing secondary school that teaches consistently in English, regardless of their children's pre-existing knowledge of or ability to perform well in the language. For the pupils and students themselves, this often means that they have to 'pretend' that they know English and that they understand what they are being taught in school, while in reality they often fail to comprehend the content and meaning. Teresa King, whom I wrote about in Chapter 1, explained this in our interview, which we conducted in Kiswahili.

TK You know, if you have graduated from one of the *government* primary schools where every lesson is taught in Kiswahili – when you enter the secondary school *suddenly* every lesson will be in English. Now you will be studying two things at the same time: the language and the subject. This means that you will be cramming [*unasoma*] and repeating [*unakariri*] so that you can give the answer in the exams. Sometimes we Tanzanians are *very intelligent*, more than other people, but we are just learning by heart [*unasoma*], *just claiming*.
HD What exactly is it that you *just claim*?

---

[48] In his claim, the prime minister alluded to the fact that Dr Rwakatare herself had attended government schools during her education and was nevertheless able to communicate (and study) 'internationally' (i.e. in the US). See Dr Rwakatare's *mbunge* homepage at www.parliament.go.tz/index.php/members/mpcvs/1560/2010-2015 (accessed 19 August 2019).

[49] 'Majadiliano ya Bunge. Mkutano wa Kumi na Sita. Kikao cha Kumi na Tisa – Tarehe 2 Julai, 2009', National Assembly of Tanzania, 2 July 2009, p. 21, www.bunge.go.tz/polis/uploads/documents/1464197307-HS-16-19-2009.pdf (accessed 14 October 2019).

[50] The impact of the language gap is felt in both structurally weak government schools and private schools. After one of the classes at the Al-Farouq Islamic Seminary for Boys – one of the Muslim schools in my study, where teaching took place mostly in Kiswahili (see Chapter 5) – I noted in my field diary: 'How are students supposed to write an essay in English during the national exams if they never exercise writing in English during class? If all the arguments they can refer to are their own notes from the lecture and the blackboard, which often consist only of keywords and phrases?'

TK You [are] *just claiming 'what is biology'*. Someone who has graduated from Standard VII does not know English, he or she will see how it is defined: that *biology is the study of living and non-living things*. She or he ... will be learning by heart how these words are written – [in the exam] one will write '*biology is the study of living and non-living things*', but one will not know what *living things* actually are. There are people who have a *high capacity* to *claim*, a person will *claim* that he or she has understood [*anapata*]. This is the reason that if you use a different language [in the exam] than from your *notes* in class, this person will fail [*anakosa*] ... Maybe if they *change* the *system* and start with *English and everything* on the *primary* [level], then people will have this basis [*ule msingi*]. You know, this is how we *Tanzanians* are.

In his book *Pedagogy of the Oppressed*, Paulo Freire (2005 [1970]: 71) states that modern education 'suffer[s] from narration sickness'. This condition is defined by the relationship between 'a narrating Subject (the teacher) and patient, listening objects (the students)', while the content of this relationship 'become lifeless and petrified'. Freire's critique of education is highly relevant in the context of Tanzania's language gap, where students are often not able to understand what they are being taught (or told). They have to use their 'brains'[51] not only for complying with their schools' requirements but also in order to succeed as members of a social group that is associated with a higher educational status and a certain way of cultural life.

Under these conditions, the strategies of Tanzanian students to 'cram', 'memorise', and 'learn by heart' (*kusoma, kukariri*) – without actually 'knowing' or 'understanding' (*kupata*) the content of what they recite – can be compared with the kind of mimicry that was established in colonial settings in order to 'get by' in relationships of inequality and dependency; these dynamics of dependency persist in the 'transnational, postcolonial age' (Ferguson 2002: 558), with its series of global structural reforms (Mazrui 2004a: 47–8). However, in other regards the students' situation is fundamentally different from the colonial setting, in that there is no '(white) colonial other' whom they have to or want to impress, or whom they could challenge or subvert with a perfectly performed mimicry. Thus, in a context where mimicry and imitation 'become excessive and uncontrolled' (Ferguson 2002: 553), these strategies mainly hurt the pupils themselves: while they may be trying to impress their teachers, fellow students, and families by 'claiming', their performances and simulations become utterly meaningless if they

---

[51] In Tanzania, Dar es Salaam is sometimes referred to as 'Bongoland' (*bongo* translates as brain): the place where people only survive by being 'cunning' and 'shrewd' (Sommers 2001: 2).

consequently fail in national examinations or the demands of higher education, at home or abroad.

Conclusion

This chapter has explored how the educational market of faith-oriented schooling in contemporary Tanzania has been shaped by the increasing popularity of church-run schools, which have been able to appropriate privatisation processes for their own (as well as their students') benefit, as their better-off students are usually better able to succeed in an internally stratified and contradictory educational system. The close entanglement of educational and socio-religious inequalities in today's Tanzania has been moulded by the history of Christian and Muslim encounters and the associated politics of schooling in colonial Tanganyika. The subsequent postcolonial reform processes were driven by ideologies of equality and mass education and, more recently, by deregulation and quality improvement, which favoured 'free market solutions over government interventions' (Mundy et al. 2016: 6). Since the 1990s, shifts in the educational sector have led not only to a growing socio-religious stratification of the educational landscape but also to the institutionalisation of a language gap that negatively affects students' transition to higher education and is perceived to reinforce their 'realization that their culture, its images and symbolic representation are of reduced value and significance' (Qorro 2006: 11).

In Chapter 3, I explore how the colonial and postcolonial histories of Christian and Muslim encounters and schooling in Tanganyika/Tanzania relate to the religiously diverse cityscape of Dar es Salaam today. In particular, I describe how religious pluralism in the city has become increasingly contested on the political level, and also diffuse. Part of this story involves the Tanzanian government becoming acutely invested in regulating the field by scrutinising 'suspicious' religious actors in the public domain (see Dilger 2020). In the final sections of the chapter, I discuss these attempts at regulating religious diversity in relation to the registration and vetting of Christian and Muslim organisations, which have become tied not only to global events and processes such as the War on Terror or the (unequal) establishment of transnational faith-oriented development interventions, but also to the haunting memories of the historical dissolution of the EAMWS in 1968 among Muslim revivalists.

3 Staging and Governing Religious Difference in the Haven of Peace

> They break the sixth commandment in churches [MATH 5:27]
>
> And worship false gods to get money in front of Gertrude Rwakatare's altar
>
> While at Bishop Kakobe's [church] they fall in front of the altar eeeeeeeeee ...
>
> Religion has become big business. *From the song 'Amka Tanzania' by Bongo Flava rapper Roma (2007)*[1]

> [M]any voices who monopolize the pulpits in churches and mosques have become voices that preach hate and intolerance against those unlike them and against women. Yet these are the voices that the government (and donors) feels obliged to engage to gain some form of legitimacy in terms of religious endorsement for their agendas. *Salma Maoulidi*, Censoring Religious Hate Speech *(nd)*

In Dar es Salaam over the last decades, encounters between Christians and Muslims have been shaped by the growing presence of Evangelical individuals and organisations, most prominently from the steadily booming neo-Pentecostal field (Hasu 2006; 2009; Dilger 2007; 2009). These neo-Pentecostal organisations have developed powerful religious – and sometimes also economic and political – networks, using their position to lobby not only against some of the 'mainline' churches but also against the allegedly growing influence of Islam in the country. According to them, revivalist Muslims want to turn Dar es Salaam – whose name means 'Haven of Peace' in Arabic – into Islamic territory and Tanzania into an Islamic state.

At the same time, Muslim revivalist individuals and organisations have also gained strong visibility in Dar es Salaam since the early to

---

[1] '*Amka Tanzania*' can be seen on the 'Tanzania' video, directed by Abbuy 6.1B and produced by Nah Real and Yuddi (Kama Kawa Records), Interscope Film Effects, www.youtube.com/watch?v=x1MtKGYjHzY (accessed 14 May 2019). I would like to thank Kelly Askew for allowing me to use parts of her transcription of this song for this book. '*Amka Tanzania*' is Kiswahili for 'Wake up, Tanzania'.

mid-1990s, competing not only with each other and with 'traditional' Islamic groups such as BAKWATA[2] (Loimeier 2007) but also with the neo-Pentecostal churches' sometimes aggressive approaches to proselytisation in the city (Ahmed 2008). In recent years, encounters between these two strands of Christianity and Islam have resulted in often heated public debates and even in acts of violence, which have raised concerns among both the government and the city's inhabitants (Wijsen and Mfumbusa 2004; Mbogoni 2005).

While the activities of both Muslim and Christian revivalist organisations have not been shaped by external influences alone, many of them have benefited from transnational ties with actors in North America, Europe, the Arab world, and several countries on the African continent (cf. Ahmed 2009; Stambach 2010a; Dohrn 2014). Both Christian and Muslim revivalist groups have initiated social service projects (Dilger 2009; Leichtman 2020) – and in this the field of education has become central for their engagement with the material and moral lives of the urban population (Dilger 2013a). In addition, while other religious organisations – most significantly the Catholic church – have also become involved in creating civil society initiatives and articulating political claims, it is the Christian and Muslim revivalists in particular whose moral and political agendas make it into the limelight of public debate. Both groups often make use of media technologies and other forms of public engagement, including neo-Pentecostal crusades, Muslim leaders' 'open air preaching' (Ndaluka 2014c: 155), and political manifestations and statements.[3]

This chapter describes how the development of the educational system in Tanganyika and Tanzania – and its entanglements with socio-religious inequalities over the last century (see Chapter 2) – has become embedded in the wider politics of staging and governing religious diversity and difference in Dar es Salaam since the 1990s. I argue that the efforts of 'new' Christian and Muslim actors to establish themselves in the educational market should be understood in the context of inter- and intra-religious competition, polemics, and criticism (cf. Soares 2016: 681ff.) in

---

[2] Baraza Kuu la Waislamu Tanzania (National Muslim Council of Tanzania).
[3] An exception to this is the public debate that the Roman Catholic church sparked in 2009 with its pastoral letter on civic education. While the church aimed to advise the urban public on how to elect 'good leaders regardless of their religions and ethnic group', several members of parliament urged it to withdraw the document as it allegedly posed 'a threat to the country'. 'Repent, Kingunge tells Catholics', allAfrica, 13 August 2009 (original source: *The Citizen*), https://allafrica.com/stories/200908140726.html (accessed 21 August 2019). In response to the church document, the Association of Imams in Tanzania published its own electoral guidelines (*waraka*: letter, epistle) in order to 'prepare Muslims in the country to keep in mind the interests [*maslahi*] of ... Islam' in the upcoming elections (Shura ya Maimamu Tanzania, Kamati Kuu ya Siasa 2009: 11).

the public arena that have shaped the field of Christian–Muslim encounters in the city.[4] I also show that the desire of many revivalist Christian and Muslim actors to compete and expand their spiritual, moral, and geographical territory in Dar es Salaam (Dilger 2014a) presents not only a challenge for the state to establish order (for example, in regulating religious instruction in schools or (de)registering religious organisations). It also presents a challenge for Christian and Muslim activists and organisations themselves, as the structural forces of moral and political ordering put pressure on them to legitimate and further expand their claims. To understand these dynamics, it is illuminating to look back at the historical antecedents of such potentially highly conflictual debates, including the still contested 1968 dissolution of the East African Muslim Welfare Society (EAMWS) by the Tanzanian government.

Religion, Economy, and Politics: Neo-Pentecostal Churches in Dar es Salaam

The Pentecostal presence in Tanzania dates back to the late 1920s, when the Swedish Free Mission and the Holiness Mission founded their first mission stations in central and south Tanzania respectively. But it was not until the late 1960s that churches such as the US-based Assemblies of God and the Elim Pentecostal church attracted larger groups of followers, partly due to their mediation of social and economic tensions arising from Ujamaa policies. According to Frieder Ludwig (1999: 190), it was the Pentecostal congregations, and not the former mission churches, that responded to the spiritual and social 'vacuum' created by the government's villagisation programme. They thereby managed to establish new church branches in the newly created settlements. After the end of the socialist regime, in the mid-1980s, it was again the Pentecostal churches that benefited from the challenges of globalisation and the negative socio-economic effects of structural adjustment programmes. However, while the Pentecostal movement in Tanzania grew steadily, counting more than 500,000 followers in the mid-1990s, it also became increasingly diverse as a result, splitting into innumerable sub-churches (Ludwig 1999).

Today, the Pentecostal movement in urban Tanzania encompasses a rich agglomeration of diverse congregations that are tied to a wide range of national and international religious traditions. In particular, it comprises a growing group of neo-Pentecostal churches that were founded mostly by Tanzanian pastors and bishops, independently of an

---

[4] Such positions are also expressed in popular and activist culture, as can be seen in the epitaphs at the start of the chapter.

international mother church. Some of the 'classical' Pentecostal denominations were grouped together in the Council of Pentecostal Churches of Tanzania (CPCT) in the early 1990s, but various neo-Pentecostal churches were excluded because the council defined some of their religious practices and ideas as 'non-Pentecostal'.[5]

As in other African countries (Meyer 1998b; Gifford 2004; Maxwell 2006), the appeal of the neo-Pentecostal movement in Tanzania has been associated with the social, economic, and spiritual uncertainties that have shaped people's lives in the context of neoliberal reforms and growing inequalities since the 1980s (Dilger 2007; Hasu 2007). In particular, the structural adjustment policies implemented under pressure from the World Bank and the IMF had a tremendous impact on people's lives in Tanzania. These reforms not only led to rising living costs and the impoverishment of rural areas, thus reinforcing migration to urban centres, but also reduced formal employment opportunities – mainly available to men until then – and stagnated salaries (see Tripp 1997: 30–59). Consequently, in the late 2000s, many of the largely female followers of the neo-Pentecostal churches in Dar es Salaam came from the urban underclass and the lower middle class: in other words, those most strongly affected by urbanisation and globalisation.

Particularly attractive to these less wealthy followers is the movement's gospel of health and well-being, which promises relief from occult forces such as spirits and witches that haunt urban citizens in their everyday struggles (Dilger 2007; Hasu 2007; Lindhardt 2009). Furthermore, these churches are popular with many for the development-related activities they have initiated for their followers and other urban people. Some of these churches have started to build schools, health centres, and financial institutions (Hasu 2007: 231; Dilger 2009); others have set up networks

---

[5] Interview with David Mwasota, Dar es Salaam, 8 October 2008. Among the churches that were not included in the CPCT initially were the Full Gospel Bible Fellowship church, led by Bishop Kakobe, which became widely known for its proclaimed 'AIDS healings' in the early 2000s (Dilger 2007) and for the bishop's intervention in the 2000 general election on behalf of the opposition party (Dilger and Malmus 2002: 199–200). Also excluded was the Glory of Christ Tanzania church, led by Pastor Gwajima, which was renowned for its claims to be able to return 'zombies' (*msukule, wasukule*) to life (Hasu 2009: 74), and Efatha, which runs its own television network (Hasu 2007: 231) and operated its own bank between 2009 and 2018. 'Central bank closes five banks', *The Citizen*, 4 January 2018, www.thecitizen.co.tz/news/Central-bank-closes-five-banks-/1840340-4250698-o7wwpsz/index.html (accessed 20 August 2019). Such exclusions have not always been permanent: in 2014, a report by the Pentecostal online platform *Gospel Kitaa* noted that the Full Gospel Bible Fellowship church and Efatha had become members of the CPTC. 'Hitimisho la Mfungo wa Siku 40 kwa Wapentekoste Tarehe 15 PTA', *Gospel Kitaa*, 14 February 2014, www.gospelkitaa.co.tz/2014/02/13/hitimisho-la-mfungo-wa-siku-40-kwa/ (accessed 20 August 2019).

of support and care on the community level (Dilger 2007), organising food banks and charity events for the 'neediest' in the city. For instance, the Dar es Salaam Pentecostal church (DPC) – a branch of the Pentecostal Assemblies of God, Canada, which has existed in Tanganyika since 1956 – has been organising 'charity days' since 2008. At these events, the DPC not only distributes food and clothes but also arranges medical examinations and free treatment for 'needy' church members and the surrounding community (Dilger 2014a; 2014b).

But neo-Pentecostal churches' followers are not only from the underclass and the lower middle class; they increasingly also target the wealthier upper middle class in their efforts to attract new followers and sustain their social service projects. For instance, in 1992, the DPC started a 'special programme' in order to attract English-speaking, well-educated members of urban society; since then, it has offered Sunday services in both English and Kiswahili. Especially among the English-speaking church members, urban professionals were strongly represented in the late 2000s; they came from a variety of working backgrounds (media, medicine, non-governmental organisations (NGOs), government offices, etc.) and national origins (Zimbabwe, Ghana, Kenya, Sweden, Ukraine), and some held degrees from international universities. It was these – better-situated – members of the English-speaking congregation who started to cater to the 'needy', primarily Kiswahili-speaking followers through the charity days mentioned above – and who thus laid the foundation for dividing the church into two parts, one more affluent and the other socially disadvantaged (Dilger 2014a).

Another example of the growing social differentiation *within* neo-Pentecostal churches is the Mikocheni B Assemblies of God church, which was led by Pastor Gertrude Rwakatare until her death in 2020. The Mikocheni B church is closely connected to – and also sustained by – a network of business professionals and government employees in the city whose privileged positions are felt within and beyond the church on multiple levels. During my research, this group of church members – women and men involved in private businesses or holding government positions – occupied the front pews at Sunday services. This 'inner circle' of church members also had privileged access to 'private' healing prayers in the church offices. They formed an entourage that accompanied Rwakatare's ritualised entry into the Sunday service and were distinguished from ordinary church members in that their (usually higher than average) weekly donations (*sadaka*) were announced publicly and by name to the congregation.

Apart from being the owner of the St Mary's school network (see Chapter 4), Dr Rwakatare was involved in various business enterprises and advocated for religion to play a stronger role in politics. As the leader of her church, she conducted a week-long 'prayer for the nation' around Christmas 2013, with the aim 'to unify' Tanzanians.[6] Furthermore, as Special Seats Member of Parliament, she made requests on behalf of Christians and other groups, especially women, who were underrepresented in political debates.[7] She also used her position to promote the involvement of Christianity in politics in general, for instance on issues such as abortion and homosexuality, which she strongly opposed, and she met regularly with a group of about 50 other parliamentary representatives who '[prayed] together during lunch and dinner time'.[8]

Muslim Differences and Revivalism in the Haven of Peace

Like the neo-Pentecostal churches and organisations, a broad spectrum of Muslim organisations and individuals are involved in a range of socially and politically transformative projects in Dar es Salaam today. Their activities are based not only on 'a normative (reformatory) discourse', but also on 'modes of programme-oriented agency which propose to translate a specific programme of change ... into social realities' (Loimeier 2010: 136). While these revivalist agendas and activities have become embedded 'in a matrix of international networks and media-based representations', they are at the same time 'situated in local contexts, wherein their advocates attempt to translate their interpretations for reality on the ground' (ibid.: 138).[9]

In his article on the history of Islamic reform in Tanzania and Zanzibar, Loimeier (2010: 150) argues that reformist tendencies on the East African coast were articulated as early as the late nineteenth century by Sufi sheikhs from the Qadiriyya, Shadhiliya, and Alawiyya orders: they introduced changes in Islamic practice with regard to new forms of *dhikr* (ritual prayer) and the celebration of the *Mawlid* in honour of the prophet Muhammad's birthday. While this first generation of Sufi reformers was

---

[6] 'Assembly prays for the nation as the new year approaches', *The Citizen*, 18 December 2013, www.thecitizen.co.tz/News/Assembly-prays-for-the-nation-as-the-new-year-approaches/-/1840392/2116022/-/60xubg/-/index.html (accessed 14 May 2019).
[7] For Dr Rwakatare's interventions in parliament on the subject of education, see Chapter 2.
[8] Interview with Gertrude Rwakatare, Dar es Salaam, 16 October 2008.
[9] The diverse ideological agendas and socially transformative missions of Muslim revivalists concern not only actors from the Sunni and Sufi Shafi'i schools of jurisprudence, but also those from the Shi'a, Ibadhi, and Ahmaddiya communities. However, as the latter are not involved as actively in public political debates as the former, they are not included here. At the same time, however, some of the Shi'a organisations have established their own schools and hospitals and conduct *da'wa* and medical missions (see Bilal Muslim Mission 2007; 2008; van de Bruinhorst 2007: 95; Scharrer 2013: 101ff.; Leichtman 2020).

fairly well integrated into the German and British colonial administration, it was the Sufi sheikhs of the 1930 and 1950s who established new educational centres such as the Muslim Academy on Zanzibar (founded in 1951) (ibid.: 150–1). These reformers also became involved in the struggle for independence and collaborated closely with President Nyerere in establishing BAKWATA. At the same time, they marginalised the preceding generation of Sufi reformers who had partly opposed the politics of President Nyerere (ibid.: 151–2).

Tensions among different Muslim factions increased in the subsequent decades, especially through the foundation of organisations that initiated their own educational and socio-political projects and denounced BAKWATA as a 'government organisation'. Following the Warsha ya Waandishi wa Kiislam (Muslim Writers' Workshop) in 1975, numerous bodies were established in the late 1980s and early to mid-1990s, including the Baraza Kuu la Jumuyia na Taasisi za Kiislamu (Supreme Council of Islamic Organisations and Institutions in Tanzania) (Loimeier 2010: 153), the Tanzania Muslim Professionals Association (TAMPRO), the Islamic Propagation Centre, and the Shura ya Maimamu (Council of Imams) (van de Bruinhorst 2007: 98). This network of organisations collaborates for political reform (ibid.: 98–9) and is sustained especially by a generation of Muslim sheikhs and other individuals with ties to Sudan, Saudi Arabia, Kuwait, Iran, Egypt, and Turkey, as well as to the USA and various European and other African countries (Ahmed 2009; Loimeier 2010: 154). Many of these organisations' employees – who also engage in new modes of activism in order to advance their socio-political agendas – define themselves as much via their educational and professional backgrounds as their religious identity. In contrast, BAKWATA religious leaders have often completed 'only' religious or theological training and, according to the reformers, lack administrative and technical skills.

Among this new generation of Muslim activists are outspoken critics of practices within the field of revivalist Islam itself, for instance the 'religious hate speech' of Muslim (and Christian) leaders (Maoulidi nd) and the position of Muslim women in Tanzania (Maoulidi 2002). However, other Muslim revivalists oppose the 'esoteric episteme' of Islamic learning within Sufism (Loimeier 2010: 154) and lobby against the practice of *dhikr* and certain forms of the *Mawlid*. Many also object to the flourishing Islamic healing market in Dar es Salaam, which is replete with little shops selling amulets, healing books, and herbs and roots for medical purposes (Wilkens 2009: 31ff.).[10] At the same time, this group also includes

---

[10] Despite such internal disputes, all Muslim revivalist positions in Tanzania are shaped by Sufi influences, as about three-quarters of all Muslims in the country belong to Sufi

sheikhs with an explicit affinity for South and East Asian forms of detoxification and energy healing.

Finally, the most prominent – and most publicly audible and visible – groups of Muslim revivalists are those that use Islam as 'a framework for political action' (van de Bruinhorst 2007: 99). These reformers publicly oppose certain Christian churches and organisations and the Tanzanian state's alleged domination of Muslims (ibid.: 95). Among these Muslim revivalist groups are the Uamsho (the Awakening) and the *Ansaar Sunna*, which Van de Bruinhorst (ibid.: 96) describes as a 'pietist' project teaching 'the right way of the Prophet and Salafiyya (pious ancestors)'. However, while these organisations have also vehemently criticised 'state-paid Muslim functionaries' (Loimeier 2010: 154) – among them previous generations of Sufi sheikhs who obtained influential government positions after independence (Nimtz 1980: 87–8) – they are often explicitly supported by sheikhs from the Sufi spectrum, as reflected in the Islamic Propagation Centre newspaper *An-Nuur* (van de Bruinhorst 2007: 95).

The socio-political concerns of this last group of Muslim revivalists – which also has partial overlaps with the second group in particular – are based essentially on three closely intertwined issues. First, there is a strong preoccupation with the political state of Tanzania and with (religiously based) social and political inequalities, as these were established before and after independence. While Muslims were central to the struggle for independence (see Chapter 2), they were marginalised in the distribution of political power in the post-independence government, and high-ranking positions were assigned mainly to the better-educated Christian leaders, many of them Catholics. The allegedly deliberate marginalisation of Muslims, and its impact on the socio-economic status of Muslims today (Said 1998; Dar es Salaam University Muslim Trusteeship 2004), are focal points in the discourse of Muslim activists in contemporary Dar es Salaam (Heilman and Kaiser 2002: 701–2). In addition, this perception of discrimination against Muslims by the government has been increased by the state's surveillance of Muslim groups that established close links to charity organisations in the Arab world in the early 1990s and also became involved in providing health and education services. The potential link between social service provision and *da'wa* (proselytisation) activities (Ahmed 2009: 427) has been observed critically and has led to the national government putting in place a number of restrictive measures (as is discussed later in the chapter).

brotherhoods. These are in turn part of the Shafi'i school of Islamic jurisprudence to which most Sunni Muslims also belong (van de Bruinhorst 2007: 95).

Such encounters with the controlling state feed into Muslims' sense of being marginalised with regard to schooling (Jumbe 1994: 121ff.),[11] employment, and economic opportunities (see also Loimeier 2007) – in short, of being deprived 'of their active citizenship' (Ahmed 2009: 426).

Second, according to Muslim revivalists, Tanzania has been a 'Christian state' for many decades, with the churches having expanded their historically established dominant position in the context of the social and economic crises of the 1970s and 1980s. In this, the reformers rely heavily on writers from within the Catholic church who suggest that the final years of Ujamaa were crucial for establishing the church's role in Tanzanian society (Jumbe 1994: 116), as it became an important player by providing relief assistance when the state had been weakened (Sivalon 1995: 187). The role of churches in social service provision was cemented further in a 1992 memorandum of understanding between the Christian Council of Tanzania and the Tanzania Episcopal Conference, on the one hand, and the United Republic of Tanzania on the other. This memorandum established: the Christian Social Services Commission (CSSC), with its focus on education and health; a commitment not to nationalise schools or hospitals in the future; close cooperation between international donors, the Tanzanian government, and the churches; and the 'willingness [of the government] to endeavor to include financial assistance to church-run social services in its bilateral negotiations, particularly with the government of the Federal Republic of Germany' (Sivalon 1995: 189). In the eyes of Muslim revivalists, this close alliance of the Tanzanian government, international (Western) donors, and the former mission churches was an internationally sanctioned way of turning the East African country into a 'Christian state' (see Jumbe 1994: 114ff.).[12] Such alleged aspirations are critiqued in the Muslim media and at public rallies in Dar es Salaam, where activists lobby for the introduction of sharia law and advocate for Tanzania to join the Organisation of the Islamic Countries (OIC).[13]

Third, and closely related to the second point, Muslim revivalists compete with neo-Pentecostal organisations over political, social, and

---

[11] See also 'NECTA Irekibishwe Haraka', *An-Nuur*, 7–13 September 2012, http://de.scribd.com/doc/105282102/ANNUUR-1033#scribd (accessed 14 May 2019).

[12] Indeed, the colonial system of subsidising church-run hospitals through government grants continued during Ujamaa and after Tanzania's transition to a multiparty democracy (Ludwig 1999: 90ff.).

[13] Such efforts are vehemently opposed by the Pentecostal bishops of Tanzania, who threatened in 2008: 'If the Parliament passes [a law on the introduction of] *kadhi* courts and agrees to Tanzania's joining of the OIC; then we Christians are going to request from the Parliament to pass a "section" for Christians to include our own court in the constitution' (PCT 2008).

spiritual/moral territory (Dilger 2014a; 2014b), as well as over the resources to create their own institutions and infrastructure and thereby overcome their status on Tanzania's societal and political periphery (see Kresse 2009: 78–9). As described above, Muslim revivalist organisations have established a wide range of transregional ties with actors in the Arab world and North Africa, and these provide them with funds for the building of mosques, schools, and hospitals, as well as scholarships for students in educational institutions in their own countries (Scharrer 2013: 60). At the same time, however, Muslim revivalist groups complain that they are largely excluded from access to the resources of European and North American development organisations and from the distribution of development funds through the Tanzanian government more widely. For instance, the general secretary of TAMPRO claimed in an interview in 2009 that around 90 per cent of the funds for HIV and AIDS in Tanzania in the category of 'faith-based development' are channelled through Christian organisations, despite the fact that, according to him, Christians and Muslims represent equal shares of the total population.[14] Some activists therefore became involved in establishing the Tanzania Muslim Welfare Network in 2010; this is carefully presenting itself as a 'trustworthy Muslim funding recipient' and has succeeded in attracting funds for HIV-related projects through its collaboration with the Tanzania Commission for AIDS (TACAIDS) (Becker 2014: 38ff.).

Governing Religion in a Secular State

So far, I have argued that over the last three decades the encounters between Christian and Muslim revivalist actors in Dar es Salaam have been shaped by competition, polemics, and criticism, as well as by mutual accusations of aiming to establish a 'religious monopoly' in the country. Both sides have claimed that the national government is biased towards the other. Against this background, the government has sought not only to emphasise 'religious neutrality' in the public sphere (Casanova 1994: 55) but also to govern the increasingly diffuse field of religious voices, actors, and resources (Dilger 2020; see also Bader 2009: 32). According to the constitution of 1977, Tanzania is a secular state in which 'every person has the right to the freedom of conscience, faith and choice in matters of religion, including the choice to change his [sic] religion or faith' (Tanzania 1977: Article 19). Furthermore, given the

---

[14] Interview with Pazi Semili, Dar es Salaam, 26 August 2009.

contested history and politics of Christian–Muslim relations in colonial times, and their goal of national unity, post-independence governments have been careful to stress religious equality.

In addition to balancing the presence of government representatives at religious events – and meticulously observing the alternating religious affiliations of presidents since the first multiparty elections in 1995 (see Chapter 2) – religious neutrality in post-independence Tanzania has been emphasised especially through the decision not to include 'religion' as a category in the national census since 1967 'on the grounds that [statistics on religious affiliation] were politically sensitive and could undermine national unity and security if not handled with care' (Ndaluka 2014d: 2). However, although the state has sought to establish order by not interfering in the religious field at all, these attempts at neutrality sparked strong criticism from revivalist Muslim groups and speculations about the 'true' figures of religious affiliation abound in Tanzania (Loimeier 2007: 148–9; Scharrer 2013: 54).

In particular, Muslim revivalists claim that the 1967 census – according to which 32 per cent of Tanzanians were Christians and 30 per cent Muslims, while 37 per cent held 'local beliefs' (Heilman and Kaiser 2002: 698) – was 'altered intentionally to reduce the percentage of Muslims in the population, since the 1957 census showed Muslims outnumbering Christians by a ratio of 3:2' (ibid.: 698). Similarly, some Muslim revivalist groups have claimed[15] that, according to a survey on 'Africa south of the Sahara', 60 per cent of the Tanzanian population was Muslim,[16] which seemed plausible to them, as, according to them, many Muslims in Tanzania live in polygynous marriages and therefore have more children. While such claims about being the 'religious majority' in the country are hard to sustain in the absence of reliable empirical evidence,[17] they have become the basis of Muslim activist demands that Tanzania should become an 'Islamic state' in the future (Scharrer 2013: 54). These activists also claim that 'Muslims might become increasingly

---

[15] For instance, at the presentation of the 'Guide for Muslims for the elections 2010' by the Shura ya Maimamu Tanzania (2009) on Dar es Salaam's central assembly ground, Mnazi Mmoja.

[16] 'Dola na Tatizo la Udini Tanzania', *An-Nuur*, 15–17 August 2000, www.islamtanzania.org/an-nuur3/277/277-13.htm (accessed 14 May 2019).

[17] The Muslim revivalists' claims about being the majority in Tanzania are contradicted not only by the 2010 survey by the Pew Forum (see Chapter 2, fn 5) but also by some scholars' claims that attribute Muslims' lower fertility rates to continued marginalisation (Omari 1984: 374ff.). On the importance of discussing the lack – and potential contradictions – of survey data in relation to the anthropology and history of religious plurality in Nigeria, see Nolte et al. (2016).

discontented as they witness a disproportionate share of privilege enjoyed by Christians' (Mazrui and Tidy 1984, quoted in Chande 1998: 199–200).

Despite its stance of being 'religiously neutral', the government of President Nyerere took measures to contain the potential for religious conflict by permitting only those religious organisations that served the enforcement of 'national morality' (Westerlund 1982: 94). Following this logic, the government installed BAKWATA in 1968, passed the Law of Marriage Act (in 1971) that prohibited Muslims from marrying multiple wives without the permission of their previous spouse(s) (ibid.: 94), and nationalised (most) Christian and Islamic schools in 1969 in order to give all Tanzanian students the world view of a secular-socialist education. However, with political and economic liberalisation, and the concurrent pluralisation of the religious field since the early 1990s, the potential for interreligious conflict increased further. Since then, governments have launched multiple efforts to shape the religious field according to their own agendas, often in close alignment with their international donors' and partners' interests (as in the case of the establishment of the CSSC in 1992, which actively included the former mission churches in social service provision).

Explicitly restrictive measures have been targeted particularly at Muslim revivalists. Especially after the terrorist attacks on the US embassies in Dar es Salaam and Nairobi in 1998, as well as in the wake of the events of 9/11, this course of action gathered momentum. The Prevention of Terrorism Act was passed in 2002 (Scharrer 2013: 66) and vetting by state authorities of Muslim organisations – and financial flows from Kuwait and Saudi Arabia – was intensified (see Chapter 6; on comparable developments in West and Central Africa, see Kaag and Sahla 2020). In the year 2000 the book *Mwembechai Killings* by Hamza M. Njozi was banned on the grounds that its contents were inflammatory (Wijsen 2014: 200–1). Among the neo-Pentecostal churches, Bishop Kakobe from the Full Gospel Bible Fellowship church was banned from campaigning for one of the opposition parties in the 2000 national elections and was threatened by the government with the closure of his church if he continued to do so.[18]

However, the governance of religious diversity in Tanzania is not restricted to revivalist Christian and Muslim actors; it also addresses the position of religious practices and organisations in the public sphere – and in relation to the state – more broadly. As examples of this, in the following sections I discuss: first, recent debates on religious instruction

---

[18] 'Tanzania: Dar bans clergy from election campaigns', *The East African*, 5 October 2000, https://allafrica.com/stories/200010050396.html (accessed 14 May 2019).

in (secular) state schools, which has also become a topic of contestation in other parts of Africa; and, second, the politics of (de)registering religious organisations by the state authorities. Third, I take up the example of the government's closure of the EAMWS in 1968, an event that continues to be hotly debated among revivalist Muslims and has become emblematic for their continuing 'negative' perception of postcolonial (as well as colonial) history (see Linke 2015: 185).

Religious Instruction in Public Schools

In South Africa, religious instruction has been defined recently 'as an educational and not a religious or confessional practice ... as the only legitimate and reasonable pedagogy for plural societies' (Tayob 2018: 2). In this context, efforts to institutionalise this new approach to religious education in the education sector exposes the tension between including dominant religious symbols and traditions in the everyday operations of a school and the rejection of 'learners from minority religious traditions' for violating school codes and norms (Tayob 2017). Furthermore, state authorities struggle with not only the challenge of defining *what kind* of 'religious diversity' is tolerated in schools, but also how to represent 'religion' itself in the context of secular education (Tayob 2018).

Comparable struggles can also be noted in Tanzania, where religious instruction is still not a mandatory subject in public and private schools. The teaching of '*dini*' (religion) is offered on a voluntary basis at all levels of the educational system to individual groups of pupils according to their faith; it may involve singing, praying, or teaching from the religious scriptures. However, there is no clear guidelines on who qualifies as a teacher of *dini* – religious leaders or contracted teachers – nor is there clear institutional support for teaching these subjects. In religiously motivated secondary schools and seminaries, on the other hand, religious instruction can also include the subjects of Islamic Knowledge (alternatively called Islamic Studies), Bible Knowledge (O level), and Divinity (A level) – though again without relying on a fixed curriculum or texts approved by the state. These latter subjects are then examined through the National Examination Council of Tanzania (NECTA) during the national exams, but the lack of an agreed curriculum continues to create considerable uncertainty.

In 2005, the Ministry of Education and Culture (MoEC) announced that it was going to standardise religious instruction in public and private schools and introduce an additional, compulsory subject entitled 'Religion and Ethics' (*dini na maadili*) for all levels of education. In the same year, the MoEC led a study tour to Uganda, where representatives of the umbrella organisation EDIMASHUTA[19] were 'to learn from others so as to ... improve the existing curriculum and prepare a new curriculum of teaching religion and ethics in Tanzanian schools' (EDIMASHUTA 2005). However, while the tour included representatives from the MoEC, NECTA, the Tanzania Institute of Education (TIE),[20] and different religious groups – including the Tanzania Episcopal Conference, the Christian Council of Tanzania, and BAKWATA (NECTA 2005) – it was met with fierce criticism by Muslim revivalists. In addition to complaining that they had been excluded from the debate on religion and ethics, revivalists claimed that the inclusion of ethics (*maadili*) in religious instruction – for instance, in the context of topics such as corruption (*rushwa*) or terrorism (*ugaidi*) – would 'mix up' (*kuchanganya*) the writings of the Bible and Qur'an. As a result, religious instruction would become an academic subject like, for instance, geography, instead of offering the opportunity to teach about religion (*dini*) and faith in God (*imani ya Mungu*).[21]

The debate about the exact definition and scope of religious instruction – and who has authority to provide definitions for the subject 'religion and ethics' and 'religion' itself – was still ongoing during my research in 2010, and it triggered severe doubts among Muslims about the government's agenda with regard to teaching religion in public schools (Mwananchi 2013). Nevertheless, the TIE released two documents in 2008 that formulated guidelines for the preparation of religious education syllabi for all educational levels by representatives of the Christian and Muslim faiths. In addition to information about the content and didactics of religious teaching, these syllabi (*mihtasari*) are required to include topics such as human rights, HIV and AIDS, road safety, or the fighting of corruption (TIE 2008a; 2008b). However, the *mihtasari* from 2008 did not eliminate concerns among the various parties involved about the documents' status for teaching *dini* in schools; in 2010, when I asked an employee of the Ministry of Education and Vocational Training how NECTA was preparing the exams for these two

---

[19] Originally, the debate on the standardisation of religious instruction had been started in the early 2000s by UMAKA – an interreligious association in the Kagera region that had articulated the need for a syllabus on this topic and for the teaching of religion and ethics in relation to HIV and AIDS (UMAKA 2004). This initiative was then extended by the MoEC to the national level through the foundation of EDIMASHUTA. EDIMASHUTA's full name is Umoja wa Elimu ya Dini na Maadili Shuleni Tanzania (Association of Religious and Ethics Instruction in Tanzanian Schools).
[20] The TIE is an organisation under the Ministry of Education and Vocational Training.
[21] 'Somo la Dini na Maadili: Mpango wa Siri Kubwa', *An-Nuur*, 14–20 June 2013, https://zanzibariyetu.files.wordpress.com/2013/06/annuur-1075.pdf (accessed 14 May 2019).

subjects without a binding curriculum, she shrugged and said: 'Even the employees of NECTA say, "We are just doing it."'

Numbers and Files: Registering – and Deregistering – Religious Organisations

The governance of religious difference in Tanzania also includes the act of registering (and deregistering) religious organisations; this has become central for defining the increasingly tense relationship between religious groups and the controlling postcolonial state since the early twenty-first century (Dilger 2020; see also Bader 2009: 35). In 2009, I conducted a survey of the Ministry of Home Affair's (MoHA) Registrar of Societies Office registration books in the context of the politics and dynamics of registering religious organisations from the early 1980s onwards.[22] This close examination not only confirmed that there was an overall continuous increase in the registration of religious organisations between 1980 and 2009 but also showed that there was even a kind of 'religious resurgence' (Robertson and Chirico 1985) in the government books around the mid-1990s, which then declined steeply in the late 1990s and early 2000s (Figure 3.1).

Of course, the mere act of submitting an application does not indicate anything about the actual religious practice of the respective organisation or the concrete effects that a registered organisation has on community life in Tanzania. And many smaller churches are never registered, as they are counted as branches (*matawi*) of their mother churches. However, these figures do show that, around the time of political and economic liberalisation in Tanzania, a growing number of religious actors made a deliberate effort to become government-recognised entities. The MoHA books also show that government 'scrutiny' of registration applications increased around 2000, with some religious groups not being registered at all and other applications being rejected or revoked. Figure 3.2 demonstrates that the number of 'open registrations' – those cases where the MoHA invested more time than normal for vetting a religious organisation – increased steeply from the turn of the twenty-first century. Furthermore, there was a striking peak in the number of rejected or

---

[22] Officially, all religious organisations in Tanzania have to register under the Societies Act of 2002 at the Ministry of Home Affairs. For this process, they are required to submit a constitution of their organisation or group; the names of ten founding members; and the names, curricula vitae (CVs), and photographs of their governing board (Tanzania nd). Furthermore, they are asked to provide a document from a governing authority, such as the district commissioner or their 'parent ministry/institution', in support of their application (ibid.).

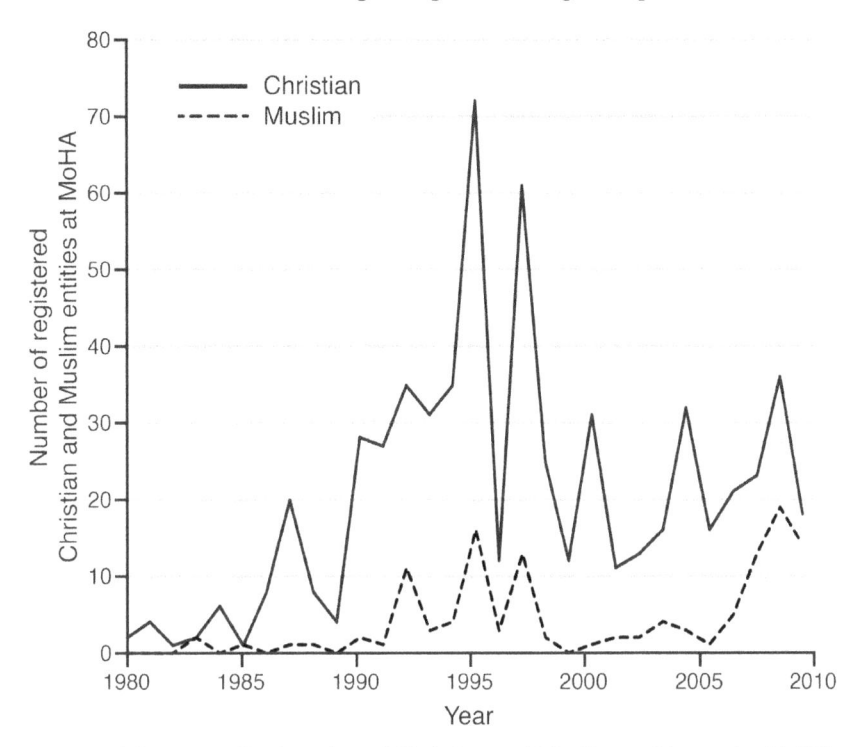

Numbers and Files: Registering – and Deregistering 79

Figure 3.1 Registration of Christian and Muslim entities at the MoHA (1980–2009).

revoked applications from religious organisations in the years 2000–2, with 24 applications from Christian groups falling into this category (Figure 3.3).

Admittedly, it would be brave to argue a causal connection between the Tanzanian government's vetting of religious groups and world developments such as the 'War on Terror' or the growing attractiveness of faith-based organisations in global development based on the registration books alone. When I asked MoHA employees for an explanation of the increase in open registrations around the year 2000, they were largely unaware of such shifts. But even if there were a causal link between the politics at the MoHA and global developments in religion and politics, the registration books would not have supported the claims of some Muslim revivalists in Tanzania that the national government was especially biased against Islamic actors in the area of registration (but see below). On the contrary, it was mainly Christian organisations whose registration processes were marked as 'open' in the MoHA books – there

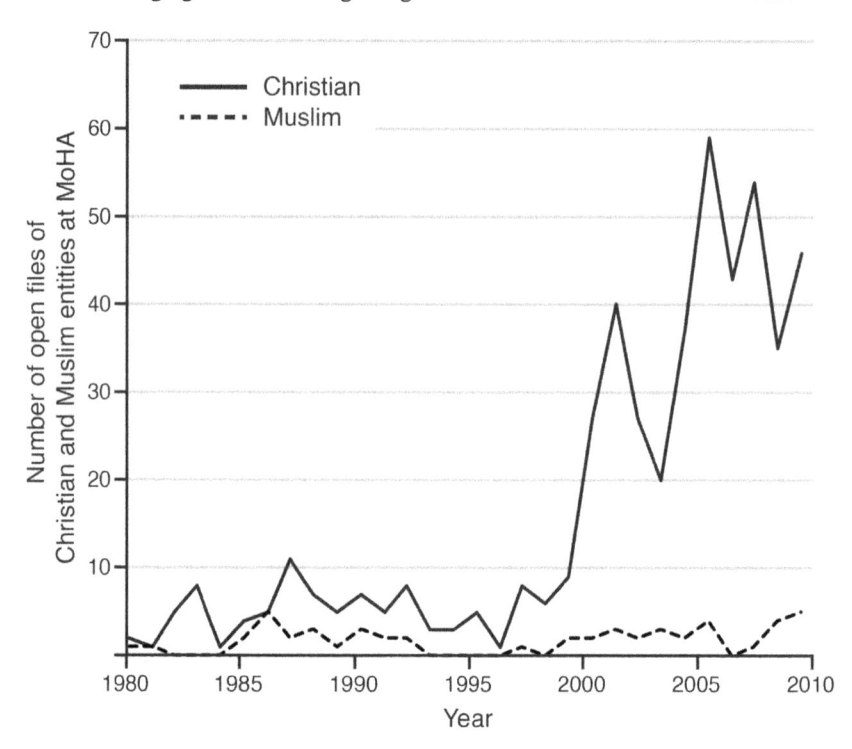

Figure 3.2 Open files of Christian and Muslim entities at the MoHA (1980–2009).

were 492 Christian and 51 Muslim 'open' applications between 1980 and 2009 (Figure 3.2) – despite the fact that they had submitted complete application files.[23] Furthermore, most of these open cases were applications from neo-Pentecostal or Evangelical organisations, with many of their names including terms such as 'faith', 'life', 'revival', 'ministries', 'fellowship', 'Philadelphia', 'harvest', 'praise', 'international', or 'outreach' (Figure 3.4).

One of the MoHA employees explained that the vetting of religious organisations was conducted by the Ministry of Defence and National Service, and that they were allowed to practise even before the registration process was completed as otherwise it would be 'difficult to vet them at all'. Furthermore, she remarked that, while 'earlier' religious

---

[23] While significantly fewer Muslim organisations applied for registration at the MoHA, they faced proportionally fewer delays in registration than their Christian counterparts in the early 2000s.

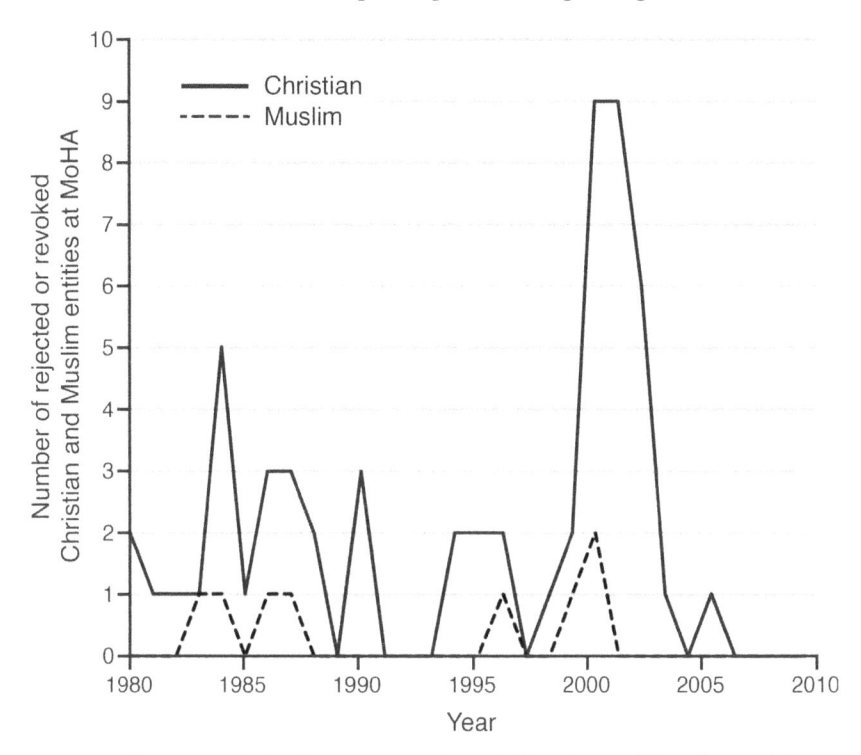

Figure 3.3 Rejection or revocation of Christian and Muslim entities at the MoHA (1980–2009).

organisations had been registered 'straightaway', 'these days [i.e. 2009] one would look carefully at the work of such organisations as many of them are liars [*waongo*]'.

In order to prove her point, she showed me the file of a neo-Pentecostal church that had applied for registration in October 2005. Along with a temporary district-level permit that allowed the church to practise until a conclusive decision was made by the MoHA, the one-inch-thick file contained several articles from Tanzania newspapers reporting on rumours that one of the church members had embezzled US$20 million. The file also contained a letter of support from a US church – probably the applicant's mother church – that emphasised that 'no funds of such an extent had ever been transferred to Tanzania' and that the addressees should stop paying attention to such rumours (literally: 'You Africans have to stop that'). Finally, the file contained the constitution of the proposed church and the CVs of its leaders, along with a document entitled 'Special Prayer' that praised the 'good work' of

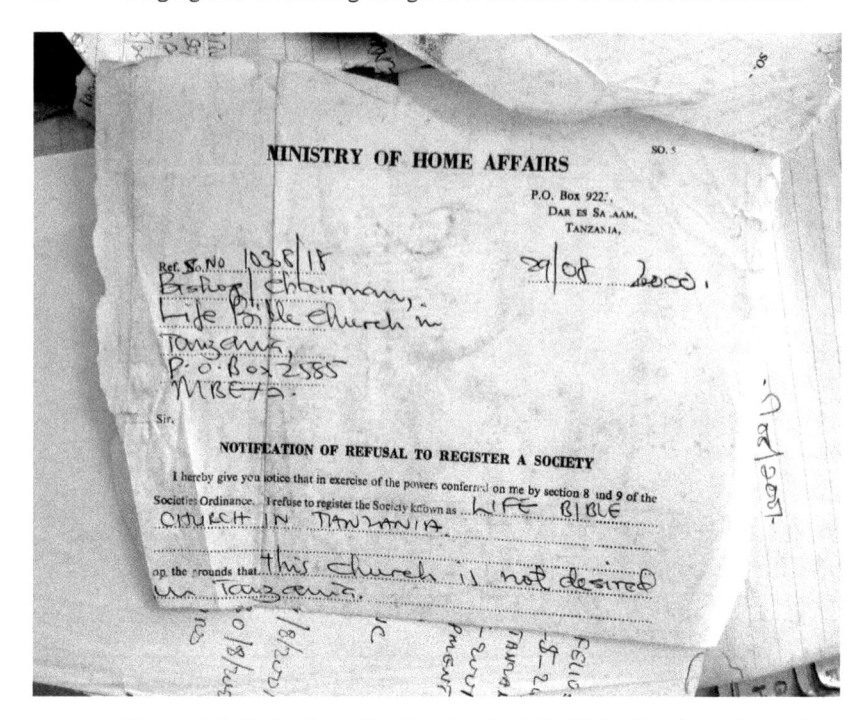

Figure 3.4 Refusal notification for the Life Bible church in Tanzania (Mbeya), dated 29 August 2000 ('This church is not desired in Tanzania').

the government authorities and each of the cabinet members, the army, and the court. However, while the church 'prayed' strongly for each representative of the government (*tunamwombea*), the vetting process dragged out, and the church had still not been registered during my visit to the MoHA in August 2009.

Incorporating Muslim Organisations

While the MoHA's registration books did not display an obvious bias against Muslim organisations, they did reveal that very few Muslim organisations even applied for registration. When I asked the employees why this was, I learned that – contrary to the website of the MoHA, which claimed that it registered all religious societies in Tanzania – most Islamic organisations were actually registered through the Registration Insolvency and Trusteeship Agency (RITA), which was established under German colonial rule in 1917. Today, RITA is 'an Executive

Agency under the Attorney Generals Chambers in the Ministry of Justice and Constitutional Affairs ... [which] aims at ... incorporation of trustees, safeguarding properties under trust, of deceased persons, insolvents, and minors to enable the law to take its course'.[24]

Neither the employees at RITA nor those at the MoHA were able to explain conclusively how the practice of registering Christian and Muslim organisations differently had been established. One MoHA employee claimed that Christian organisations had to register with RITA, too, after completing the process at the MoHA; however, in practice the Christian entities rarely submitted a second application to RITA[25] and Islamic organisations usually applied exclusively for incorporation as trustees. A RITA employee claimed that the specific structural characteristics of Islam and Christianity had led to different forms of registration within the Tanzanian bureaucracy. According to him, the Christian faith is more hierarchical than Islam, which led churches and Christian organisations to register as societies, especially if they were branches of a mother society that had been registered previously with the MoHA.[26] Mosques and madrasas, in contrast, applied independently as they often did not have a mother organisation through which they could acquire land or property. The latter explanation had some plausibility with regard to the earlier mission churches, whose headquarters had been established in Tanzania for many decades. However, it was less convincing as far as the neo-Pentecostal churches were concerned, as they often registered at the MoHA completely independently of any mother church.

While no conclusive explanation can be provided for the different registration patterns of Christian and Muslim organisations, the actual procedures at RITA and the MoHA were similar. Applicants were asked to submit a form with the names of the trustees, along with the entity's constitution, and an application fee (TZH 100,000 in 2014). Applicants also had to submit a letter of recommendation from their respective district commissioner and, in the case of religious organisations (for instance, mosques or madrasas), from 'relevant supreme religious Institutions'.[27] The registration books did not confirm a third claim made by the MoHA

---

[24] See the RITA website at www.rita.go.tz/page.php?pg=82&lang=en (accessed 21 August 2019).
[25] For instance, when they acquired property and land for which they needed registration as a trustee.
[26] Societies Act 2002, Chapter 337, 2[2].
[27] See www.rita.go.tz/page.php?pg=94&lang=en (accessed 21 August 2019). Some RITA employees claimed that such letters were usually provided by BAKWATA (see also US Department of State 2014), while others stated that letters from other religious bodies were also acceptable. In most of the applications I reviewed, no letter of support from *any* religious body was included.

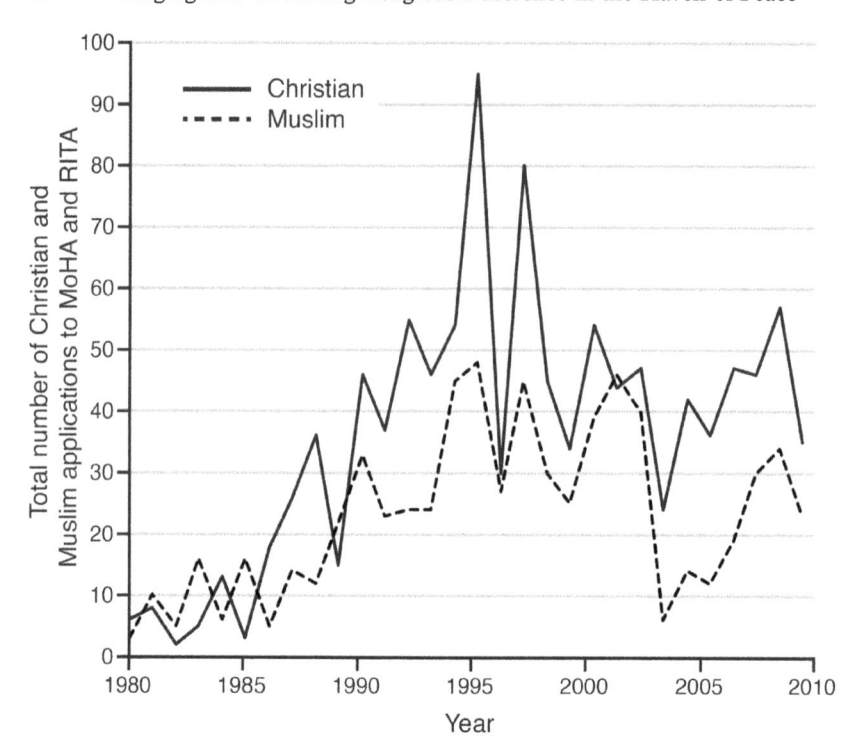

Figure 3.5 Christian and Muslim applications to the MoHA and RITA (1980–2009).

and RITA employees: namely, that incorporation as a trust at RITA was 'easier' and 'quicker' overall than registration as a society at the MoHA. While RITA's registration books did not provide any information about the open status of applications, they did display multiple instances of organisations being 'revoked' and 'declared as unlawful'.[28] The RITA books also corrected the previous impression of the MoHA files, which had suggested that significantly fewer Muslim organisations than Christian ones were registered in Tanzania after the end of Ujamaa. Figure 3.5 displays the combined registrations at the MoHA and RITA and shows

---

[28] However, between 1980 and 2009, applications from only one Christian and two Muslim organisations were refused or revoked at RITA. This stands in stark contrast to a media report from 2009, which claimed that the government threatened to deregister 100 Christian and Muslim organisations because they did not fulfil their duties as trustees. 'Serikali yatishia kuzifuta taasisi zikiwemo za dini', JamiiForums, 3 September 2009 (original source: *Gazeti la Mwananchi*), www.jamiiforums.com/threads/serikali-yatishia-kuzifuta-taasisi-zikiwemo-za-dini.37898/ (accessed 20 August 2019).

that the numbers of applications from Christian and Muslim bodies between 1980 and 2009 were quite similar and often followed parallel trends in 'weak' and 'strong' application years.

The 'Special' Case of the East African Muslim Welfare Society

The most prominent example of an Islamic organisation that was declared 'unlawful' in post-independent Tanzania is the EAMWS.[29] As mentioned above, this case is widely remembered among Muslim revivalists and has been referred to by scholars of religion as an 'Islamic crisis' (Rasmussen 1993: 58; Chande 2008: 108). In fact, the continued evocation of the event as one reason for activists' claims about the systematic marginalisation of Muslims in the country may explain how this particular memory has thrived in the context of perceived 'hostility' from the state and from the public at large (see Buyandelger 2018: 79).

The most detailed account of the course of events is probably provided by Mohammed Said (nd[a]);[30] this account also sustains the dominant narrative among Muslim revivalists that the EAMWS was deregistered by the Tanzanian government because of 'its ultimately pan-Islamic outlook' (Westerlund 1982: 95) and that it was then 'replaced' with the 'government organization' BAKWATA (Ndaluka et al. 2014: 64; see also Rasmussen 1993: 58; Ludwig 1999: 97–8; Chande 2008: 108–9).[31] In 'Islam and politics in Tanzania', Said argues that the end of the EAMWS was initiated at the society's annual conference in 1966, when a 'splinter group' openly opposed the leadership of the Aga Khan and lobbied for an 'indigenization of the constitution of the EAMWS' (Said nd[a]). This motion was supported by the TANU government, which regarded the (international) EAMWS leadership as 'a threat to its own political domination over [the] Muslim majority' in the country

---

[29] Christian organisations were also deregistered: for instance, the Jehovah's Witnesses and their publication *The Watchtower* were declared 'unlawful' for a period of five days during Ujamaa in 1965 (Höschele 2007: 400; see also Westerlund 1982: 95).

[30] Said's book was published at www.islamtanzania.org/nyaraka/islam_and_politics_in_tz.html; all direct quotations refer to this online source.

[31] In 2012, the Muslim newspaper An-Nuur summarised the events in the following way: 'The government broke all Islamic organisations with power, as for instance the EAMWS, and established BAKWATA instead, whose agenda and positions are basically to protect the government's interest rather than to support religion.' 'Serikali Itakuwa Imejifunza Jambi Zoezi la Sensa', *An-Nuur*, 7–13 September 2012, http://de.scribd.com/doc/105282102/ANNUUR-1033#scribd (accessed 14 May 2019).

(Said nd[a]; see also Chande 2008: 108).[32] Furthermore, the TANU government criticised the fact that the EAMWS was financed primarily through the Aga Khan and the relatively wealthy Ismaili Asian Muslim community in Tanganyika and abroad. It claimed that such funding made the EAMWS 'an instrument of the big bourgeoisie which was being controlled by the capitalists who are exploiting the common people' (Said nd[a]; see also Chande 2008: 108). In its efforts to create a split within the Tanzanian section of the EAMWS, the TANU government removed Tewa Said Tewa – then president of the Tanganyika Council of the EAMWS and simultaneously a minister under Nyerere – from his government position and made him an ambassador to China. The TANU government also backed the rise of Adam Nasibu, the regional secretary of the EAMWS Bukoba branch, who pushed for a revision of the EAMWS constitution by stating 'that socialism was compatible to the teachings of the Holy Quran' (Said nd[a]).

In late 1968, the Tanganyika Council of the EAMWS formed a commission in order 'to probe into the crisis' (Said nd[a]). However, the commission's work was hampered by the government's 'propaganda machinery against the EAMWS leadership' as well as by public agitation incited by the 'dissident group with Adam Nasibu as its main spokesman' against the Aga Khan (ibid.). When Tewa Said Tewa, president of the Tanganyika Council, and Bibi Titi Mohammed, his vice president, asked President Nyerere for support, they were 'scolded ... like naughty school children' (ibid.). At the beginning of December 1968, nine out of 17 regional groups had withdrawn from the EAMWS, which paved the way for the establishment of a new 'pro-government organisation' (ibid.). Finally, the dissident group's time arrived when the TANU government claimed that the EAMWS's financial report was incorrect, following which the Aga Khan resigned from his position as chief patron of the society. On 13 December that year, an Islamic National Conference was held in Iringa, and BAKWATA was established as the new National Muslim Council. On 19 December, the EAMWS was declared 'unlawful' and all its 'moveable and immoveable property were ... vested to BAKWATA as from 30.6.1969'.[33]

Both Muslim activists and scholars of Islam structure their account of the events related to the EAMWS around two main axes: (1) the conflict

---

[32] Indeed, the EAMWS had been able to accumulate growing influence in society through the building of mosques and schools; it supported 86 schools in Tanzania in 1966 (Ludwig 1999: 97; see also chapter 2).
[33] 'Registered trustees of the East African Muslim Welfare Society', Tanganyika Office of the Registrar-General, 1969, File No. I/350.

between the Bukoba branch and the Tanganyika headquarters of the EAMWS; and (2) the class-, ethnicity-, and/or race-based conflict between 'Pan-African Muslims' and their 'Asian financial supporters', which was essentially driven by the political agenda of the TANU government (Chande 2008: 108). While activists and scholars also mention the role of individual actors within the EAMWS – especially Tewa Said Tewa, Bibi Titi Mohammed, Adam Nasibu, and the Aga Khan himself – they tend to exclude other figures who played a part in the events of 1968 and the preceding years, figures whose names are suggested by the 'Registered trustees' file kept by RITA.[34] Furthermore, the file indicates that tensions escalated not only between the Bukoba branch and the Tanganyika Council of the EAMWS but also between the Tanganyika Council and the Supreme Council of the EAMWS, which was under the direct patronage of the Aga Khan.

Back to the Files: An Alternative Account of the End of the EAMWS

The RITA file opens with the EAMWS' certificate of incorporation, dated 12 May 1962. This lists four trustees: the Honourable Chief Abdulla Said Fundikira (Dar es Salaam), Alibhai Mohamedali Karimjee (Dar es Salaam), Count Fatehali Dhala (Mombasa), and Hassen Kassim Lakha (Kampala). The EAMWS constitution from 1960 states that, apart from the propagation of 'Islam in East Africa by all reasonable means', one of the principal aims of the society was 'to render assistance for the advancement, betterment and welfare of such East African Muslims who in the opinion of the Society need assistance in education secular and religious, religion, social, health and other similar spheres'. After documents noting the replacement of two of the original trustees in 1964,[35] the next entry in the file is a letter by Tahir Ali (dated 27 June 1967), advocate of the registered trustees of the EAMWS, informing the Office of the Administrator General that 'a Tanzania Council of East African Muslim Welfare Society has recently been formed and it appears that they have selected their own trustees'. Ali writes:

It has come to our above-mentioned client's notice that instead of registering themselves as a separate Society the Tanzania Council applied to the Registrar of

---

[34] Ibid. Notable among these figures were Abdalla Said Fundikira (trustee and president of the EAMWS Supreme Council), V. M. Nazerally (honourable organising general secretary of the EAMWS), D. J. A. Dowdall (administrator general of trustees), and Tahir Ali (advocate of the registered trustees of the EAMWS).
[35] In addition to Fundikira and Dhala, two new names are listed as trustees: Prince Badru Kakungulu (Kampala) and Mr Abdulkarim Yusufali Karimjee (Mombasa).

Societies for a change of name from East African Muslim Welfare Society to Tanzania Council of East African Muslim Welfare Society. Our clients have taken appropriate steps to rectify the matter with the Registrar of Societies ... If the Tanzania Council of East African Muslim Welfare Society apply [sic] to register themselves as a separate body it should be noted that the constitution makes no provision for appointment of separate Trustees of the Tanzania Council.

Ali's concerns were confirmed by the 1968 application of the 'Registered Trustees of Tanzania Council of E. A. Muslim Welfare Society' for incorporation as a trust, an application that had been stamped by three notary publics between June and November 1967 and then signed by Al-Haj Tewa Said Tewa, Al-Haj Saleh Masasi, and Anver Ali Karimjee on 3 February 1968. Furthermore, the application also contained a request to vest 'all lands, properties that are acquired in the name of the Tanzania Council of E. A. Muslim Welfare Society' into the proposed body corporate; this line was struck through by the administrator general, D. J. A. Dowdall, on 3 March 1968 and overwritten in turquoise ink with the word 'None'. On 21 February 1968, Dowdall wrote a letter to the four trustees of the EAMWS in Tabora, Dar es Salaam, Kampala, and Mombasa, informing them that he had:

refused to proceed with the application on the ground that the certified copy of the Constitution, Rules and Regulations of the East African Muslim Welfare Society do not provide for the appointment of a Tanzania Council of the Society[36] nor do they allow for the incorporation of trustees for such Tanzania Council ... On the 17th February, 1968, Al-Haj Tewa Said Tewa called on me following receipt of my letter of refusal and indicated that it was intended that the Constitution, Rules and Regulations of the East African Muslim Welfare Society should be amended in order to allow inter alia the incorporation of Trustees for Regional or District Councils of the Society and in particular for the Tanzania Council with Headquarters in Dar es Salaam ... Would you please confirm, firstly, as to whether or not it is intended to amend the Constitution, etc., of the East African Muslim Welfare Society, and, secondly, if it is so intended, what precisely are the amendments, and thirdly, if it is so intended, when it is anticipated that such amendments shall be duly accepted and passed and become part of the Constitution of the East African Muslim Welfare Society.

While the file contains no response from the addressed trustees, V. M. Nazerally, the honourable general organising secretary of the EAMWS, 'beg[ged] to reply on their behalf as well as of the Society' on 24 February 1968. In his letter, which was written on the letterhead of the EAMWS with post office boxes in Kampala and Dar es Salaam, Nazerally

---

[36] This is not entirely correct, as the constitution did allow for the establishing of regional and district councils; however, the property of the society was to be held by 'four trustees to be elected by the members of the Society at a General Meeting'.

confirmed that 'it [was] indeed intended to amend the Constitution' and that he thought 'that there is a general acceptance of the proposed amended Constitution by Tanzania and others'. Attached to the letter, which was copied to the four trustees of the EAMWS as well as to Al-Haj Tewa Saidi, the president of the Tanzania Council, and Al-Haj Aziz Khaki, its secretary general, was the draft of the amended constitution. While the headquarters of the EAMWS were to remain in Dar es Salaam and 'His Highness the Aga Khan Mowlana Shah Karim El-Huseini' was to remain the chief patron of the society, the amendments included three changes that would have entailed a significant shift in the existing power structure of the EAMWS:

(1) the abolition of the Supreme Council, which in the original Constitution had 'full power to superintend and conduct the business of the Society' and was also entitled 'to appoint one or more of its members from time to time to go on inspection tour to the different Provincial Councils', which otherwise operated 'under the direction and control of its Territorial Council and/or the Supreme Council';
(2) the transfer of all decision-making power to the executive council, consisting of three 'substantive members (the President, the Honorary Organising Secretary General, and the Honorary General Treasurer)' as well as several 'ex-officio members' (including the trustees of the society and the presidents of each principal council in Kenya, Tanzania, and Uganda); and
(3) the principal councils' rights of nomination for the posts of the substantive members and to appoint a trustee or trustees 'for any institution in its territory which has been established by the Society or with the Society's support or aid'.

On 3 March 1968, the administrator general replied that he was going to proceed with the incorporation of trustees for the Tanzania Council of EAMWS. His decision was seconded by a letter from Nazerally dated 5 March 1968, confirming the proposed amendment relating to the right of the 'Principal Council to appoint Trustees for any Institutions, which they desire to establish, and for which Trustees are required'. Furthermore, Aziz Khaki, secretary general of the EAMWS Tanzania Council, informed Dowdall on 9 March 1968 that the matter raised by the administrator general[37] had been 'discussed between Al-Haj T. S.

---

[37] The letter of the administrator general to which Khaki referred (dated 7 March 1968) is missing in the file, but 'the appointment' he probably alluded to was the appointment of trustees as suggested in the Tanzania Council's original application for incorporation.

Tewa, Mr Nazerally and [himself] and it was agreed that the appointment should refer to all Secondary Schools, Islamic Centres incorporating Mosques, and Muslim Community Centres established in Tanzania, under Tanzania Council of E. A. Muslim Welfare Society'. However, while the matter had apparently been solved satisfactorily, a letter from A. S. Fundikira, the president of the EAMWS, stopped the process abruptly on 4 April 1968. The letter, which was typed on the letterhead of East African Airways and was written in response to Dowdall's query of 21 February, read:

> I am aware that certain changes to the Constitution of the East African Muslim Welfare Society are contemplated but I am not quite sure of the exact nature of these changes. I would therefore be unwilling to agree that the application from the Tanzania Council of the East African Muslim Welfare Society for incorporation should be proceeded with at this stage. It would be advisable to await the actual amendment of the Constitution of the Society itself to be effected at a General Meeting of the Society before incorporation of the Tanzania Council is allowed.

While no further entry followed Fundikira's letter, the cover of the EAMWS file at RITA closed the case with three short remarks written in red (Figure 3.6): '1. Declared unlawful 19.12.1968 Government Notice No. 434 on 20.12.1968; 2. Both moveable and immoveable property were vested to the Administrator General – by Government Notice No. 435 of 20.12.1968 with effect from 19.12.1968; and 3. By Government Notice No. 169 of 28.6.1969 [beginning of new line] All the moveable and immoveable property where [sic] however vested to BAKWATA as from 30.6.1969.'

Was the Dissolution of the EAMWS also the Result of an Internal Conflict?

The letters and documents in the EAMWS file at RITA show that the conflicts and power relations that led to the dissolution of the society in 1968 were probably even more complicated than is usually presented in scholarly and activist accounts. First, when reading the documents, it becomes obvious that it was not simply the Tanzanian government that 'dealt with the EAMWS' (Ludwig 1999: 98) and banned the society by backing the efforts of Adam Nasibu – the regional secretary of the EAMWS Bukoba branch – who 'had managed a coup against the president of the EAMWS' (Said nd[a]). Rather, there were also significant internal quarrels between the Tanzania Council and the Supreme Council of the EAMWS. These quarrels concerned the distribution of power and entitlements within the society; this conflict passed into the offices of the TANU government via the filing of an application for

Figure 3.6 Photographs of (a) the cover of the EAMWS file at RITA and (b) the letter by A. S. Fundikira dated 4 April 1968.

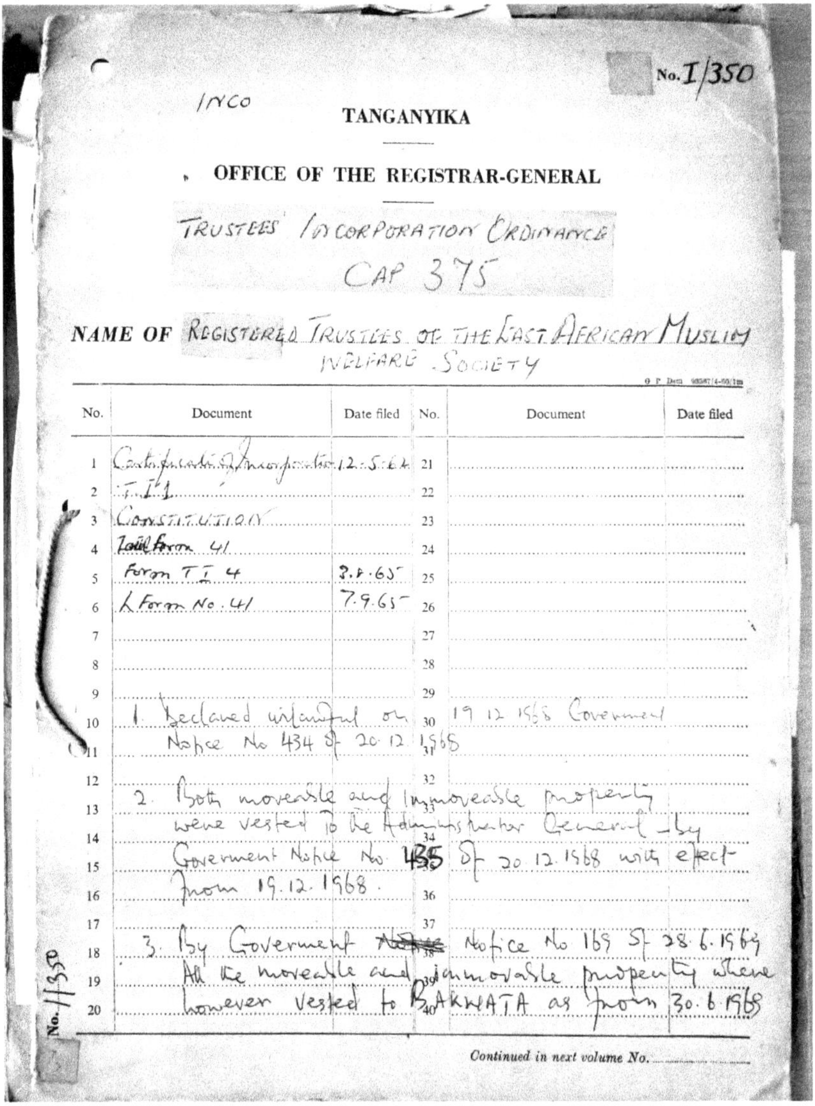

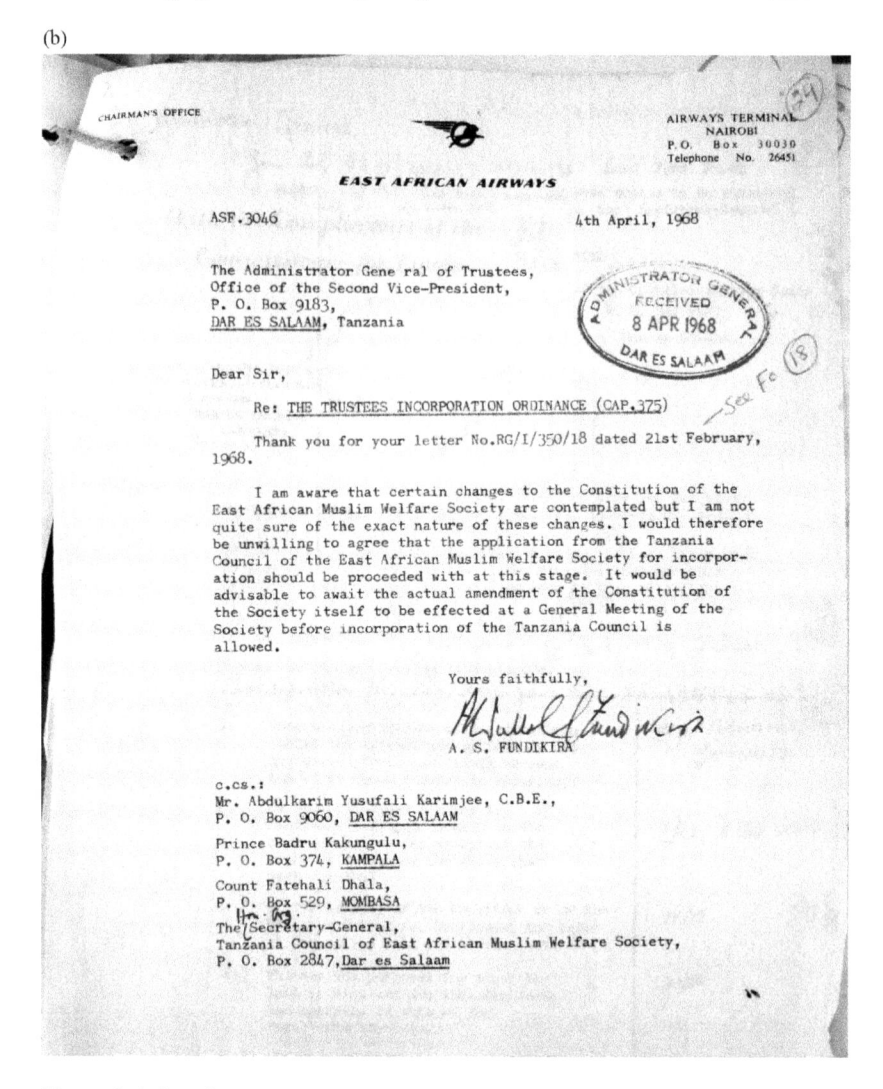

Figure 3.6 (cont.)

incorporation as a separate trust (and possibly for the replacement of the original body corporate), as well as the submission of amendments to the EAMWS constitution that had not been approved by the main society.

Second, the documents raise questions about the widespread portrait of the EAMWS as a 'pan-Islamic and nonsectarian' organisation that 'was capable of unifying Muslims, especially coastal elements, into a bloc that could pose a threat to Tanu' (Chande 2008: 108). They also challenge the claim that the conflict within the EAMWS was sustained primarily by 'two fractions of the organization': 'one group of mainly African Muslims [who] supported ... [Nyerere and his socialist Arusha] declaration [and] another group of Asian Muslims, who were mostly business men [and] were negatively affected by the socialist policy' (Ludwig 1999: 98). In this latter regard, the role of Abdallah Said Fundikira, president of the EAMWS since 1961, is particularly interesting. Fundikira – a Nyamwezi chief from the Tabora region – was not only a fellow student of Nyerere at Makerere but was also the president's most serious opponent in the scramble for political leadership before and after independence (Eckert 2007: 192). In 1961, he was appointed minister in Nyerere's first cabinet but resigned in 1963 when the government ruled – against his vote – on the nationalisation of land (ibid.: 193). After a stint as chairman of the board of East African Airways between 1967 and 1972 – from where he sent the letter to the administrator general – Fundikira became involved in several private businesses, only to return to the political scene in 1990 when he founded the opposition party Union for Multiparty Democracy (UMD). In 1999, he returned to the ruling party, the Chama Cha Mapinduzi (CCM), and was appointed member of parliament by President Benjamin Mkapa after the general elections of 2000 (Ewald 2011: 369).

The particular role of Chief Abdallah Said Fundikira shows that the internal conflict in the EAMWS cannot be explained by clear-cut ethnic, racial, or class-based distinctions. Fundikira belonged to the group of 'African Muslims' who were opposed to the TANU government and ranked among those Muslim protagonists in the struggle for independence who were later sidelined by Nyerere, including Tewa Said Tewa, Bibi Titi Mohammed, and members of the Sykes family (cf. Heilman and Kaiser 2002: 701). Furthermore, he also pursued his business interests and seemed aligned with the agenda of the Asian businesspeople who were negatively affected by the political changes of Ujamaa (Ludwig 1999: 98). Finally, while Fundikira reportedly was aiming to create a close collaboration between the 'Ismaili' and 'African' Muslims within the EAMWS (Eckert 2007: 193), his position was subverted by Tewa Said Tewa, who actively pushed for the dissolution of the Supreme Council of the EAMWS. To make the affair even more complicated, the moves of Tewa and the Tanzania Council were supported by Nazerally, the honourable general organising secretary of the EAMWS, who seems to have belonged to the Ismaili community and actively supported the dissolution of his own organisation.

Conclusion

A dominant view among many Christians in Tanzania is that their country 'is one of the very few countries where Christians and Muslims have lived peacefully for centuries' (Rukyaa 2007: 181). Many attribute this to President Nyerere, who, they claim, 'never deliberately promoted any religious group while he was in power, and upheld the philosophy of equality' (ibid.: 192). According to this view, the decline in this good interreligious relationship is attributed to 'Muslims starting to attack Christian teachings in public, and some Christian groups retaliating' (ibid.: 192). Such a view is also widely shared in annual media reports marking the death of the Mwalimu ('Teacher') on 14 October 1999; these celebrate Nyerere's achievements in establishing political tolerance and a sense of togetherness in Tanzania.[38] Of course, revivalist Muslims would strongly dispute this. Most of them – along with those Muslims who are not openly politically engaged (including the students and teachers of the schools I visited) – would insist that interreligious conflict and injustice had already started during colonial times and were perpetuated and sustained after independence.

The claims and counter-claims that fuel debates about Christian and Muslim life in Tanzania produce a need to introduce new evidence into the discussion, especially in regard to the impermeability of social and political structures relating to religious difference. They also lead to the government's 'desire to order' the increasingly diffuse field of interreligious relations among a wide range of actors. Alongside religious actors, who claim moral and spiritual superiority and work to establish new institutions to overcome injustices and provide opportunities in the realm of health, education, and business, the government aims to control faith-oriented activities that are often driven by transnational political agendas. Such processes of interreligious politics and governance are configured by the interests and activities of multiple – often competing – individuals and organisations on local, national, and transregional levels.

As far as the dissolution of the EAMWS is concerned, the evidence from the file at RITA that I present in this chapter is hardly conclusive on the course of events between the months of May and December 1968, after Fundikira sent his letter. Still, the documents raise questions about how the various actions and aims of individual members of different EAMWS entities shaped the process that led to the dissolution of the society. They also reveal how multiple lines of social, ethnic, political,

---

[38] 'President's call on political tolerance', *The Citizen*, 15 October 2009.

Conclusion 95

economic, and religious differentiation contributed to the weakening of the society from within, and thus to the complexity of governing religious bodies in Tanzania in the late 1960s – and up to the present day. Furthermore, as my survey of the MoHA and RITA registration books from 1980 to 2009 shows, in such a politically sensitive context, quantitative data may shed new light on issues such as religious plurality and introduce new lines of ethnographic inquiry for dealing with, and responding to, inter- and intra-religious diversity and competition (cf. Nolte et al. 2016: 561).

I now turn to the ways in which Christian and Muslim actors in Dar es Salaam have established educational institutions over the last three decades, against the background of colonial and postcolonial histories of religious difference and education in the country. In particular, I show that these educational initiatives are not only a response to the political and spiritual-moral agendas of a certain faith or denomination – or to market opportunities and (individual) professional ambitions – but also to the desire to provide new avenues for 'learning values' and moral becoming in the 'Haven of Peace'.

Part II

Moral Becoming and Educational Inequalities in Dar es Salaam

4 Market Orientation and Belonging in Neo-Pentecostal Schools

The second part of the book presents case studies of the six schools of my research in Dar es Salaam to illustrate how students' and teachers' moral becoming were embedded in the schools' explicit or implicit faith orientation and specific approaches to the teaching and learning of values. It also argues that the quests for a good life in these schools are closely entwined with these institutions' structural positions in both the educational market and the local, regional, and transregional networks (of faith or other schools) that determined a school's visibility and desirability, as well as how it presented itself to potential students and the wider public.

The St Mary's school group is one of the largest privately owned networks in Tanzania. It was founded by Dr Gertrude Rwakatare, the late pastor of a large neo-Pentecostal church in Dar es Salaam, in the mid-1990s. In 2010, it comprised eight primary and secondary schools nationwide, as well as a teacher training college in Dar es Salaam. The first issue of the school network's magazine, entitled *Quality Education in Tanzania, a Vision Come True*,[1] explains that the founding of the first school, St Mary's International Primary School, was closely connected to Tanzania's educational situation at the time:

Asked why she joined the education sector [Dr Rwakatare] is quick to say: 'I joined the education sector because I had the nation at heart. I was touched when I saw buses at Namanga [a Kenyan border town] taking students to Kenya and Uganda to acquire quality education' … [T]hese students would be foreigners in their own country since they study foreign History, foreign Geography and foreign Cultures. Thus, St Mary's international schools were born.

In their early years, St Mary's ranked among Tanzania's top-performing schools. St Mary's International Primary School in particular was known widely for employing English as the language of instruction at the primary level and for preparing its graduates for higher education and, potentially, a successful career 'in foreign embassies and international

---

[1] *St Mary's Mirror*, 2002–3, p. 3.

organisations'.[2] During my fieldwork, the reputation of the St Mary's schools had declined considerably. I often heard people in Dar es Salaam talk critically about the schools' business-oriented approach, Dr Rwakatare's widely known disputes with teachers about the formation of a union, and her dismissal of teachers for no particular reason.[3] At the same time, several of the schools were still attracting significant numbers of families who were willing to pay the high school fees in order to secure a good education for their children. In addition, in 2002, the St Mary's schools networks had established a number of schools to cater to those families with fewer financial means who were still seeking a 'quality education' for their children.

In this chapter, I describe how two schools in the St Mary's network – St Mary's International Primary School in Tabata and Kenton High School in Mwenge – were established in the specific socio-religious and socio-political contexts of Dar es Salaam, thereby reflecting not only processes of educational segregation but also dynamics of spiritual revivalism and 'insecurity' (cf. Ashforth 1998) in the wake of global economic and educational (Mundy et al. 2016) restructuring. As the first part of the chapter shows, the two schools catered to students and families from different socio-economic backgrounds, and in their everyday practices they contributed to class formation among the students and staff. They were also marked by specific pedagogical styles, including a 'caring discipline' ethos, through which they responded to the expectations of students' families for returns on the investments they had made into their children's future. Furthermore, there were significant tensions among the teaching staff; these resulted not only from concerns about national and ethnic favouritism in the context of transnational labour mobility in the East African Community, but also from a rigid system of surveillance and self-evaluation, and the generally weak position of teachers with regard to employees' rights and social security.

The second part of the chapter highlights how – despite these internal frictions in the context of market orientation and an extensive 'audit culture' (Shore and Wright 2015) of monitoring staff performance – the St Mary's schools established networks of local, national, and international belonging among their students and staff, which were often experienced on multiple levels as well as in relation to the institutions' socio-material and ideological environments. In particular, belonging was enhanced among both students and teachers because of the schools' reputation for providing 'high-quality' academic and 'moral education',

---

[2] Ibid.   [3] 'Uongozi St Mary's Matatani', *Majira*, 4 July 2009.

which was realised both during the morning assemblies and through the teaching of values in Kiswahili and English lessons. Furthermore, while the St Mary's schools did not claim publicly to be 'Christian schools' and offered very little formal teaching of religious content, implicit articulations of faith played a significant part in everyday practices of moral becoming. This was the case not only in the context of the fellowshipping practices of some of the teachers, but also with regard to the healing prayers that were conducted especially for female students from Muslim families, who were perceived as being particularly exposed to the attacks of evil spirits.

Establishing Religious Infrastructure in 'the Bush'

In Dar es Salaam, the privatisation of schools since the 1990s has been linked to the restructuring, over many decades, of sparsely populated districts that were categorised either as 'bush' or 'government land' and sold to private investors after the official end of the socialist project in 1985 (cf. Cooksey and Kelsall 2011: 25).[4] A school's location in the city was thus determined in part by property prices, which were especially unaffordable for newcomers to Dar es Salaam (cf. Fitzgerald 2017: 54, 112), a city whose 'physical shape' was defined largely by its two colonial governments (Kironde 2007: 97).

The schools of the neo-Pentecostal churches were often founded by 'religious entrepreneurs' (see Lauterbach 2016; Seabright 2016: 213) from (partly lower) middle-class backgrounds who established themselves in the wealthier ranks of Dar es Salaam's urban society in the mid-1990s (Dilger 2007: 65; Hasu 2007: 230). Their educational projects were sited either on the margins of the city or in those parts of Dar es Salaam that were not densely settled at the time when their schools were built (Dilger 2013a: 467; Dilger and Janson forthcoming 2022). The choice of more remote locations was also shaped by government guidelines that required the allocation of sufficient land for recreational facilities when constructing a new school.

The St Mary's schools exemplify this trend in land use by religious newcomers. For Dr Rwakatare's first school, the International Primary School, she selected a sparsely populated neighbourhood in Tabata on the former outskirts of Dar es Salaam, which until the 1980s had been used for agricultural purposes. Then, she acquired the former grounds of

---

[4] According to Cooksey and Kelsall (2011: 29), corruption was also often involved in the private accumulation of land, and public assets were given away below their value in the process.

the Tanzanian National Insurance Company, and, in 2006, she established an orphanage that provided shelter and education for about 700 children in the immediate environs of St Mary's International Primary School. Next to the orphanage was the Al-Farouq Islamic Seminary for Boys, which was founded by the Africa Muslims Agency in 1997 (see Chapter 5). The areas next to the tarmac and dust roads around the primary school were also home to the St Mary's Teachers' Training College and numerous neo-Pentecostal churches and traditional clinics that promised 'healing'.

In public statements and in her conversations with me, Dr Rwakatare downplayed her connections to influential personalities and organisations at home and abroad. But while she described the founding of her school network as a national task, she relied on local and international networks of support, including the US-based NGO The Christian Working Woman as well as several members of her own church, which counted around 10,000 members in 2010 (Dilger 2009).[5] Her church, the Mikocheni B church in Mwenge, has thrived, drawing from a growing urban middle and upper class for congregants and developing its own radio and television programmes. Dr Rwakatare has also drawn on her political connections, particularly since 2007, when she was appointed Special Seats Member of Parliament by President Kikwete (Chapter 2).

In the context of the economic hardships faced by many in the city, some of the activities of religious entrepreneurs such as Dr Rwakatare have become not only a potential solution to social and spiritual problems but also targets of suspicion. Neo-Pentecostal churches especially, which promise prosperity and claim to be able to free followers from the influence of evil spirits, have also become the object of people's anxieties. In the case of St Mary's International Primary School, there were persistent rumours that the land on which the school was built was haunted by spirits (*majini*). Some of my interlocutors at the school ascribed the presence of these *majini* to the backgrounds of the pupils themselves, who may have brought them from their rural homes (as discussed later in the chapter).[6] Others, however, claimed that Dr Rwakatare herself had forged an alliance with witches and evil spirits as a way of getting rich – a not uncommon allegation against neo-Pentecostal pastors who appeared to have accumulated significant amounts of wealth over comparatively

---

[5] Although it is formally linked to the Assemblies of God, the congregation operates independently from the mother church.

[6] On the possession of Muslim schoolgirls through 'angry' spirits in Niger, see Masquelier (2018: 301).

short periods of time (Dilger 2007: 82, fn 12; Lindhardt 2009). One of the schools' former teachers referred to this in a conversation:

MR WALKER In Tanzania with these private schools, people believe that if you build a school or buy a plot, you make an agreement between the owner and those *majini*, so that they help you to attract many students and to get rich.
HD But the owner of this school is a pastor?
MR WALKER Some of the pastors in this country use magical powers. [Laughs.] Also, if you want to go to another school as a teacher, you will tell [the school owner] only if you have already received a contract from this other school. If not, they can manipulate the *majini* so that you stay in [their] school.
HD What do these *majini* get for their services?
MR WALKER They want blood. They want the flesh of people. There was one bus driver; he was under the bus and repairing the bus. Suddenly, he fainted and died.

The St Mary's Schools as Social and Moral Signifiers

In Dar es Salaam, a school's physical location marked its social position in the wake of urban and educational transformations; it became a 'moral signifier' in the intersecting processes of class formation, inter- and intra-religious competition, and urban transformation in the city (cf. Rowe 2017: 37). In general, students and families preferred the location of a school in a rural area – or a city's periphery – where young people were assumed to be able to focus exclusively on their studies instead of being lured into the 'immoral' distractions of city life. This discourse on the perceived immorality of urban space was expressed in public concerns about premarital sexual relations and the risk of HIV, which were assumed to be widespread in urban Tanzania (Setel 1999: 183; Dilger 2000: 171; see also Figure 4.1).[7] Students also expressed a desire to be housed with likeminded young people of their own age, a contrast from their family homes where they had to adjust to the rhythms of their siblings and other children. One student, 12-year-old David, explained the advantages of being a boarding student at St Mary's International Primary School: 'My father asked me if I want to go to another school but I wanted to stay. Here, you get time to review your books.'

---

[7] While crime rates in Dar es Salaam were increasing in the years before my research (Louw et al. 2001), my interlocutors' concerns at the neo-Pentecostal schools were more with the city's perceived moral dangers. These concerns were partly sustained by comparatively high rates of HIV infection, especially among sex workers and drug users (PEPFAR 2019: 6), and of teenage pregnancy (Pfeiffer et al. 2017) in the city. At the same time, the alleged 'moral decay' of Dar es Salaam has shaped popular perceptions of the metropolis for many decades (Dilger 2005: 57–9) and even during colonial times (Ivaska 2011: 62).

Figure 4.1 'Make a true decision: keep your education in mind!' Mural in Dar es Salaam, 2010.

However, not all the parents of the St Mary's schools' pupils were either interested in or able to afford boarding school. For these families, schools had buses to pick up the pupils close to their homes in the morning and drop them off in the evening. The headmaster of St Mary's International Primary School explained to me that the school-owned transport system kept the pupils' minds 'fresh' and prevented students from 'mixing' with other children and people in a *dala dala*, the city-run minibus.[8] This experience was strikingly different from the *dala dala* rides to some of the other schools of my study, including Kenton High School (see below).[9] Apart from the long waiting times, many of these pupils, who were easily recognisable by their uniforms,

---

[8] I was able to witness the comforts of the school's transport system personally when I was included in one of the bus drivers' schedules for a period of two weeks. During the drive between my home and the school, which took about 40 minutes, I was able to relax in the softly cushioned seats, escaping the city's dust behind tinted windows. The children next to me joked and talked happily, or got some additional sleep despite the often deafening music, mostly hip-hop and rap, played by the bus driver.

[9] Kenton High School did not have a boarding section of its own and many parents could not afford the additional school bus fees.

were taken only reluctantly by the *dala dala* drivers as they paid only half of the standard ticket price. Students often had to stand throughout the ride or were asked to sit on the laps of other passengers, especially girls, which did not assuage the concerns of their parents and schoolteachers about 'interacting too closely' with other people in the city.

In general, the social position of St Mary's International Primary School reflected the ongoing dynamics of internal stratification among Dar es Salaam's private primary schools, which were all competing with the even larger number of free but less well performing government schools in the city.[10] School fees for the day school in 2009 were set at TZH 1,080,000 per year (about €570); this included school buses, meals, and supplies excluding textbooks. However, while studying in the costly St Mary's International Primary School could be afforded by only a limited number of families, such social differentiation was not acknowledged by the owner of the school. When I asked Dr Rwakatare whether social segregation could lead to conflict in a rapidly transforming society, she denied that there were 'wealthy' people in Tanzania at all and claimed that '[we] are all struggling'.[11] At the same time, according to her, social differentiation was a 'natural process'. She said: 'We can't go back to socialism. Even in Scandinavia or in your country this hasn't worked. If you look at our hand, you will see that one finger is longer, the other one is shorter. They will always differ.'

The 1,800 pupils of St Mary's International Primary School came primarily from the middle and partly from the upper classes and shared a certain sense of 'achievements and orientations' (James 2019: 43). This social profile was confirmed every morning when expensive four-wheel-drive vehicles dropped off those pupils who were not brought by the school bus. Among the Grade 7 students, most of the fathers and mothers – who were usually both working – earned income from business, government, or other white-collar jobs. A few parents were employed as doctors, university professors, or at an international embassy. Furthermore, the students reported engaging in activities that were typical of the emerging middle class in the city, including reading story books, watching television, playing football or videogames, and swimming or going to the beach.

Finally, Grade 7 pupils had clear expectations of what the future would hold for them. Many of them expected to graduate from university and

---

[10] Attending a public primary school in Tanzania has been 'free' since 2001, except for the often considerable costs of uniforms, textbooks, and transport.
[11] For more on the processes of social differentiation within Dr Rwakatare's own church, see Chapter 3.

hoped to become doctors, lawyers, or pilots. Similarly, all aimed to study in one of the country's top-rated Christian secondary schools – or in one of the few top-performing Muslim secondary schools – after graduation. The topic of choosing one's future secondary school mirrored both the trends of the educational market and those of individual classrooms. The statements by Abdul and Nathan (both 12 years old) illustrate how students at the primary school articulated their ambitions for their personal future:

ABDUL I want to go to St Marian later. It takes the cream people – people who are clever. I want to be a doctor later.

NATHAN I want to go to Marian Boys or Feza Boys. These two schools are among the most famous schools. I want to become a representative of Tanzania and work for the success of the nation. You know, Tanzania is a poor country. I want that it makes progress like the G8 countries. My cousin is studying in the US. I want to do it like him – but not in the US, but Europe.

Kenton High School as a 'Local' School for 'the Poor'

While St Mary's International Primary School was designed to train Tanzania's 'cream people', Kenton High School in Mwenge, which has admitted students since 2004, set out with a very different agenda. Mr Adam, the principal of Kenton, who came to Dar es Salaam from Uganda in 1999, recalled that the idea for founding the school was born at an international school conference in South Africa, which he and some of the other headteachers and principals of the St Mary's school network attended with Dr Rwakatare. Right after the conference, Dr Rwakatare – to whom Mr Adam referred as 'Mama' – acquired the plot of land in Mwenge[12] and started building the school:

[At the conference] in 2002 – we were free on that day, sitting around the swimming pool or in the hotel bar. [I expressed] the idea for starting a local school, for those students from poor families, people who cannot afford schools like St Mary's [International] High School. When we came back Mama … [built the school] because by then, there was an outcry. People were looking for quality education. Many people wanted their children to go to St Mary's.

---

[12] Kenton High School was located in the Mwenge area, one of the busiest hubs on the former (relative) outskirts of the city. The area was also home to three of Dar es Salaam's largest neo-Pentecostal churches: Bishop Kakobe's Full Gospel Bible Fellowship church (Dilger 2007); the Efatha Ministry, which had its own bank and TV station (Hasu 2007); and Dr Rwakatare's church, located in the Mikocheni B neighbourhood.

In 2010, Kenton High School had 600 students taught by 26 teachers in total. The school fees were set at TZH 620,000 per year in 2010 (about €330), to which fees for medical exams, uniforms, supplies, and registration were added. The costs for transport via the school-owned buses, which was optional, were set at TZH 240,000 per year. Furthermore, some of the students opted for additional evening teaching in Form IV ('tutoring'), which had to be paid separately.[13] The fact that the school was founded as a 'local school' indicated the close correlation that the school management – as well as the students and teachers themselves – established between 'locality' and 'class'. Thus, while the clients of St Mary's International Primary School had been categorised by its headmaster as belonging mainly to the (internationally oriented upper) middle classes of Dar es Salaam, the students of Kenton were assumed by its management to come mainly from 'poor local families' who were not able to afford some of the other, costlier private schools in the city.

At first sight, the difference between the social backgrounds of the pupils from the primary and the secondary school was not as striking as the 'international–local' dichotomy might suggest. Most parents of the Form IV Kenton students were employed in business and government, and a few were doctors and lawyers. However, significant differences did exist between the two schools with regard to the students' preferred high school[14] and life goals. Even though half of the Kenton students had a sibling who attended one of the popular Christian schools in the country, the majority preferred a government school for their future high school. This was related to the fact that few of them assumed that their parents, or other family members, would be able to pay the school fees of one of the more prestigious Christian high schools. Furthermore, while all Form IV students expected to graduate from university – and had high hopes regarding their future employment (e.g. doctor, engineer) – their concrete expectations for their future lives were often more modest. For example, Kenneth (20 years old) said:

[I want] to do better in my studies in order to get a better future, to have any kind of work, you know. And to live independently [so that] I can support myself and my sisters, and my family in general.

The most striking difference between the two schools concerned the command of English; this was of particular concern among both Kenton

---

[13] In contrast, attending a government school at the secondary level was comparatively cheaper at TZH 20,000 for day schools and TZH 70,000 for boarding schools at the time (Godda 2018: 3).
[14] The Kenton school calls itself 'High School' but comprises only Forms I–IV. Thus, in my survey I asked Form IV students which other high school (Forms V and VI) they aimed to attend after graduation.

High School students and their teachers. Many of the students who attended the school had graduated either from a government primary school where English was taught only as a foreign language or from a private school that 'claimed' to teach English but did not have enough well-trained teachers, leaving students insufficiently prepared for learning in English at the secondary level. As one 18-year-old student noted: 'Most of the students who are coming here, they are from government primary schools where their English is not their medium of communication.' Thomas (17 years old), who preferred to speak Kiswahili during our interview, claimed that he spoke mostly Kiswahili to his friends at school:

You cannot *force* [*huwezi ukamforce*] someone to speak *English*, maybe he does not know it [well], or he is afraid to be joked about [*kutaniwa*]. In class, you may *perform* well in Kiswahili, but in the other lessons you fail.

The teachers of Kenton High School attributed some of their students' poor command of English to their low social backgrounds, and they used various strategies to help such students 'catch up'. Ms Gracious, a 26-year-old teacher from Uganda, said:

We have students from government primary schools where they were taught in Swahili. So to teach them in English is the biggest challenge. I advise [them] to read small story books, so that they get [to a certain] level. I have a student who was – nothing. But right now, she performs well and listens [to] English. [B]ut some of them are not cooperative: you tell [them] 'read' and they do not do it. So that makes them fail.

At both the St Mary's schools, many students were well aware of their own socio-economic status, as well as the potential impermanence of different levels of the privilege that is an inherent part of 'middleclassness' in many urban African settings (Lentz 2015: 23). Some of the former students of the primary school had experienced personally how wealth and social status were often transitory in the context of quickly shifting economic circumstances. In one of the families I talked to, the children had previously attended St Mary's International School but the parents were no longer able to cover the costly tuition fees: the father – a well-paid government employee – had been sent to jail for corruption. The children of another family, who attended the same school, had to switch to a less costly government school when their father lost his job due to chronic illness. Thus, while private schools such as St Mary's International Primary School and Kenton High School have become entrenched in the logics of the neoliberal market economy, students' quests for a good life were shaped by their shifting social circumstances. In such instances, students and families realised that social mobility – which has become linked so strongly to educational investments since the mid-1990s (cf. Stambach 2017: 2) – can go in either direction, substantially affecting their individual and collective life chances.

Infrastructural Differences and Caring Discipline

The fact that the students' families at the St Mary's schools paid comparatively high school fees for their children's education and future raised specific expectations with regard to the returns on these 'educational investments' (Hunter 2019: 87). Mr Kariuki, the headmaster of St Mary's International Primary School, explained that students spent the whole day at the school and parents therefore expected their children to be well taken care of, with regard both to facilities, classrooms, and food and to their academic performance and their acquisition of 'good' behaviours.

The care that the St Mary's schools extended to their students was manifest in the aesthetic and material standards of their buildings, which simultaneously created 'boundaries and differences' (De Boeck 2012) across the two educational sites, as well as in the educational marketplace. Both schools were painted white and pink with red corrugated roofs, but the material infrastructure at the primary school was of higher quality than that of the high school. At the primary school, the doors and window frames of the classrooms were painted sparkling blue and the floor was covered with blue and white chequered PVC flooring. Some walls were covered with faith-oriented murals; additionally, the interior yard contained tall trees encircled by benches as well as painted wooden sculptures of Tanzanian wildlife (Figure 4.2). At Kenton High School, in contrast, over the course of 2010, the ivory-painted walls of the classrooms became grey, the reddish PVC floors faded, and the red and green flowered curtains lost their colour as well. Furthermore, while the primary school was equipped with a computer room that put it on a par with other expensive private schools in Dar es Salaam, Kenton High School's library held largely outdated textbooks and novels. Nevertheless, the campus of Kenton High School radiated a welcoming atmosphere, too, with its large pitch for playing football and its abundant trees surrounding the site.

The 'caring environment' at the St Mary's schools to which the headmaster referred was also evident in a pedagogical approach that was said to be distinct from most government schools and also many other private schools in the city. Their 'caring discipline' emphasised the importance of instilling confidence in pupils, the proximity of students and teachers, and the value of an 'empowering pedagogy' (Frueh 2020). In particular, the St Mary's schools highlighted the value of 'teaching knowledge', which Mr Kariuki identified as the main reason for the strong

Figure 4.2 School buses and pupils in St Mary's International Primary School's inner yard, Dar es Salaam, 2009.

performance of his school. In contrast, teachers at government schools were 'drilling [students] for exams', he said, but they did not make them internalise knowledge or encourage them to express their own views. Such encouragement, he argued, depended strongly on teachers' ability to 'connect' to pupils through a caring relationship.

When I attended some of the classrooms over several weeks, I found that pedagogical styles depended largely on individual teachers and specific class situations. In several instances I observed elements of top-down teaching and rigid repetition and memorising of content, not dissimilar to what was described as the common pedagogical approach of government schools (see Chapter 2). Discipline was enforced among pupils through a set of intimidating practices that included student monitors registering attendance and maintaining silence in class,[15] the

---

[15] Students at both schools were encouraged early on to help enforce discipline by running for one of the offices in the school government (head boy, head girl, class captains at Kenton High School; monitors and prefects at St Mary's International Primary School). In the 2002–3 *St Mary's Mirror*, students described how such positions trained them to become 'academic giants' (pp. 12–13) and 'leaders in the future' (p. 31). Mohamed Wadi, from one of the other St Mary's schools in Dar es Salaam, stated: 'I have served as

public posting of students' performance in each classroom, and unannounced assignments. In one situation where several students had failed to deliver their homework, the teacher said: 'I will take you to the principal. I don't know what punishment he will give you. I give you homework and you don't do it!'

At the same time, however, I observed multiple instances of active efforts to involve all students in the learning process. Some teachers tried to motivate quiet students to reply to their questions, others reminded pupils of the importance of 'sitting properly', and they provided feedback on their pupils' individual performance. Most teachers were remarkably patient with their students and invested significant effort in helping them understand the subjects of their lessons. Some brought images to class in order to illustrate a particular phenomenon or made their pupils curious about the issues they had not understood (by asking them to read more about it, for instance). Others asked students to keep trying until a problem had been solved, and they rewarded students who performed well by leading a round of applause.

Furthermore, similar to the Catholic mission school of Simpson's research in Zambia (2003: 60), the pedagogical approach at the primary school was shaped by its emphasis on being physically and emotionally 'close' to students. Teachers mixed with their pupils during the breaks and stated that they 'liked to eat what the pupils eat'. Moreover, some teachers enhanced their proximity to students by making jokes in class and being comparatively relaxed regarding students' minor failures in complying with the school regulations, for example with dress codes. Finally, most teachers emphasised the importance of group solidarity and ensured that none of the students in their class were excluded by others, posing questions such as 'Are we together?' or – in Kiswahili – '*Tumeelewana?*' (Have we understood each other?). If students mocked a classmate, teachers intervened and pointed out that such behaviour was 'not good'.

At Kenton High School, the teachers' caring attitudes were also acknowledged by the students themselves, some of whom had heard of the school's reputation even before starting there. Kenneth, a 20-year-old male student, recounted how he had heard that Kenton High School was a good school and how he valued his teachers' commitment and care: 'St Mary's [is] widely known as one of the good schools ... The teachers are more in contact with the students, yeah.'

When I asked the teachers at the St Mary's schools why they adopted a caring attitude in their teaching, their explanations differed significantly

Head Boy for one year and I think it has been a great job ... All it takes is to maintain the students' discipline and the naughty students to be handed over to the teachers ... I hope to become the Vice President of Tanzania.'

from those of the students; they also differed between the primary and the high school. At the primary school, the teachers claimed that they wanted to prepare their pupils to meet the future challenges of their personal and professional lives by learning morally and socially responsible 'lifestyles'. In contrast, the teachers at Kenton High School adopted an almost paternalistic approach, emphasising that their students came from 'risky' and 'harmful' environments from which they needed protection. The principal of Kenton High School, who had studied social work in Uganda before becoming a teacher, said:

The students [here] are facing a lot of problems, at home [and] in school. So they need to be talked to, they need to be hugged. They are surrounded by drugs. [The girls] are dropping out due to pregnancy. They need [someone] who is talking to them. Actually those are the reasons that made me go for [this job].

'The Most People Least Valued': Parents' Investments and Teachers' Pressures

Especially at St Mary's International Primary School, the teachers I talked to expressed a strong commitment to their work and described it either as a pedagogical style of caring for their students or as the result of a Christian work ethos. In this regard, they complied with other Christian private schools' 'explicit' ethical frameworks (Bochow et al. 2017: 451), which were based on the reputation that their teachers were highly disciplined and 'worked harder' than those at government schools. But their engagement was also motivated by the higher salaries such schools usually paid. One teacher at the primary school explained that the salaries at his school shaped his own and his colleagues' work ethos:

The difference [from government schools] is the way [the teachers] care for the students. In the government schools [the] salary is less. In private schools [the teachers] care for the students well because they are getting money.

Market-based expectations of effective and well-performing schoolteachers, who deliver a good return on the investments made by their students' families, were internalised by the teachers, who told me how busy they were during their working hours and how arduous their job was. When students or their parents confronted them with a problem, some teachers first responded that they were 'very busy', although they later attended carefully to those problems and were generally highly committed to finding solutions. In one instance, a teacher greeted a colleague with the question, 'You are very busy, aren't you?' The colleague was preparing something for the school's administrators and replied jokingly: 'They are on my neck. Every five minutes they come and ask if it is ready yet.'

As my conversations with the teachers progressed, it became obvious that the trope of being busy – and the apparent satisfaction with the higher salaries at private schools – overshadowed other, more critical discourses on the neoliberal excesses of Tanzania's educational market. Thus, on the one hand, many of my interlocutors criticised the relatively low salaries in the government education sector, where payments were regularly delayed. It was against this background of critical discourse on government schools that teachers found Christian schools such as St Mary's more attractive with regard to salaries, better teaching conditions, a strong work ethos among the staff, and their overall higher academic reputation. Furthermore, one of the female teachers at the primary school, Ms Kitula, asserted that the university graduates who had been deployed to rural areas by the government in the late 1990s sought to transfer to private schools because they were often situated in urban environments: 'Many teachers like myself went to the private schools when they were established. Because it is difficult to live in rural areas when you are not used to it. There are no good hospitals, clean water.'

On the other hand, however, teachers – especially Tanzanians[16] – complained about the generally low social status of teachers in the country, saying that they were 'the most people least valued'. Even Ms Kitula complained strongly about the working conditions at St Mary's International Primary School, which, she claimed, had deteriorated significantly since she started there in 2002. According to her, many of the teachers had moved on to other private schools, since their salaries had not been increased for several years. The system of token payments, a kind of 'performance incentive' – given, for instance, on the successful completion of annual final exams – had been discontinued in 2006. She confirmed extensive media coverage reporting that the teachers, who did not receive work contracts, were forbidden from joining unions and thus had little power to negotiate salaries or pension payments. Echoing a growing 'neoliberal critique' of contemporary education (De Saxe 2015), she claimed that the school's policies had been defined entirely by the logics of the free market economy. She said:

MS KITULA We [teachers] even went on strike in 2006. But [the management] simply dismissed them. There are no contracts. In 2006, we were given forms to fill in for pensions, but they made us fill in that we started in 2006 – even those who started earlier.
HD How could this happen if the owner of the school is a pastor?

---

[16] For more on the international backgrounds of some of the teachers at St Mary's, see the next section.

MS KITULA She is establishing business after business – but then she doesn't follow up. She just says: 'If they have got greener pastures, they can just go. We will hire another teacher.'

Another teacher, Mr Walker, quoted earlier, was equally critical:

It is a big problem at this school [to negotiate the salaries]: Maybe you can go as an individual [and negotiate], but not as a group. I haven't received a contract here since [I started in] 2007. We can say that we are doing cheap labour here. This is no social service, this is a business. We have no security here.

The insecurity of employment due to the absence of work contracts, along with the lack of a union to negotiate salaries,[17] led to competition and fluctuation among the staff, who largely saw their position at the schools as temporary. Several teachers confirmed that internal rankings covered classes, subjects, and teachers and were circulated within the primary school, thereby creating a scale of well-performing teachers. Furthermore, they were aware of the hierarchical landscape of schools in Dar es Salaam, which in turn defined their ambitions concerning their own futures. Being well aware of their reputation as hard-working teachers, they had hopes of eventually joining one of the 'top schools' in the city. One of the teachers concluded our conversation with the question: 'If you get a better opportunity, who can hold you?'

Teacher Mobility, Ethnic Tensions, and Audit Culture

The growing competition for 'good teachers' in Dar es Salaam's educational market has also become connected to the dynamics of teacher migration within Africa, which often takes place 'within the regions or to neighbouring countries where standards of living are slightly higher than the origin country' (Yonemura 2010: 2). As already mentioned, St Mary's International Primary School in Dar es Salaam was established with the goal of offering 'quality education' in English; it hoped to discourage families from sending their children abroad – especially to Kenya – for advanced education (cf. Abdulaziz 1991).

To realise this goal, Dr Rwakatare hired teachers from Tanzania's neighbouring countries who were fluent in English; she even travelled to some of these countries herself to recruit teachers in person. Over the years, the St Mary's network has recruited a significant number of teachers from the East African Community, especially from Kenya and

---

[17] Many teachers engaged in income-generating activities outside their school employment, for example by running small businesses or offering tutoring to students, including those from the St Mary's schools.

Uganda, and also from the Democratic Republic of Congo and Burundi.[18] Some of these teachers were promoted to leadership positions within their schools and established small national – or ethnic – enclaves in their institutions by recruiting additional teachers from their home countries. The primary school, for example, was led by a headmaster from Kenya and employed a group of Kenyan teachers; similarly, Kenton High School, led by Mr Adam from Uganda, had hired a large number of Ugandan teachers.

For these teachers from abroad, their position – like that of their Tanzanian counterparts – was often only a transitory stage in their quest for a good life; many of them dreamed of moving on either to a better school in Dar es Salaam or, preferably, in their home country. However, while their professional ambitions resembled those of their Tanzanian colleagues, their reasons for leaving their home countries, and how they defined the relation between state schools and private schools there, were very different. The teachers from Kenya and Uganda both claimed that the employment situation 'back home' was better overall in government schools than in the private sector. For instance, Mr Maina from Kenya said that government schools there offered more 'benefits' than private institutions, with higher salaries, access to loans, and pension payments. He had come to Tanzania as there had been a surplus of teachers in Kenya at the time of his graduation, which forced many graduates to wait a few years until they were able to secure a position in a government school. Similarly, Ms Gracious from Uganda, who was the dean of students at Kenton High School in 2010, said:

> If you get into a government school, then you are okay. In Uganda we have these prominent schools like Mengo, Makerere College. When you enter in such schools, you have that security, you have a job and you depend on that.

The relationships between the Tanzanian teachers and those from abroad were shaped in particular by three factors that established an internal hierarchy among the teaching staff, with the Tanzanian teachers usually at the bottom. First, the Kenyan and Ugandan teachers were described – by all teachers, irrespective of their country of origin – as being more qualified than their Tanzanian counterparts. They usually taught the prestigious 'hard' subjects such as biology, mathematics, and other sciences, while their Tanzanian colleagues taught the 'soft' subjects, including civics, history, and Kiswahili. Furthermore, the Kenyan and Ugandan teachers were usually more fluent in English than their Tanzanian counterparts, which was what had made them desirable hires

---

[18] The latter teachers were hired to offer classes in French.

in the first place. Correspondingly, many felt that their Tanzanian colleagues were less prepared for leadership positions than their international counterparts. Such attitudes of superiority were expressed by two high-ranking Kenyan staff at St Mary's International Primary School:

MR MAINA Kenyan teachers became the pioneers of English-medium schools. They were marketable.

MR KARIUKI I am sorry to say this but Tanzanians – I try to train the Tanzanians. When I left [the school temporarily], I [appointed] a Tanzanian as headmaster, but things did not go well. This is why I came back.

Second, while the Tanzanian teachers acknowledged the 'marketability' of the international teachers, they complained that the internal hierarchy made them particularly vulnerable. Before the start of my fieldwork, several teachers were dismissed from the primary school, either because they had not complied with orders from the school administrators or because there had been a surplus of teachers due to low enrolment rates that year. Even though a teacher from Kenya was among this group, the Tanzanians felt that such dismissals were based on national and ethnic favouritism, as two new teachers from Kenya were hired a short time later. The Tanzanian teachers had little hope that this system could be challenged, as it had been established by the school owner herself. One teacher, Mr Walker, put it like this: 'Many [leaders] started with Mama here at the headquarters. These people became headmasters and principals; some of them are in other branches [of the school] now. Some of them are also in her church.' Among the Kenyan teachers themselves, there was little solidarity with the Tanzanian teachers. Instead, there was a shared sense that the Tanzanian teachers were hostile to the international teachers. As Ms Mwangi, a 25-year-old teacher from Kenya, said: 'Life is good here, except – don't quote me wrong – they don't like Kenyans here. They think that we are taking away their jobs.'

Third, mistrust and tension among the teachers increased, especially at the primary school, when an internal system of evaluation was introduced by the school management shortly before my arrival.[19] The school administrators claimed that 'close monitoring' of the teachers' work was a way to improve staff performance. They argued that some of the teachers needed 'guidance' in their professional development and that they still had to earn the salary that they were paid. As the headmaster and the academic deputy put it:

---

[19] The teachers' scepticism initially also extended to my own position as researcher at both schools, as some of them thought that I was a school inspector evaluating their classes. The atmosphere became more relaxed after I had responded to all their questions during collective meetings in the teachers' rooms.

Table 4.1. *Quotes from performance evaluations*

Section heads	Deputy headmaster	Teachers
'Absenteeism of pupils and lack of morning preparations are sources of these [poor] results.' 'I will be strict in clearing up if all topics are covered, homeworks, morning preps and enough exercises are given.' 'Quite poor performance [of named teacher]; a lot should be done to rectify this next time.'	'Good work portrayed. A self-motivated teacher.' 'Science averages are below the agreed average. The teacher should give subject tests regularly.' 'In Grade 1 there should be no pupils scoring below Grade D. Much effort is needed.' 'The teacher should find out why pupils absent themselves from school.'	'I shall give more attention to the weak pupils.' 'The school should provide teaching aids for the sciences.' 'The performance is good but I have to put more effort in History Grd 4 by giving pupils more exercises to improve their standards.' 'More exposure is needed equipping the library with more story books and ensuring pupils use English language. However, am doing my best to ensure good performance.'

MR KARIUKI A main challenge is that some of the teachers may not be teaching in the right way. Teaching is a noble job. You need someone to guide them.
HD What happens if a teacher performs poorly?
MR JONAS We give them a letter of warning. You know, this school is maintained by the market. This will be an eye-opener for him or her.

While school administrators denied that the evaluations had a negative impact on the teachers' employment status, the systematic monitoring had become part and parcel of a pervasive 'ethics of accountability' (Shore and Wright 2015: 23) that assessed – and ensured – the teachers' efficient performance at all levels of the school. In Table 4.1, select quotes from one of the end-of-year performance evaluations demonstrate how the three section heads,[20] the deputy headmaster, and the teachers themselves commented on issues such as absenteeism, students' grades in various subjects, and the performance of individual teachers. Each group of actors identified other concrete steps to improve the performance and discipline of teachers and students. As these quotes make clear, especially from the

---

[20] The seven grades at St Mary's International Primary School were divided into three sections: two lower sections (Grades 1 and 2, Grades 3 and 4) and one upper section (Grades 5–7).

perspective of the teachers, responsibility for taking measures for improvement should not be placed on their shoulders alone.

Intermediate Conclusion

The first part of this chapter has shown how two schools in the St Mary's school network have been established in Tanzania's neoliberal market economy since the mid-1990s and how their particular structural position in Dar es Salaam has been shaped both by urban restructurings and by growing social stratification (see Hunter 2019). Among the students and teachers, these processes were tied closely to perceptions of class difference, which differed strongly across the two schools and were simultaneously embedded in the dynamics of (upward and downward) social mobility. These dynamics also gave rise to the cultivation of a learning environment that engaged students and made them 'understand' what they learned; furthermore, the teachers made strong efforts to meet the expectations of their students' families, who had made significant investments in their children's future. Finally, among the teachers, highly insecure employment conditions created a strong sense of competition and insecurity and enhanced tensions, especially among the Tanzanian and international staff of the two schools.

The second part of this chapter highlights how the St Mary's schools fostered a sense of belonging to an overarching academic and moral community, despite the frictions that were experienced in both educational settings. Students and teachers articulated multiplicities of belonging (see Kempf et al. 2014: 1–2), navigating the complex dynamics of their schools' inward and outward orientations in highly situated ways. Moral belonging was enhanced through formalised school rituals, and both schools taught values in the classroom in often highly interactive ways. Students' and teachers' moral becoming also happened implicitly, for instance through the religiously informed symbolism within the schools, as well as the teachers' 'fellowshipping' networks. These everyday practices of faith orientation established a direct connection between the schools, on the one hand, and the neo-Pentecostal churches in Dar es Salaam on the other, not least through the healing of 'possessed' female students from Muslim families.

'Feel at Home in This School': Identities and Networks of Belonging

While students – and especially teachers – experienced multiple frictions and pressures in the St Mary's schools, their educational settings also fostered a sense of academic and moral belonging. Belonging at the St Mary's schools implied a formalised affiliation (as employee or paying client), but it also referred to a sense of being connected to, and identifying with, groups and localities within and beyond the schools, and it became manifest in acts of solidarity and care (see Mattes et al. 2019b). While relationships of belonging at the St Mary's schools were self-chosen and self-ascribed, they were also embedded in multiple social contexts (see Röttger-Rössler 2018) and in complex hierarchies and power relations.

The students of St Mary's International Primary School and Kenton High School articulated aspects of belonging, first and foremost, to their family and kinship networks, which transcended the immediate bonds with their parents and (blood) siblings. The majority of Grade 7 students at the primary school had been born in Dar es Salaam, but some of them had parents living abroad, for instance in Ethiopia and Germany; however, when I asked them about their 'home' (*nyumbani*) or 'tribe' (*kabila*), almost none of them claimed an attachment to Dar es Salaam or the *kabila* mainly associated with the city (Zaramo) – or, conversely, with a place outside Tanzania. Rather, the students indicated that their home was in cities such as Moshi, Morogoro, or Mwanza, or that they visited their grandparents, who belonged, for instance, to the ethnic group of 'the Wahaya', for Christmas.

The picture at Kenton High School was similar: a minority of the Form IV students had been born in Dar es Salaam (42 per cent) and only 26 per cent claimed a home attachment to the city or, alternatively, to 'the Zaramo'. Like the primary school students, they also claimed belonging mostly to the places from where their parents had migrated and that were tied closely to their kin's ethnic groups. Such claims of belonging showed the persistence of ethnic identities in a country that has emphasised national over ethnic belonging, especially through the Ujamaa policies during its socialist years (Tripp 1999). They also reflected the continued importance of rural–urban ties, even among the middle and upper classes in Dar es Salaam (see Geschiere and Gugler 1998; Dilger 2013b).

Relationships of belonging were also forged within the space of the school, often closely entwined with the material and immaterial aspirations that students and families articulated in the context of wider class formation processes. In particular, the pupils of St Mary's International Primary School had a range of school-specific experiences that cultivated their sense of belonging to the city's emerging, internationally oriented middle class. These bonding experiences included, for instance, trips to different sites within Tanzania where they learned about their country's heritage, as well as to places such as the United Kingdom, South Africa, and Korea, where they learned about these countries' educational and cultural lifestyles and met students abroad.[21] For some pupils, such trips ignited a desire to study at an international institution in the future. Others argued that it was important to continue their higher education at one of the universities or colleges in Tanzania. Mgeni A. Ngongolo, a graduate of the school's network, described her educational years in an essay in the *St Mary's Mirror* in a highly affective way:

> I am twenty-one years old, pursuing a Bachelor of Arts Degree in Political Science and International Relations at the University of Dar es Salaam. I am actually one of the pioneer A' [sic] Level Students of St Mary's High School … I advise the students not only to think about universities abroad. Most students spend a lot of time discussing about foreign universities and colleges and at the end of the day they fail and join inferior colleges rather than universities.[22]

While no study trips were undertaken at Kenton High School, ties of belonging were also emphasised among the students and teachers – although the sense of belonging at the school was more local in scope than the one at the primary school. For example, at one of the morning assemblies, Mr Jonas, the academic deputy, stated: 'The body of students is one family, the body of teachers is one family, and even the body of support staff is one family. Feel at home in this school.'

This metaphor of the common body was also extended to the Tanzanian nation, which was a central reference in articulations of connectedness in both schools. Thus, as in other schools in the Western and Southern African region, a close moral and emotional bond was evoked in the framework of an overarching national identity (Coe 2005; Fumanti 2006; Phillips 2011), which was manifested in the raising of the Tanzanian flag in the schoolyard and the display of the president's photograph in the schools' central offices. Furthermore, the schools started each day with the singing of the national anthem (in Kiswahili) – 'the prayer for the nation', as one teacher described it – and, in the case of the primary school, the 'patriotic song' (Kiswahili) and St Mary's own anthem (English). In all these songs, allegiance to the Tanzanian nation and the close entanglement of the school's identity with the motherland's future were stressed (Figure 4.3).

Finally, relationships of belonging were forged in reference to faith-oriented identities and practices. In particular, the Christian pupils of the

---

[21] *St Mary's Mirror*, 2002–3, pp. 28–9. The trips were partially funded by the parents (who paid for the airfare) and partially by institutional partners abroad (who paid for accommodation and food).
[22] *St Mary's Mirror*, 2002–3, p. 18.

Figure 4.3 Pupils performing in Maasai and in national costumes at the morning assembly of St Mary's International Primary School, Dar es Salaam, 2009.

boarding section at the primary school told me that practices of 'moral and spiritual education' – which were otherwise not strongly formalised in the school – were prominent at the Bible school that was available to them on Sundays. Muslim students enrolled at the St Mary's schools could practise their faith in the schools too, although for several of them this was a more troubling experience than for their Christian counterparts. During Ramadan, Muslim pupils could fast and receive special food; Muslims in the boarding section received prayer mats to pray in the dormitories and could also pray on Fridays during the 'pastoral programme' unit (see below). However, after Ramadan ended, they had to return to praying on Sundays with the Christian students and were not allowed to pray in the dormitories. For some Muslim students, this was a challenging situation and they discussed it repeatedly. Several of these students were also particularly curious about the situation of Islam in Germany and asked about my own religious identity, things I was rarely asked about by Christian students. Ahmed, who was 12, started one of our conversations with a volley of questions: 'Are you fasting? Are you Muslim? Are there Muslims in Germany?'

Teachers' Networks and Faith Orientation in a Transnational Setting

Like the students, some of the teachers at the St Mary's schools claimed belonging to the various networks established in the space of the schools. Even the Tanzanian teachers who complained about employment insecurity and mistrust within the multinational staff setting reported that there were regular interactions among the teachers that extended well beyond the confines of the school. These interactions included mutual invitations to weddings or funerals as well as exchanges with other teachers in the St Mary's school network at football games or education seminars. In this latter regard, St Mary's International Primary School functioned as the mother school of the network and the teachers expressed pride in working at such a 'high-quality' institution. Furthermore, even those teachers who were critical of the school administrators' practices joined their colleagues in calling Dr Rwakatare 'Mama' and in using metaphors of kinship and relatedness when talking about the communities of teachers and students at the two schools.

However, this sense of mutual connectedness was even stronger among the teachers from abroad. I have already described how nationality and ethnicity became markers of both contestation and belonging in a context of transnational professional mobility and hierarchies (see Bakewell and Binaisa 2016). In addition, many of the teachers from Kenya and Uganda lived in one of the schools' staff quarters, provided especially for international teachers and for unmarried, predominantly male teachers from Tanzania. Living in close quarters, the teachers engaged in a number of joint activities, such as watching television, cooking, attending football games, and going swimming at the weekend. This established a sense of belonging in a context where they felt partially alienated (ibid.), not least due to the use of Swahili, which not all of them knew well. Ms Gracious from Uganda explained this to me:

MS GRACIOUS It's quite different here in Dar es Salaam. I mean, you are black and you don't know Swahili! It's kind of ironical. So, it was hard going to the market, buying things, [whose name] you don't know.
HD How did you solve it? Do you live in one of the staff quarters here?
MS GRACIOUS Yeah. It makes it easy ... because we don't have to communicate too much in Swahili. You can find a person, you feel you have a connection with.

In addition to ethnic and national belonging, religion was also important for developing a sense of mutual connectedness among teachers in the transnational setting (see Settler and Engh 2018). Through the practice of joint fellowship or prayer, teachers in the staff quarters even overcame some of the dividing lines that they had ascribed to ethnic favouritism in hiring decisions. Mr Walker, a Tanzanian who had been very critical in this regard, lived with several Kenyan teachers and reported: 'Every Saturday, we have a lesson of praying. It is a big house there [where we live]. There is always someone who is leading – who is praying and reading the Bible.'

Other teachers became equally drawn into 'fellowshipping' and connected their adoption of this practice to an encompassing spiritual and moral transformation in their lives. Ms Mason from Uganda (34 years old), who had been raised in an Anglican family, recounted that her move to Dar es Salaam had effected a spiritual challenge in her to which she responded by fellowshipping with other teachers as well as by joining an Evangelical church:

[When we moved here,] things were different. This is a coastal region, there are many foreigners, there are things like witchcraft, so I decided to give my life to Jesus. In an Islamic school, my upbringing would be demolished. In a Christian school, I feel in my own place. I feel like I am at home spiritually.

Other teachers reported similar experiences of sharing practices of faith in the common residences, although all of them also attended their individual church services. Thus, Ms Gracious had been brought up in a Catholic family and had been drawn, along with her siblings, into the Pentecostal faith at a Catholic boarding school and then continued in this community of faith after finding a new Pentecostal congregation in Dar es Salaam. She claimed that fellowshipping with her school colleagues was an important way of providing mutual encouragement and solving problems: 'In the evenings [we] read the Bible and exchange words of encouragement. Many people have their own problems, some are depressed. We encourage each other.'

Finally, Mr Mukuru from Kenya explained that the community of teachers provided moral guidance in a 'foreign' context where he needed a continuous reminder of the values he had accepted during his own educational formation at a Catholic school:

You know, in a Christian school you get guidance. This moulded us – I still hold the same values. Especially here in Dar es Salaam I live alone – there are no parents, no wife, no kids. [At my school they] taught us not to engage in drinking and activities like sex before marriage. They also taught us how to socialise with people from different communities and with different characters.

A Total Education: Minds, Bodies, and Spirits

Competition and unstable economic circumstances – as well as the perceived 'immorality' of urban life in a partly different national context – have become an integral part of the everyday experiences of teachers and students, and many emphasised the importance of combining academic and moral guidance in materially and spiritually troubling urban environments. At the two St Mary's schools, the rhetoric linking 'quality education' both to success in life and to the teaching of (religiously informed) values aimed to build a community of 'well-adjusted, knowledgeable and responsible' future citizens for the sake of the Tanzanian nation. In their mission statement, the schools promised to achieve this goal through a 'total' education that included attention to the value of cultural and religious difference and 'academic perfection'.

The morning assembly was one of the key sites for instilling discipline and values in the students (see Simpson 2003: 46–7). Each day, before the start of the morning classes, all students were summoned to the central courtyards for assembly, where the recitation of a prayer and the singing of the national anthem and other songs fostered a distinct sense of academic and moral belonging. The assemblies were also used for discussing issues that required correction according to the school administrators. Typical problems at Kenton High School included students' failure to communicate in English consistently or to buy textbooks for their classes. At the primary school, assemblies might address students' misbehaviour during breaks or their improper 'lining up' for the march to the dining hall.

At both schools, such scrutiny also focused on how students took care of their bodies and how they dressed. Dress codes and bodily discipline are core issues in Tanzanian education, and government schools, too, teach students how to dress properly and how to respect 'the African way of life' in dressing oneself (Stambach 2000: 56). During the morning parade at the primary school, pupils were carefully screened by the teachers for cleanliness and the styling of hands, fingernails, hair, and uniforms; the rules for each were noted meticulously in the 'Cardinal School Rules', which had to be signed by the students and their parents on admission to the school. Those students who failed to comply were singled out and corrected in front of the others.

In general, however, such codes of body care and dressing were dealt with somewhat more liberally at the St Mary's schools than at the Catholic and Muslim schools of my study. This pattern mirrored the overall comparatively liberal approach to dressing that was promoted in the teachings of Dr Rwakatare in her church. The middle- and upper-class women of her church dressed in colourful, shiny clothes, sometimes trousers, wore make-up and fashionable hairstyles, and adorned themselves with jewellery. This was significantly different, for instance, from the way in which women dressed at the Full Gospel Bible Fellowship church, led by Bishop Kakobe, who reminded female worshippers to dress 'decently' (in other words, to cover their heads, to eschew trousers, and to not wear jewellery). At one of her services, Pastor Rwakatare countered such proscriptions, without referring to Bishop Kakobe's church explicitly, saying:

Shall a woman smell badly because you tell her that perfumes are of the devil [*ya shetani*]? In the Bible, there is no law which forbids women to wear trousers – this is a law of the church. What about the Indian women who wear belly top dresses? Are they all sinners? Each person has his or her own character [*kila mtu ana tabia yake*]. The most important issue is that you teach people to avoid sin.

At Kenton High School, this liberal approach to dress and style caused occasional trouble at the morning assemblies. Here, the girls' uniform consisted of brown, knee-length shorts and a white blouse; the boys wore brown trousers and white shirts. All students were supposed to wear brown neckties with white stripes, white socks, and black shoes. Diverging from this dress code, some girls wore golden earrings or hairbands and braided their hair according to the latest fashion. Several female Muslim students wore long black gowns or headscarves that covered the whole of their upper body (not just the head and neck, as prescribed). Some of the boys wore their trousers below the hips, and when they bent their backsides were exposed. At the morning assemblies, such 'failures' were announced in front of all the students and teachers. On one occasion, the principal remarked: 'Some girls look like Christmas trees.' After reminding the young men to 'always shave', he declared: 'If I see any of these things again, students will be sent back home!'

Teaching Values in Class

Classrooms represent an ideal venue for teaching the values and norms of a society and/or the group and the ideological context to which they are connected (Simpson 2003: 87ff.; Xu 2014). The 'explicit' teaching of values within the curriculum of the St Mary's schools occurred especially in the Kiswahili and English lessons. At the primary school, the Kiswahili teachers used little stories and sayings (*nahau*), poems (*mashairi*), and proverbs (*methali*) to explain the core values of 'good living' (*kuishi vizuri*). These included, for instance, the value of sharing (*kushirikiana*), the immorality of stealing (*kuiba*), and the importance of not losing hope in life itself (*kutokata tamaa*).

One teacher provided a more abstract reflection on Kiswahili terms that represented key values and virtues, including the terms for 'morals' (*adili*: everything right and good), 'luxury' (*anasa*: pleasure, enjoyment), and 'desire' (*ari*: the state of wanting to accomplish something and not allowing oneself to fail). The teacher then asked the students to provide illustrations for each of the terms and to clap when the contribution was particularly strong: for example, one student suggested 'Our hospital has hung up *mabango* [billboards] concerning the harm of smoking' and was rewarded with applause. Other pupils were corrected, however, when they used their illustrations for making jokes about their peers. This was the case, for instance, when Ahmed said: '[X] has a lot of *anasa* [enjoyment].' As the other pupils laughed, the teacher remarked: 'It is not good to say about a fellow student that he has a bad character if he does not have it. This is bad.'

At Kenton High School, core values of human life were discussed in the English lessons when novels such as *Passed like a Shadow* by Bernard Mapalala or *Weep Not, Child* by Ngũgĩ wa Thiong'o were read. The Mapalala novel describes the story of a Ugandan family whose members die of AIDS one after another, survived only by one young woman who falls in love with an AIDS counsellor. After asking the students to identify the protagonists and themes of the book, Ms Gracious asked them to reflect further on some of these themes (poverty, betrayal, death, ignorance, promiscuity) and to think about how the novel's main characters had failed to live up to the core values of human behaviour and their responsibilities as fathers, mothers, siblings, and spouses. In particular, she involved them in a conversation about 'conflict' that gradually evolved into a discussion on relations of failed care and support in times of HIV and AIDS – although she provided some of the answers to the increasingly challenging questions herself:

MS GRACIOUS What kind of family conflicts are represented in the novel?
STUDENT Being irresponsible.
MS GRACIOUS Good. What is the father supposed to do?
STUDENT To show love to the children.
MS GRACIOUS This father [Adiyeri] is not doing it. When he comes, he is drunk and battering the child. If his child lets the dishes fall, he is supposed to show love and care. But he is doing his own things, drinking and being a womaniser and all that. How is Amooti [the wife of Adiyeri] described? [No response from the class.] She is described as short and talkative. So if she sees that Adiyeri has another woman, she freaks out. She doesn't care for him when he falls sick … When Adiyeri dies, who felt sorry? [No response from the class.] Didn't you feel sorry? Of course, he has done some bad things, but he hasn't deserved to die.

'This Is Not a Christian School': (In)formalising Faith

Faith-oriented schools in Tanzania have long had the reputation of exerting a specific disciplinary effect on their students' and teachers' bodies and souls (Stambach 2010b; 372). According to Anastasia Martin from the Christian Social Services Commission,[23] such promises and expectations are also translated into the work ethic of the teachers and administrators of these schools in the country and have become part of their 'identity' – as well as a necessary condition to survive as a fee-dependent school – in the educational market: '[Christian schools] have a vision – they refer to the work of Jesus Christ: He was a teacher and a doctor. Even those schools which are not good are trying to be good. If not, you lose your identity.'

However, in addition to the practice of fellowshipping, which was widespread among the teachers in the staff quarters, there was little agreement among the students and teachers on whether the St Mary's schools were 'Christian schools'. Most of my interlocutors rejected such a label, and the academic deputy master of Kenton High School, Mr Mumbi, said: 'This is not a Christian school. It is affiliated to St Mary's. But it was established for the locals who cannot afford St Mary's High. Not as a Christian school.' Mr Walker, who was himself a member of the Moravian church, agreed: 'For me, this is not a Christian school. People say it is a Christian school because the owner is a pastor. But we don't have [religion] as a subject here, there is no teacher for this.'

Claims about the St Mary's schools' alleged faith neutrality were partially undermined by the fact that the teachers from abroad had been hired as 'missionary workers', something they ascribed to the fact that visas for missionary workers were cheaper than for other, regular work categories and that it was easy for Dr Rwakatare, a Christian pastor, to obtain this type of visa. More importantly, there was a widespread – albeit diffuse – perception among the teachers and students of both schools that the St Mary's schools were 'somehow' connected to the Christian field, as they were owned by the pastor of one of the largest neo-Pentecostal churches in Dar es Salaam. This association was reinforced further by the neo-Pentecostal symbolism that dominated the spaces and everyday routines, especially at the primary school. Thus, walls of the school buildings of St Mary's International Primary School were painted with messages of faith including 'God is Able' and 'My Home is a House of Prayer: Jesus Christ'. Similarly, murals on the perimeter walls of the neighbouring St Mary's Bright Future Orphanage Centre were painted with large-lettered, colourful phrases such as 'Jesus loves you', while an advertisement for Kenton High School read 'Stop suffering, K. High School is your answer' (see also Figure 4.4). This slogan echoed one of

---

[23] Interview with Anastasia Martin, Dar es Salaam, 10 October 2008.

Figure 4.4 'Forward ever, backward never.' Mural on the perimeter wall of Kenton High School, 2010.

the core promises of neo-Pentecostal churches in Dar es Salaam, a similarity that was brought home to me in one of my first conversations with Mr Kariuki, the headmaster of St Mary's International Primary School, who was also one of the elders at Dr Rwakatare's church: 'If you want to be successful, if you want to be rich, come to our church.'

Beyond such materially visible manifestations of the St Mary's schools' Christian (and neo-Pentecostal) orientation, however, faith had a rather implicit presence in the everyday operations of the two schools. Both institutions admitted students from various religious backgrounds and there was no clear preference for any one denomination within the highly diverse Christian spectrum. Out of the 52 students in Grade 7 at the primary school, 14 were Roman Catholic, 11 Muslim, and 27 'Protestant'.[24] At Kenton High School, among the Form IV students, nine identified as Roman Catholics, nine as Muslims, and 14 as Protestants; four of the last

---

[24] These included Seventh Day Adventists, Evangelical-Lutherans, Moravians, and a few Pentecostals.

category were Pentecostals. The teaching of religious content at the schools was not formalised, and there existed no formal subject such as Christian education (but see the next section). Equally, while the libraries at the two schools were fairly well stocked with novels and textbooks on different school subjects, there was no shelf for books on religion.

Under these circumstances, issues of faith were enacted and negotiated mostly in the informal conversations and interactions among students and teachers at the schools. This 'moral becoming within the domains of everyday life' (Mattingly 2014: 27) through Christian rhetoric and symbolism was strongly present in informal conversations during class and at lunchtime. In one instance, one of the Grade 7 pupils proposed to 'play church' during the break but was interrupted by her fellow students ('Stop preaching!'); teachers and students made the sign of the cross on themselves before lunch, discussed the content of church services, and invoked God when jokingly scolding a teacher who claimed to be unable to speak Kiswahili ('We have heard that you speak Swahili! God is watching you!'). Finally, some of the staff joined in singing Christian songs that were popular at Dr Rwakatare's church when cleaning up the dishes; these had titles such as '*Ametenda maajabu na siwezi kueleza*' (He performs wonders that cannot be fathomed).

The statement of Happiness, a 12-year-old boarding student, summarises how important the connection was between the categorisation of St Mary's International Primary School as an academically well-performing institution, on the one hand, and implicit personal as well as collective ascriptions and experiences of faith on the other. I asked her why she hoped to attend a Christian school after graduation:

HAPPINESS Because I want to learn more English. I want to perform well, to get Division 1. I cannot go to a local school because I don't understand what they tell. Nowadays, English is better than Kiswahili.
HD Is your belief important for doing well in school?
HAPPINESS I am Roman Catholic. You cannot learn without praying to God first. If you pray to God, he will make you perform better.

Teaching Values and Faith in 'PPI'

In various parts of Africa – including Tanzania (see Chapter 3) – a kind of religious instruction is currently being established that 'encourages [pupils] to grow in their inner spiritual and moral dimensions' by learning about different faith traditions (Tayob 2018: 146). This shift towards the non-denominational teaching of values was also described by the students and teachers of the St Mary's schools. Apart from referring me to the teaching of values in Kiswahili and English lessons, teachers at both schools claimed that lessons about morally appropriate behaviours were also taught in a specific class period that they identified as 'PPI'. However, when I asked them to explain what the abbreviation stood for, they were largely unable to. Some teachers claimed that PPI was a form of 'religious club' or 'counselling', but others conceded that they knew neither what the abbreviation meant nor what was taught during the lesson period.

When I asked the primary school administrators about PPI, it turned out that the 'pastoral programme instruction' unit, as the period was called, had been introduced shortly before I started my research. According to the headmaster, Mr Kariuki, students were taught about core challenges of life through 'counselling' and were given 'advice' about being selective in their TV watching, relationships (including especially sexual relations), and lifestyles in general. He claimed that being exposed to the allegedly 'risky' and 'immoral' context of Dar es Salaam provided the students with a unique opportunity to learn about lifestyles that would not 'distract' them later on in life: 'I like my children to get exposed.[25] Children get pregnant because they do not know. Through counselling we make them fear the consequences, not the act itself.'

However, when I went deeper with my research, it turned out that PPI was not so much a time for the intellectual reflection on values but rather a space where students practised and learned about their respective denominations and faiths together. At the time of my fieldwork, Mr Gregory from Uganda was teaching PPI at the primary school and was thus able to explain its content:

We teach the children how to believe well on the side of religion, the goal is to have God-fearing children. Our children here are sometimes lacking discipline – performance goes together with discipline.

At Kenton High School, one 20-year-old male student said that during PPI they split up the students into three groups: Muslims, Pentecostals, and 'all other Christians'. Mr Mumbi, the deputy master, added that PPI was taught by teachers from the school and not from 'outside', as was the case in other schools, including those of the government (see Chapter 3). The following excerpt from my field diary illustrates how PPI was conducted at Kenton High School on a Wednesday morning in March 2010:

First, I attend the PPI of the Muslim students. There are about 160–170 students in the room, which is packed. More than half of the students are boys; the girls,

---

[25] As discussed earlier, however, the primary school students' contact with other inhabitants of Dar es Salaam was limited due to the use of school buses or private cars.

who all wear their headscarves, are seated collectively in the back rows. Outside there are about 40 students who didn't fit into the room and pursue the 'lessons' through the window grills, on chairs they brought with them. From the floor above, we hear the almost constant singing and clapping of 'the Christians'. The teacher from Burundi, who also teaches French, is a Muslim and supervises the period. After an introductory prayer (in Arabic), he asks one of the older boys to guide the session. The boy, obviously unprepared for this task, clears his throat several times and starts to speak in Kiswahili about *sitara* (the covering of the human body through dress),[26] *usafi* (cleanliness), and the general preservation (*kuchunga*) of the Islamic faith in society. During the around 25 minutes of my attendance, there is no space for questions, but many follow the speaker attentively. The leading boy establishes his authority while he speaks and corrects some of the younger pupils intermittently, which in turn causes embarrassed laughter among the senior students. However, his role is generally well accepted – even if there remains a constant murmuring in the background. Compared to the songs and clapping from above, the rather monotonous 'preaching' of the speaker seems rather sober and down to earth.

I move on to the dining hall where 'the Pentecostals' have assembled. At the back of the room, 'God is able' is painted on the wall, framed by bunches of grapes on the left and right. Girls and boys sit next to each other – and some of them (boys with boys and girls with girls) have rested their hand on their neighbour's shoulder. As I arrive, one of the teachers asks one of the senior boys to step forward and speak to the other students ('We are preached to,' a girl next to me whispers). There are about 200–250 students in the room. The boy points repeatedly to the Bible (which he has obtained from the Academic Deputy beforehand) and the importance of faith and *Mungu* (God) in the everyday life of the school. He slowly finds comfort in his role. At the end, he moves to the centre of the hall and imitates the preaching style of a church service. As in the Muslims' group, there is no space for questions from other students. The period ends with a song that I know from church services at Rwakatare's and Kakobe's churches, as well as a prayer that is spoken by a female student. Outside, I encounter one of the students who I have interviewed the day before; he greets me enthusiastically with 'my friend'.

My attendance at the PPI periods confirmed much of what I had been told by the teachers and administrators of Kenton High School. There was little formalisation of the content, and the students in their subgroups joined in prayers and were instructed about core issues of (their own) faith in their everyday lives within and beyond the school. However, the teaching of values and religious content was even more arbitrary than I had expected from what I had been told, as it depended on the ad hoc assignment of individual senior students for this task. Furthermore, the groups of students did not necessarily assemble according to their own religious affiliation; rather, they made choices about the group they

---

[26] *Sitara* means 'concealment, covering' in Kiswahili (see Chapter 5).

attended according to their individual preferences. In some cases, it was exactly this flexibility that made PPI an enjoyable part of life for the students at the school. Thus, when I asked Kenneth (20 years old) why he had attended the 'Pentecostal' period despite the fact that he was Roman Catholic, he replied as follows:

KENNETH Well I'm not so sure if it's Pentecostals or Lutherans, but I know it was not the Roman Catholics. I decided to go there because I liked it, even though I'm Roman Catholic. I liked it. Because they are praying and singing about – I mean, praising God. So I really liked it.
HD Is religion important for you?
KENNETH Oh yes. I feel I need to believe in something. I can't be just sitting here and I'm not Muslim, I'm not Christian. It is like absurd, you know?

'We Are Going into Battle': Possession and Healing in the Space of the School

While the St Mary's schools fostered students' and teachers' sense of moral and faith orientation far beyond the school settings, they also helped them to engage in a 'spiritual battle' against invisible forces – 'agencies that thwart progress' (Strong 2017: 83). In particular, instances of spirit possession and healing were an important part of the moral becoming at the two schools. Possession by malevolent spirits (*majini*) in educational settings was not exclusive to the St Mary's schools: in March 2010, *The Citizen* reported that there had been a panic among teachers of a primary school in Mwanza 'after dozens of pupils … uttered in strange tongues before they fell down unconsciously'. The incident attracted a number of pastors from Pentecostal churches and the African Inland church, who conducted healing prayers jointly. One 'specialist in psychiatry' explained the phenomenon in terms of a 'mass conventional [sic!] disorder … in a community mostly comprising teenagers' who feared 'punishment' and 'threats' at their school.[27]

While psychiatric interpretations remained absent in explaining spirit possession at the St Mary's schools, the phenomenon was partially connected to the pressures that some students experienced with regard to examinations. Happiness, the 12-year-old girl quoted earlier, was the only student I talked to at the primary school who had experienced *majini* possession in her own body. She came from a religiously mixed family where the father of her (now) Christian mother had been a Muslim. During the exams in 2008, she had troubling dreams of talking to her late grandfather. Her mother consulted her grandmother and a local

---

[27] 'Teachers panic when pupils turn hysterical', *The Citizen*, 6 March 2010.

'witchdoctor' and the attacks on her body were identified as the requests of a malevolent *jini*. She went to a healing church to be prayed for and was also healed during prayers at her school:

HAPPINESS I was having the *majini* myself last year. It was when I was doing exams, they were coming – they wanted me to eat the blood and meat from someone. At night, I was talking to my late grandfather. One morning, I told my mother about it. She went to my grandmother in the village and my grandmother went to a witchdoctor. He said that I must eat the blood of someone. But my mother said: 'You must go to church and pray.' I went to a Lutheran church in Magomeni, and they prayed for me. When they prayed, I fainted, and when I woke up I asked my mother what happened. Since then I started to pray to God.
HD Were you scared by the *majini*?
HAPPINESS Yes, I was scared. But then I started to pray.

Several teachers emphasised that it was only girls – and among them, Muslim girls – who were affected by the *majini*. They ascribed this to their family backgrounds, where spirits of late ancestors were allegedly trying to 'protect' their descendants in the context of a Christian school. Mr Walker explained:

Most Muslim students have those *majini*, which is not good for a Christian school. From my experience, those *majini* are taken from grandmothers – they like to give them to the children as protection. If two *majini* meet in one class, they will compete – one starts to shout and then the other one.

For other teachers, however, especially Pentecostals, *majini* possession also hinted at occult activities by the school owner who was trying to harm the children in order to enrich herself (see the section above). Mr Kaduri, one of the teachers involved in the teaching of PPI, said: 'Some of the older teachers told us that the owner of the school brings [the *majini*]. You know, people say you can't get rich without doing bad things.' Ms Mason added:

[The *majini*] say that they come from the ocean, but it is only talk. We interrogate [the *majini*]: 'Where do you come from?' And they shout: 'You are killing us, you are harming us! We have been sent by so and so.' We are going into battle with these spirits through the prayers.

At Kenton High School, the discourses on possession by *majini* were even more elaborate than at St Mary's International Primary School, although they echoed some of the tropes that shaped experiences of spirit possession at the primary school, too. One of the teachers, Mr Masome, claimed that spirit possession was caused essentially by wealthy families trying to get even richer, which made the phenomenon a particular challenge for private schools:

HD Somebody told me that there are many [*majini*] in Dar es Salaam.
MR MASOME They are many, yes. But it depends on those people themselves. They get their wealth in a bad way, so there must be something you agree [to], which if you don't fulfil then they follow you. It is often [among] rich people.
HD Would this also happen in government schools?
MR MASOME In government schools it is very [rare]. Most people in the government [schools] are poor people. Students fall down only if [they are] sick.

The students at Kenton High School were also well informed about instances of spirit possession at their school. In particular, they had a higher awareness overall of the diversity of the spirit world on the East African coast (Giles 1999; Dilger 2007: 67–8), although only a few were able to identify individual *majini* by name or by their specific characteristics. Thus, when I asked the students whether there were different types of spirits that entered students' bodies, they largely confirmed this. However, it was only Thomas (17 years old), who also attended a Pentecostal church on Sundays, who provided me with more concrete information in this regard:

THOMAS They differ from each other [*yanatofautiana*]. There are *majini* who are [called] *mufilisi*; this one makes people poor. Then [the spirit of] *uchafu* [dirt], I don't know his name; he makes a person being dirty.
HD Where do these *majini* come from?
THOMAS I think they come from hell [*kuzimu*]. From the devil [*shetani*].
HD Where does this *mufilisi* live? In East Africa or in the whole world?
THOMAS In the whole world. And often these spirits are sent by someone [*yanatumwa*], someone can just order [*-agiza*] them to make that someone else makes bad things, and the person doesn't know it.

Conclusion

Since the late 1990s, students' and teachers' quests for a good life in Tanzania have been shaped by the educational institutions of neo-Pentecostal churches and pastors, whose establishment has become embedded in processes of urban transformation and segregation, regimes of neoliberal schooling, and the demands of the educational market for 'high-quality' education. The learning and teaching of values at these schools have been shaped by a capitalist logic of schooling that aims at the 'transmission of economic status from parents to offspring' (Bowles and Gintis 2002: 5) and moulds the learning and working environment through pervasive systems of monitoring and disciplining. While these capitalist logics of education have been largely formed in the US/American and West European context, models of privatisation, market orientation, and competitiveness have been established in the wake of economic globalisation in all parts of the world (Mundy et al. 2016: 5).

At St Mary's International Primary School and Kenton High School in Dar es Salaam, this trend towards a market-based model of schooling is closely related to specific processes of moral becoming, which included a strong awareness of class distinction as well as the articulation of particular forms of moral and bodily discipline among their students and staff. In this context, learning was 'not simply the acquisition of skills and knowledge' but became 'a process of identification and belonging' (Coe 2005: 162) that extended far beyond the schools themselves. Thus, in opposition to the mission school of Simpson's study in Zambia, which maintained 'a boundary ... between the "world"' and the Community' of the school (Simpson 2003: 62), the St Mary's schools reinforced a sense of belonging not only within the Tanzanian nation but also to an emerging urban middle class with international connections and aspirations (in the case of the primary school) or, conversely, to a 'local' class of less well-positioned urban citizens who still perceived themselves as privileged (in the case of the high school). In all these regards, these quests for a good life in the St Mary's schools were characteristic of Dar es Salaam's heterogeneous and fragile middle class (see Darbon 2019) as they could be interrupted by unexpected life events and/or the sudden inability to meet the high costs of a 'top education' in the educational market. Among the teachers, this sense of fragility was also present as their professional trajectories were shaped by the highly competitive logics and hierarchies of the labour mobility of the East African Community.

Religion and faith played an ambiguous and contested role in the practices of moral becoming at the St Mary's schools and in the dynamics of learning and teaching values in the educational setting (cf. Mattingly 2012; 2014). Thus, while the schools were widely perceived as 'Christian schools' due to their link to Dr Rwakatare and her church, students and teachers often disputed such a categorisation; this was also underlined by the somewhat diffuse status of the PPI lesson in the schools' schedules and by the students' and teachers' mixed religious and denominational backgrounds. Nevertheless, the schools' Christian, and even neo-Pentecostal, orientation was central for students' and teachers' moral becoming in both explicit and implicit ways. This became visible not only in the imagery displayed in the school buildings and the use of prayers and songs in everyday interactions within the schools, but also – and in stark contrast to this – in the way in which Muslim students' freedom to practise their faith was restricted to particular festive seasons and the formal context of PPI.

In addition, both schools became home to new networks of personal and professional belonging among the teachers. These were informed not only by processes of ethnic and national identification in the transnational setting (see Bakewell and Binaisa 2016) but also by the practices of fellowshipping in a spiritually and morally challenging urban environment (see Settler and Engh 2018). Furthermore, spiritual healings from malevolent spirits, which are common in Dar es Salaam's neo-Pentecostal churches, were important occasions for the everyday embodiment of values in the context of religious diversity and an increasingly stratified educational market. They also became a powerful moral counternarrative to the excesses of the St Mary's schools' neoliberal market orientation, which – in the views of students and teachers – has become embodied by the school owner and some of her wealthy clients.

In Chapter 5, I show how experiences of faith and belonging are, in some ways, very different in educational settings that identify as purely 'Islamic'. The two schools of my study were established by the Africa Muslims Agency and the Kipata mosque, and both are gender-segregated schools. However, while the two seminaries cater only to families of the Islamic faith – and also claim to belong to the *umma*, the global community of Muslims, while simultaneously negotiating lines of differentiation *within* the Islamic field – they involve different experiences of social exclusion and inclusion in Dar es Salaam. In the boys' school in particular, feelings of religious difference were tied to an overall perception of marginalisation that the students – and also the teachers – experienced in society and in the city; at the Kipata seminary, in contrast, the struggles of the female students to become 'good Muslims' were tied closely to their belonging to an aspiring Muslim urban middle class, not dissimilar to the pupils at the St Mary's primary school. Finally, both schools moulded the students' and teachers' moral becoming through specific disciplinary and didactic approaches, which – especially at the boys' seminary – were often more authoritarian than at the other schools of my study.

5 Marginality and Religious Difference in Islamic Seminaries

Islamic seminaries in Dar es Salaam have emerged in a context of perceived marginalisation that, according to Muslim revivalists, has deprived Muslims of their rightful access to social services and full rights as Tanzanian citizens (Loimeier 2007). As discussed in Chapter 2, Islamic education has a long history in Tanzania *beyond* the madrasa schools, where the Aga Khan-related East African Muslim Welfare Society (EAMWS) established a significant number of Muslim schools between 1945 and 1968. The successor of the EAMWS, the Baraza Kuu la Waislamu Tanzania (BAKWATA), continued to build education and health institutions for Muslims. However, in 1981 an intense dispute erupted between the Tanzanian government and BAKWATA after a group of 'enthusiastic young Muslims' staged a coup against BAKWATA's leadership and turned Dar es Salaam's Kinondoni Secondary School into an Islamic seminary (Njozi 2002: 9–10). With this step, the rebels aimed not only to restrict Christian students' access to the BAKWATA-run school (Said nd[b]); they also wanted to protest against the fact that President Nyerere had become the de facto 'invisible religious leader' of Muslims in the country (Njozi 2002: 8).

Dissatisfaction with BAKWATA's leadership has continued within and beyond BAKWATA and its schools (Chande 1998: 146ff.). Several of the teachers and staff of the schools in my study – and many of the employees and leaders I talked to at the revivalist Muslim organisations in Dar es Salaam – had attended BAKWATA-owned schools during their childhood and youth.[1] However, later on in their lives they joined, or established, one of the revivalist NGOs or educational institutions in the city that – for various reasons and to varying degrees – were critical of BAKWATA's claim to be representative of the entire

---

[1] In 2008, there were 21 BAKWATA-run secondary schools in Tanzania, two of them in Dar es Salaam: the Al-Haramein High School and the Kinondoni Secondary School. Interview with Suleiman Sheikh Lolila, BAKWATA Director for Health and Social Welfare (now BAKWATA Secretary General), Dar es Salaam, 4 October 2008.

Tanzanian Muslim community. Today, Islamic seminaries[2] operate in a highly diversified landscape of Islamic organisations and practices that aim to improve people's material lives at a time of growing socio-economic inequality. They also strive to offer an alternative to the morally troubling 'excesses' of the free market economy and the allegedly overwhelming presence of Christian actors in the public domain (see Chapter 3). The Islamic 'infrastructures' in Dar es Salaam (cf. Larkin 2013: 328; Kirby 2017) include Islamic banks and humanitarian NGOs as well as the moral-political interventions of Muslim revivalists, preachers, and missionaries. These diverse practices and institutional forms encompass Sunni, Shi'a, Sufi, and Ahmadiyya Islam and are simultaneously embedded in local and transregional networks of faith (Ahmed 2009; Dohrn 2014), which in turn reflect the long-standing histories of different strands of Islam along the East African coast (Simpson and Kresse 2008).

In this chapter, I discuss how two Islamic seminaries were established in Dar es Salaam in the mid-1990s and mid-2000s, in a context of multiple political and moral-spiritual tensions that characterise the relationship between Muslim revivalist organisations, on the one hand, and BAKWATA, the Tanzanian government, and the urban (especially Christian) population on the other. The first Islamic seminary I studied was established by the Africa Muslims Agency (AMA) in the Tabata area next to St Mary's International Primary School; the other by a revivalist mosque located in the centre of Dar es Salaam. Both organisations are linked to the *Ansaar Sunna*, which was influenced strongly by Muslim students returning from Saudi Arabia in the 1980s and which has been highly critical of the government's stance towards Muslims and its alleged favouring of Christian organisations in post-independence Tanzania (Becker 2006: 591).

I argue that these seminaries' explicit ethical frameworks, which were expressed in their founding constitutions, teaching practices, and the sermons of their on-site mosques, gained meaning in relation to the local and translocal networks of Islamic faith in which these schools were embedded, as well as within the urban educational market and the Tanzanian state's heightened scrutiny of Islamic schools in the wake of 9/11 and other terrorist threats. Furthermore, both schools were established as gender-segregated seminaries and shaped gender-specific perceptions of religious

---

[2] The schools of my study are run as seminaries and admit only Muslim students. They are thus different from those educational institutions that have an Islamic orientation but do not advertise it (for instance, the Feza schools that are run by the Gülen movement and admit students from different faiths (see Dohrn 2014) and the Shi'a Islamic seminaries that operate exclusively on behalf of the significantly smaller non-Sunni communities).

difference, which were tied to notions of social marginalisation and harsh disciplinary measures in the Al-Farouq Islamic Seminary for Boys, and a specific type of market orientation towards Muslim middle-class families at Kipata. Finally, both schools instilled in their pupils and teachers a sense of being morally and religiously distinct and trained them in bodily practices that prepared them to find a position as a 'good Muslim' in a context of a spiritually, morally, and materially challenging urban environment. As the two seminaries were not established under the same institutional structure, they are dealt with separately in this chapter.

The Al-Farouq Islamic Seminary for Boys

Even before starting my fieldwork at the Al-Farouq Islamic Seminary for Boys, I had become acquainted with the school's head organisation, the AMA,[3] through the registration books at RITA and the MoHA (see Chapter 3). While most of the other schools of my study (or their head organisations) did not have their own files at the MoHA or RITA, the AMA did (as did the Kipata mosque). The first entry for the AMA in the RITA file dates from 1989, when the organisation was granted the right of occupancy for a plot in Tabata (Dar es Salaam) for 99 years, for the purpose of building a 'Secondary School (religious)'. The AMA constitution proposed to 'apply the Trust Fund for educational, cultural, social welfare and health purposes ... for the benefit of the Muslim community'. It also aimed to 'raise, collect and receive subscriptions, fees, funds, grants, donations, bequests, endowments in cash or in kind for the furtherance of all preceding objects in Tanzania or Abroad'. Finally, it aimed to 'co-operate and liaise with the Government of the United Republic in all matters in the furtherance of the preceding objects'.

Over the next few years, the AMA established mosques, wells, hospitals, and schools in different parts of Tanzania (Ahmed 2009: 429). However, it came under growing pressure after the bomb attacks in Dar es Salaam and Nairobi in 1998, and 'red flags [were] raised against several questionable entities' (Jamestown Foundation 2003; Tamim and Smith 2010: 118) in the East African region. The AMA leadership submitted a list of names to the MoHA, thereby demonstrating that persons who had become suspicious to the government were no longer active. It also submitted three financial reports proving that the AMA's annual spending for charitable purposes in Tanzania had been between US$1 million and US$2.4 million since the mid-1990s. In one of the

---

[3] The AMA is also known as Direct Aid (Kaag 2013).

reports, the AMA director emphasised that the collaboration between the agency and the government had always been positive, but that the AMA faced growing challenges after tax exemptions had been removed, as this resulted in a steep decline in charitable donations from Kuwait. He also stated that police officers had searched the AMA offices and asked for a careful verification of information that was provided about the AMA by third parties.[4]

Given the strained history of the relationship between the AMA country branch and the government authorities in Tanzania, I was surprised how warmly I was welcomed by the Dar es Salaam office to conduct my fieldwork in their school in 2009.[5] The AMA premises in Dar es Salaam included the Al-Farouq Islamic Seminary for Boys, which was established in 1996 (ordinary and advanced secondary level), a primary school (English medium),[6] an orphanage, and a health centre. The school operates under the direct supervision of the AMA Dar es Salaam education coordinator but has its own management structure (including headmaster and deputy, master of academics and assistant, and master of discipline and assistant). The students also have their own governing body (*serikali ya wanafunzi*), although it was not very active in 2009. They also had their own mosque where the students and staff assembled for prayers.

All services received funding from the AMA headquarters in Kuwait, which – apart from helping to maintain the personal and material infrastructure – sponsored the accommodation and medical treatment of orphans in the AMA medical centre as well as the education of students from poor family backgrounds in the AMA-owned schools. However, after funding had declined steeply since the early 2000s, the AMA welfare programmes had to rely on other funding sources. Large plaques on their buildings showed their connection to various donors abroad: 'Ben Hamuda's Office for Private Companies and Charitable Services' (library), 'His Royal Highness Prince Saud Ibn Naif Ibn Abdul-Aziz' from Saudi Arabia (medical centre), and the 'Al-Jabr Commercial Company' (women's vocational centre). Furthermore, a growing

---

[4] Source: MoHA files (fieldnotes, 14 September 2009).
[5] One might argue that it would have been difficult for the AMA office to decline my request for assistance, given that their refusal might have increased suspicions of their work. However, my impression was that most of the staff and students of the AMA office and the Al-Farouq seminary had a sincere interest in showing me how they worked, taught, and studied, and the challenges they faced in their endeavours.
[6] One of the reasons for establishing the primary school in 2009 was to provide an on-site school for the children in the AMA orphanage. However, the primary school also admitted children from families that were not previously connected to the AMA.

number of students paid fees for education, placing the AMA schools somewhere between a charitable organisation and a market-oriented one. In its early years, the AMA branch in Dar es Salaam had sponsored up to 500 students each year, while in 2009 only 60–70 pupils were exempted from the payment of school fees; between 160 and 170 boys were living at the orphanage.

Declining Performance and Structural Challenges at Al-Farouq

While marketisation as one of the logics of 'global schooling' (Anderson-Levitt 2003) had become increasingly ingrained in the operations of the Al-Farouq Islamic Seminary in 2009, processes of market orientation have conflicted with the low social profile of the school as a charity. During my research, the school had 365 registered Muslim students, most of them paying their own annual school fees of TZH 300,000 (day) or TZH 600,000 (boarding) at the ordinary level and TZH 350,000 (day) or TZH 650,000 (boarding) at the advanced level. Those students without the ability to pay their fees were screened for their financial and social background in the AMA head office, which decided whether their school fees were to be either fully or partially funded by the agency.[7]

According to the headmaster, Mr Shabani, the school's central challenge was to meet the expectations of students' parents. This was, he said, a simple rule of the market according to which 'religious schools' had to 'stand out'. In particular, parents expected that their children would acquire 'moral credentials' (Hoechner 2018: 161). They also expected, he said, that their children would not 'join bad groups of people' but would 'become good members of society' after graduation; this expectation, according to him, was particularly strong among the parents of the boarding school students, who, in addition to the midday prayers, attended evening prayers in the on-site mosque and received comprehensive religious teachings.

At the same time, the headmaster was quite aware that the appeal of acquiring 'moral credentials' was not sufficient to recruit, or retain, new (paying) students and he was highly displeased with the seminary's weak academic performance in the late 2000s (see Table 5.1). The AMA and Al-Farouq administrators had various explanations for the school's decline. In particular, they argued that the school was less competitive compared with other – private and non-governmental, but also some high-performing government – schools due to its weak material infrastructure (e.g. its laboratory and library) and the high turnover of teachers (see also Possi and Maselle 2006: 468ff.). This competitive

---

[7] In addition, the earlier performance of a student was said to play a role in this decision.

Table 5.1. *Declining examination results and number of exam candidates at the Al-Farouq Seminary*

Year	Total	Div. I	Div. II	Div. III	Div. IV	Failed	Absent
2005	52	1	4	20	27	0	0
2006	61	1	4	12	38	4	2
2008	95	0	7	16	43	25	4
2010	54	0	0	4	34	15	1
2012	42	0	0	1	13	28	0
2013	54	0	0	11	29	13	1

Source: NECTA (2005; 2012; 2013).
Note: Ordinary level = CSEE (Form IV).[8]

disadvantage was ascribed in part to the declining funding situation since the early 2000s,[9] but mainly to the fact that the school management had little leeway in dealing with these challenges. In early 2009, there was talk among the teachers that many of them would leave due to their dissatisfaction with their salaries. While other schools in Dar es Salaam had already reacted to this long-existing problem of teacher retention (Towse et al. 2002) by increasing their salaries, this was not possible at Al-Farouq as all far-reaching decisions about budgets were made in the headquarters in Kuwait. The school administrators applied to increase their teachers' salaries, but before the decision was made, six teachers had already left the school.

As a market-oriented enterprise, the seminary struggled to meet the expectations of its target groups, who had a rather low social profile; as an Islamic seminary, it faced competition from Christian, government, and other Muslim schools; and as an AMA charity, it was finally subject to the bureaucratic hierarchies of the NGO under which it had been established. There were various strategies with which the Al-Farouq management – as well as the AMA country office – responded to these challenges. They tried – within the limits above – to 'revise' their teachers' salaries regularly and to offer certain benefits in order to increase their 'spirit of work', as discussed in the following section. The teachers also valued the various school networks that the Al-Farouq seminary had established and in which headmasters – and teachers – shared experiences and strategies concerning

---

[8] No numbers were available for the years 2009 and 2014. The CSEE is the Certificate of Secondary Education Examination.
[9] Mr Shabani said that the funding from Saudi Arabia had stopped completely in 2009.

certain educational developments. In particular, the school was part of the Inter-Islamic Schools Network, which included eight other Islamic seminaries in the city.

Teaching at Al-Farouq: Between Material Interests and 'Volunteering'

The extensive local and translocal networks of the AMA were valued by some of the Al-Farouq teachers as a kind of cultural capital, which facilitated their academic and professional advancement within multiple overlapping networks of Islamic faith. Some of them had been trained in one of the newer Islamic schools and universities in Tanzania and/or the East African region. Others had attended one of the BAKWATA schools in Dar es Salaam, from where they pursued educational opportunities abroad, including in Sudan, Egypt, Saudi Arabia, and Pakistan. Still others had been trained in government schools and became connected to Al-Farouq through friends and colleagues.

In this wider context of Islamic networking and faith orientation, several Al-Farouq teachers felt that their work had a social and spiritual meaning beyond simply earning an income. The Arabic teacher, a man in his late fifties from the rural Pwani region, stated that many Al-Farouq students came from poor families. He found it rewarding to meet the expectations of parents who wanted their sons to 'get at least some knowledge about their religion'. Other teachers referred to their profession as 'work for God', 'volunteering' (*kujitolea*), or 'work for society' (*kazi ya jamii*) – although in most instances these comments were a statement about both faith and the reality of a low-paid job. As Mr Ibadi put it: 'You work for the benefit of the society – not for your own benefit.' For him, teaching in an Islamic seminary was a temporary solution, as he saw his employment at Al-Farouq in opposition to his material and professional interests.

Most Al-Farouq teachers originated from families with a poor socio-economic and educational background, and they were often among the first within their families to complete secondary education. For all of them, but especially for the part-time teachers, their salaries were usually insufficient to sustain their families; most had additional sources of income, such as working as private tutors or running side businesses – for example, a computer training centre or a little shop (*duka*). One teacher in his mid-twenties said: 'I am here for profit [*kimaslahi*] – not for religion.' Mr Ismaili (aged 48) said: 'A teacher will stay long in a place if the income [*kipata*] is good. The status of a school rises when the salaries are raised.' Thus, contrary to what has been suggested elsewhere (e.g. Possi and Maselle 2006), the teachers at Al-Farouq were not more altruistic with regard to their profession than their Christian or secular (Towse et al. 2002: 650) counterparts.

The Al-Farouq administrators were well aware that the issue of income played a major role among its staff, especially as their monthly salary was somewhat lower than the pay at government schools. The headmaster reported that there was growing salary competition among the private schools in Dar es Salaam and that their teachers were looking continuously for 'greener pastures'. In 2005, the AMA teachers had gone on strike because of '*maslahi*' (profit); many teachers left the school as a consequence. After Mr Shabani became headmaster in 2009, the school management and the AMA head office implemented a number of measures in order to compensate for the school's comparatively low salaries. Beyond sponsoring education and health services for select teachers and their families, they reduced the number of part-time teachers as they were usually involved in side businesses or late to class.

However, higher salaries were not the only issue of contestation among the teachers at Al-Farouq. Some were dissatisfied with the overall management of their school and complained about a 'lack of communication' with the teachers themselves. One teacher added that most of the AMA directors had been 'Arabs' from Sudan, Syria, Iraq, Morocco, and Egypt who did not know 'the environment of Tanzania' and did not speak Kiswahili (see Ahmed 2009: 428). He did not believe that the AMA did not have the money to raise salaries, given that the incomes of 'the foreigners' were higher than those of the local teachers. Another teacher was more positive on this subject and said that the AMA country director had 'understood' that the salaries had to be increased in order to match the cost of living in Dar es Salaam.[10]

Despite their strong critique of the AMA management, along with their complaints about low salaries at Al-Farouq, some teachers stayed many years at the school. They valued living near their families in Dar es Salaam and not, for instance, in one of the upcountry districts where many had their first teaching jobs. They also saw the benefit in being able to pursue further education with the support of the AMA; especially for teachers from a poor background, this was often their only chance for higher education. Finally, some teachers found the schedule at Al-Farouq much more relaxed than at other private schools, which gave them freedom to pursue their other income-generating activities and/or

---

[10] During my research in 2010, however, the Al-Farouq teachers were still waiting for the results of these negotiations as salary decisions were not made by the director but by the AMA headquarters in Kuwait.

take care of family matters. Mr Issa (aged 36) had graduated with a BA in economics from the University of Dar es Salaam and had the choice of teaching at 'better' schools in the city with these qualifications. Nevertheless, he had stayed at Al-Farouq since 2002:

> I stay here, even though my income is small, but together with my casual earnings it is sufficient. I have my wife and my parents here. My father and my mother need my help; they are sick. My brother needs me to support his education. If I move all of them to the countryside, the costs will increase considerably.
>
> But it is true, there are schools where you get a good salary, even a computer. To work [at Al-Farouq], you need to have a heart for doing service [*kujitolea*]. In 2004, the academic master of Feza Boys offered me a job. An interesting offer, but there I would not have the possibility to further my education – because there you finish work at 6 p.m. Here at Al-Farouq, the school finishes at 2.30 p.m.

Learning to Be a Good Muslim at Al-Farouq

In many parts of Africa, public perception of Islamic education is predominantly in comparison with secular or 'modern' education, which is connected historically to the schools of the colonial state and the mission churches (Launay 2016: 1ff.). The teachers at Al-Farouq were well aware that Muslim seminaries did not have a good reputation in Tanzania; (select) government and (mostly) Christian schools were associated with material 'reward' and 'success' (Chande 1998: 213). Consequently, they downplayed the role of faith in the space of the seminary, as a close connection between the school and 'religion' or 'Islam' could have had a negative impact on how they wanted to be perceived as professionals. They were also concerned about the political reputation of the school, as they – and the students – were aware of public perceptions that connected Islamic schools to terrorist threats.[11] Responding to such concerns, Mr Abdulrahmani (25 years old) stated that Al-Farouq was not very different from a government school; he also emphasised that the students' parents often had no particular interest in issues of faith:

> Yes, students are praying at the *masjid* [mosque], but even at public schools they are allowed [to pray at the mosque]. When you look at their families, some fathers want their children to be taught Islam, they think that they can learn something

---

[11] See Hoechner (2018: 43) for similar perceptions of Qur'anic schools in Nigeria, and Kaag and Sahla (2020) for mistrust of Islamic charities in West and Central Africa in the wake of 9/11. At Al-Farouq, I was initially startled when I saw some odd scribblings on the walls and chairs in the classrooms referring to 'Osama bin Laden' or 'ALQAIDA CAMPS'. However, while these scribblings were few and far between, they stood next to handwritten slogans such as 'We sell ice cream and cold water' or 'Arsenal FC'. They were thus to be understood as part of the popular culture of a socio-politically marginalised school rather than explicit political statements.

about moral behaviour, to take care of their family. But you know, many parents don't want their children to become *shehe* or *ustadh*;[12] they want their children to study secular education.

Mr Nassir (aged 30), who had previously taught at a BAKWATA school and, after graduation from the AMA-owned University College of Education in Zanzibar in 2007, was hired by Al-Farouq, concurred. The only difference between 'government' and 'Islamic' schools, as he saw it, was that Islamic seminaries taught 'values' (*maadili*), which he defined as being part and parcel of 'Tanzanian culture' and thus something to which *all* students should subscribe:

> The *syllabus* and the *curriculum* here are not different from the *basic* values of religion [*dini*] or tradition [*mila*]. Some children come here with a certain attitude [*mwendo fulani*]. Maybe he uses abusive language [*matusi*] or has a bad character [*tabia mbaya*] that can lead him to doing dirty things [*mambo machafu*] like sex [*ngono*] or adultery [*zinaa*]. According to the Tanzanian tradition this is not good – this is all the same for Christians and Muslims.

At the same time, however, the teachers were perfectly aware that Al-Farouq was an *Islamic* seminary and that there were parents and families who expected the school to train their children academically and morally as well as religiously. Again, some of the teachers were critical of this expectation, as they felt that some of the parents did not know about the importance of a secular education. '[T]hey don't want to make their [children] study hard,' said Mr Abushir, 'they just want them to learn religion; this affects most Muslim institutions.' In a similar vein, the assistant academic master, Mr Bashir, claimed that Muslims did not make a sufficient effort to perform well; instead, he said, they just 'lean[ed] back' and complained about their marginal status. '[We Muslims] are not *serious* with the issue of education. We Muslims are only talking and blaming: "Oh, these Christians are getting everything from the government." But they get it because they are sweating.'

Beyond these critiques, teachers and students at Al-Farouq had usually more positive associations with the topics of Islamic faith and being Muslim. The staff and students enacted their common belonging to the Muslim *umma* through the joint attendance of midday prayers and, in the case of the boarding students and the teachers who resided on the AMA premises, morning and evening prayers. They also greeted each other occasionally with '*salaam aleikum*' or addressed each other, in a joking and appreciative manner, as '*mashehe*' (sheikhs), in the case of students,

---

[12] *Ustadh* is the Arabic term for a scholar who is familiar with issues of Islam and faith, but who – in contrast to a *shehe* (Arabic: *sheikh*) – does not preach in a mosque.

or as '*mwalimu mtukufu*' (holy teacher), in the case of teachers. Usually, such appellations were connected to particular situations, in which the addressee had proven to be particularly knowledgeable about matters pertaining to Islam or Muslim life – or, conversely, was being reminded of his religious background and the values of the Islamic faith. Certain individual students and teachers distinguished themselves from others through their style of dress: while the students commonly dressed in dark blue trousers and white '*nusu kanzu*' (a hip-length shirt resembling the Muslim *kanzu*), some of them covered their head with a '*baraka shi'a*', a tight-fitting black cap that resembled the caps of Shi'a Muslims, or a '*kofia*', a cylindrical cap worn by many Muslim men for prayer. One of the students, who wore a particularly sophisticated *kofia* with a gold and red brim, was addressed by one of the teachers as 'Mwarabu' – 'Arab Muslim' – a sign of recognition in this context.

In accordance with such positive connotations of being Muslim, students emphasised the importance of the Islamic faith and how attending the seminary helped them in becoming 'good Muslims'. For instance, the religious and moral dimensions of learning and being taught at Al-Farouq were very important for Hasan (23 years old). After having attended BAKWATA's Al-Haramain school for three years, Hasan's brother – his main guardian after their parents' death – was no longer able to afford the school fees. When I asked him why he and his brother opted for an Islamic seminary, he replied as follows:

HASAN The school fees here were lower. Also, I am a young man, I was to get some manners [*maadili*] of my faith, because in other schools religion is marginal.
HD So do you follow the teachings of Islam?
HASAN Regarding the matters of prayer [*ibada*], I don't want to deceive you. I am praying [*nasali*] – but sometimes the whole question of prayer is like a test [*mtihani*] and we fail to pray as prescribed. Furthermore, often we pray only in school, but when we return home, the whole question of prayer remains undone.

Faraz (17) had been 'brought' to Al-Farouq by his father – a 'religious man' (*mtu wa dini*), as he said – after he had not been selected to attend a government school following the primary school exams. He emphasised how important the issue of faith had become for 'giving guidance' to his life and for being part not only of the 'community of Muslims' but of humankind as a whole:

[Being with other Muslims] helps me to recognise that we Muslims are supposed to be as one [*kuwa na umoja*], how we are supposed to be and live. We learn the life that we are going to live later. And this is not only for the Muslims – all human beings [*binadamu wote*] are one, only their beliefs [*imani*] are different.

Religious Difference and Social Marginalisation Entwined

The issue of religion was central to the students' self-identification and was simultaneously linked closely to the young men's ethnic identities. Thus, while the majority of the students were born in Dar es Salaam, the rest originated from the predominantly Islamic coast, south-west, central, or northern Tanzania, and finally Zanzibar and Pemba. The reported *kabila* (ethnic affiliation) of the majority was Mzaramo or Mnyamwezi, while five identified as Arab and Shirazi. Although almost all students said that their parents were Muslim, a significant number specified the religious denominations of their parents further as 'Sunni', 'Answaar', 'Bakwati', or 'Bahrain'.

The emphasis on religion and ethnicity in the students' identity constructions was inseparable from their overall lower social status, which was reflected in their family backgrounds. Thus, the majority of the Form III students' fathers earned their income as small-scale traders and drivers; were employed by the government or in private factories or companies; or worked as farmers or fishermen. Those mothers who contributed to their family's income were small-scale traders or owners of small shops, while others were employed in the service industry or in government offices. The remaining mothers worked as farmers or housewives or were unemployed.[13] In comparison with the other secondary school students of my study, the students at Al-Farouq had more modest expectations for their futures. While most of them aimed for a university degree, their preferred employment included accounting and business; others hoped to work in communication technology, in the family business, or as police officers.

Perceptions of being religiously and socially 'marginal' (Loimeier 2007) or 'peripheral' (Kresse 2009) within Tanzanian society were central to the students' and teachers' moral becoming. Their 'profound sense of dependency' (Mostowlansky 2020: 247) referred not only to the Tanzanian state – which itself depended strongly on international aid – but also to the Islamic charity sponsoring the school. Thus, the seminary's close proximity to the AMA office and the unmistakeable presence of donors' plaques on various school buildings were a constant reminder to the pupils and staff that their seminary had the goal 'to uplift the standard of life, morality and education of the most deserving and needy in the Continent of Africa'.[14] Several students and teachers, and occasionally teachers' family members, were recipients of educational grants and/or

---

[13] Some of the 'unemployed' women may have contributed to the household income through odd jobs or trading activities that were not necessarily listed as 'work'.

[14] See the AMA website at https://africamuslimsagency.co.za/vision-and-mission/ (accessed 29 March 2019).

free treatment at the AMA-owned dispensary. From time to time, pupils carried white bags of *mitumba* (used clothes) across the campus, distributing them among the younger children and the orphans of the seminary; teachers sometimes left the school with one of these bags, too.

In my individual conversations with the students, the interrelatedness of religious difference and social status – and how it affected the young men's position at the seminary and in life more generally – was especially relevant in relation to the students' structural position in the wider educational market. Thus, neither of the two students I quoted above (Hasan and Faraz) had been selected to attend a government secondary school after primary school, thereby limiting their opportunities for higher education. Their options for secondary education were constrained further by the fact that their families were able to pay only modest school fees. Hasan valued the rigid schedule at Al-Farouq not only because it helped him fulfil his obligations as a Muslim but also because he had embodied knowledge of what it was like to hang out with his unemployed peers 'on the street' and not be able to attend school due to a lack of resources.

In addition to individual interviews with students, we engaged in often heated collective discussions during class breaks or when one of the classes was cancelled. Through their constant shifting between their self-positionings as Muslims, Tanzanian citizens, or members of a lower social class, the young men outlined a moral map of the world that largely confirmed what they already knew: they lived in a world full of differences and hierarchies where they were usually – though not always – at the lower end of the scale. Thus, in individual interviews, students insisted that the infrastructure at Al-Farouq was better than at government schools, for instance with regard to the seminary's laboratory. Faraz said: '*Private* [Islamic schools] have laboratories – such things are not available in government schools. *Private* is better.' But when I raised this issue in groups of students, they complained that – compared with other private (especially Christian) schools – 'there was nothing' at Al-Farouq. Not only was there a constant lack of books and laboratory equipment, but because of the frequent turnover of teachers, there was often no follow-up on topics that had been introduced by teachers who had left the school. This was different from 'Europe' (*Ulaya*), they claimed, where students 'received practical training' in the laboratories and therefore 'understood [the lessons] well'.

The students were also concerned that Al-Farouq teachers were often not able to teach in English consistently, which left them ill prepared for the exams, and they especially voiced complaints about the issue of transport. Most of the students came to school with the *dala dala*, the primary means of public transport across the often highly congested city at the time. The pupils reported long waits and travel times, which, they said, made their body 'ache' (*kuumiza*). They compared this to the Christian schools that provided private buses. As one student put it: 'In [Christian] schools the students are brought home after school, but we ride the *dala dala*. I leave school at 2.30 p.m. and often have to wait half an hour for transportation. In some *dala dalas* you have to stand up the whole way home – two or three hours. By the time you get home your whole body aches.'

While the students at Al-Farouq had thoroughly internalised knowledge of their own socio-religious marginalisation, such feelings of being 'peripheral' did not necessarily give rise to irritation. Thus, one of the students, who complained vehemently about the issue of public transport, concluded in a sober tone: 'We are the people from below [*sisi ni watu wa chini*]. Ordinary people are just moving [with public transport].' Similarly, other students were rarely bitter or frustrated about the topics or outcomes of our conversations. Rather, they discussed issues of social difference and marginalisation in a joking or humorous tone. Thus, while the Al-Farouq seminary was a space for experiencing, and expressing, multiple instances of dependency, it simultaneously allowed the young men to arrive at an arrangement with these injustices that went beyond complaint, in an institutional setting that promised at least temporary escape from this situation.

Moral Becoming in a 'Dangerous City'

The sense of both religious and social alienation (Becker 2016: 160) was constantly experienced by Muslim students and teachers at Al-Farouq, and their critical discourse on Muslims' marginal status extended well beyond the space of the school into the wider conditions of the postcolonial world. The young men involved me in discussions about why Muslims and black people were discriminated against in Germany (and how they themselves would be able to survive if they ever had the chance to go there), whether there were prisons in Germany, and how the multiparty system functioned in my country when Tanzania had only one party that clung to power with force.

Some of these topics were also discussed during class. The history of colonialism and its destructive impact on African societies – as well as the Berlin Conference of 1884–5 and the Nazi regime – were regularly referred to by students, and to some extent by the teachers, too. Thus, in one of the history lessons, the teacher lectured on 'the impact of the colonial economy on African societies' and asked the students about positive and negative effects of colonial rule. When one student suggested 'education' as a positive outcome, the teacher was reluctant to take it up but finally stated that 'specialised education in agriculture and livestock' had not existed in precolonial Africa.

However, the teachers' and students' moral perceptions of socio-religious marginality were expressed most pertinently with regard to their position in an alienating – and partly threatening – urban environment. One teacher told me that Muslims were treated differently in their everyday encounters with Christians and other people in Dar es Salaam and reported that this had become part of his daily bodily experience: 'Sometimes you sense that they greet you differently because you are a Muslim – for instance, when they shake your hands.' Some students put it more dramatically, claiming that especially the Christian public perceived Islamic schools as educating 'future terrorists'. They painted bleak visions of their future, with some of them being concerned about being exposed to the 'moral temptations' (*vishawishi*) and dangers of urban life, including the use of drugs and the risk of getting infected with life-threatening diseases (Figure 5.1). They argued that, if they performed poorly in school, they would 'die an early death' (*kufa mapema*) in their 'urban neighbourhoods' (*mitaa*).

Such accounts[15] of everyday life in Dar es Salaam translated neatly into class discussions on life in contemporary Tanzania, which were tied closely to the students' own life experiences – and their moral perceptions of them – in Dar es Salaam. In one of the Kiswahili lessons, the teacher established a list of 'negative behaviours' in society with the help of the students. Their suggestions included terms such as 'gangsterism' (*ujambazi*), 'rape' (*ubakaji*), 'prostitution' (*umalaya*), and 'adultery' (*uasherati*). '*Uasherati*,' the teacher explained, referred broadly to all kinds of actions that are 'not good' – including 'homosexuality' (*ushoga*), which was 'against creation' (*kinyume ya kimaumbile*). An appalled murmur was heard among the students as if speaking the word '*ushoga*' alone had broken a taboo. The teacher continued to explain the 'deeper causes' of some of these 'behaviours' and argued that 'prostitution' and 'gangsterism' were usually a result of poverty, which, in turn, was the outcome of the government's lack of care for its citizens. He concluded: 'Mussa and Peter would not go drinking if they went to school. However, they were driven away from school because they could not afford the school fees.'

The social ills of everyday life in Dar es Salaam, which were said to affect (poor) Muslims in particular, gave rise to a form of moral

---

[15] It was difficult to assess how much such accounts were based on the students' concrete experiences of life in Dar es Salaam, or whether they built on a discourse among young men who cultivated a self-image of leading a risky – and for me, as a white and significantly older researcher, 'different' – life. Nevertheless, the issues described here were more than young men's bragging about their risky lives in urban Tanzania, but rather a ground for moral becoming that did not exist at the other schools of my study.

Figure 5.1 'Avoid bad groups [of people]!' Mural in Dar es Salaam, 2010.

becoming at Al-Farouq that was an integral part of this discursive conglomerate. For many students and teachers, the explicit religious and ethical framework of the seminary and its embodiment in day-to-day schooling were a protection against the vagaries of everyday life and the socio-economic conditions they were exposed to. One teacher, Mr Ibadi, claimed that 'good morals' (*maadili mazuri*) – and the values of 'unity' (*umoja*), 'compassion' (*huruma*), and 'solidarity' (*mshikamano*) that were taught and enacted at Al-Farouq – were important for meeting the challenges of a 'changing world'. In this world, he claimed, 'different cultures' interacted and 'drunkenness' (*ulevi*), 'crime' (*ujambazi*), and 'disobedience towards parents' (*kutosikia wazazi*) prevailed; parents, he added, expected the school to 'shape their children into human beings' who 'fear evil' (*kuogopa maovu*).

Mr Abdul claimed that the students who came to Al-Farouq had already 'been lost' (*wameshindikana*). Many of them were 'just dropped by their parents' who did not care about 'their progress' and were just hoping that their children were 'straightened into the *Islamic perspective*' by the school. Similarly, Mr Ahmed, the AMA education officer, argued

Figure 5.2 Learning about ethical and unethical behaviours in class (class notes in English on the right). On the day in question, the students were eager to learn central kinship terms in German and taught me some Arabic terms in return.

that the seminary's ethical framework of moral and religious teaching compensated for the 'lack of care' that many of the students experienced in their homes:

It is very important to have schools that provide Islamic teachings. Many students come from homes where the parents are divorced or have died. Often, the students are not watched at home and watch too much TV. Only very few parents report if there are problems at home or if a student does not perform well. If we knew about these issues we would follow up and provide *counselling*.

Al-Farouq established a dense web of moral learning that included the communicative 'co-presence' (Pels 2013 [1999]) of students and teachers in which they negotiated moral values and knowledge about their own social status and position in life (Figure 5.2). As part of their religious education, the young men at Al-Farouq attended Islamic Knowledge and Arabic classes (each two periods per week) as well as the noon prayers at the on-site mosque. Skipping the mosque service was said to be equivalent to 'breaking the school rules'. Boarding students assembled four times daily for the mosque prayers and received Qur'anic teaching in the dormitory ('hostel') in the early morning. Faraz referred to his previous stay in the hostel when he explained:

> At the hostel, they taught the Qur'an usually around 5 a.m., first before the prayer, then again after prayer. Then you went to have a shower, drank your chai, and then you entered school [at 7.45 a.m.]. There were two groups [reading the Qur'an]: the orphans who always sat together, and we others who sat apart, either with someone who knew [about the Qur'an], or with someone who just happened to come by and teach us.

The students emphasised that the religious education they received at Al-Farouq provided them not only with a general moral orientation but also with concrete answers to questions they had about how to practise their faith in their everyday lives. Thus, some of the young men reported that they had learned in school about the five pillars of Islam: the profession of faith (*shahada*), prayer (*salah*), alms giving (*zakat*), fasting (*sawm*), and pilgrimage (*hajj*). For Ibrahim (aged 17), learning to correctly recite the Qur'an and the proper way to pray (*dua*) helped him to believe that God (*Mungu*) protected him at night. In one Islamic Knowledge lesson, a teacher explained the purpose of the hajj, the journey to Mecca that every Muslim should complete once in his or her life, the difference of the hajj from the *umra* ('small hajj'), and the way one should clothe oneself during the ritual trip. The students listened attentively to the teacher and had many questions, for instance about the participation of women in the hajj, which were answered patiently by the teacher.[16]

Becoming Good Muslim Men: Marriage, Prayer, and Sex

Islamic renewal often occurs in settings of intense social and economic inequalities that impose multiple constraints especially on 'young men's possibilities of gaining respectability and recognition' (Schulz and Diallo 2016: 226). Under these conditions, marriage is often perceived as 'the crucial step for adult status' (ibid.: 230), even more so than potential

---

[16] Further questions were answered in detail by the books that were used in Islamic Knowledge classes. These books were the only acknowledged teaching materials for Islamic education in secondary schools at the time and had been prepared by the Islamic Education Panel, partly under the supervision of BAKWATA and the Ministry of Education in Zanzibar (see Islamic Education Panel nd). However, the students separated 'religious knowledge' strictly from their other lessons. For this reason, some were highly critical of one teacher who made multiple references to religion in his biology class. They argued that this should be kept separate, as they wanted to learn about biology in the biology class.

educational and occupational achievements. Similarly, the students at Al-Farouq were certain that they would 'marry early', although for most this was not a matter of individual choice. In multiple group conversations, they asked me how the process of finding a spouse was 'organised' in Germany. When I responded that partners were selected mostly individually, they found this 'very appealing' (literally 'tasty'; *tamu sana*) and stated that in Tanzania marriages would usually be arranged through one's family (see Beckmann 2010: 625). Others claimed that they were pressured by their parents to marry early in order to be protected from 'the temptations' of 'the streets' and from diseases such as HIV and AIDS. One of the big challenges they faced was gathering money for bridewealth (*mahari*), as many came from poor families. At the same time, however, few were explicitly critical of early marriage – even though Mahmoud (aged 19) stated that married life was 'costly' and that he wanted to study and find employment before getting married:

If you have a wife before you started working, it will give you problems because the wife needs clothes, food, and other things. This is why I won't marry before having studied and starting to work. You study first, you put yourself in a clean spot [*ujiweke safi*] so that you know: I have arrived in a good place.

In general, the teachers at Al-Farouq conveyed the model of a 'patriarchal masculinity focused on order, not disruption, and particularly on the domestic sphere' (Becker 2016: 159). In the classroom, the topic of marriage – and relationships with girls and women in general – was addressed in Islamic Knowledge classes. In one class I attended, bridewealth, the importance of both spouses' consent to marriage, and the 'proper way of getting married according to Islamic law' were discussed. The teacher answered questions about having sexual relations with a woman, which, he said, was only 'legitimate' (*halali*) once the bridewealth had been transferred. He also emphasised that a woman was not allowed to divorce her husband if he was not able to procreate; this was different from the 'voluntary' decision of a man not wanting to have children, in which case his wife was allowed to file for divorce.[17] In all his explanations, the teacher differentiated 'Islamic' traditions meticulously from 'Hindu' or 'Christian' ones, claiming, for example, that divorce was not allowed among 'the Christians'. In other instances, however, he referred to 'local' or 'African' values: for example, he stated that 'in our African societies' men were responsible for the transfer of bridewealth.

---

[17] It remained unclear whether a husband was allowed to divorce his wife in the case of *her* infertility. Furthermore, it was taken for granted that women did want to have children.

The topics of women and marriage also figured prominently during the sermons in the on-site mosque; this reflected a wider trend of Islamic preaching in Tanzania since the late 1990s, which has focused on 'things as [sic] marriage law, women's modesty, and the education of children' (Becker 2016: 160). While I was not allowed to enter the mosque itself, I was able to listen to the sermons outside via loudspeaker. In one sermon, the imam outlined the core definitions of a 'good Muslim woman' according to Islam and described the challenges that Muslim women faced in a 'polluted world' (*ulimwengu ukichafuka*). He also defined the responsibilities of husbands to 'take care' (*kutunza*) of their wives and to explain to them 'the instructions of Islam' (*masharti ya Islam*), as otherwise they would be the ones 'to blame' for their wives' behaviours. In this vision, women were called upon to stay at home and take care of their children and husbands – even though, the imam admitted, some of them were today 'allowed by their husbands' to leave their homes or get jobs. The husband's 'trial' (*mtihani*), on the other hand, was to protect 'the honour' (*heshima*) of his wife. He reasoned:

> All you Muslim men, if you come from work and find your wife playing cards with the neighbours, she has not prepared your food. I think that what you have to do is show your rage, show your anger that this person has not prepared your lunch when you come from work. How many women do we see in the streets where they are surrounded by men – one here and one there and [other women] are braiding her hair. This is the reason that we have to look closely at how you live with your wife and take certain measures ... It is *your* responsibility to make sure that your wife lives as God wants it; this is your trial, as the woman has been brought to the world to cause trouble and destroy it. Let us correct each other [*turekebishane*]. We Muslims need to talk with our wives about all these things; there is no question of divorce for such reasons, my Muslim brothers, let us speak with our wives, let us speak *with love* [*tuongeze mapenzi*].[18]

Regular exposure to such patriarchal understandings of Islam influenced the students' understandings of marriage, women's desired behaviour, and the expectation that they should abstain from premarital sexual relations. At the same time, they negotiated their perceptions of women – and their potential attractions to them – in everyday conversations and interactions. On the school premises, there were several women working in the AMA office or attending the vocational training centre. Many of them wore the niqab – the dress that covers the full head and body except the eyes; the students referred jokingly to this as 'American ninja'. In contrast, when we walked together to a football game in a different part of Dar es Salaam, a revealingly dressed young woman crossed our path; when one of

---

[18] Emphasis added.

the students mumbled '*mtihani*' (trial), the rest of the group laughed about the 'challenges' they knew they shared in their everyday lives.

On a more personal level, most of the students admitted to having girlfriends, although the majority insisted that they had not engaged in sexual relations with them *personally*. It was hard to tell whether such claims were always true, and one student asserted that 'others usually have sex with their girlfriends'. On the one hand, the reasons that the students provided for their abstinence were linked closely to the ethical discourse about 'good' Muslim men and women, and the risks and dangers of the contemporary world at large, as it was taught in the mosque and the classroom. One student stated that his religion 'prohibited [premarital sexual relations] strictly'. Another student said that he was 'focusing' on his faith (*kujizatiti*, to be firm in the things that one is doing) and that he had 'this fear that is imposed by religion'.

On the other hand, however, students were struggling with how to behave in the relationships with their girlfriends by transcending religious and cultural scripts of 'traditional masculinity' and respecting their partners' (perceived) needs. One student claimed that he was afraid of making his girlfriend pregnant or contracting a disease (thus implying that he had the desire to have sex with her). Similarly, Mahmoud (19 years old) claimed that he had not had sex with his girlfriend out of respect for her: if he conceded to his girlfriend's wishes to have sex with him, he said, he would soon 'leave her' as this was 'the culture of Tanzanian men':

MAHMOUD [She] loves me, but I can't make love with her, because she is studying and has her goals in life. And I am studying and have my goals in life, too. There is also the *culture* in Tanzania that when a man makes love with a woman [he] will leave her, because she has no use any more [*haifai*].
HD So you say that to reject her wishes is to care about her [*kumjali*]?
MAHMOUD Yes, to care about her. Because ... I would destroy her goals in life – and I still love her and I don't want to destroy her plan. I want to study and when I have found work I am going to marry her and then we can have sex.

As this last sentence shows, even if the young men were struggling with patriarchal notions of masculinity, they still thought of themselves as making the major decisions in a relationship when it came to marriage and sexual relations.

Encouraging and Disciplining Students

While the students of Al-Farouq subscribed largely to their school's ethical framework, which emphasised the need to work hard and observe the prescriptions of their faith in order to become good Muslims, they often struggled with the school's strict demands. Thus, the staff and teachers of Al-Farouq complained repeatedly that pupils transgressed the school's rules and challenged its discipline. In addition to their disappointment about the students' poor performance in the national exams (Table 5.1), there were reports of neighbours complaining about students making 'trouble' outside the school's premises during the class periods, and teachers reported that students came late to class, made noise in the classroom, and violated the school's dress code.

The teachers and administrators of Al-Farouq had different ways of dealing with such transgressions and students' poor performance. There were measures that aimed at improving the students' discipline by enhancing their motivation for learning, including exempting the best-performing students in each cohort from paying school fees for the subsequent year and sponsoring those graduating with very good results for their university studies. Individual teachers also encouraged their students on an everyday basis to perform well and to engage with the content of lessons. Although instruction at Al-Farouq was dominated by a top-down teaching style and the copying of notes from the blackboard,[19] most teachers used a friendly tone with the students and addressed them occasionally as 'brother' (*kaka*). Several teachers also worked hard to involve the students actively in their lessons by ensuring that they understood what they had just been taught: '*Tupo pamoja?*' (Are we together?).

Just before the national exams, the assistant academic master, Mr Bashir, motivated the students for the upcoming tests. In one of his speeches, he explained to the Form IV students how the exam process was structured and emphasised that they should not rely on prayers for their success. He also appealed to them as a collective – as the 'student body of Al-Farouq', as 'Muslims', and as 'young men from a disadvantaged social background' – stating that they needed to perform well for the sake of the reputation of their school and for the families who had invested in them:

> If you are going to take your exams next week, keep in mind that you can either build [*kujenga*] or kill [*kuua*] the name of Al-Farouq. The results [of the exams] will be published in the newspapers all around the country. How will you feel if someone asks you: 'Have you graduated from Al-Farouq where there are lots of zeros?' Remember to study hard, not just pray to God. Remember where you come from and where you live. Maybe you are the first person in your family who has studied through to Form IV. Now, if you don't perform well, your father will see that you are wasting his money.

At other times, the teachers used more drastic measures to discipline the pupils; they found these methods essential for moulding students into

---

[19] Most teachers at Al-Farouq had not received didactic training.

'proper' Muslim men. As Rudolph Ware (2014: 43) has argued, the body is a central site for the transmission of Islamic knowledge and ethics in Qur'anic schools in West Africa, and corporal punishment is often regarded as a 'positive, and foundational ... part of the educational process' (see also Last 2000: 376; Boyle 2004: 113ff.; Hoechner 2018). At Al-Farouq, the teachers also relied strongly on physical drills: at the morning assemblies, the academic master gave orders in an almost military tone, waving a rod in front of the students or making them run a couple of laps around the school premises in order 'to wake up'. Some teachers also caned students in front of others or had them crawl through the courtyard under the burning sun. Occasionally, teachers returned midterm tests to the students in the courtyard and punished those who had performed poorly with the cane. The architecture of the school thereby recalled Jeremy Bentham's image of the panopticon, as referenced by Foucault (1994), as other teachers and students were able to observe these harsh forms of discipline from their respective classrooms and offices (see Figure 5.3).[20]

In contrast to the Qur'anic schools in West Africa referred to above, however, the practice of caning was debated fiercely at Al-Farouq, and in Tanzania more widely. Corporal punishment – which was introduced under British colonial rule (Mbilinyi 1980: 238) in order to enhance 'submissiveness' as part of 'character training' (ibid.: 267) – is lawful in the country as long as it is administered by the head of a school, although this condition is rarely observed in the everyday practice of educational institutions.[21] At Al-Farouq, only a few teachers found caning students necessary for the young men's 'social becoming' (Fay 2019: 324) – and, if they did, they referred less to Islam than to their 'Tanzanian culture'. One teacher labelled 'Tanzanian students' as '*wahuni*' (singular: *mhuni*), a term that has come to symbolise 'the pathology of personhood associated with cities, markets, travel, and business' in contemporary Tanzania (Setel 1999: 166; Dilger 2000: 175) and can be translated with the English terms 'vagabond', 'outcast', or 'thug'. He insisted that *wahuni* had to be disciplined by caning: 'Without the stick, they do not comply.'

---

[20] For details of the panopticon-like setup of a Catholic mission school in Zambia, see Simpson (2003: 81ff.). On public shaming as part of moral socialisation, see Fung and Chen (2001: 423ff.) and Funk et al. (2012: 234).

[21] In 2013, the national *Daily News* quoted the deputy minister of education and vocational training, Mr Mulugo: 'Mr Mulugo said absence of corporal punishment contributed to the decline of discipline in schools, and consequently may have contributed to the ongoing fall in the performance in exams.' 'Public schools to continue using corporal punishment', *Daily News* (online edition), 9 April 2013, http://allafrica.com/stories/201304090024.html (accessed 14 May 2019). On the continued government support of corporal punishment on Zanzibar, see Fay (2019: 328).

Figure 5.3 Courtyard of the Al-Farouq Islamic Seminary for Boys as seen from one of the classrooms.

The teacher who applied the cane most prominently in school claimed that beating students with a stick was necessary in order 'to correct them' (*kurekebisha*) permanently: Mr Salmini explained:

> In our Tanzanian culture, if a child doesn't get threatened [*kutishwa*] it can't cease certain behaviour. It needs to be scared from doing it again. The children here come from different family backgrounds; we want them to become all the same, as part of one culture. First we talk to them. If the child doesn't listen, we punish it so that he doesn't do it again. You will see that there are children who abuse us, they fight with each other, they become the most bizarre thieves. Now we correct them. With the stick [*bakola*]. To cane is to build our culture.[22]

Most teachers and students at Al-Farouq were either undecided on caning or criticised it strongly. In particular, the majority of students were adamant that caning had negative effects on them, especially since most of them were adults. Mahmoud explained: 'In our culture you have to cane a child

---

[22] Even some students supported caning, arguing that there were students who had 'failed' and on whom the use of the stick was justified. One student claimed that some of his peers were 'not honest with the teachers' and needed to be punished.

so that he or she becomes good. But if it is a person like here – this is an adult. If you cane him, you humiliate him [*unamdhalilisha*].' Other students insisted that, instead of 'building them', the practice of caning 'destroyed them'. Abdullah (aged 18) stated that caning was 'shameful' and 'hurt psychologically'. Hamza (also 18) said that he felt like an 'outcast' and 'vilified' when he was caned:

HD   How did you feel when you were caned?
HAMZA   I felt bad … I felt that I was a *mhuni*. I felt that my dignity was broken [*nimejivunjia heshima*] – even for the teachers their dignity decreases.

Intermediate Conclusion

Up to this point, I have shown how the Al-Farouq Islamic Seminary for Boys has been established in a particular structural and ideological environment within a growing landscape of revivalist Muslim organisations – and long-standing histories of socio-religious othering and educational stratification – in Dar es Salaam. The seminary's position in the educational marketplace was shaped not only by its strong dependence on the AMA with its headquarters in Kuwait, but also by its identity as a charity and its limited ability to compete with other private – and government – schools. Furthermore, the specific position of the AMA seminary was reflected in the self-perceptions of teachers and students of their socio-religious status and their experiences and practices of moral becoming in the city. However, while the students embodied the ethical teachings of their school with regard to (patriarchal) notions of masculinity and proper Muslim behaviour, they were also critical of some of their school's practices, which they found incompatible with their social and moral upbringing as (almost) adults. In turn, several teachers felt that their employment at an Islamic seminary was in opposition to their professional and material ambitions.

In the following sections, I show that teaching and studying in a 'new' Islamic seminary in Dar es Salaam may vary greatly between different educational settings. I explore this through the Kipata Girls' Islamic Seminary, which was established by the Kipata mosque, closely allied with the Ilala Seminary for Boys, and which belongs to the same ideological context of *Ansaar Sunna* as Al-Farouq. Unlike the AMA school, however, the Kipata seminary appealed especially to a growing group of aspiring middle-class Muslims in the city who wanted a rigid moral education for their daughters rooted explicitly in their faith. I argue that this context of market orientation was entwined closely with the teachers' motivations to work at the school, as well as with their didactic approaches and the students' moral practices of becoming 'good Muslim women'.

The Kipata Girls' Islamic Seminary

The Kipata seminary was located in the buzzing centre of Dar es Salaam's Ilala district. Surrounded by a number of construction sites, and right across from a shop selling school books and Islamic literature, the seminary was located on the third floor of the green-and-white painted building of the Kipata mosque. When I first started doing fieldwork there in 2009, I was accompanied by a Tanzanian Christian friend who was an acquaintance of the headmistress. We passed the mosque on the ground floor, where an elderly man in a white *kanzu* and with a *kofia* on his head was teaching a young boy; on the first floor, a few boys were singing and reciting the Qur'an. After passing an iron gate on the third floor, we entered the school's premises. I noticed that the classrooms had been freshly painted in white and that the doors and window frames looked new. Passing the prayer room on the right, we reached the headmistress's office.

Mwalimu Mariam, the headmistress (*mwalimu mkuu*[23]), welcomed us and consented readily to my request for permission to conduct fieldwork at her school. She had completed her primary and secondary education at various government schools in Dar es Salaam before graduating from the Ubungo Islamic Teachers' College in the city. After teaching at an Islamic secondary school for four years, she completed a degree in education at the AMA-owned University College of Education in Zanzibar. In 2008, she was hired as the headmistress of the Kipata girls seminary, where she also taught biology, geography, and Islamic knowledge. In 2009, Kipata had been operational for one year and had 35 students in Form I.[24] Like other Islamic seminaries, Kipata taught all the secular subjects plus Islamic Knowledge and Arabic.

The Kipata seminary was founded by the executive committee of the Kipata mosque, which had been on the same site in Ilala for 'more than 50 years', according to the headmistress.[25] In 2009, a total of eight (mostly female) teachers were employed at the seminary – with several of them working on a part-time basis. The teachers were all paid by the mosque committee, which raised its funds through school fees (TZH 350,000 annually), *sadaka* (alms), material donations (e.g. construction

---

[23] The female teachers at Kipata were addressed by the students and other teachers with their title and first name. I quote them accordingly.

[24] Further students were attending Pre-Form I, which prepared them to enter secondary school the following year. The seminary's plan was to teach students through to Form VI in the future.

[25] While the Kipata mosque was incorporated as a trust at RITA in 1994, Said (2014) reports that Ally Kleist Sykes (1926–2013) had prayed there as a young boy.

materials), and various 'projects' (*miradi*), such as the renting out of mosque-owned property to shopkeepers. Like Al-Farouq, the Kipata school was part of a wider network of Islamic educational institutions that are tied to the *Ansaar Sunna*: 'that is, followers of the Sunna, the authoritative practice of Prophet Muhammad' (Loimeier 2007: 143). The Kipata school had particularly close ties with the Ilala Islamic Seminary for Boys, which had been established under the Shafi'i mosque in 2005. While students from the Ilala Islamic school would occasionally pray at the Kipata mosque, the pupils of Kipata were using the laboratories at the Ilala seminary until their own labs (for chemistry, biology, and physics) were completed. Teachers were also exchanged between the schools on a regular basis.

In their constitution,[26] the registered trustees of Kipata Mosque Gerezani in Dar es Salaam formulated as one of their main objectives: '[To] perform all Muslim religious rites, ceremonies, prayers and worshipping in and around the Mosque.' They also aimed to 'provide education to the Muslims in the Holy Qur'an and other Islamic subjects'. The executive committee opted to establish a girls' school as there were already several Islamic seminaries for boys at the time; Kipata became the second Islamic seminary for girls in the city.[27] Mwalimu Mariam told me that the 'girls are performing better on their own', as they were more motivated to compete with each other. Her biggest motivation was 'to help' women in society as they were still 'behind in development', as she put it. Kipata offered special 'practicals in science' across all levels of the school, and it also invited female university students to speak to Kipata pupils about how they had succeeded.

Teaching at Kipata: Between Professional Ambitions and Moral Responsibility

Schulz (2013: 398) has argued that the recent structural transformations of the schooling system and the simultaneous educational interventions of reformist Muslims in Uganda have 'enabled Muslim women to conceive of themselves as intellectually accomplished and outspoken citizens' of the country. Thus, while reformist Islam is generally associated with the contestation of established Muslim and societal practices, it can

---

[26] This was submitted along with the application for incorporation as a trust at RITA in 1994.
[27] The first Islamic seminary for girls in Dar es Salaam was the Kunduchi Girls Islamic High School, which was registered in 1990. See www.school.co.tz/s0622/school-profile (accessed 24 August 2019).

help shape female modernist subjects 'in the sense that they fashion themselves as educated subjects and aspire to become members of a cosmopolitan Muslim elite' (ibid.: 412).

At Kipata, the headmistress stressed the 'modernist' orientation of her seminary too. In particular, she claimed that the teachers were different from the earlier generation of BAKWATA teachers who, she said, had been mostly 'religious leaders' with little interest in 'secular education' or 'management' (for this critique, see Chande 2008: 158). While the majority of teachers had been educated in government schools, most had been trained as teachers in the network of new Islamic educational institutions within and beyond Tanzania. One male part-time teacher had studied at the International University in Khartoum, which was affiliated with the University College of Education in Zanzibar and was sponsored by the AMA. Mwalimu Zainab, who taught Islamic Knowledge and English, had completed her teacher training at the University College of Education in Zanzibar and appreciated the way in which 'Islamic behaviours' were an integral part of everyday life on the island. She was impressed not only by the incorporation of prayers in the university schedule but also by the widespread wearing of the hijab. This, she said, was very different from Dar es Salaam, where the wearing of the *baibui*[28] was an 'exception': 'Here [in Dar es Salaam] you are always constricted, there [on Zanzibar] you just have to do it.' It was also on Zanzibar that Mwalimu Zainab met the later headmistress of Kipata, Mwalimu Mariam, who invited her to apply for the position.

The self-conscious emphasis on the importance of combining 'Islamic' with 'modern' education was reiterated by the headmistress of the school, who said that her teachers were 'committed to all': teaching religion, morals, *and* secular subjects, as well as building their professional careers. At the same time, the teachers I talked to at Kipata unanimously emphasised the value of teaching in an environment that followed the 'rules' of Islam. 'The manners [here] are good, they are Islamic,' stated Mwalimu Zainab. While some teachers did not want to specify the denominational orientation of Kipata, others said that the Kipata mosque and seminary were part of *Ansaar* Islam, which, they added quickly, was not to be confused with the Salafiyya tradition. According to Mwalimu Naima, a number of Muslim schools had been founded since the early 2000s because government schools were not able to train students in religious and moral matters. Praying was not just an 'individual decision' at Kipata, she said, but rigidly inscribed in the daily

---

[28] A *baibui* or *buibui* is a long black garment covering the whole body and worn over a woman's dress (see Fair 1998: 82–7).

schedule. Like the women in Schulz's (2013) research in Uganda, Mwalimu Naima aimed to train her students as educated women acting 'modestly and thus in compliance with Islamic norms of female decency' (ibid.: 412). She said: 'On the Day of Judgment, I will be asked: "If you wear the hijab, why haven't you taught them?" I have the responsibility [*majukumu*], and these girls were going half-naked. Did not Jesus have his disciples? [These students] are following my manners [*mwenendo wangu*].'

There was no immediate correlation between Mwalimu Naima's immediate family background and her growing inclination towards matters of faith during adolescence; in this, she was similar to other teachers. Her parents and nuclear family had not been very religious; rather, it was through an uncle, who had sponsored her education in an Islamic seminary, that she had been drawn to the faith. Similarly, Mr Othmani, a part-time teacher at Kipata, had grown up in a largely non-religious family and had been educated exclusively in government schools. There, teachers of religion had made him interested in issues of faith, so much so that he became convinced of the advantages of teaching at a religious seminary. He stated:

MR OTHMANI   In government schools, there are many problems like pregnancy or students escaping from school. Discipline is becoming a big problem in these schools. But not here [at Kipata]. [Religion] shows us the right way to live with others. It makes peace [in] our society, it tells us what is good and bad. We teach [the students] how to be good people.
HD   And what about yourself?
MR OTHMANI   For me, it is important because it helps me to know my responsibility within society. My parents – I never talked to them about religion. In A level, there was a teacher teaching during the religious period in school – so it was my peer group at school and the teacher who made me to be what I am living today.

Learning Piety in a Sex-Segregated Seminary

The Kipata seminary saw itself on a par with other Muslim – as well as secular – private schools in the city, which, in the administrators' opinion, had a general advantage over the government schools. Thus, the headmistress, Mwalimu Mariam, stated that the majority of government schools in Tanzania lacked teachers, so students had to compensate for cancelled lessons with privately paid tutors. Of course, she added, students at Kipata had tutors, too; however, tutoring at her school was primarily for 'improving' student performance and not for getting a grasp of the subject matter 'at all'.

The Kipata school was especially attractive to the growing number of Muslim middle-class families in Dar es Salaam, who were seeking to reconcile their 'generalized ideas about "progress" and ... middle-class aspirations' with notions of 'religious virtuosity' and faith (Osella and Osella 2010: 207). According to Mwalimu Mariam, the combination of 'secular education' (*elimu ya* secular) and 'religious education' (*elimu ya kidini*) was particularly relevant for Muslim parents at the secondary level, as their daughters no longer had time to attend the madrasa; the religious teaching at Kipata guaranteed that their daughters learned 'discipline' (*nidhamu*) and to differentiate 'what is good, what is bad'. Such knowledge, she added, was highly important in a city such as Dar es Salaam where there were lots of 'temptations' and where girls and young women were constantly exposed to encounters with men (for example, the *dala dala* conductors).

While Mwalimu Mariam found boarding schools to be better overall for girls than day schools, as they spared female pupils many hours in the city's public transport system, she said that many parents were not able to afford boarding school fees, which could amount to TZH 1,000,000 or 2,000,000 annually. At the same time, however, the Kipata seminary administrators did not think of the school as a cheap alternative. Rather, the school's second headmistress, Mwalimu Naima, emphasised that 'not everyone' was able to afford the school fees of TZH 300,000 – this was beyond the reach of many 'poor' Muslim parents. Thus, the school revealed a trend of social differentiation within the landscape of new Islamic seminaries in Dar es Salaam that was also reflected in the social and economic backgrounds of the students' families.

Similar to Al-Farouq, most of the 30 Form I students were born in Dar es Salaam, with the rest designating as their place of birth one of the cities on the Tanzanian coast or in other parts of the country. Interestingly, however, all of them located their 'home' (*nyumbani*) outside Dar es Salaam, which meant that their families had all migrated to the city during previous generations. While the 'tribal' (*kabila*: ethnic) backgrounds of the students were mixed, five students said that their families originated from South-East Asia, India, Pakistan, or Saudi Arabia. The fathers of the Kipata students earned their income in similar jobs to the fathers of the Al-Farouq students, mostly as small-scale traders or businessmen, as drivers, or in one of the other blue- or white-collar jobs in the city. In contrast with the students at Al-Farouq, however, the majority of the Kipata students' mothers also worked – mainly as traders, businesswomen, or teachers – and only six were 'housewives'. Like the students at Al-Farouq, a significant number of the Kipata pupils had not been selected for a government school after graduation from primary school, forcing them and their parents to find another way to get a secondary education.

One of the main topics at Kipata was how students were to become proper Muslim girls and women through moral *and* academic education. In this regard, the teachers found it important that the students were being educated in a female-only environment. One male teacher, Mr Selim (aged 25) stated that sex-segregated schools were highly advantageous for student development:

MR SELIM   [Sex-segregated schooling] is good; it reduces *intersection*. Often, *kids are not capable to control themselves; maybe they can have illegal relations.*
HD   What are *illegal relations?*
MR SELIM   *Sexual relations before marriage.* This helps with *performance* at school because they *concentrate* on the lessons.

The students at Kipata were equally positive about studying in a girls-only environment. In particular, they felt 'free' to articulate their ideas in the classroom, while they said they 'were afraid' (*kuogopa*) to express themselves in the presence of boys. I asked Aisha (15 years old) about the difference between the mixed learning environment of her previous government school and the sex-segregated classes at Kipata:

[At the government school] we mixed ideas with the *boys* – it was good, but it is better in a girls' school. *Sometimes you can feel free* – more than with *boys. Also, [in] mathematics [the] boys* knew everything better than the girls.

Haleema and Salma (both aged 15) claimed that female students often accepted that boys performed better and that competition with other girls at Kipata had increased their own motivation to do well at school. At the same time, Salma was adamant that female students were not less intelligent than boys, but were sometimes even more intelligent:

HALEEMA   There is competition [in class]: that is, if you study with other people in the same class you won't accept to be surpassed [*kupitwa*] by your peers, either women or men. But if you study in a *mixture,* and a man beats you, you will just say, 'This one is a man, he has outperformed me because of his capabilities [*uwezo wake*].' But if I am surpassed by my female peer, it hurts me in my soul.
HD   Are boys more intelligent?
SALMA   We think that their intelligence is stronger [*akili sana*]. But others are just average [*kawaida*], maybe – I don't know physically [*kimaumbile*] – but there are also girls whose capabilities are even bigger than of boys.

The presence of male teachers at Kipata was a matter of concern mainly among the male teachers themselves and caused them to reflect on their own interactions with the female students. Thus, Mr Othmani (25 years old) greatly appreciated that there were 'restrictions' in the Muslim schools that established strict gendered codes for the behaviours and appearance of students:

MR OTHMANI At the government schools there are no restrictions. Here they avoid closeness between the teachers and the students. The girls need to wear hijab. And the men wear long trousers, not short ones.
HD What do you mean by 'avoiding closeness'?
MR OTHMANI They have restrictions for male teachers, not to be so close. For example, even to touch the hand of a girl like this [he grasps my hand] is avoided. I can act like I did [in class] today [when joking with the girls] when there are many students in class, but not if there are only a few students. When I am outside class and encounter them, I just greet them [from a distance]. But here in class, I can even ask them about their problems and their lives at home.

Faith-specific expectations about both female *and* male modesty (Beckmann 2010: 620) were also a concern for the school administrators in the context of the interaction between the female students and me as a male researcher, especially when I asked for a space that protected the confidentiality of my interviews and politely declined the offer to conduct them in the teachers' office. Ultimately, I got permission to conduct interviews with the girls in one of the empty classrooms. This room (see Figure 5.4) was located next to the headmistress's office and the prayer room, and it had two windows onto the hallways; this initially made me uncomfortable, as the teachers and students could easily observe us through the windows. At the same time, however, the noise of the surrounding classrooms – along with the constant rattling of the construction machines in the street – covered our voices so that they could not be heard beyond a distance of one or two metres, thus assuring my interlocutors and me that our conversations remained confidential.

The Value of Religion for Prayer and Dress

According to Mahmood (2006: 32), in the wake of global events such as 9/11 and other terrorist attacks, supporters of Islamic revivalism have been associated – both in scholarship and in public discourse – with 'social conservatism and their rejection of liberal values'. In contrast, Mahmood argued that the women she researched in the mosque movement in Cairo had carved out spaces of moral agency for themselves that allowed them to embody specific virtues of their faith in often highly active ways. My interviews with the students at Kipata made clear that, even at their young ages, they were also more than 'passive and submissive beings' (Mahmood 2001: 205) when it came to the embodiment of religious values in their lives.

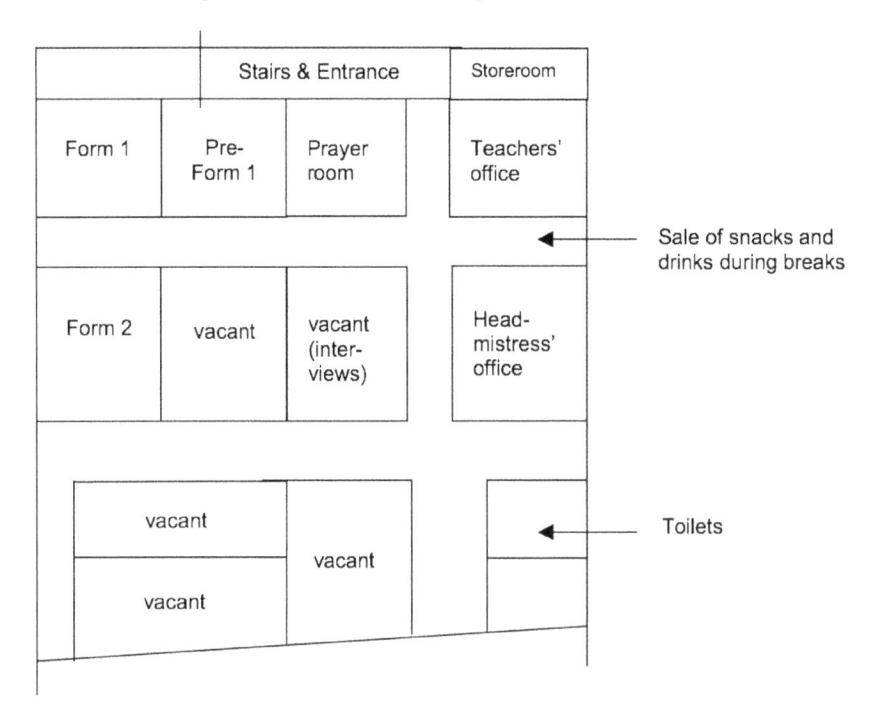

```
|         | Stairs & Entrance      | Storeroom   |
| Form 1  | Pre-    | Prayer       | Teachers'   |
|         | Form 1  | room         | office      |
|         |                        |             |
| Form 2  | vacant  | vacant       | Head-       |
|         |         | (inter-      | mistress'   |
|         |         | views)       | office      |
|         |                        |             |
|    vacant        |                |           |
|                  | vacant         |           |
|    vacant        |                |           |
```

← Sale of snacks and drinks during breaks

← Toilets

Figure 5.4 The location of the interview room in the Kipata Seminary for Girls (third floor, Kipata mosque).

In particular, our conversations showed that all of them knew their position on religious matters and had played an active role in choosing Kipata for their secondary education. Some of them had searched mainly for a better-performing school than the community or government school for which they had been selected. Others had explicitly wanted to attend an Islamic seminary, despite the fact that they had been selected for a well-performing government school. The parents of Aisha (aged 15) would have preferred her to continue studying in a government school, but she had convinced them otherwise:

AISHA I didn't like going to the government school. I wanted to study in a religious school [*shule ya dini*] and *improve* my faith.
HD How did you feel at that other school?
AISHA I felt just normal [*kawaida tu*] because there were other Muslim students. But I knew that there will be the Day of Judgment [*siku ya kiama*] where those people who have fulfilled the religion of Islam will not be punished. My parents *emphasise* religion a lot, but still they wanted me to go to a government school. I don't know why.

HD Do you go to the madrasa?
AISHA Yes, when I come from school I go to the madrasa close to my home, it is *mixed* with boys and girls. Here we finish the lessons at 5 p.m. I get home at 6 p.m. and then I go to madrasa until 9 p.m. Then I have dinner.

A central topic for the female students' moral becoming was the issue of dress and bodily comportment, which is seminal for Muslim women's proper behaviour in other areas of Tanzania too (Becker 2016: 171). In fact, at Kipata the emphasis on decent dress has become part and parcel of the 'particular modernist subjectivity [the teachers and] students articulate and perform in regard to both peers and a broader, "religiously mixed" public' (Schulz 2013: 412).

Many students at the seminary were highly uncertain about the various terms designating the covering of Muslim women, despite Mwalimu Naima's repeated explanations. According to her, the Arabic term '*stara*' refers to the '*principle* of covering', expressed in Kiswahili as '*kujisitiri*' (reflexive form of *kusitiri*: to keep a secret, hide, protect). 'Hijab', she explained, is the generic term for different pieces of dress for covering the body. These included the '*juba*' – alternatively called the 'umbrella' – a gown tied tightly around the face and covering a woman's shoulders, arms, and hands, and extending down to her knees. The students themselves wore adjusted versions of these dresses as their uniform; their white *juba* was shorter than the style worn by adult women, ending just above the hands or fingers. The olive-brown skirt of the students went just past the knee and was worn on top of trousers of the same colour, along with white socks and black shoes. Under the *juba*, one could sometimes see a (usually white) cap that covered the hairline. I asked Mwalimu Naima whether the *kanga* and *kitenge* that some of the mothers coming to Kipata wore around their head and upper body were also a form of *hijabu*. She vehemently rejected this idea: '[The *kanga* and *kitenge*] is just for decoration; this is no *hijabu* – you are asked to veil yourself well.' When a student entered the office during our interview, Mwalimu Naima tested her immediately on what she knew about *hijabu* and was disappointed when the student mixed up the terms and defined '*stara*' as a piece of dress. 'We are teaching this. This is even in the books,' the teacher reminded her.

The students described wearing *hijabu* with the Kipata uniforms as a liberating experience, which they contrasted with the practice at non-Muslim schools where the hijab was usually shorter or forbidden. Maryam (aged 15) said that she 'felt free to be with other Muslim students' and 'to cover herself more'; for her, this was the reason why the Kipata students were 'not afraid' of other people's opinions. Salma reported that, at her previous government school, the Muslim girls were forbidden from wearing the *juba* and wore only a kind of headscarf that barely reached beyond their shoulders. Along with the fact that there was no room for prayer at this particular school, she felt 'restricted' (*-banwa*) there. The Kipata seminary, Salma said, helped her develop 'a good character' and made her able to teach the core values of her faith to her younger siblings:

SALMA Here we are taught many things in *Islamic* [Knowledge classes] so that later on I will be able to teach my younger siblings.
HD What can prayer and Islamic Knowledge help you with in your life?
SALMA In religion, we learn that prayer [*swala*] is a must [*lazima*] for Muslims. If you pray, you are protected against dirty things [*mambo machafu*].
HD What kind of dirty things?
SALMA For example, I orient my prayer strongly towards my fellow students and friends. I can't tell lies, I can't talk about other people. I won't have this character.

While Salma said that her faith and the practice of prayer helped her to focus on 'her own things', she also emphasised that she was not shutting herself off from her (non-Muslim) friends and that her interactions with people of different religious backgrounds were a core element of her everyday life. In this regard, she asserted that the liberating experience she enjoyed in the context of her faith at the seminary had influenced her everyday moral comportment in her wider (multi-religious) social and urban environment:

You know, in Dar es Salaam, it is just normal: the Christians have their things, the Muslims have their things, but we are united in society. For instance, I study in an Islamic school, but when I return home I have my Christian friends there. I go and ask them for materials, maybe for a certain book. We teach each other, maybe my friend knows things although she is a Christian.

'We Have the Highest Discipline'

What struck me during my time at Kipata was that the students were rarely reprimanded or punished by their teachers. As in the other, strongly market-dependent schools of my study, the moral self-fashioning as a seminary for 'modern' middle-class Muslims seemed to be incompatible with the practice of corporal punishment (on a similar trend in South Africa, see Morrell 2001). Mr Selim, a teacher quoted above, said: 'Caning is one type of punishment that makes the pupil fear, but doesn't change her.' One student, Salma, confirmed that caning was applied in serious cases only, and that if students had to be caned, the Kipata teachers usually fetched the headmistress's husband, a teacher at the Ilala Islamic Seminary for Boys, to do the caning. Nevertheless, bodily discipline was also stressed at the Kipata seminary, as Mwalimu Naima remarked:

If they make trouble, I give them different kinds of punishments. One of them is that they have to stand on one leg and with the other they have to write 'Kipata Girls Islamic School' in the air; this either makes them dizzy or they get tired. Sometimes I make them clean the floors for two hours.

The teaching at Kipata resembled that of St Mary's International Primary School, as it was conducted almost entirely in English and the teachers applied a rather interactive teaching style. Once, in one of the chemistry classes, I sat (as usual) in the last row of the classroom and focused on the teacher's explanations concerning the 'bonding of elements and electrons'. As she wrote and explained her notes on the blackboard, the teacher also involved the students by asking them questions. After about 20 minutes, she set an in-class assignment and passed through the rows of students answering individual questions. The teacher took her time over longer explanations, finishing each with the question 'Is it clear now?' In the final part of the lesson, the teacher had some of the students write their solutions to the assignment on the blackboard, and then she gave a concluding summary in Kiswahili. During the whole lesson, the girls took notes and were highly focused; only a few whispered occasionally to their neighbour.

Other teachers at Kipata were dedicated to an interactive teaching style too, and they engaged the students with questions and the repeated reassurance of: 'Are we together?' ('*Tuko pamoja?*'). Others tried to establish a relaxed atmosphere by making jokes and appealing to the students to participate ('*Changamka!*' – 'Wake up!'). Not all of them had completed a degree in education; Mr Selim, for instance, held a degree in accounting and was now teaching mathematics at various schools (including Kipata) and tutoring centres. When I asked him where he had learned his style of teaching, he replied:

MR SELIM I used to learn from the other teachers [at the tutoring centre] – they gave me practice [on] how to teach; some are from schools, others are from colleges. They have mixed backgrounds there, from government, private and religious schools.
HD How do you know if you are teaching well?
MR SELIM You need to know the students, how their psychology is. First, I have to know what they are to be told according to the syllabus. Then I teach them. Then I have to look whether they understood by asking questions or making them participate. Some of my students go to university now. Thus, I think I can [teach].

A final example of a classroom situation where the students engaged actively in the learning process was Mwalimu Naima's Kiswahili lesson. The topic of the class on the day in question was the writing of a letter, and Mwalimu Naima started by asking if any of the 39 girls present had already had the experience of writing a letter. She addressed each of the students by name and had them stand up when they quoted sample sentences from their earlier written letters. Some of the best sentences were read aloud by the whole class and assembled interactively into a structure that provided an orientation for writing a letter to 'relatives, parents, and friends'. Finally, one girl was called to the blackboard and was asked to write a fictive letter to one of her friends, making use of the structure they had reviewed. The girl wrote the following letter.

To 'Name of the friend'
Ilala Islamic Sec. School
Dar es Salaam

From: Kipata Girls Secondary School
Dar es Salaam

13.10.2009

For my dear friend [*Kwa rafiki yangu mpendwa*],

Asalam aleikum, how are you doing? I am doing well and am healthy but you are far away from me [*wewe ulio mbali na mimi*].

The purpose of this letter is to let you know about the education [*taaluma*] here at our school. We are taught well and our teachers have sufficient experience [*zoefu wa kutosha*], also we students have the highest discipline [*nidhamu ya hali ya juu*], we respect the teachers [*tunawaheshimu walimu*]. We hold the environment of our school clean, so our school is clean [*safi*].

So this is how it is at our school. I don't have more to tell you than only this. I would also like you to write me a letter [about] how the education [*taaluma*] at your school is.

It is me, your friend Saida

This 'classroom event' (Wortham 2008: 46) demonstrates how the process of learning values at Kipata occurs in both explicit and implicit ways. Mwalimu Naima's lesson highlighted some of the seminary's explicit ethical values in relation to the emphasis both on friendships and family relations and on the active involvement of students in the learning process. As Mwalimu Naima told me after the lesson, she achieved the 'best results' by starting from the assumption that the students 'have something in their heads' and making them express these thoughts through group discussions, asking questions, and writing a letter. The letter that Saida wrote shows how such a didactic approach – and the values of friendship and being/staying connected promoted by the teacher – translate into implicit dynamics of moral becoming in which the students articulate additional values of the school and their life. This embodiment of 'institutional ethics' through everyday classroom interactions (see Lambek 2010: 4) thereby reveals not only the values of the close relationship of Kipata with the Ilala seminary, which is highlighted by the choice of Saida's imaginary (Muslim) friend at this particular school. It also reflects the various values that the seminary promoted *beyond* the Kiswahili class, such as 'respect', 'cleanliness', and 'discipline', which provided much of the content of Saida's letter. While these values were not highlighted or addressed in the class discussion on the assignment, which focused rather on 'proper' ways of staying connected with a friend through a letter, they were a key part of the implicit ways in which the students – and their teacher – talked about and embodied the ethical frameworks of their school.

Conclusion

Learning values in the growing number of Islamic seminaries in Dar es Salaam has become a diverse phenomenon in itself. This diversity is enhanced by the different structural positions that Muslim schools hold in the educational marketplace, as well as in the (local and translocal) institutional networks through which they were established (Ahmed 2009; Dilger 2013a; Dohrn 2014). The Al-Farouq Seminary for Boys was founded under the AMA, with its headquarters in Kuwait, and catered especially to the less privileged Muslims of the city (and beyond). In contrast, the Kipata Muslim Seminary for Girls was established by the Kipata mosque, which had a long-standing history among Dar es Salaam's Muslim population (Said 2014), and appealed to the growing number of middle-class Muslim families in the city who were ready to invest in the best possible moral and academic education for their children.

The different structural positions and historical trajectories of the two schools (i.e. being attached to a transnational Muslim NGO or to a mosque; having recently started as an aspiring school or with a partly conflicted history of more than 12 years) had an impact on the ethical frameworks of the schools, as reflected in the constitutions and mission statements of their founding institutions, as well as in their didactic approaches and the syllabi used in their teaching. But they also moulded the implicit dynamics of moral becoming in the seminaries' everyday practices and interactions in the context of patriarchal understandings of being a 'good Muslim man' or 'woman', certain forms of discipline, and the way in which students and staff related to their larger urban environments.

Conclusion

At Al-Farouq, the teachers and students adopted a more distanced position towards working and learning in an Islamic school; this was linked closely to their perception of the marginal status of the Muslim community in postcolonial Tanzania. This sense of marginality translated into the Al-Farouq students' moral experiences and practices of being religiously *different*, and into distinct notions of Muslim masculinity and youth in the specific context of Dar es Salaam. In this latter regard, the students appreciated that their seminary provided them with a sense of unity and of being valued in a world that they perceived as both hostile towards and dangerous for young Muslim men. Simultaneously, some students – and teachers – were highly critical of their seminary's everyday operations, which they found incompatible to some extent with their personal desires and interests (for instance, with regard to caning).

At Kipata, gendered experiences and practices of becoming a 'good Muslim woman' also shaped the process of learning and teaching values, and the staff were highly dedicated to the ethical project of training their students as 'modern female Muslim subjects'. The teachers, and also the students, valued the context of a mostly female environment in which they felt free to express themselves as Muslim women and girls. In particular, the teachers and students reflected actively on the role of dress and bodily comportment, which were seminal for both their belonging to the global *umma* and, more implicitly, their relationship to Islamist traditions within Tanzania.

It is important to note that while both seminaries created spaces for becoming a 'good Muslim', they were not detached or isolated from society. This idea that their faith was not only individually liberating (Mahmood 2006) but also a socialising force in their everyday lives was experienced even at Al-Farouq, where the students felt excluded from a world in which they had little opportunity for upward social mobility. Still, such feelings rarely translated into bitterness or frustration among the young men, but instead blended with other facets of their – and their teachers' – belonging and faith orientation as part of (i.e. not in opposition to) a pluralist Tanzanian society and/or 'African culture'.

In Chapter 6, I focus on two schools of the Catholic church that were re-established as 'church schools' in Dar es Salaam's historical city centre in 2005 and 2008 respectively. These schools' exposed location reflects the long history of missionary education in Tanzania, but the two institutions – a primary and a high school – are different from these earlier educational settings in that they are now operating in a highly competitive educational marketplace. Teachers and students are highly aware of their own and their schools' privileged status in this market, and they cultivate an ethos of both elevated social status and charity, which also creates inequalities and frictions within the institutions themselves. Furthermore, moral becoming in these educational settings implies participation in faith-specific rituals and lessons by teachers and students of different religious and denominational backgrounds. In these contexts, my interlocutors reflected on the value of being socialised in a multi-religious society in which they have been trained, often since their childhood, to comply with the requirements and expectations of different faiths.

6 Privilege and Prayer in Catholic Schools

The Catholic church still has a dominant place in the educational market in Tanzania today. As discussed in Chapter 2, the role of the Catholic mission societies and orders in education was shaped by their prominent position under the colonial British administration after 1919 and, most importantly, in the wake of the Phelps Stokes Commission report in 1923. During the subsequent decades, the colonial administration came to greatly value the work of the Christian missionary societies in the areas of education and social development. By the dawn of independence, in 1958, the Commissioner for Social Development, J. P. Moffett, wrote that 'no praise can be too high' for '[t]he labours of many of the pioneer missionaries' (Moffett 1958: 387).

After independence and the establishing of Ujamaa, the relationship between the churches and the Tanzanian government generally remained good, despite initial irritations among church leaders about a 'Marxist approach in [Tanzania's] development strategy' (Sivalon 1995: 184). But even though the Ujamaa government nationalised the mission schools in 1969, this barely affected the good working relations between the churches and the national government. Thus, while some church officials were actually quite pleased with the nationalisation of their schools, 'since the running of these educational institutions had become a tremendous drain on the churches' (ibid.: 184), the new political system continued to involve the church in the provision of select social services (ibid.: 185). Furthermore, the forced resettling of rural populations to Ujamaa villages in 1973 provided some of these churches with the opportunity to expand control over their own rural parishioners (Jennings 2008: 86–8).

The first part of this chapter outlines the broader historical context in which the 'new' generation of Catholic schools have been re-established as prominent educational institutions in Tanzania since the early 1990s. I argue that a political discourse on the 'excellent' position of Catholic schools – as promoted, for instance, by the Christian Social Services Commission (CSSC) – was appropriated by the staff and students of the schools themselves, as they shared an overarching moral sense of belonging to the country's 'top schools'. However, this perception of the privileged social status of the two schools was also connected to processes of stratification within and beyond educational settings. Thus, while the teachers sometimes felt belittled by students and their parents due to the teachers' lower socio-economic status, they engaged – together with the students – in an ethical discourse on 'compassion for the poor' that was translated into the organisation of a charity trip by the primary school to an orphanage in the city in March 2010.

The second part of the chapter shows how certain ethical values – which were an important part of the schools' mission to 'serve God and the nation' – were taught and embodied in the schools through particular didactic techniques and disciplinary styles. I show that everyday practices of moral becoming were realised not only at the morning assemblies and through various forms of punishment, but also in the context of the classroom; this included teaching and learning on appropriate gender relations and forms of 'love'. Related practices and subjectivities were also tied closely to the specific denominational framework of the schools, and students and teachers participated regularly in church prayers and rituals that made them reflect on – and embody – the ethical values of 'respect' and 'community' in the multi-religious context of Dar es Salaam.

'Why Do We Have Holes?': Church Engagements with Social Welfare

In 2008, I met the then auxiliary bishop of Dar es Salaam, Methodius Kilaini, in his office. This was located on the premises of St Joseph's cathedral, in the centre of Dar es Salaam. According to Kilaini, the church's history of social service provision was a story of continued success that was interrupted neither by the two World Wars nor by the Ujamaa regime. Kilaini emphasised that the Catholic church had fostered an almost unequivocal admiration for President Nyerere, whose socialist policies were interpreted as a 'fulfilment of old Christianity where there are no rich or poor'. No 'religious person', he said, could have objected to this dream, although it was economically 'a disaster' in the end. In contemporary Tanzania, he added, the church 'invested in society', not only through its social service projects but also by teaching people to maintain a critical distance from the government. This, he argued, was inherently different from the Ujamaa period, when the church did not interfere in political issues.

Through their 'new' development activities in wide parts of Africa, faith-based organisations are both complementing and competing with state structures in areas of social welfare (Bornstein 2005; ter Haar 2011). In Tanzania, the former mission churches' engagements in social services have been coordinated by the CSSC (see Chapter 2), which remains central for managing its member organisations' health and educational activities. In 2015, the CSSC education board also advised church-owned schools to think about developing alternative sources of income – although it made no explicit reference to the costly school fees charged by many church-owned schools. At the same time, the board reminded the schools of their need to remain accessible to students from socio-economically disadvantaged backgrounds, thereby echoing the CSSC's original goal to work together 'for social development' in Tanzania (Figure 6.1).

Since the 1990s, the Catholic church, as well as other former mission churches, have faced new competition in their various activities, especially from the neo-Pentecostal churches. This competition has materialised in these churches' social development activities, which include networks of schools (see Chapter 4), health centres, and financial institutions (Hasu 2007; Dilger 2009).[1] Despite such competition, the Catholic church remained confident about its continued socio-political role in Tanzania. When I asked the Auxiliary Bishop Kilaini how he would describe the Catholic church's engagement in the country – as 'development', 'charity', or 'social justice' – he vehemently opted for 'development' guided by 'social justice'. According to Kilaini, the Catholic church today played a crucial role in 'human development' and the 'formation of persons for social and material progress'. The church had also established 'unique structures' in all developing countries through which its various sub-organisations were able to reach people directly. 'We have passed the period of charity,' he concluded. The Catholic church, Kilaini insisted, was no longer satisfied to 'fill potholes'; instead, it asked '*Why* do we have holes?'[2]

From Mission to Market: The St Joseph's Schools

The two St Joseph's schools – a primary school and a secondary school with advanced-level classes – are located on a campus in the buzzing

---

[1] This competition is strongly felt in the context of the long-standing (Wilkens 2009: 26ff.) spiritual appeal of these churches. The principal of the college of the Anglican church and the priest of a Catholic parish in Dar es Salaam both confirmed that individual congregations were extremely concerned that their members might leave for neo-Pentecostal churches with their 'promises of miracles'. Furthermore, the church representatives reported instances of Charismatic revival within their own churches.
[2] Emphasis added.

Figure 6.1 The CSSC, government, and (international) partners fighting 'poverty', 'diseases', and 'illiteracy' in a CSSC leaflet.

centre of Dar es Salaam, right next to the Indian Ocean, where Tanzania's multiple colonial, missionary, and post-independence histories (Chapter 2) intersect in unique ways. On one side, the campus borders St Joseph's cathedral and the offices of the archdiocese of Dar es Salaam. On another side is the touristic harbour area, where ferries to Zanzibar depart. Finally, on its north-eastern side, the school borders Atiman House, founded by the White Fathers from France who settled in Dar es Salaam in 1922. Next to Atiman House, which is integrated into the structures of the former harem buildings of Sultan Masjid of Zanzibar, there are a number of old (German) colonial buildings, including the old post office and – further along the seafront – the seat of the Tanzania high court. The area also hosts the National Bank of Commerce, several large hotels, the office building of the vice president, and the Evangelical-Lutheran Azania Front church.

The buildings in which the St Joseph's schools are located today were erected by the German order of the Benedictines, who arrived in Dar es Salaam in 1887 and helped establish the archdiocese of Dar es Salaam. After the end of World War One, in 1921, the Vatican asked the Capuchin order and the Baldegger Schwestern – a religious order of nuns under the Franciscan order and originating, like the Capuchins, in Switzerland – to take over the work of the Benedictines. In 2010, I interviewed two of the Baldegger Schwestern in their home, which is next to the primary school and located in a former military hospital building that had been erected by the Benedictines. The conversation with Sister Sandra Stich started in the living-cum-dining room, which was decorated sparsely with a crucifix and the photograph of an elephant. Later, I was invited for dinner with the four sisters residing in the house, and while we enjoyed soup, sausages (*Würstchen*), and potato salad (*Kartoffelsalat*) I listened attentively to the sisters, who had witnessed several decades of history in the schools and in Tanzania more widely.

Sister Sandra arrived in Tanzania in 1962, after earlier Baldegger Schwestern had established a primary school (after World War One) and a secondary school (in 1956) in the former premises of the Benedictines. Initially, she told me, the secondary school was attended mainly by 'Asians' and 'very few Africans', but then the government introduced a quota system in the mid-1960s that considered religious and ethnic backgrounds in the selection of students. In 2010, Sister Sandra still spoke highly affectionately about Nyerere's notion of self-reliance, which, she said, was good because 'the people still knew that they have to work'. During Ujamaa, Sister Sandra supervised 16 self-reliance projects at the primary school, including the production of sandals and a French fries enterprise. After nationalisation in 1969,[3] she left teaching and became involved first in a youth movement and then in establishing a school for tailoring.

Sister Sandra was sceptical about the schooling situation in contemporary Tanzania. Not only was there little emphasis on 'creativity' and

---

[3] The nationalisation of the St Joseph's schools included the transfer of the school administration to Tanzanian teachers. The school buildings and the land on which they stood, however, remained the property of the archdiocese of Dar es Salaam and the sisters continued residing in them. According to Sister Sandra Stich, President Nyerere wanted to return the primary school to the church as early as 1972, but the church did not want to take it back as it was already 'broken' (*kaputt*).

'handicraft' in the teaching at primary schools, she said, but the education system had also become a self-referential upward spiral that often ended in unemployment. Education had become dominated by school fees, which often could be paid only by the 'upper class'. In her critique, Sister Sandra also included the St Joseph's schools, which were returned to the archdiocese in 2005 and 2008 respectively and were now under the administration of religious orders from Kenya and Tanzania. She thought that the students at the recently established high school in particular 'lost connection' to 'real life':

I understand the sisters, they have to pay the salaries and the students' accommodation [in the boarding section]. They also have school buses. But why shouldn't these students come to school by public buses? Get up early [bissl früh aufstehen]. The students lose the connection, completely. One day, one boy arrived with a big trolley. What is such a suitcase for in the school? But this is also a kind of competition, isn't it? Nyerere said that competition is capitalistic. Young people need to compete, but not in having but in being [nicht im Haben, sondern im Sein].

Sister Leonora – the Tanzanian headmistress of St Joseph's 'high school', which began operating in 2010[4] – offered a different view of the school and the way it had established itself in Tanzania's educational landscape. Sister Leonora was born in the mid-1970s in the Kilimanjaro region, where she completed her primary education in a government school. During her secondary education in a Catholic school in Dar es Salaam, she joined the order of the Little Sisters of St Francis of Assisi, and, in 2010 – after completing a BA and an MA in education – she was called by Cardinal Pengo to be headmistress of the newly opened St Joseph's Cathedral High School. The cardinal's vision was that the Little Sisters would first take over the supervision of the newly established high school and in the future would also run the primary school, which in 2010 was still under the supervision of the St Joseph's sisters from Kenya. In 2010, Sister Leonora had been in charge of the high school for only a couple of months. She recalled how she had first entered the school in 2009, shortly after the government secondary school had ceased operating in 2008:

SISTER LEONORA It was terrible, it was dirty. You could not even pass through the classrooms because it was dusty.
HD But they had still used the building in that condition?

---

[4] The *ordinary* level of the St Joseph's secondary school was opened in 2008; it was run under separate supervision and located on the margins of the city. In 2010, the *advanced* level of the secondary school was established on the city campus and was referred to as the 'high school' by St Joseph's students and staff.

SISTER LEONORA Yeah, you know, in Tanzania, when something belongs to the government no one has that [feeling that] 'This is ours, this is something which you have to handle with care.' For example, you can see in the primary school, we have 250 students. If you go to a government school, the same building, the same classes, they will take even 3,000 students.

Looking back, Sister Leonora associated the start of the high school mainly with the challenges that the school faced. To her, St Joseph's had to offer a number of services – including transportation, good accommodation, and school meals – in order to establish itself successfully in the educational market. In 2010, the activities at the high school demonstrated that 'religious entrepreneurship', which has been associated mainly with Pentecostal upward social mobility (Ojong 2008; van Dijk 2010; Lauterbach 2016), had also become embodied by Catholic orders and nuns in the East African context. The sisters' entrepreneurial spirit could be felt in and around the buildings of the high school, where the classrooms had been freshly painted in a creamy white, blackboards were bordered with a light grey frame, and new fans were buzzing on the ceiling. While the second floor of the building was still waiting for refurbishment, the inner yard had been carefully landscaped with colourful flowers and a bright green lawn.

Such efforts to establish St Joseph's Cathedral High School as a distinct educational institution were perceived more critically by the (Kenyan) sisters of the primary school, however. One of the school's administrators recalled how the ordinary level of the secondary school was established at the insistence of Cardinal Pengo when the first cohort of students from the primary school approached graduation. Despite backing from the highest church ranks, however, financial support from the archdiocese was negotiated only with difficulty, and any funds that were ultimately provided were granted as loans. In 2010, the ordinary level of the secondary school faced a severe crisis after a school inspection set strict conditions for its continued operation. In this context, the administrator at the primary school was highly sceptical about the idea of opening the advanced-level 'high school', as it would, according to her, face similar challenges as the ordinary level of the secondary school in a very short time.

Belonging and Being Unique in a 'Church School'

Despite such scepticism, the high school had a successful start overall and very quickly the students and staff had the impression of being the 'chosen other' (Simpson 1998) when it came to studying and working in one of Tanzania's top-performing schools.[5] In 2010, the high school had 208 registered students – 70 girls and 138 boys – with 133 students (girls and boys) residing in the school dormitories. The high school had two streams, science and arts, for which the students' families paid annual school fees of TZH 1,700,000 and TZH 1,600,000 respectively. In addition, the fees for the hostel – including meals and transportation – amounted to TZH 150,000–165,000 per month, and costs for school uniforms were TZH 35,000. The maximum annual payment for a student's education at the high school amounted to TZH 3,715,000 (about US $2,690) at the time of my research.

The social profiles of the 43 Form V students reflected why the students' families were able to afford the school fees, and how their parents' 'employment status play[ed] a central role in intergenerational class (im)mobility' (Hunter 2019: 200). The majority of the students' fathers were businessmen or were employed in finance or accounting; the remainder worked in engineering, law, or other white-collar jobs. Most mothers were also working, either in business or finance/accounting or in various other positions in the public and private sectors. While most students were born in Dar es Salaam, the majority claimed that their actual home was in Mbeya, the Kilimanjaro region, Arusha, Bukoba, and other, comparatively wealthy, regions of Tanzania.[6] Most students identified their ethnic backgrounds as Chagga and Haya – groups that have the reputation of being successful in business.

However, the schools played a central role in (re)producing not only 'a materially "successful" elite' but also 'an expanded Catholic middle class' (Grace 2003: 48). Thus, the students' religious backgrounds were much less diverse than, for instance, at the St Mary's schools (Chapter 4). Most Form V students were Roman Catholic; less than a third belonged to the Protestant churches (Evangelical-Lutheran, Seventh-Day Adventist, and Anglican), and only one student identified as Muslim. The majority of the students' siblings attended a Christian school. While St Joseph's Cathedral High School students had entered their school only recently, they were convinced that they would receive a 'good education' there. Some claimed that Christian schools had good teachers and learning materials, were well managed, and made them 'spiritually strong'. Florence (aged 17) explained why she chose the school:

FLORENCE [M]y parents wanted me to go to Loyola. But when I heard [that] St Joseph had A levels, I told them that I would like to come here.

---

[5] According to Sister Leonora, St Joseph's Cathedral High School had 700 applicants for its first cohort. In 2012, the ordinary level of the St Joseph's secondary school was ranked number 14 among the 'high-performing schools' in Tanzania (NECTA 2012).
[6] Two came from Kenya and South Africa.

HD What exactly did you know about the school?
FLORENCE The first contact [with St Joseph's occurred] at the O level. St Joseph secondary school [and my former school, Canossa] were sort of rivals. And Canossa is a good school. So, St Joseph being a rival is like we're at the same level. [Also] I believed that St Joseph as a new school run by the Catholic church – that maybe the teachers, we being the first, they will do their best to make us pass. Also, it's under the cardinal's organisation – it is the [only] school [like that].

Not all the students had had the intention of attending St Joseph's Cathedral High School, though. Tahir (aged 18) – the only Muslim student in Form IV – would have preferred to attend a well-performing government school or, alternatively, the Feza boys' school, which he referred to as a 'Muslim school'. However, when he was not admitted to Feza due to insufficient grades at ordinary level, he opted for St Joseph's Cathedral High School:

First of all [we learn] to be good people here, [more] than in government schools [where] you can do many things that are immoral, like smoking. Also, if you see the results of Form IV from last year, the top ten schools in Tanzania were, first, private schools and, second, they were Christian schools. The only [well-performing] Muslim school in Tanzania is Feza Boys'.

The socio-economic and religious backgrounds of the pupils at St Joseph's primary school were almost identical to the profiles of the Form V students.[7] The majority of the 35 Grade 7 pupils were born in Dar es Salaam and had their home regions in Moshi, Bukoba, Kilimanjaro, and Iringa. Their fathers worked in business, engineering, or economics and finance, while the mothers worked in business or in various white-collar jobs. The overwhelming majority of the parents were Catholic; significantly fewer fathers and mothers had a Protestant background and very few were Muslim. A slight difference from the high school students existed with regard to the even higher proportion of siblings attending either Christian or (rarely) Muslim schools. Again, the overwhelming orientations of the Christian students were Catholic. While some of the Grade 7 pupils were still quite young, there were often specific reasons why they were attending a Christian school. In the case of Jane (13 years old) and her sister (aged 11 and in Grade 5), their parents had first inspected the school before registering them. Jane explained that her parents 'saw how the teachers are teaching. Also, the

---

[7] According to Sister Leonora, there was a strong continuity in students attending the St Joseph's schools across all levels (i.e. from nursery through to primary, secondary, and high school). In the high school, 80 per cent of the students were graduates from the St Joseph's secondary school.

performance of the service and the people here. My parents, they're all Catholics.'

While Jane's parents had selected the school for their daughters, this was different in the case of Sophia (aged 11). I talked to her jointly with Paul (13), who, like Sophia, was born in Arusha. Both of their fathers were businessmen; Sophia's mother was a lawyer and Paul's mother an office employee. Sophia spoke fluent English with an American accent as her father had studied in the USA.

SOPHIA   When my dad asked me 'Which school you wanna come to?' I said I want to go to St Joseph, because really I need to be in touch with my God, yeah.
HD   Why is this important for your life?
SOPHIA   It's a good spiritual guidance with my life, because in the Bible we get all types of things, you call that living problems.

Paul was equally convinced that St Joseph's had been a good choice for his primary education and reflected on how his current school was preparing him for admission to an even better secondary school. That school should be a Catholic school, too, he said, as religion played an important role in his life (he was an altar boy in his church). Paul's preference for this prospective school, the St Marian School for Boys, was shared by Sophia, who aimed to go to the school's girls' section:

HD   Are you planning to go to secondary school next year?
PAUL   Yes, Marian Boys. They have excellent teachers. They are in the top ten.
HD (TO SOPHIA)   And you?
SOPHIA   The same [Marian Girls], because everyone there wants to be the best. It is the first one in exams. You have to go where it's exceptional class.

Teaching in an 'Elite School'

The teachers of St Joseph's shared the students' perception that they were working at one of the growing number of Catholic 'elite schools' in Tanzania (Connell 2016: 40). A strikingly high number of teachers at the primary school had taught previously at St Mary's International Primary School (see Chapter 4). In their comparisons of the two schools, some emphasised that working at the Catholic school had clear advantages. Not only did they feel more secure in their employment because they received contracts at St Joseph's; they also reported receiving higher salaries and bonus payments, and having 'more free time' for pursuing individual life plans. Mr Joseph, from Kenya, stated:

It is true, you have good chances to get a job if you come from St Mary's because they know that you work hard. But it is too hectic there, they have too many students, even seven streams in one grade. They are after the money.

Other primary school teachers confirmed that private schools such as St Mary's were run like businesses. They compared this to the St Joseph's schools, where they felt they were treated 'with dignity'. Mr Kaduri (aged 33) said:

> It is the dignity they [extend] to us, the workers. When you join them, you become part of the employer; they treat you as a human being, not as an object to be used. But other primary schools, they [throw you] out after three days.

The teachers at the high school were equally positive about their employment at St Joseph's. Again, some of them compared it to the St Mary's schools, which they said were often perceived as a 'Christian school' in public discourse. Disputing this, Ms Malinda (25 years old) claimed that only church-owned schools were actually 'Christian schools':

> People in Tanzania believe that once you take your child to a Christian school, that child will [learn] good morals. That's why they call themselves 'Saints', they make people believe that this is a Christian school. I believe that Christian schools are only those schools that are owned by the church. Not by simple persons.

For many teachers, teaching at St Joseph's was an important milestone in their personal and professional trajectories – although their career ambitions were closely aligned with their concerns about their parents' and siblings' well-being. Mr Kaduri's father worked as an accountant at a small bank in Kilimanjaro and his mother had taken care of her six children while running a small business on the side. As the firstborn son, he said that, 'according to African culture', he was responsible for ensuring the well-being of both his parents and his younger siblings, including by paying for their education. The importance of supporting one's family was also highlighted by Mr Usman (aged 27), the only Muslim teacher in the high school in 2010. Mr Usman came from a 'poor family' and his parents and siblings had supported him in his own education. Thus, it was now his obligation 'to look out for them' in return, before thinking about his personal future. When I asked him about his dreams, he laughed and said:

> A famous businessman, that is my dream, possessing my own house, fancy cars. But first I have to work to support my family. When the parents [work] for you to get [an] education, they expect something in return. So, I have to pay the price, because my parents and siblings supported me unconditionally during my studies.

The perception of belonging to a distinct work environment was also actively cultivated among the teachers and school administrators, who often interacted well beyond the school setting. In the primary school, the teachers came together for farewell parties before the end of term; these were arranged by the headmistress and included the sharing of food and drinks as well as the handing out of bonuses. There was also a small group of male teachers – known as the 'bat' (*popo*) club – who were all unmarried; they went dancing in clubs at the weekends. In the high school, teachers shared important life events with each other: for instance, they collected contributions among the staff for funerals and also on the occasion of send-offs and weddings, to which they invited their fellow teachers and administrators, who appreciated this attentiveness.

For the school management, this 'making of a community' was more than just colleagues getting along with each other; it was equally important as a strategic resource in the educational market. Mr Lema, one of the leading personnel at the high school, stated how meaningful such interactions were for the teachers to work at St Joseph's: 'We are building their morale through events like these. We are making a community so that they feel motivated to work here.' Sister Leonora explained that a sense of belonging to the workplace was essential in a highly competitive labour market: 'Paying teachers is not enough. Because when they shift and leave the students after one year, we have to find another new teacher who has to come here and get familiar with the students.'

Ambiguous Belonging in Settings of Inequality

In the context of middle-class formation in many African settings, the sense of belonging to a privileged group of people is interwoven with the dynamics of differentiation *beyond* (Bourdieu 1996 [1984]: 363–4; Pauli 2018) as well as *within* (Lentz 2015: 26) a given social field. Among the teachers at St Joseph's, this 'middle-class boundary work' (ibid.) within the space of the schools included perceptions of inequality, which they articulated with regard to the elevated socio-economic backgrounds of students and parents.

Teachers at both the primary and the high school came from rural areas outside Dar es Salaam and their parents earned their income in lower-level public sector and service jobs, as small-scale traders and farmers, and, in the mother's case, as housewives. The St Joseph's students came from middle- and upper middle-class backgrounds; lived with their families in Dar es Salaam's wealthy areas, often in expensive flats or houses; and were brought to school by the school bus or were dropped off in fancy cars. Their teachers witnessed how the costly school fees translated into the formation of young people as future privileged citizens who were taken on excursions abroad or to Arusha, Dodoma, and Tanga in order to visit important political and historical sites. In this context, the teachers experienced the class disparity as 'a loss of respect' (cf. Hartmann 2008: 69) and found it 'hard' to discipline the students.

Ms Mshauri (30 years old) said: 'If they made a mistake [and you] punish [them, they] become harsh. Some students even say: "My mother is paying you, so ..."' Mr Robert (34) lamented the fact that, due to their elevated socio-economic backgrounds, most primary school students lost contact with 'the world'. He also complained about the condescending attitude of some of their parents:

> We work for [the students]. They don't know anything about the world. They are dropped here by their parents, they are picked up in the evening. [Some parents] assume that because they pay the school fees, they [can] treat the teachers as houseboys. Whenever you meet outside the school campus, they ignore you.

In the high school, the teachers' perception of their lower social status was even more pronounced. Mr Kaduri said that it was 'challenging' for him to teach students from wealthy families because they 'looked down' on him. He connected this not only to the higher social status of the students but also to the generally poor reputation of the teaching profession in Tanzania. When I asked him how he felt personally about the role of Christian schools in the increasingly stratified society, he picked up on the critique from within the church that Catholic schools had lost their purpose of training students for the 'common good' (Connell 2016: 25; see also Chapter 1):

> MR KADURI Kids from wealthy [backgrounds] believe that money can manipulate teachers. Sometimes they look down at you, maybe you wear jeans. And he or she wears a watch of [TZH] 50,000, so [they think that] in fact I am taught by a very poor teacher. [For the rich people,] teaching as a career is meant for [people] who are less intelligent and very poor. So we are [creating a] classed society.
> HD It seems like the church is playing a role in this process, too.
> MR KADURI As a Christian I don't see it as a good thing. I wish that I could teach [in rural areas], because people from the villages have no good teachers. But unfortunately I cannot, because I need the money.

Other teachers also found it challenging to teach students from wealthy families, but for different reasons. Mr Malemi (27 years old) thought that wealthy students enrolled in top-performing schools only 'because of their money' and that they were not as 'intelligent' as 'ordinary' children. Similarly, Mr Usman compared the high school students at St Joseph's with pupils he had taught previously at Benjamin Mkapa, a well-known government school in Dar es Salaam. These students, he claimed, were 'more serious' about their studies because they wanted to advance socially:

> Most students at Benjamin Mkapa were from poor families. They were very eager to learn and to apply the knowledge that can help them and their families get out

of poverty. But students from the wealthy families [think]: 'Even if I fail, my dad or my mum would do something about that.'

Cultural Distinctions of Class and Social Responsibility

Notions of class distinction were deeply inscribed in everyday life at St Joseph's schools, including among the students themselves. In both the primary and the high school, interactions and conversations among students were shaped by 'processes of identification' (Scharrer et al. 2018: 24) as an emerging middle and upper middle class, which became manifest in particular interests and an increasingly international orientation. Students were highly curious about social and political issues, and often related them to their own positions, in an interconnected world. How could they study abroad, the high school students wondered? And were scholarships available for Tanzanian students? The primary school pupils were particularly fascinated by the Berlin Wall, international pop culture, and Germany's biggest soccer stadiums and clubs.

In both schools, self-perceptions of the emerging (upper) middle class in Dar es Salaam were also tied to the students' family backgrounds, which were partly internationally oriented, and to their lifestyles at home. Several students had relatives working or studying abroad, with some having completed an MA or PhD in the USA, Europe, or Asia. In the primary school, fathers had been employed with a company in Malaysia or had studied engineering in Poland. Students talked about the 'British' versus the 'Tanzanian' curriculum and discussed a forthcoming school trip to the United Kingdom that was co-sponsored by the British Council and a Tanzanian private company. The primary school pupils' preferred leisure activities were reading novels, swimming, watching movies, singing in a choir, and playing games. The high school students shared these interests, but added 'listening to music' and 'chatting with friends'.

Finally, the students' educational and professional ambitions reflected a particular (upper) middle-class habitus. All 43 Form V high school students (except one) stated that they expected to attend university, and the majority intended to work in law, business, accounting, diplomacy, or in other fields in the private economy. Similarly, in the primary school, most Grade 7 pupils aimed to attend university or college. Their desired future work was also mainly in finance and accounting, business, law, or engineering – although some wanted to become doctors or pilots.

While the St Joseph's students were highly aware of their privileged status, the way in which they related their elevated social positions to other young people or groups in Tanzanian society differed across the two schools. Among the primary school pupils, conversations about social differentiation – and one's own privilege – were especially pronounced. Ernest (aged 13) lived with his father (a ministry employee) and his mother (who was 'just at home') in one of the affluent wards of Dar es Salaam's Kinondoni district; both his sisters also attended Catholic schools. I asked him whether the high school fees that his parents paid added to his own ambition to perform well:

ERNEST It puts pressure on me. Because from Grade 1 to 6, it's a lot of money. My father paid for me so that I [can attend] a better school and my future will be better. Because now in Tanzania if you don't do well, you end up selling maybe tomatoes or eggs. [It is good if] you have a better job and a car.

HD Do you think you have to work hard? Your parents have money and a job – you could say, 'I can [depend on] my parents, they will help me anyway.'

ERNEST Yeah, this [is what some] kids [think]. But let's say that everyone is mortal; so you cannot say that your parents [will] live [forever]. So, you say, 'Ahh, I want to be [like] my father, I want to be the head lawyer, yes.'

At the high school there was less critical reflection among the students about being part of a privileged group, probably because the school had started to operate only recently and the students were still getting to know each other better. However, the staff of the school reflected critically on the growing discrepancy between the ideals of the Catholic church and the actual societal implications of their everyday work.[8] Thus, the headmistress, Sister Leonora, said that, while it was important to create a distinct school environment with particular services in a highly competitive educational market, she was also highly aware of the social effects of such competition:

You know, I am a Christian, but sometimes I think that the church divides society. I studied at the university and the students who had gone to the Christian schools looked down on the others. But we can't stop doing this just because there are some things wrong.

With regard to its position in the stratified educational market, the high school administration saw the school in an ambivalent position. On the one hand, the headmistress was confronted with a continued lack of resources even with the very high school fees, which were not sufficient to cover the teachers' salaries, student meals, transportation, accommodation, and various extracurricular activities. On the other hand, the school administrators felt a strong responsibility towards less privileged families and offered a limited number of free places at the school for

---

[8] For similar dynamics of critical self-reflection with regard to their own privilege, and corresponding social responsibilities, among members of the Pentecostal churches in South Africa, see James (2019).

well-performing students from poor backgrounds. While the cardinal of the archdiocese supported the initiative through church funds, the school administration kept the names of the sponsored students secret. 'Only the top management knows,' the headmistress stated. 'All [these students] came from government schools, but performed very well. We called their parents and told them: "Go and buy uniforms and books if you can." But we don't tell this to the others because if the others know that they are helped they look down on them.'[9]

Sister Leonora's statement reveals that middle-class formation at St Joseph's went hand in hand with the emergence of a 'critical citizenship' (James 2019: 40ff.) that aimed to improve other people's lives beyond their families and congregation (Lentz 2015: 35). In particular, the responsibility that the administration and teachers – as well as the students – felt in relation to their privileged position was addressed in the wider institutional discourse on the ethical value of charity that has come to shape the attitudes and behaviours of the Christian middle and upper classes in Dar es Salaam. In the following, I present a case study of a charitable trip that the primary school pupils undertook to a local orphanage in March 2010, thereby claiming responsibility for taking care of the 'happiness' of 'poor' children in the city. The case study shows how the children of the school embodied and performed the moral self-perceptions and values of a growing middle and upper class in urban Tanzania. The students not only enjoyed socio-economic privileges but also cultivated a Christian ethos of being charitable, which began to be enacted in the daily routines and practices of their educational environments.

'We Love You so, so Much, Our Orphans'

During the days preceding the Easter holidays in March 2010, the pupils of St Joseph's primary school were preparing for their annual trip to the local orphanage, during which they aimed to bring 'gifts' (*zawadi*) to 'children in need'. Some of the children brought clothes, food, and used school books from their homes, all of which were stored in large plastic bags in the school library. The headmistress was pleased with the children's commitment and remarked: '[These pupils] are good in giving. We are going to the poor.' She invited me to accompany the pupils and

---

[9] While scholarships for individual students were kept secret in the school, some students and teachers *did* know about them. One primary school pupil informed me about two 'orphans' in her class who were 'sponsored by the sisters'. She said that the 'whole class made an effort to make them feel welcome in our school'.

teachers on this trip, which was announced in classes as a 'charity day' or as having the purpose of 'serving the nation'.

On the morning of the charity trip, the boys and girls of Grades 3 and 4 loaded the bags of gifts into the school-owned buses, and, one hour later, we were on our way to the Kurasini National Children's Home, the children singing and highly excited. We were received by one of the (Muslim) orphanage's leaders, who expressed his hope for a lasting 'friendship' (*urafiki*) between the St Joseph's pupils and the Kurasini children. As we were given a tour of the orphanage, the excursion turned from a pure 'friendship' or charity event into a learning experience for the St Joseph's pupils and teachers about the socio-material reality of urban life among Dar es Salaam's less privileged population. We visited one of the girls' dormitories, where about 40 beds were placed, as well as the boys' bedrooms, with four to six beds each. While the teachers were interested in the big charcoal oven on which large pots of beans were boiling, the children were fascinated by one of the cows grazing next to the kitchen building – and jumped back with a horrified 'Eww!' when the cow began to defecate. Finally, they ran onto the playground, where they were observed, from a distance, by some of 'the orphans' and the orphanage staff. To the disappointment of the school's headmistress, however, it turned out that only the preschool children of the Kurasini home were present on that day, as the older children – who would have been more compatible in age with the St Joseph's pupils – were at their respective primary and secondary schools.

At the end of our visit, we gathered in the assembly room where the preschool children expected us, sitting in rows on small wooden chairs and dressed in neat red clothes. The St Joseph's pupils were lined up, facing 'the orphans' directly, and started to sing songs in Kiswahili and English. One of the songs praised their school, parents, and teachers – and the orphans themselves – in several verses, and culminated in the line, 'We love you so, so much, our orphans.' While 'the orphans' were too young to understand the English songs, and probably would have found the line of the subsequent prayer ('God bless mum and dad') challenging, they clapped eagerly after each performance and responded with the song '*Karibuni wageni*' ('Welcome, our guests') as a sign of appreciation.

The subsequent distribution of gifts, as administered by the Kurasini staff, was observed critically by the headmistress, who expressed slight disappointment about the event later on (Figure 6.2). In a personal conversation with me, she said that the children of the orphanage had not been prepared as well for the visit as they had been for the preceding year's event. In fact, the St Joseph's students themselves did not seem very interested in the actual distribution of gifts and ran quickly back to

Figure 6.2 The distribution of gifts to 'the orphans' during the St Joseph's school's charity trip.

the playground as soon as given permission to do so. However, back in the bus on their way to their school they appeared extremely cheerful and looked forward to sharing their experiences with their fellow students, who received them eagerly with the question 'Were they [the children at Kurasini] happy?'

Becoming Compassionate

In the days after the trip to Kurasini, the pupils of St Joseph's were still deeply impressed by the event and shared their experiences eagerly with me. It became clear that the excursion to the orphanage had been for them a core moment of embodying the specific 'affective orientations' of their religious environment (Dilger et al. 2020: 17). Thus, similar to the way in which people in Botswana have cultivated 'an unselfish "Christian love" to motivate proper care for needy children' in the context of HIV and AIDS (Dahl 2009: 24), the pupils referred to their school's ethical values, such as compassion and helping others. They presented themselves as members of a privileged social group who not only had the ability to define who was deserving of such support but also had the means to help others in living a decent life. In such moments, the young students became aware that they were not dependent 'objects' of charity in a globalising world (Bornstein 2001). Rather, the trip to the orphanage, and the way in which the children reflected on it, became part of their socialisation as members of a predominantly Christian upper middle class that was formulating an increasingly charitable – and pitying – perspective towards the more disadvantaged groups of its own society.

Most children I talked to were first of all very 'sad' and even wanted to 'cry' about the life situations of the orphans. Veronica (aged 10) said: 'It's really sad, because those children there, they are usually sad. Their parents are gone. Sometimes I feel like crying about it.' Similarly, Jane (13) said that she 'felt sorry' about the orphans, 'how they live. It isn't pleasant there.' When I asked the students to compare the lives of the 'orphans' with their own homes and families, they were highly conscious of their own privilege with regard to food, care, and education. Carolyn (13) said: 'You know when you just think about their parents. And then think about us. I can tell my dad I need a bicycle or… But there is no one to tell their problems. Or someone to share with your sorrows.' When I asked Jane why she thought that 'the orphans' did not live with their parents, she was convinced that the Kurasini children had experienced mistreatment:[10]

JANE   Some parents, they don't like [them]. Some parents just throw them in the toilets. That's really happening.
HD   How do they feel when you come there? Give them presents and gifts?
JANE   They are very happy that people help them, they know that they need help.

The students' compassion and pity for the orphans were connected to an urge to 'help'. Some pupils emphasised that the children at Kurasini were in need of support and they wanted to 'tell them that they are not alone'. The pupils were aware that they had only a limited ability to change the orphans' life situations. Still, they felt that it was their responsibility to help them even with the little means at their disposal. Ernest (13 years old) said that, according to the Bible, 'You are supposed to feel sorry for your friend.'

Ernest's statements highlight that the pupils of St Joseph's were strongly committed to the way in which the leaders of their school framed the excursion to the orphanage as an act of 'charity' and 'compassion', hoping that their students and teachers would become engaged in ethical

---

[10] While some of the children at the orphanage did not have any relatives, others had been abandoned by their parents.

practices surrounding the value of friendship and helping those with less social and economic capital. At the same time, however, the anecdote above highlights that the excursion itself brought to the fore other moral priorities, which were not always congruent with the school's official agenda. The teachers' curiosity about the way 'the needy' actually lived seemed to diverge from the idea that they were driven primarily by 'compassion for the poor'. The pupils, on the other hand, enjoyed opportunities for playing and socialising with each other on the orphanage's playground as much as the actual encounters with the young 'beneficiaries' or the distribution of gifts. Thus, the case study highlights that the heuristic distinction between the way in which ethical values are made explicit in institutionalised (discursive) school frameworks and the implicit everyday moral practices of students and teachers is often challenged when it comes to 'real-life' situations and interactions at the schools (cf. Woods 2013: 9; Mattingly 2014: 19; see also Chapter 1).

Intermediate Conclusion

The first part of this chapter has described how the two St Joseph's schools – which have been established as 'top schools' in Dar es Salaam's stratified educational market – have shaped notions of privilege among their students and teachers. The pupils and staff have become implicated in the formation of a growing urban (and mostly Christian) middle class that is cultivating a distinct sense of social belonging, which includes specific moral and affective orientations, interests, and ambitions (see Lentz 2015; James 2019). However, this group of 'chosen others' (Simpson 1998) is not homogeneous; it is also characterised by internal differentiation. Thus, while both schools have become involved in faith-driven practices of charity that are oriented towards the poorer parts of Dar es Salaam's urban population, the structural context of the two schools has also fostered notions of inferiority among the teachers in relation to the students and their families, who often show off their elevated social status at the schools.

In the following sections, I show how the explicit ethical values of the Catholic school – which were articulated in the mission statements of the two institutions and included, among others, notions of order and discipline, national belonging, and bodily conduct – were cultivated and performed within the space of the schools. I demonstrate how this occurred especially through specific disciplinary techniques as well as in the context of the classroom, which provided an opportunity for the articulation of, and mutual reflection on, these values by students and teachers. I also show that the ethical frameworks of the schools were embodied by students and teachers through their performances of faith-specific prayers and rituals, which simultaneously exposed diverging ways of enacting the value of 'community' in the multi-religious settings of the schools.

Disciplining Students 'For God and the Nation'

Simpson (1998: 81ff.) has shown in his research on a mission school in Zambia that the students' activities there were regulated through a fine-grained system of establishing order and discipline. This was not only shaped by the ethical framework of the Catholic school in the postcolonial context but also focused specifically on the body as the central site of proper self-care and conduct. Similarly, at St Joseph's, the teaching of values was deeply incorporated into the academic life of both schools and simultaneously connected to an explicitly Christian ethos of order and bodily discipline.

Mr Joseph, from the primary school, stated that the pupils at church-based schools 'behaved well' because they knew that 'God is always watching us'. Mr Malemi, who taught at the high school, claimed that the St Joseph's students were 'taught by good teachers' who gave them 'guidance' and 'discipline'. The moral disciplining of students and the goal of a strong academic performance were tied intimately to the schools' ethos of training pupils as members – and future leaders – of society and the nation, and for 'serving God'. The high school's slogan was 'For God and our nation', and its mission statement said that the school aimed to provide an environment that was 'conducive to excellent learning, civil maturity, accountability, moral integrity, personal responsibility, and human dignity'.

A central moment of moral disciplining at the St Joseph's schools was the morning assembly (cf. Simpson 2003: 109ff.), where the core values of bodily appearance and academic performance, as well as the school's commitment to the nation and a Christian way of life, were internalised by the teachers and students. Throughout the assemblies, moral values were evoked in the interactions between staff members and pupils, as well as through the active involvement of pupils in the formulation of these values and in appealing to their fellow students to 'behave well'. Assemblies were often strongly emotional experiences in that they included instances of public shaming (cf. Fung and Chen 2001: 423ff.) along with the singing of the national hymn and Christian songs. Furthermore, moral disciplining was inscribed into the school's spatial arrangements (cf. Simpson 2003: 82), as students and teachers gathered in areas close to the school's administrative offices from where all official orders and disciplinary measures were issued.

At the primary school, morning assemblies were held in front of the headmistress's office, facing the pole flying the Tanzanian flag and an elevated platform from where the teachers gave instructions and selected pupils performed songs, readings, and prayers for the student body (Figure 6.3). The assemblies usually started with the checking of the pupils' uniforms and bodies, thereby reminding the students of the rule that 'cleanliness is next to Godliness'. Non-compliant pupils were singled out and made to stand apart from the group; some were asked to report to the administration later, where they were caned with one blow on the buttocks or the hand. Others were blessed by the headmistress, who stood next to the flagpole, shaking their hands and placing her hand on their heads. After the screening, students sang the national hymn and Christian songs ('I have decided to give my life to Jesus', 'Are you happy to praise the Lord?'), thus pledging their loyalty and commitment to the Tanzanian nation state and the Christian way of life.

After joint prayers (including the Lord's Prayer) as well as public announcements on school matters and pupils' performances, a reading from the Bible was usually delivered by one of the students and followed up with a statement from the head boy or the head girl. The head students' statements revealed how the teachers' – and God's – 'panoptic gaze' (Simpson 2003: 190) was internalised by some of the children through practices of (self-)disciplining. For example, one morning, head boy Ernest (aged 13) commented on the preceding Bible reading, whose message he summarised as: 'A man who works hard gets what he wants.' He reminded his fellow pupils to work 'very hard' for their upcoming exams and concluded:

The Bible tells us that God sees us everywhere and that he knows everything that we are doing. When I was young, I thought that God cannot see me when I enter the house [the teachers and other pupils laughed quietly]. But later I learned that he can see me. So please let us do good things so that God can bless us.

At the high school, morning assembly took place in an open hall next to the administrative offices. These assemblies also started with a check of the students' cleanliness; select pupils marched through the rows of students, who showed them their hands with their fingernails facing upwards and their white handkerchiefs on top. The teachers intervened only occasionally when they felt that a student's appearance or uniform required admonition. After the national anthem,[11] the dean reminded

---

[11] In the high school rituals, there were no prayers or songs yet, as the school had been established only recently. One teacher explained that the administrators had invited the students to submit proposals for a school song and prayer as the teachers wanted to involve the students in building the school: 'The student whose song is chosen will become part of the school history.'

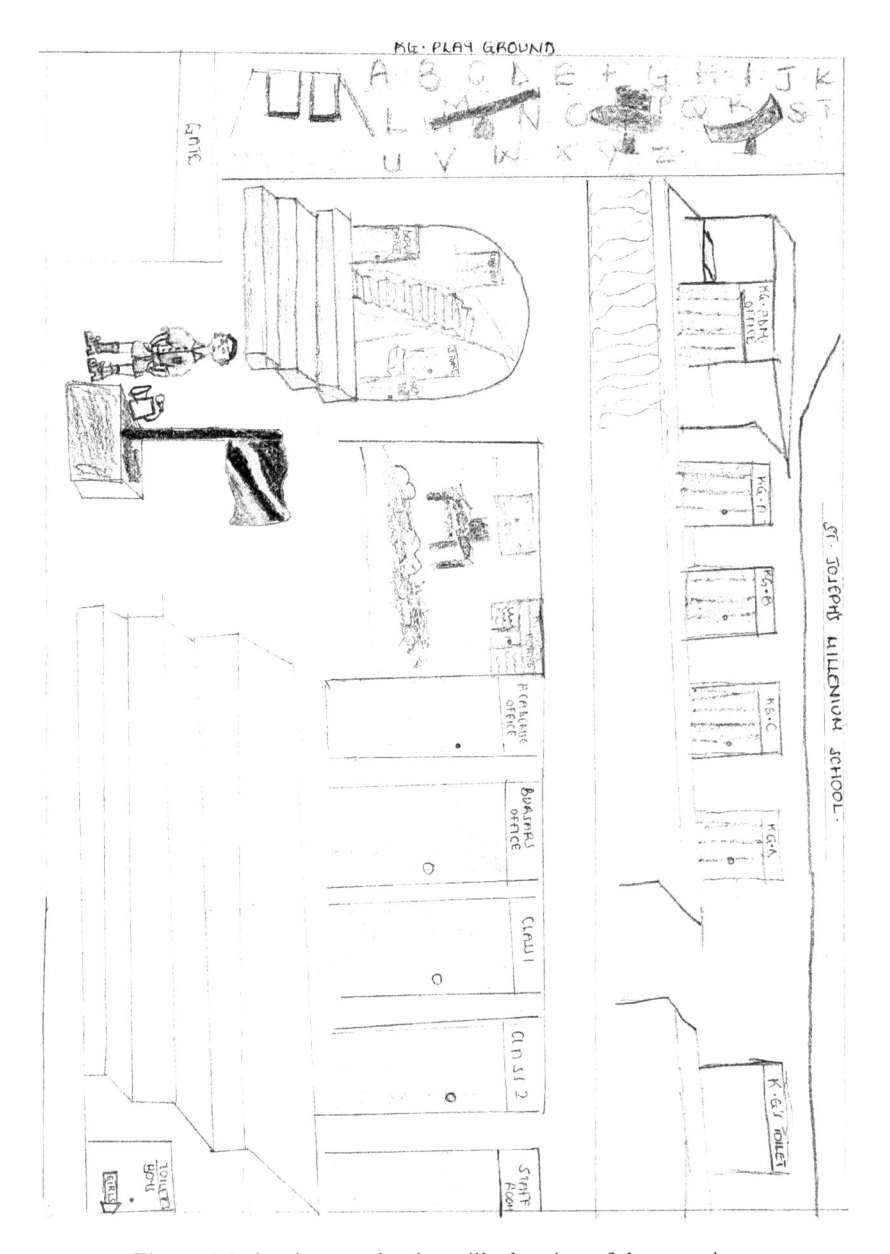

Disciplining Students 'For God and the Nation'   199

Figure 6.3 A primary school pupil's drawing of the morning assembly grounds.

pupils of key regulations: the prohibition on mobile phone use, the rule to speak English at all times, the school fees policy, and the obligation to attend school activities irrespective of other commitments.[12] During my research, some pupils did not attend the school's mandatory Saturday classes because they belonged to the Seventh-Day Adventists. The dean reprimanded them: 'You and your parents knew how the school regulations were. So if you think that it is a sin to come to the classes on Saturday, please find an alternative [school]. Render to Caesar what is Caesar's and to the Sabath what is the Sabath's.'

Another topic often addressed at the high school assemblies was school uniforms. Boys had to wear dark blue trousers with black shoes, along with a white polo shirt bearing the school logo on the front and 'St Joseph Millennium High School' on the back. The female students wore a long white skirt together with a white blouse with the school logo on the front; this was complemented by a long collar that draped across the back. The students were rebuked – and in some cases corrected or sent home – when their neck ties were tied incorrectly, their shoes were the wrong colour, or their skirts were too short. On one occasion, three students gave short speeches to their fellow pupils about appropriate behaviour at school; the two female students were commended by the dean but the male student was criticised for his 'bad performance' and scolded for his improper dress, with the dean adjusting his tie and collar in front of the others.

Maintaining Distance, Punishing Transgression, and Students' Self-Governance

As in the mission school of Simpson's study in Zambia (2003), the demeanour of St Joseph's teachers towards the pupils oscillated between an attitude that was highly affectionate and caring and one that was explicitly disciplining and distancing. At both schools, some teachers engaged in intensive individual conversations with students, asking them about the challenges they faced or urging them to perform better in the future. One high school teacher who liked debating and making jokes with the students was quite sad when they returned to their families at the end of the term and said: 'I will miss my students – I have got used to exchanging ideas with them.' The dean, who lived in the boys' dormitory, stated: 'We feel deserted – although it is a relief [that they are gone].'

---

[12] Corresponding with their students' different ages, there were slight variations in the rules and regulations of the two schools. In particular, the high school's regulations were more detailed with regard to the use of mobile phones, and students could be expelled for 'marrying and getting married' as well as 'all kinds of sexual harassment'. In all other areas, the two schools used almost identical language in their regulations.

At the same time, the teachers also maintained a distance from the pupils in order to establish respect. Especially at the high school, the teachers valued a spatial separation between the students and the staff, not least because of the widespread feeling that social hierarchies were somewhat inverted. At lunch, for instance, the high school teachers ate in their own room. One teacher said: 'Here in Africa it is good to maintain respect between teachers and students, so we separate them.' Another teacher told me:

> If we allow them to eat together with us, the discipline is going to fall down. And also, as you know, according to our profession, we believe that there should be a social gap between a teacher and a student. If there isn't a social gap between a teacher and a student, the concept of respect – eh, actually it won't be there.

While the teachers and administrators at St Joseph's had precise ideas about their students' proper conduct, they also maintained a fine-tuned system of punishing transgressions of school regulations. Apart from reprimanding students at the morning assemblies, there were meetings with parents to discuss the performance of individual pupils, and, in some cases, students were sent home. Furthermore, students were subjected to other disciplinary measures within the school, where the pupils' bodies again became the main site for establishing control and enforcing discipline (see Simpson 2003: 116).

At the high school, in several instances students had to kneel down on the floor next to the student dean's office; once, a group of about 20 students had to kneel on the assembly grounds. The dean claimed that this kind of punishment was less 'psychologically affecting' than caning, which was rarely applied in the high school. At the primary school, where I had seen only a few pupils kneeling as punishment, the headmistress explained that this practice was preferred at the high school due to the age and social backgrounds of the students. Sister Lucia said: 'You can't cane them because some are even similar in age to the teachers. Some come from rich families. If you tell them something, they can ignore you. Some of them look at you as if you are a cartoon.' The high school students themselves experienced the kneeling punishment as an emotionally disturbing and shameful experience, however; some felt that they had personally offended their teachers and needed their 'forgiveness'. Richard (18 years old) talked about the punishment in a conversation:

RICHARD [Kneeling down is] bad: [you are] kneeling, others are standing, it's like a shame. It's like being pointed at – you, that you are wrong.
HD This morning, I saw someone crying.
RICHARD Yeah, of course, it's really embarrassing. I don't know – it's not inhumane, but it's a punishment. It makes a person feel very bad: 'Why does it have to be me?' Or: 'Why is the teacher not forgiving us?'

The 'everyday student regimentation' (Simpson 2003) at St Joseph's schools was also ensured by the prominent role of the student government, whose representatives monitored interactions within the schools and reported 'troublemakers' (ibid.: 98). At the primary school, representatives on the student government were elected annually in a secret ballot, and positions included a prefect girl and prefect boy for each grade; these were responsible for taking their class to the dining hall and selecting pupils to read prayers and Bible lessons at the morning assemblies. The class monitors, on the other hand, reported Kiswahili speakers to the teachers, noted student absences in attendance books, and watched for discipline and tidiness in the classroom in general. Finally, the head boy and head girl met with the prefects regularly and discussed general problems (such as the widespread speaking of Kiswahili) with them.[13]

Within the 'order of things' (Simpson 2003: 118ff.) at the schools, the strong reliance on the student government representatives for maintaining discipline established quasi-autonomous spaces of moral self-disciplining among the students – especially when the teachers were absent.[14] At the primary school, when the class had one hour of 'free' time after the end of the day, the students usually completed their homework or other assignments before getting picked up by their parents or the school bus. In one such situation, the male prefect admonished the pupils not to make 'noise' and to watch each other's behaviours, while the female prefect emphasised her peer's commands with the dramatic waving of her ruler. In another instance, a prefect asked his fellow students about global warming and encouraged them 'to cheer up'. At the end of the session, he said to the class: 'Let's stand up and pray!' As if they were in a Charismatic service, the students raised their hands and joined the prefect in prayer, beginning with 'In the name of the father, the son and the holy spirit' and then reciting the Lord's Prayer.

These anecdotes show how the representatives of the student government interacted with, and were respected by, their peers in specific classroom

---

[13] The high school had an even more elaborate student government than the primary school, which involved the additional positions of secretary to the head boy, head girl, and class prefects, as well as two gender prefects, two social prefects, two academic prefects, and one dormitory prefect. The student dean told me how important it was to involve pupils in managing their everyday life at school: 'We have a big student government because we want to give them responsibility. They should learn to represent themselves – not to be spoken for by others.'

[14] A certain autonomy among the St Joseph's students was also visible when they walked through the room during exercises or admonished each other when a student became uninvolved ('Wake up, Denis!').

situations. At the same time, their particular responsibilities were also defined by the school administration itself through swearing-in rituals that officially recognised these positions. In 2010, the prefects, monitors, and head boys and head girls of the primary school were sworn in during a ceremony that was part of a larger farewell party for the students before the holidays. The elected students swore not only to 'cooperate well with the teachers' but also to aim for the realisation of the school motto, mission, and vision, vowing: 'For the betterment of the school and the nation at large, God the Almighty help us!' The academic mistress reminded all students to cooperate closely with the student government: 'The prefects are the eyes of the teachers. If you disobey them, you disobey the teachers. This is a big crime.' In a concluding speech, she established an explicit connection to the patron of the school and appealed to the students:

St Joseph was a man of God. Do you follow his example? Are you praying at home? As head boy or head girl you must set an example. Can you report noise-makers when you have the loudest voice in class?

Learning Values in the Classroom

The teaching approaches at the primary school were partly a continuation of the morning assemblies and other instances of moral disciplining in that they relied on 'ritualized practices' (Wulf 2012: 40) that rendered the core values and hierarchies of the school explicit. In the classroom of the primary school, colourful posters on bulletin boards reminded the students of the school's learning mottos: 'Hard work and prayer = success', 'This is your home, take care of it', and 'We lead, others follow', for example. Teachers were greeted by the pupils at the beginning of the lessons with their name and one of the school mottos, resulting in combinations such as: 'Good morning, Sister Lucia. Our school motto is virtuous and faithful!'

The teachers' interactive teaching approaches bore a striking resemblance to the teaching styles of the St Mary's and Kipata primary schools. Thus, in multiple classroom situations, teachers asked pupils to step forward and write answers to their questions on the blackboard; those who did well were rewarded with applause, while others were corrected when they did not face the class properly or spoke too softly. Through the constant emphasis on the importance of a good academic performance – and a didactic approach that relied on a mixture of motivation, admonishment, and reward – the classrooms at the primary school radiated an atmosphere of constant pressure.[15] This was enhanced by many small

---

[15] These dynamics were also extended to the classes as a whole, for instance when Grade 6 performed particularly well during one term and was rewarded with a trip to Dodoma,

quizzes and a strong fixation on grades, which resulted not only in the teachers constantly marking tests but also in much excitement and tumultuous expressions of joy and disappointment by the pupils when grades were announced in class and individual students either lauded or reprimanded for their performance.

However, the St Joseph's primary school also employed a rather playful approach in its teaching that was quite different from the other primary schools of my study. Thus, some teachers used playful exercises such as 'rapping' in a foreign language or singing short (Christian) songs ('I will make you fishers of men if you follow me!') in order to prevent students from getting tired. Furthermore, the teachers also relied on group-oriented teaching that fostered interactions among the pupils themselves. At the primary school, each grade was subdivided into four to six groups that carried the names of minerals, animals, or game parks in Tanzania. In Grade 7, for instance, the groups were labelled Serengeti, Ngorongoro, Mikumi, and Manyara. During the lessons, these groups were asked to work on certain exercises from the textbooks – sometimes in competition. In all these instances, the teachers intervened only when the pupils strayed too far from the topic. When I asked Mr Joseph about the group work approach for teaching, he explained:

They started this in recent years; before it was just lecture, lecture. But now the government of Tanzania[16] has found that the children – they have something in their minds and [you start] from there. That's why we use [group teaching].

Finally, the performance of the primary school pupils was enhanced using a range of group activities in which they interacted and competed with other schools in the city, such as mock exams. Particularly important in this regard was the network of Catholic schools that all performed well in the National Examination Council of Tanzania (NECTA) rankings; this network met to discuss shared challenges and to exchange learning materials in preparation for the national exams. The students also engaged in drama activities that were conducted both in the school and in competition with other schools in the city. Again, such activities were venues for the sharing and articulation of values through the students, who – with the support of one teacher – mostly wrote the songs and plays themselves. Most performances dealt with socio-political issues or undesirable

where they visited a session of parliament. The comparatively high costs of the trip had to be covered by the parents.

[16] I was not able to confirm whether this shift in didactics had indeed been initiated by the government. My research in the other schools, as well as reports about teaching approaches in government institutions, gave the impression that state schools still relied strongly on lecture-style teaching.

behaviours and conveyed a specific moral message. In one instance, I accompanied the Grade 7 pupils to the Living Arts Tanzania festival in Dar es Salaam, where they performed a song about albino murders in Tanzania (cf. Brocco 2016). At the farewell party before the holidays, they performed a play about 'arrogant pupils' who chased their teachers away, thinking that they did not need them. The other students clapped and sang along enthusiastically and laughed about the characters, who finally regretted their wrongdoings and reconciled with their teachers.

'Do Angels Exist?': A High School Class Event

The didactic approaches at the high school were somewhat different from the teaching philosophy in the primary school. Especially in large classes, which sometimes had more than 50 students, several teachers employed lecture-style teaching without any opportunity for the students to ask questions. But there were also highly interactive lessons in which the students were confronted with deep philosophical questions by their teachers and negotiated their subject positions in relation to broader 'existential concerns' (Lambek 2010: 6) through processes of mutual reflection, consideration, and questioning.

The latter was the case in the General Science class, which included in its curriculum 'philosophy and religion', 'contemporary and cross-cutting issues', 'democratic processes and practices', and 'life skills'. In one lesson, Mr Kaduri introduced the core ideas of 'philosophical thinking about idealism and materialism' with a lecture. According to him, 'materialism' was a mode of thought that emphasised the importance of proving all phenomena that were relevant for human life 'scientifically'. 'Idealism', on the other hand, would allow for diverging explanations of human existence, including those based on religion. He illustrated the difference between these two modes of thinking by giving the example of death and the afterlife, suggesting that idealist approaches gave moral guidance to humans as they articulated ideas about 'good' and 'bad' ways of living. Materialism, on the other hand, stood for scientific ideas such as evolution theory.

As the view of secular science was positioned in explicit opposition to the Christian cosmology of human creation, interest in the topic grew among the 52 students. The student next to me asked, rather unconvinced: 'Are there really people who seriously support materialism?' Another student, Heri, was also alarmed and initiated a lengthy discussion in which the students split into a 'science' faction that debated with a 'Bible' faction. A female student named Clara challenged Heri, and the other students contributed comments or laughed supportively when one of the debate leaders made a strong point:

HERI According to the Bible, God created man using soil. It is not an idea. Don't ask me, ask Moses. What if everything Newton says is a lie? Newton is not alive.
CLARA There are some calculations that can prove [his theory].
HERI But it is the same as with Moses, because Newton was shown a revelation from God.
CLARA But they judge it as an idea because it is not scientifically proven. Can you go to the laboratory and prove that [the creation of man through God] happened? How can you prove that God is there? [At this point, some students who had supported Clara's ideas so far expressed indignation.]

As the debate became increasingly heated, the teacher steered it in a different direction, though still challenging the students to think deeply about some of the assumptions they had taken for granted. In an effort to illustrate the difference between materialist and idealist approaches further, he used the example of angels:

TEACHER Do you believe in angels?
STUDENTS (COLLECTIVELY) Yes.
TEACHER What colours do angels have?
STUDENTS (SEVERAL) White!
TEACHER Have you seen them? Have you touched them? [The students were unsure.] Who has seen an angel? [Two students lifted their hands.] What colour does the *shetani* [Satan] have?
STUDENTS (COLLECTIVELY) *Nyeusi*! [Black!] [The discussion switched to Kiswahili.]
TEACHER Why are the angels white and Satan black? [The students laughed.]

At this point, most of the students agreed that ideas about the colour of angels and the *shetani* originated from the European/colonial perception of the African continent. One female student abruptly turned to me: 'Why is it that everything people in Europe think about Africa is bad or evil? I heard that there is a lot of discrimination against Africans in Russia and Germany.' I was taken aback by this unexpected turn in the debate as the students had not paid much attention to my presence so far. I tried to adopt a moderate stance in my answer. While there were multiple instances of racism and discrimination against people perceived as 'foreign' in Germany, I said, many migrants also lived well in the country. I was not sure whether my answer had convinced the students, but one of the Muslim students concluded: '*Shetani ni mwekundu*' (Satan is red). The teacher and students laughed.

Religious Selves at the School and 'in Love'

References to religion and faith played an important role in the moral becoming of teachers and students in both schools, and the Christian – and often specifically the Catholic – faith was central to the learning of values at St Joseph's. Material references to the Christian faith were most visible with regard to St Joseph's cathedral next to the campus and in the bookshop selling Catholic literature at the entrance to the schools. They were also present in the sisters' dresses and the students' uniforms, with the latter wearing the St Joseph's logo on their shirts and blouses or having necklaces and bracelets with small crosses and iconic pictures of Catholic saints as pendants. One teacher occasionally wore a shirt with the vertical letters 'PUSH' on the front, which were spelled out horizontally as '**P**ray **U**ntil **S**omething **H**appens'.[17] Finally, the administrative offices were decorated with Christian paraphernalia combined with references to school life in both national and international settings. For example, the primary school's headmistress had a large photograph of the former Tanzanian president Jakaya Kikwete above her desk, alongside portraits of Cardinal Pengo, the school's owner, and Auxiliary Bishop Methodius Kilaini. The wall was decorated further with pictures from a school trip to the UK, while the opposite wall featured a portrait of former Pope Benedict and a cabinet with statues of the Virgin Mary and St Joseph.

References to the Christian faith were also part and parcel of the – explicit and implicit – everyday teaching and learning practices in the two schools. As well as being required to attend church services, the pupils at the primary school prayed collectively in class before lunch. Furthermore, some younger students engaged playfully with the topic of religion: for example, two of the boys in Grade 7 wore a band of paper underneath their collars to make them stiffer, thereby evoking comments from their peers that they looked like and aspired to become priests. In one instance, a female student ran through the classroom with a Bible and 'blessed' other students by laying her hand on their heads. Finally, reflections on and practices of faith were also institutionalised in the formal curricula of the two schools through the subject of 'Religion' (*dini*); 'Divinity Studies' was taught only in the high school.

In the primary school, Religion was taught by the St Joseph's sisters. The class comprised collective prayers, crossing oneself at the beginning and end of each lesson, and focused on the teaching of the core values and practices of the Christian faith, with strong references to the Catholic church. The lessons that I attended were conducted in Kiswahili[18] and were always highly interactive, with the sisters encouraging the students

---

[17] The teacher said that he had bought the shirt at a Pentecostal 'mission event' and that 'it had changed [his] life'.

[18] 'Religion' was the only lesson where Kiswahili was used (except for the Kiswahili lesson itself).

to share what they already knew from their homes or Bible classes. In one lesson, the topic was 'the calling of the church' and the pupils were eager to give examples of 'priest' and 'a life of orders' (*maisha ya masharti*), as lived, for instance, by the sisters. In another lesson, the sister focused on the seven sacraments of the Catholic church and explained the different ways of 'marrying' in Tanzania – through a priest, the government, or a customary rite with the family. She did not pursue one student's comment that one could also marry in the mosque, but emphasised that the sacraments were directly 'under Jesus Christ' and that most of them – including marriage, baptism, confirmation, and priesthood – could be given only once in life.

During my research at the high school, I was able to attend only one of the lessons for the Catholic students; when I asked about classes for the Muslim students, it was not clear whether a teacher was available at all or where exactly the class took place.[19] On this particular day, the students organised the lesson themselves; the dean, Mr Vincenzo, joined the group later but then assumed a central position in the discussion. At the beginning, the leaders of the group presented the topic of the lesson: 'Is it good to have a love relationship as a teenager?' The group split up into two factions that were to represent two sides of the argument: 'Catholic church' and 'the world' (or 'modern society'). After some initial hesitation, the students adopted their positions quickly, and as they debated it became increasingly unclear whether their arguments were just part of their assigned role or their personal opinions. That the proposed topic had the potential to produce a highly controversial debate – and necessitated a 'moral choice' on the part of the students (Mattingly 2012: 162–3) – became clear immediately after the two factions poignantly articulated their opening statements about 'love among teenagers':

CHURCH It is not allowed [to engage in a relationship]. It has been written that even if you just look at a boy or girl, it is a sin.
WORLD Love is not a sin, it is what you feel.

The group leader intervened in the debate and asked the participants to define what they actually meant by 'love'. One male student referred to the Bible and said that '*mapendo*' was the feeling of caring for somebody. He linked the love for God and the love for one's fellow human beings, but distinguished *mapendo* from the act of 'making love'. Similarly, another student claimed that one needed to distinguish between

---

[19] The unclear positioning of Religion classes for Muslim students in the high school was due to the fact that the school had started only recently and had not yet found a permanent teacher for the Islamic section.

'*mapendo*' and '*mapenzi*', where the latter was the 'legitimate' kind of love between a married couple. According to him, the love that students had been talking about so far was '*tamaa*' (desire, lust) – a feeling driven primarily by the body. While he implied that *tamaa* could be 'controlled' by the mind and/or faith, a third male student interjected to say that physical feelings were not something one could 'fight' (*kupinga*):

STUDENT 2   There is the love [*upendo*] of loving one another as relatives, and then there is the love of loving someone as your wife. But you here are not lovers [*mapenzi*]. You as youths [*vijana*] have *tamaa* to satisfy the body, that's all [*basi*].
ALL   Let us praise Jesus Christ. For eternity. Amen.
STUDENT 3   There are some things you cannot fight. That means that if you are thirsty you have to get water.

As the debate became repetitive – and the 'World' arguments garnered growing support among the students – the dean intervened with a long lecture on 'What is love?' (*Upendo ni nini?*). In it, he focused on the notion of 'real love' as an 'attraction' (*mvuto*) from the 'heart' (*moyo*) and a result of 'God's grace' (*neema ya Mungu*). He encouraged the students to pray hard so that God would show them 'the right choice', and not to listen to their own desires, which were often caused by material or physical attractions (in the case of girls and boys respectively). If marriage, as the essence of love, occurred on the basis of physical attraction, he assured them, it usually lasted only briefly:

MR VINCENZO   It is God himself who shows you that 'This is your right choice.' You will know it due to the way you are taught the rules [*kanuni*] [of the Catholic faith]. You will know that 'I love this girl' or 'I love this boy' due to the voice [*sauti*] that speaks from your heart ... There are people who enforce it [*wanalazimisha*], but I know that they won't have peace. If they do it by force, to be with a husband who has a car, or with a girl whose physique [*umbo*] is ... At the end of the day such marriages usually don't last long – after one week there is chaos [*mparaganyiko*]. Any questions [*swali*]?
ALL   Love [*Mapendo*]. Forever [*Daima*].

The students, who had listened attentively up to this point, expressed uncertainty about how to meet the high expectations articulated by Mr Vincenzo. How would they know whether they had made the right choice or how to differentiate between their own 'fake' feelings and feelings originating from God's grace? They were also very concerned about the appropriate age at which they were supposed to find true love and marry, and they were surprised when Mr Vincenzo told them to wait until they were 25 years old. Some students next to me chuckled quietly and blinked at each other as the debate came to an end:

STUDENT 1 What time in life is appropriate [*muafaka*] for marriage?
MR VINCENZO At least the time of marriage is 25 years. Especially for us who study: you will study [first], pray, and then God will show you.
STUDENT 2 What if I get the sign from God now?
MR VINCENZO You can't serve two masters at a time. First school, then marrying.
SEVERAL STUDENTS Eh!?

After the Religion class, I talked to Florence, the Catholic students' group leader, about the discussion. She was not very happy with the debate, not only because most students had not contributed but also because many of them had been deeply troubled afterwards about the prospect of having to wait until they were 25 years old before getting married or having a relationship:

FLORENCE I wasn't really satisfied because … most students were a bit shy to defend their side. Because they thought [the others might] think that they have those relationships [themselves]. I think it's hard because at the end the teacher came and gave us the final word. Most of them were also surprised because they never knew that 25 would be the age of having a relationship.
HD Is this realistic, 25?
FLORENCE No, it's not realistic! And that's why students were a bit shocked. Some were like, 'It might happen [that way] – but, let's say for 1 per cent of the youth.'

Patriarchal Views of Gender (Relations) in Divinity Studies

Christianity has long been central in shaping people's understandings and expressions of love, relationships, and sexual intimacy in African contexts (Bochow and van Dijk 2012; Spronk 2012: 113–14) and faith-oriented schools have incorporated teaching about these issues into their moral education lessons (Bochow 2020). However, while the explicit ethical frameworks of the St Joseph's schools – and lessons in the 'standard rules' (*kanuni*) of the Catholic faith – were highly relevant for the high school students' orientation in relation to love and gender relations, their everyday moral becoming was equally shaped by their active negotiations of their teachers' and schools' expectations.

At St Joseph's, relations between men and women were a central topic in the Divinity Studies class that took place on the same day as the 'love' debate. Divinity Studies in Form V was taught by the student dean, too. He held an elaborate view of the way in which this subject was different from Religion and how to involve students actively in learning about the importance of the Bible for their everyday lives. According to Mr Vincenzo, Religion focused on the ethics of individual religions and denominations, whereas Divinity Studies was based on the teachings of the Bible and the Catholic church. Thus, while students of all Christian denominations attended Divinity Studies, it conveyed primarily Catholic teachings; these included, for instance, the differentiation between 'venial' (minor) and 'mortal' (grave) sins and their consequences. According to Mr Vincenzo, humans lived in a state of 'condemnation' whereby all the problems they faced, such as diseases or disasters, were a result of the 'expulsion of the first human beings out of the garden of Eden'. Against this background, students should obey the church's commandments so that they could 'live a happy life' and transition into an 'eternal life in which we all believe' after death. In all these teachings, the school followed a syllabus that was prepared, Mr Vincenzo told me, by 'pastors who are under the panel in the Ministry of Education'.

Mr Vincenzo prayed at the beginning and end of each of his lessons in order to 'involve the Lord and the power of the Holy Spirit' in the discussions. He also involved the students in critically reflecting on the Bible excerpts they read and made sure that all of them had understood the relevance of the values they learned. In this regard, he framed Divinity Studies within a wider approach of educating the students at St Joseph's as 'responsible citizens' beyond the 'restrictions' taught by individual religions:

> We teach them how to live as faithful and good Christians, who are useful to the church and the entire nation. We also teach them how to live as good Christians without segregating that 'this is a Catholic [thing], this is a Protestant [thing]'.

In one of his lessons, Mr Vincenzo engaged the students in an interpretation of the Bible reading on Samson and Delila. After outlining the plot of the story, which had been assigned to the students for homework, he used it as a starting point for reflecting on the characters of men and women generally. He elaborated on notions of masculinity that, he said, implied an endless desire for women: 'Some men are never satisfied. If they love one, they want another because they think she is different.' This desire, he continued, was the weakness of all men who were 'heroes on the outside' but 'under [the] control of their wife inside [at home]'. However, he concluded, while this weakness destroyed Samson, he was forgiven by God after realising that he had failed.

The bulk of Mr Vincenzo's ethical teachings that day, however, focused on Delila and the way in which her actions reflected on the character of women. Following on from the theme of 'true love' from the morning's debate, he explained that 'the harlot' Delila was bought with money by the Philistines in order to destroy Samson. When Delila saw that Samson refused to tell her the secret of his strength, she began to cry: 'How can you say "I love you" when your heart is not with me?' Mr Vincenzo lectured the class: 'You see? This is how they speak to us when we are [at home]. As it was also that serpent that approached Eve.' Throughout the lesson, Mr Vincenzo focused on the perspectives of the male students, for instance when assuming that they knew what he meant when he said 'how they speak *to us* when *we* are [at home]'.[20] He also addressed the male pupils when he discussed the characters of 'harlots': 'There are women who turn their bodies into economic enterprises. Don't we have this here in Dar es Salaam?' 'Yes,' shouted several male students, 'in Kinondoni, Makaburini, Manzese, and Sinza.'[21] 'Who is to blame here?' asked the teacher. As I was unable to understand individual answers in the ensuing tumult, I asked my neighbour what he thought: 'Of course, the women. Men are always weak to women, so [the women] can influence us.'

What struck me most during the class discussion, however, was how Mr Vincenzo and the students expressed strongly patriarchal perceptions of men and women – and their exclusively heterosexual relationships (see Van Klinken 2019: 29) – that were so obviously different from the everyday interactions between female and male students at the high school. Samson and Delila's story was one of betrayal and manipulation and portrayed the characters of women and men in a negative light, but the relations between the young men and women at St Joseph's were typified by closeness, mutual understanding, and affection. More than at any of the other schools in my study, relations between male and female students at St Joseph's seemed to be shaped by trust and physical proximity, including the placing of hands on a peer's shoulders or holding the hands of a student of the opposite sex during a conversation in the same way as they did when talking to peers of their own sex. When I asked Florence about it, she agreed that this level of intimacy between boys and girls was unusual, and also prohibited to some extent:

I was also a bit surprised because I'm coming from a girls' school. And whenever one of the nuns sees you there with a boy holding you like that, it will be chaos. But here I've seen girls and boys, some of them are best friends. From primary [school], they met here, so they interact a lot. And the way teachers take this I think they're okay with this. Not 100 per cent maybe … Because two days after we came to this school, the teachers observed this kind of relationship and they tried to say that this is not allowed around here.

---

[20] Emphasis added.
[21] These areas of Dar es Salaam were particularly known among the students for the presence of women and girls who were said to dress and behave immorally.

Against the prescriptions of their teachers and the school administration, the students had established a specific mode of interacting with each other in the space of the high school that adhered to their own values of friendship and expressed mutual affection between the sexes. As I observed repeatedly, the teachers were generally tolerant of the physical closeness between male and female students and rarely intervened when they saw pupils of different sexes standing or sitting together in familiar ways. This widely established consensus was only occasionally interrupted, for instance in one of the Divinity Studies classes, when Mr Vincenzo addressed a male student and a female student whose hands were lying one on top of the other as 'Samson and Delila'. When I asked him about this later, he said: 'I was joking and just needed them to realise something in order to make the topic understood. This is definitely not allowed here.'

'We Live Here As One': Praying across Faiths

Beyond Religion and Divinity Studies lessons, the students' moral orientations – and their sense of belonging (or not) within a Catholic school – were also shaped through the collective attendance of church services, including the Sunday services for boarding students. Both schools admitted students from different religious backgrounds, and the primary school emphasised that 'the school has made arrangements for every pupil to practise his/her religion'. At the same time, however, the primary school urged parents to follow up on their children's 'religious instructions' and the high school stated that 'students that find it difficult to cope with the regulations of the St Joseph's Cathedral High School must weigh carefully their decision to join or not to join' the school.

Students and teachers also attended church services on important holy days. On each of the four Fridays preceding Easter Sunday 2010, they prayed the Way of the Cross (*njia ya msalaba*) in the neighbouring cathedral.[22] On our way to the church, several pupils made the sign of the cross on themselves at the small chapel next to the side entrance to the cathedral, and again with the holy water contained in a basin in the main hall. The mass, which was organised exclusively for the students and teachers of St Joseph's, started with the entrance of the priest, accompanied by three altar boys and eight students from the schools. This group passed each of the 14 icons with a cross and two candles, while one student read from the Bible about the events that had

---

[22] This Catholic ritual reflects on the 14 stations of the passion and death of Jesus Christ.

happened at each station. These activities were accompanied by singing, kneeling, and reciting prayers at each of the stations. Many students and teachers held a little prayer book in their hands, the 'little school of prayer' (*chuo kidogo la sala*), as well as the booklet *Praying the Rosary with the Pope* (in Kiswahili).

Especially for the younger students, attending church services and participating in Catholic rituals were important parts of their moral becoming at school. Jane (aged 13) claimed that participating in the Way of the Cross made her 'remember to live like the sisters [at her school]' and that it was her obligation 'to help the poor'. Ernest (also 13) stated that 'the Cross' made him realise that it is important to 'love [both] one's friends and enemies'. While both Jane and Ernest were Catholic, students of other Christian denominations highlighted the positive impact of praying the Way of the Cross, too. Sophia (aged 11), whose family were Evangelical-Lutheran, said that the ritual helped her to 'relate to Jesus and all that he went through to save me', and that she 'should stop sinning'. Carolyn (13) claimed that the rituals in her Anglican church were similar (for instance, with regard to kneeling or the role of the Holy Trinity) and that the prayers helped her understand why she followed the Christian faith in her life:

CAROLYN For me I think that [praying the Way of the Cross] just brings back [the events]. You know, it makes you believe that it has really happened.
HD But why is this important today, in this society and for your future life?
CAROLYN Because it leads me to have a little time to talk with God. I go to pray, then I think: why do I do these rules? And when I don't do these rules, it's like I'm taking Jesus back to the cross. It makes me keep away from trouble.

Some teachers – especially those who were not members of the Catholic church – were more reserved about praying the Way of the Cross. Several teachers belonged to one of the Protestant churches in Dar es Salaam and claimed that they attended the Catholic mass largely because they had to 'follow the law of the school'. While they participated actively in the rituals, some said that they did not feel 'comfortable'. Mr Robert was a member of the Presbyterian church and considered praying the Way of the Cross a kind of performance rather than an expression of his inner state:

MR ROBERT It's a common sense. It's not coming from my heart.
HD Do you have to do it or could you choose not to go?
MR ROBERT You know, according to our school contract, we're supposed to.

While the non-Catholic teachers articulated some reservations about participating in some of the religious rituals at St Joseph's, their involvement was not necessarily a bodily or emotionally awkward experience for them (as it was for me, who had grown up in a modestly Protestant environment). Even Muslim pupils and teachers claimed that it was largely 'normal' for them. Veronica (aged 10) was a Muslim herself and said that her father was initially opposed to his daughter attending a Christian school. However, she had been at St Joseph's primary school since Grade 2 and had got used to 'playing' along in the church services while learning about her own faith at home:

HD   Is this not a challenge for you, to pray [the Way of the Cross]?
VERONICA   It's not a challenge. I am used to pray[ing like this]. But my father, when I was small, he didn't want me to go to Christian schools; he was concerned that I was forced by the sisters. He said that they are not the same religion.

Veronica's statement shows that religious values and affective states at St Joseph's are partly internalised in ways that can be activated for an 'appropriate' and/or respectful performance in the Catholic setting (Dilger 2017: 515), while the pupils still maintain a cognitive, partially critical distance from them. This rather pragmatic attitude of Muslim pupils to practising different kinds of faith – and the necessity of adjusting to different religious environments in a multi-religious city – was confirmed by other students and teachers from both Muslim and non-Muslim backgrounds. Florence stated that Muslim students at St Joseph's were free to practise their own faith:

It's not that they are forced to [pray the Way of the Cross]. If they feel like going, they can. For example, at [another Catholic school I attended previously], we did have Muslims and they also went to church like us. But they ... told me: 'We go there, we sing the Lord's Prayer, but deep inside we pray our religion.'

Iqbal (aged 18) said that he felt 'free' to practise his faith and to conduct his prayers in the space of the dormitory. For him, it was important to discuss faith-related challenges in a non-Muslim environment with his Muslim peers. He stressed that the Christian students and staff tolerated, and partially supported, him in the practice of his faith:

IQBAL   I normally pray in the morning before I go to school, as a Muslim but not as a Christian. Then I go to school and [when] I go back to the dorm, I pray again.
HD   Can you pray at school, for instance in a small room or something?
IQBAL   In the [dorm] room, I [ask:] 'Can you give me a break? I want to pray for some time.' And they respect what I do. So they get out and go, and I pray.[23]

---

[23] In the end, however, it remained unclear to what degree Muslim students were indeed free to practise and express their belonging to Islam in the space of the high school. In the dormitory, a student's *kofia* was confiscated when he wore it for dinner; the dean claimed that 'this wasn't tolerated' at school.

HD And if you are in the mass and follow these things, the way they preach, kneeling down, how do you feel? Is it difficult for you to do it?
IQBAL It's not difficult; it is normal. But my only wish is that I pray myself in my room, I feel different. On Fridays I like to go and meet my fellow Muslims.

The Muslim teachers at St Joseph's adopted an equally pragmatic stance towards participating in Catholic rituals and often ensured that they attended the mosque for prayer during lunch break and on Fridays. Mr Usman said that he had several Christian family members and was used to attending Christian events and that this was not uncommon in the socially and religiously highly diverse environments of Dar es Salaam.

MR USMAN I've told you that even though this is a Christian school [there are] people with different religious backgrounds and we live as a community. So, the race and any kind of 'You are Muslim, I'm Christian', we don't have that.
HD It's not something you talk about [among the teachers]?
MR USMAN It's not something we talk about, because we live here as one.

Conclusion

In Dar es Salaam's educational market, Catholic schools represented a specific kind of educational institution due to the long history of missionary schooling in Tanzania that was established during German and especially British colonial rule. While all private schools were nationalised in 1969, the former mission churches generally maintained good relations with the postcolonial state, which resulted in the swift re-establishment of their privileged position in the early 1990s. Since then, Catholic schools have benefited greatly from transnational reform programmes and privatisation processes and have regained their position among Tanzania's 'top schools' (see Chapter 2). They have also re-established faith-oriented spaces for the moral becoming – and the social reproduction – of the Christian, and especially Catholic, middle and upper classes in Dar es Salaam.

The first part of this chapter showed that there was a strong awareness of, and focus on, the social status of students and teachers in the two educational settings, who adopted a faith-oriented 'moral habitus' (Winchester 2008: 1755) of highly privileged citizens in Dar es Salaam's increasingly stratified cityscape. This translated not only into a growing awareness of less privileged parts of the urban population, who were categorised as 'needy' and were turned into objects of 'charity'. The unequal distribution of privilege also became evident within the schools themselves, where teachers sometimes felt inferior to students and their families, some of whom treated teachers as 'dependants' due to the high school fees they paid (see Hartmann 2008: 69).

The second part of the chapter focused on the way in which the two St Joseph's schools deployed disciplinary rituals and learning approaches in order to teach ethical values to their students. These techniques were similar in some ways to how values were taught and embodied at the St Mary's schools through highly interactive teaching styles in and beyond the classrooms. The St Joseph's teaching approach also shared with the St Mary's schools a strong commitment to nation building and the formation of 'good citizens', an aspect that was strikingly absent at both Muslim seminaries that I studied. Furthermore, and in contrast to all the other schools in my study, the St Joseph's schools involved students actively in the learning of moral behaviours by emphasising the role of student governments, which shared responsibility for identifying and punishing transgressions.

Finally, the St Joseph's schools explicitly foregrounded certain aspects of moral becoming in relation to the institutions' denominational framework. Their reference to the Catholic faith was a key part of the explicit material and ethical practices of the two schools – for instance, in relation to the strong presence of religious objects within the schools and the mandatory attendance of church services, but also in regard to other denominations and religions that were supposed to merge into 'one community' within the schools. At the same time, however, this foregrounding of the teachings of the Catholic church also created divergent practices of moral becoming, through which both students and teachers navigated the conflicting moral priorities of their everyday lives. This could be seen not only in debates on love, sexuality, and gender relations, as students struggled to reconcile their desires as young men and women with their ethical commitment to their faith and their teachers' highly patriarchal understandings of gender relations. It was also visible in the way in which many non-Catholic students and teachers complied pragmatically with the schools' faith-specific requirements through a 'respectful' performance of rituals and prayers, while simultaneously maintaining a critical distance and seeking other ways to practise their faith within and beyond the space of the schools.

7 Conclusion
Politics, Inequalities, and Power in Religiously Diverse Fields

In Dar es Salaam in the early twenty-first century, Christian and Muslim schools have become central in families' and students' quests for a good life, which are shaped by material, ethical, and moral aspirations (see Fischer 2014: 5). While education has figured prominently in individual and collective longings for 'different cultural possibilities' (Stambach 2000: 108) in Tanzania for many decades, educational achievements are now more important than ever for securing a decent job or career. Private Christian schools especially (Stambach 2010a), but also some Muslim educational institutions (Dohrn 2017: 54), perform well in annual school rankings and are also sought out by their lower and upper middle-class clients due to their consistent teaching in English (cf. Brock-Utne and Holmarsdottir 2004: 75ff.). At the same time, families and students – and teachers – also value faith-oriented schools – even if they were academically less successful – because of their explicit commitment to providing ethical guidance in the face of highly ambivalent social and urban environments, which, in their eyes, are fraught with moral, economic, and spiritual challenges.

What a 'good life' means and how it is enacted among students and teachers in Dar es Salaam's faith-oriented schools differ widely across and within educational settings. Teresa King, whom I introduced at the beginning of this book, said that attending a Christian school added 'meaning' to her life. She claimed that the Christian environment of her secondary school lifted her out of a state of 'mere existence' and provided her with faith in her everyday activities; so much so that she became 'saved' together with other students at her school. She also believed that her school's ethical frameworks moulded students into good citizens who would not take part in 'corrupt practices', which she associated with the graduates and staff of public schools. While not all students of my study were influenced by the faith orientation of their schools to the same extent as Teresa, they did appreciate the moral values they learned and embodied at their institutions. For these students – and their teachers – a 'good life' (*maisha mazuri*) was 'not a state to be obtained but an ongoing aspiration for something better that gives meaning to life's pursuits' (Fischer 2014: 2).

The moral people that students and teachers wanted to become – and became – in Dar es Salaam's Christian and Muslim schools were the outcomes of their biographies; their encounters with (fellow) students and teachers; and the various ethical frameworks, faith orientations, and disciplinary practices of their schools. Furthermore, their everyday pathways of moral becoming (Mattingly 2013: 306) were entwined with the political-economic forces that have shaped the 'social field' (Bourdieu 2006 [1996]) of faith-oriented schooling in urban Tanzania since the late nineteenth century.

As I showed in Chapters 2 and 3, the unequal positions of Christian and Muslim schools in Tanzania's educational market were a product of the country's colonial and postcolonial histories of education and interreligious relations (Cooksey et al. 1994: 229; Loimeier 2007: 139, 147; Mushi 2009: 84; Leurs et al. 2011: 14; Dilger 2013a) as well as more recent histories of socio-religious stratification in the wake of faith-based development, school privatisation, and transnational educational reforms (Stambach 2006: 4; 2010a; Dilger 2013a; see also Hearn 2002; Dilger 2009). They also reflected Dar es Salaam's highly diverse religious cityscape, where competition for resources, ideas, and people across the Christian and Muslim fields (Dilger 2014a) has resulted in tension and conflict, sometimes violent, since the early 1990s (Wijsen and Mfumbusa 2004; Ndaluka and Wijsen 2014). However, while such potential for conflict has led to various government interventions and regulations, students and teachers were agents of their own moral becoming (Fischer 2014: 2) and navigated *all* these structural forces confidently – and in often remarkably self-reflexive ways – within and beyond the schools they inhabited (Hirschfeld 2002).

In this concluding chapter, I compare the dynamics of moral becoming across Dar es Salaam's Christian and Muslim schools by highlighting how practices of learning values shaped and reshaped students' and teachers' relationships with the world in partly similar but often highly distinct ways (cf. Baumann and Sunier 2004: 21). I show that individual quests for a good life in these settings are entwined not only with particular institutional environments but also with the urban, national, and global economies and politics of education and socio-religious difference in an interconnected world. All these dynamics entail significant similarities with regard to moral self-positionings in Christian and Muslim schools, but they also reveal divergent understandings and practices of learning values in larger historical and socio-economic contexts. Based on these insights, I argue that a comparative perspective on faith-oriented schooling in urban East Africa calls for a new analytical approach to the study of religious diversity, one that systematically tackles dynamics of social inequality and stratification (Salzbrunn 2014: 74) and processes of power and politics more generally (Soares 2016: 679). As Altglas and Wood (2018) argue, there is a need to bring 'the social' back into the sociological (and anthropological) study of religion and religious diversity in order to understand how religious experiences, practices, and materialities are shaped and transformed in intersection with large-scale forces over time.

Ethical Classroom Cultures and Networks of Socio-Religious Belonging

The everyday learning of moral values in Dar es Salaam's Christian and Muslim schools was enacted through explicit ethical frameworks that established a normative context for distinguishing between right and wrong (Bochow et al. 2017: 451) and for providing a good – or even 'the best' – educational environment in contemporary Tanzania. These frameworks informed the official ethos for learning and working at these schools in relation to disciplinary and didactic styles, the content of curricula, interactions with other schools, the deployment of specific material goods such as school books, national and international imagery, religious paraphernalia, dressing styles, and faith practices in the space of the schools. Taken together, these various elements combined in distinct ethical institutional and 'classroom cultures' (Jackson 1968) through which Christian and Muslim educational settings distinguished themselves from government schools as well as from each other.

Explicit ethical frameworks were formulated in the mission statements of faith-oriented schools and their mother organisations, thereby linking the schools' agendas to those of churches, mosques, and religious NGOs (Chapters 5 and 6). They were also derived from national and transnational education policies, for example those that forbid the use of caning (but see the case of Al-Farouq in Chapter 5 and below) and establish grounds for competition between and across faith-oriented schools in the educational market. Finally, explicit ethical frameworks were sustained by local, national, and transnational networks of Christian and Muslim schools (Stambach 2010a; Dohrn 2014); these included the teaching and recruitment networks of the Islamic seminaries and the St Mary's schools, which extended to countries such as Zanzibar and Sudan and to Uganda, Kenya, and South Africa respectively. Furthermore, several faith-oriented schools depended on local or international religious bodies for funding – only sporadically at St Mary's and St Joseph's but more regularly at Al-Farouq[1] – and for administrative decisions (at Al-Farouq, Kipata, and St Joseph's). All of them were also integrated into local government and faith-oriented networks of schools for boosting their performance. Faith-oriented schools were tied to religious communities and their ideological frameworks, including the Catholic church and its organisations (St Joseph's), revivalist Islamic groups (Al-Farouq, Kipata), and neo-Pentecostal churches (St Mary's, though rather implicitly).

Through these various networks, faith-oriented schools established specific modes of moral and academic belonging, which comprised a sense of connection to a particular spectrum of faith(s) but also the notion of learning in and working at a distinct type of school that was regarded as superior to government (and partly other faith-oriented) schools and reflected its position in the educational market. Especially at the Christian schools, this attitude was informed by a neoliberal language of 'excellence' and 'success', which was rarely questioned by my interlocutors with regard to the impact of these expectations on their present and future lives. At St Joseph's, teachers claimed to work in 'top schools' and enacted their belonging to this exclusive environment by participating in social and family events, which were encouraged by school administrators as a motivational and economic resource. At St Mary's, the ethical values of 'working hard' and being 'morally honest' translated into the teachers' perception of being 'sought after' in the highly competitive labour market; they also developed a professional ethos of 'being busy' beyond regular work hours and, related to this, felt a great deal of pressure – this was also connected to the fact that they did not receive contracts. At the Al-Farouq and Kipata Islamic seminaries, the idea of being a distinct educational space in Dar es Salaam's landscape of schooling was also present, although the teachers and students at Al-Farouq in particular were very aware of their school's marginal status in this landscape and the disadvantages this might have for their future lives. At Al-Farouq, the management of the Africa Muslims Agency tried to compensate for such disadvantage through free educational and/or health services for their teachers, students, and their families.

In general, a strong awareness of a school's position in Dar es Salaam's educational market as a social and moral signifier (cf. Rowe 2017: 37) was enhanced by the available resources and the material circumstances under which these institutions operated and which encapsulated the role of education in processes of social stratification and elite formation

---

[1] Funding from Saudi Arabia stopped in 2009, however.

(Lentz 2015: 9ff.). At the Christian schools, and also at Kipata, the colourful and freshly renovated buildings, as well as the access to laboratories and other learning facilities (including computers at St Joseph's), enhanced the spirit of work and the sense of belonging to an 'exceptional educational class'. Such feelings were reinforced through a material emphasis on being connected to an international community of students, for instance through photographs of school trips to Europe hanging in the administrative offices at the St Joseph's primary school, or the life stories of successful graduates published in the St Mary's International Primary School magazine. The sense of belonging to a school with a distinct ethical and social spirit was shared across all schools in my study, Christian and Muslim, including at Al-Farouq, where the lack of material resources and the bleakness of its buildings were striking and were usually associated with disadvantage in the educational market. At the same time, teachers and students at all the schools had a desire to move to a 'better' educational institution when the possibility arose, apparently valuing a school's performance and material resources more than its specific ethical (or religious) agenda.

Belonging to a distinct kind of school was also forged through the enactment of explicit ethical values in highly ritualised 'classroom events' (Wortham 2006) that deployed specific didactic and disciplinary styles (Grant 1997; Fung and Smith 2010: 265–6) and moulded the moral becoming of students and teachers in particular ways. In all six schools, disciplinary rituals included morning assemblies where the students' uniforms and bodily cleanliness were screened and misbehaving students punished through different modes of public shaming (see Simpson 2003: 109ff.; Dilger 2017: 520–1). At the four Christian schools, ritualised modes of moral becoming included invocation of the Tanzanian state and the value of training 'good' citizens, something that was completely absent in the two Islamic seminaries. The Christian schools also placed a strong emphasis on involving students actively in the learning, formulation, and implementation of ethical values, for instance through public singing and praying and – in the case of St Joseph's – the writing of the school anthem. The Christian – and especially the Catholic – schools had strong student governments that monitored and enforced good behaviours among their peers, becoming 'the eyes' of the teachers and administrators (Simpson 2003: 98ff.). The student governments of the Muslim schools (if they existed) were barely visible during my research.

Interactive modes of disciplining and ethical self-formation were also articulated in the teaching philosophies of the six schools. The teachers at the Christian and Muslim schools had precise ideas about the value of engaging students in the learning process. For instance, at St Joseph's

Cathedral High School, teachers emphasised the importance of establishing 'caring' and 'affectionate' relations with their pupils – not dissimilar to those at the St Mary's schools and at Al-Farouq, where the sense of being a 'family' or 'community' was expressed through the use of kinship terms. However, while the St Joseph's teachers justified the use of this terminology, especially with regard to the long-term relationships that many students had with each other and with the school, the reference to a common 'community' reflected critically on the joint implication of pupils and staff in the production and reproduction of a Christian, specifically Catholic, middle and upper class (Grace 2003: 48). A critical view of the 'school community' was also advanced by the teachers at St Joseph's, who stressed distance and hierarchy in their relationships with the students, not only due to their older ages but also because of the students' elevated socio-economic backgrounds, which sometimes created tension.

At the Al-Farouq Islamic seminary and the Kenton High School, the necessity of engaging with students in a caring manner was also evoked among some of the teachers, but rather due to concerns about the bleak lives their pupils were reportedly living. Thus, while interactive learning models had travelled to Tanzania's Christian and Muslim schools with processes of globalisation and privatisation, their implementation varied depending on the age and gender of students, as well as the structural realities of the schools and their clients. Furthermore, all didactic approaches to educating students morally – discipline/punishment and interactive modes of (self-)care – were always embedded in hierarchies, power relations, and ideological frameworks within and beyond the schools (Grant 1997; Fay 2019).

Embodying Multiple Moral–Affective Orientations and the Value of Joking

Ethical values were learned and taught at the schools of my study through the communicative 'co-presence' (Pels 2013 [1999]: 25ff.) of teachers and students in specific material and ideological environments. Students were seen not as mere objects of disciplinary measures but as active subjects of moral becoming (Fung and Smith 2010: 267ff.) who were involved in the care of themselves (Foucault 1994) as well as in processes of inward- and outward-looking socio-moral differentiation. This co-presence involved both the minds and bodies of students and teachers and connected them in 'mimetic processes' that were foundational to the embodiment of values (Wulf 2008: 64). As Csordas (2008: 119) puts it:

To describe intersubjectivity as intercorporeality ... helps us avoid the temptation to think of intersubjectivity as an abstract relation between two abstract mental entities ... [B]ecause bodies are already situated in relation to one another ... we do not have to begin ... from the Cartesian position of the isolated cogito and later arrive at the possibility and necessity of others.

In all these processes, there was often a striking continuity between the values that were taught interactively to the students and the way students embodied and felt about these values. There was rarely open dissent or challenge of the schools' explicit ethical frameworks, not in classroom situations or formal interviews nor in the everyday interactions and conversations between students and teachers, or with me as a researcher. At the same time, the students and teachers were not 'docile' bodies without agency (Mahmood 2001: 210) when they complied with the expectations of their schools, or when some of them agreed with harsh punishments, like caning at Al-Farouq (Chapter 5). As Mahmood (2001: 212) writes, 'agentival capacity is entailed not only in those acts that result in (progressive) change but also those that aim at continuity, stasis, and stability'. Similarly, in the context of (middle-)class formation in urban Africa, people may engage in the creation, enactment, and reproduction of 'boundaries of social differentiation' (Pauli 2018: 251) – without necessarily critically reflecting on their own involvement in the production of social stratification.

That said, there were instances in which discrepancies emerged between the explicit ethical frameworks of schools, on the one hand, and their implicit moral–affective embodiment by students and staff on the other.[2] This was the case, for example, during prayers in interreligious settings at St Joseph's (Chapter 6), when teachers complained about their stressful working environments at St Mary's International Primary School (Chapter 4), when they were dissatisfied with their salaries at Al-Farouq (Chapter 5), and when students enjoyed playing on the playground more than giving gifts during the St Joseph's primary school's charity trip (Chapter 6). Equally, the St Mary's schools – which were open to students from all religious and denominational backgrounds – created anxiety about the disturbing effects of the neoliberal market but also a certain level of confidence about a possible remedy for them, through the healing of 'possessed' female students (most of whom had a Muslim family background). In such moments, the embodiment of a school's ethical framework was exposed as a partial (Turner 2015: 59) and discontinuous (Lambek 2015: 309) process in which multiple moralities and affective states coalesced. Such situations were not

---

[2] See Chapter 1 for more on the distinction between explicit and implicit ethics and how it collapses in everyday becomings of a 'good life' in the schools I studied.

experienced necessarily as conflictive by those involved, and people's compliance with a school's (explicit or implicit) ethical framework – the participation in Catholic rituals at St Joseph's or the exposure to healing prayers at St Mary's – did not imply the rejection of a different set of values or one's faith. Rather, such a pragmatic stance towards different moralities – and the desire for 'continuity' (Mahmood 2001: 12) and respect this attitude expressed in religiously diverse institutional settings – became an embodied virtue in itself.

Open disagreement with the ethical frameworks of the schools of my study was thus restricted to a very small number of topics that were particularly challenging for those involved. This concerned the – partly public – disputes about the working conditions at St Mary's (Chapter 4) and especially the practice of caning at Al-Farouq, which was officially forbidden (or at least strongly restricted) in Tanzania but still continued as a semi-official practice at the seminary. While caning was largely condoned by the school administrators, most students and teachers I talked to felt that it was 'humiliating' and 'vilifying' (Chapter 5). Potential conflicts also revolved around the topics of gender and sexual relations, especially at the secondary and high schools, some of which taught strongly patriarchal notions of proper male and female conduct and (heterosexual) gender relations.

In general, students complied with their schools' expectations for their behaviours as young men and women; they did not openly question either the dresses and uniforms they had to wear or their schools' mixed or gender-segregated environments. At the same time, many of the older students at St Joseph's – and, to a certain extent, at Al-Farouq – doubted the ethical value of postponing sexual and loving relations until marriage and found this expectation to defer their feelings unrealistic. Some students admitted to having 'illicit' sexual relations, but it was only at St Joseph's that they entered into an open discussion on the topic. And even there students were cautious about stating their opinions openly as they were concerned about being judged as immoral by their peers and teachers. In this context, they negotiated gender relations tacitly, although in direct opposition to the teachings of their school, by expressing friendship between boys and girls through everyday physical proximity.

One way of dealing with potentially conflicted moralities (see Schielke 2009) was joking. Humour played an important role at the schools as it allowed students and teachers to express a stance on, or merely raise, issues that could not be addressed otherwise, thus exemplifying the 'different forms, functions and effects of humour' (Swinkels and de Koning 2016: 8) for solving and performing moral ambiguities. At the

St Joseph's primary school, for instance, the Catholic faith was highly present in everyday routines and pupils could rarely express divergent beliefs or faiths; some did so by imitating 'Charismatics' during classroom breaks, accompanied by the laughter of their peers (Chapter 6). At Al-Farouq, there was no open discussion about the ethical value of postponing love and sexual relations until marriage. However, when I walked to a football game with a group of young men, they noted a young woman wearing a revealing dress and one of them mumbled '*mtihani*' (trial); the group laughed about the moral challenge – of reconciling their faith's restrictions with their personal (and also culturally mediated) desire – they knew they shared (Chapter 5).

Humour at Al-Farouq was also important for dealing with the moral uncertainty that my research created. This included the students' questions about the purpose of my study and who would have access to my research materials. It was difficult for them to address these doubts in the hierarchical setting of the school – even more so because they respected me as a guest. When some of them did express their doubts, and after I had answered, laughter and a joking reference to my presumed familiarity with a local staple food resolved a potentially embarrassing situation (Chapter 1). Similarly, the teacher and students at St Joseph's high school resolved an awkward class situation through laughter after involving me in a discussion on the colour of angels, which quickly became connected to questions of (post)colonial and racist othering (Chapter 6).

Social Ambiguities and Postcolonial Resentments

Students' and teachers' quests for a good life in Dar es Salaam's Christian and Muslim schools were linked inseparably to Tanzania's entangled histories of education, religious difference, and social inequalities (Chapters 2 and 3). Christian schools in particular have a privileged position in the country's educational market today. This is due not only to the strong support of Christian mission schools during British colonial rule and its continued impact on faith-based development; Christian schools have also benefited greatly from transnational reform programmes and the politics of privatisation, which have been driven strongly by the World Bank and other international organisations since the mid-1990s (Stambach 2006; 2010a; Dilger 2013a). As Mundy et al. (2016: 6) have argued, these international governing bodies have played 'a rising role during the past half century as purveyors of policy solutions to national educational (as well as economic) problems, and in so doing have created a common framework for global educational policy discourse or what Nóvoa (2002) calls "global policyspeak".'

Muslim schools, in contrast, played a less prominent role during the colonial period and were nationalised – along with their Christian counterparts – in 1969. But even the new generation of Muslim schools was marginalised in the context of market liberalisation from the mid-1990s onwards, and especially in the wake of 9/11 and the bomb attacks in Dar es Salaam in 1998. This macro-political context has become central in a long-standing Islamic revivalist discourse on the continued marginalisation of Muslims in contemporary Tanzania (Heilman and Kaiser 2002: 700ff.; Loimeier 2007; Ahmed 2009: 426; Becker 2018) and has also shaped the position of the Islamic seminaries – which were all attached to the *Ansaar Sunna* movement – in the educational market. At the same time, however, my focus on often highly individualised practices of moral becoming in Christian and Muslim schools reveals a more nuanced view of the distribution of power and privilege within and across the religious field.

At St Joseph's high school, the headmistress was highly critical of the fact that her school had become a place only for upper middle-class families who were able to afford the constantly rising school fees, thereby undermining the ethical goal of the Christian Social Services Commission and the Catholic church to fight poverty in Tanzania through development interventions. In fact, the teachers at her school felt quite overwhelmed, and sometimes threatened (see Hartmann 2008: 69), by their students' wealth, which materialised in expensive watches, fancy cars, and luxury apartments. The students were mostly comfortable with their privileged position and aspired to match their parents' professional achievements in the future. It was only in rare moments that they reflected on the exclusionary dynamics of the postcolonial world in relation to their *own* position (for instance, in the discussion on the colour of angels referred to above). In addition, the primary school pupils engaged eagerly in a middle-class ethos of 'helping the poor' and expressed compassion and pity towards Dar es Salaam's 'needy' population, without reflecting on the paternalistic implications of this discourse. This focus on charity – which had become incorporated into the schools' ethical framework as much as their claim of belonging to Tanzania's 'top schools' – seemed paradoxical given that both schools kept the (charitable) sponsorship of underprivileged students a secret due to concerns about these students' stigmatisation. It was also opposed to the Catholic church's self-perception of 'having passed the period of charity' and being a main player in promoting 'human development' and 'social justice' in Tanzania (Chapter 6).

At Al-Farouq, the sense of being marginal was shared by teachers and students. This became obvious in the omnipresent discourse on Tanzania's (post)colonial history, but also with regard to students' concerns about being stigmatised as 'terrorists' and being at risk of an 'early death' due to their dangerous living conditions. Their low social status was also manifest in their school's structural dependency on the AMA and the charitable investments of sponsors from Kuwait and the Arab world, as these were materialised in plaques and signs on campus and became evident in the delay of important administrative decisions. Finally, they compared themselves with their privileged Christian counterparts, who rode in private buses to school, while their bodies ached from the use of public transport. All this was very different at the Kipata Islamic seminary, which demonstrated how much 'middle class' has become a tangible 'aspirational category' (Pauli 2018: 249) among Muslims in Dar es Salaam, too. Not only was the seminary attended by the daughters of an upward-striving yet lower urban middle-class segment of Muslims, but the discourse on the marginalisation of Muslims in Tanzania was also largely absent, despite the fact that the school and the mosque that owned it were part of the same network of Islamic revivalist organisations as Al-Farouq. The girls at Kipata were also more hopeful with regard to their academic and professional lives, joining their teachers in a discourse on 'future possibilities' (Keane 2007: 22) that characterised their newly established school as a whole.

The sense of being privileged and of belonging to Dar es Salaam's aspiring English-speaking middle class was shared by the students and teachers at St Mary's International Primary School. However, while pupils there studied in a comparatively well-equipped school with its own international network and system of transportation, their social positions seemed more fragile than those of some of their peers, for instance those at St Joseph's. Thus, some of the St Mary's pupils were highly aware of the effects that changes in their parents' situation – due either to illness or to other social and economic vagaries of life – would mean for their own academic futures. Their Tanzanian teachers in turn faced the risk of being fired due to the lack of contracts at St Mary's and because they had to compete with Kenyan and Ugandan colleagues whose English was usually better and who could teach the much needed 'science' subjects. At Kenton High School, which had been established as a 'local' school for 'poor families' by its owner, the sense of – potential, but usually already very concrete – belonging to a lower social status was even more pronounced. While this difference between the two schools was not easily recognisable in their students' socio-economic profiles, it became palpable in the students' significantly lower expectations for their academic and professional futures.

Taken together, the processes of social differentiation in the schools of my study exposed the multiple – and often unstable – ways in which the highly diverse dynamics of class formation in educational settings (Collins 2009; Foley 2010) and the power relations within and across the religious field in urban Tanzania (Dilger 2013a) came together in practices of moral becoming. Thus, the hierarchies between 'Christian' and 'Muslim' schools – as they were presented in activist claims about the marginalisation of Muslims in education or in public perceptions of Christian 'top schools' – were experienced in often more nuanced ways in particular educational settings. But even within the same school, perceptions and experiences of privilege varied, thereby revealing not only discrepancies between the explicit ethical frameworks and the implicit moral discourses and practices of these schools but also tensions and moral ambiguities across and within status groups. Most striking was how teachers and students, some of whom were very young, reflected on large-scale political-economic forces and the effects of these on their own social positions. Through 'imaginative acts' (Weiss 2004: 194), they related their biographies and living conditions actively to abstract forces such as '(post)colonial history', 'globalisation', 'the market', or highly volatile 'class structures' (Spronk 2018: 316; see also Darbon 2019). By connecting these different layers of their experience, their moral selves came into being and they assumed a specific – sometimes resentful (Fassin 2013), often ambiguous – orientation towards the life they inhabited and aspired to.

Religious Differences and Cultural Pluralities

The moral orientations that students and teachers embodied in Christian and Muslim schools included the making and remaking of their relationship with their own and other people's faiths. The schools' admission policies differed greatly with regard to their students' religious backgrounds. The Muslim schools were run as seminaries and admitted only students of the Islamic faith; they also exclusively employed Muslim teachers. The Christian schools attracted students and employed teachers from various religious and denominational backgrounds (although Muslims represented a minority in all of them). The Catholic schools had a significantly higher percentage of students of their own denomination, whereas the neo-Pentecostal schools' clientele was more mixed. Apart from being a sign of the overall reproduction of a Christian Catholic elite at the St Joseph's schools, this was probably due to the fact that the alignment of the Catholic schools with their mother organisation was more explicit than in the St Mary's schools, which did not have a formalised relationship with their owner's church and did not promote themselves publicly or internally as 'Christian' or 'Pentecostal' schools.

The Islamic seminaries were also distinct in that their curricula emphasised the teaching of how to belong to a particular religion; some of the teachers, especially at Kipata, felt a certain calling to teach their students to become 'moral persons'. Through the subjects of Islamic Knowledge and Arabic, and the collective participation in prayers, students learned – and embodied (Ware 2014; Hoechner 2018) – how to become good Muslims in relation to issues such as marriage, the performance of the hajj, proper praying (see Pontzen 2020), and proper dress. These learning processes prepared the students for living well in a religiously diverse urban environment beyond the Qur'anic schools they attended in their home environments. The girls at Kipata 'felt free' not only due to a lack of 'competition' with boys at their seminary but also because of the absence of 'restrictions' on expressing their faith through prayers and dress, restrictions they claimed they would experience at Christian or government schools. At Al-Farouq, students were equally positive about studying in an Islamic environment but connected their self-perceptions as young Muslim men explicitly to the marginalisation of Muslims in society (Loimeier 2007). They also found it important to highlight their specific Muslim identities – e.g. as Sunni, Answaar, Bakwati, or Bahrain – an aspect that was not important at Kipata, although the seminary belonged to the same network of *Ansaar* organisations as Al-Farouq.

In the St Mary's schools, faith did not figure strongly in the institutions' official positionings, despite a public imaginary tying the schools closely to their (now deceased) owner's neo-Pentecostal church. In particular, there were no church services, nor were there formal prayers beyond the morning assemblies. Furthermore, the PPI ethics lessons retained a highly uncertain status in the primary school's schedule during my stay; at Kenton High School, the group composition for these lessons seemed less an intentional decision than an arbitrary outcome. This laissez-faire attitude to faith was ultimately not surprising in that it reflected the Pentecostal ideology's strong emphasis on individual self-expression and autonomy (cf. Meyer 2004: 461). It also mirrored the fact that both schools competed for students from a wide range of middle-class families from different religious backgrounds. At the same time, belonging to the Pentecostal faith did play a role in the implicit quests for a good life at both St Mary's schools. This became evident not only in the fellowshipping practices of the teachers, which played a particularly crucial role in an ambiguously perceived transnational setting (Settler and Engh 2018), but also in the schools' imagery and in the healings of female students with a Muslim background who were allegedly possessed by spirits. These healings became important occasions for the articulation and embodiment of values in relation to both one's own faith and the perceived immoralities and dangers of the free market economy.

At St Joseph's, learning about and practising a particular kind of faith was an explicit part of students' and teachers' ethical and moral becoming. As non-denominational faith-oriented institutions, the schools' affiliation with Catholicism was not expressed openly in their mission statement, which aimed at the education of 'virtuous and faithful youth'. At the same time, the close connection with the Catholic church was engrained deeply in the students' and teachers' minds. Not only did they know that many 'Catholic schools' were 'exceptional' but their own school's affiliation with the Catholic faith was established through compulsory prayers and masses, faith-specific discourses on 'sin' and the Bible, and the continued presence of the Catholic sisters and paraphernalia of the faith. In this context, an immediate sense of difference from other denominational and religious orientations was a constant presence. Most students and teachers pragmatically participated in faith-oriented activities 'out of respect' and/or because they were used to living in mixed religious contexts in their homes. While this reflected the partiality and discontinuity of students' and teachers' moral becoming, the performance of these activities was not 'less authentic' (Palmer and Jankowiak 1996: 234). On the contrary, the students' and teachers' participation in their schools' prayers and rituals allowed for the respectful embodiment of a different religion's or denomination's practice or teaching while maintaining a critical distance from it.

The various ways of dealing with differing faith orientations in Christian and Muslim schools reflected the many implications of living in environments where religious diversity and cultural pluralism are actively governed – and shaped – through multiple administrative and institutional interventions (Burchardt 2017: 181; Dilger 2020; see also Chapter 3). Informal practices such as the healing of possessed (mostly Muslim) girls in the St Mary's schools could account for the divisive potential of such schools in that they exposed and problematised religious otherness, despite their emphasis on respect for religious difference. Equally, the explicit focus on becoming 'good Muslims' at the Islamic seminaries might lead to an alienation from a religiously diverse society by retreating into 'enclaves' (Shavit and Wiesenbach 2012).

On the other hand, however, such practices cast religious difference as not necessarily problematic. Instead, the active embodiment of one's own and others' faith values instigated a moral orientation towards the world that allowed for a self-confident experience of (every)one's otherness in a religiously diverse city. In this regard, the value of living together well in a pluralistic society was not only an explicit ethical goal of the

Christian schools, where Muslim students and teachers valued the 'sameness' of all religions and reassured each other of the leeway they had in relation to their own faith in these contexts. It was also part of the everyday moral becoming at the Islamic seminaries, where the sense of socio-religious inequalities, which was most pronounced at the boys' school, did not translate into segregation from an allegedly 'Christian state' (*mfumokristo*). On the contrary, Muslim students became knowledgeable and confident about their faith in these schools in the context of living in a pluralist 'Tanzanian culture' in which they engaged with people from different religious and ethnic backgrounds on an everyday basis and simultaneously longed to lead a morally 'pure' and 'clean' life in spiritually and socio-economically challenging circumstances.

Inequalities, Politics, and Power: Studying Religiously Diverse Institutionalisation

Scholars of religion and religious diversity have recently criticised the field's preoccupation with discourse and cultural consumption as well as its exclusive focus on individual experiences and practices in research on 'lived religion' (Altglas and Wood 2018: 2). Salzbrunn (2014: 74) remarks that studies on religious and other forms of diversity in Europe have adopted an increasingly 'culturalist' perspective that disregards social inequalities and processes of class formation in the coming-into-being of (religiously) diverse societies. Similarly, Burchardt (2017: 181) is critical of anthropological research for focusing on the study of 'religious sensibilities and subjectivities' in the context of secularisation, instead of exploring how the construction of religious diversity itself 'is folded into the genealogical trajectory of neoliberal forms of power through which such experiences, negotiations and practices of governance are made possible'. In response to such criticisms, Althaus and Wood (2018) argue for a more sociological understanding of religion that focuses less on the object of religion itself and more on how religious orientations, practices, and materialities are produced and situated in specific societal and political-economic conditions. They call for a sociology of religion that uses 'its object as a means to understand the social world at large', thereby 'reintegrating the social – power and authority, social classes, ethnicity, embodiment and emotions, interactions and practices – into the study of religion' (ibid.: 27–8).

In the anthropology of religion in Africa, scholars have long focused on the study of either Christianity or Islam, or on their internal diversities. Only recently has there been a move towards exploring Christianity and Islam as 'lived religions' (Soares 2016: 691) within the same analytical framework. Such a conceptual shift has been expressed in the 'call for an opening up of the binary logic of an exclusive either/or that permeates the study of religion and for its replacement of an inclusive both/and paradigm' (Janson and Meyer 2016: 619; see also Soares 2006; Dilger and Schulz 2013). Over the last years, several studies have looked at 'the multiplicity of practices of pluralism' (Soares 2016: 673) in Christian–Muslim encounters, including in relation to African 'traditional religions' (Olupona 2011; Peel 2015; Nolte et al. 2017). They have shown how practices of 'borrowing, appropriation, boundary making and dissolution' (Soares 2016: 691) are key to the formation of distinct religious practices, and to the mutual positioning of different religious actors and ways of life in religiously diverse settings (ibid.: 679). Few scholars have explored how such processes occur under conditions in which Christian and Muslim actors do not necessarily interact with each other directly, but rather in shared historical and societal contexts (Dilger 2013a; 2014a; 2017; for European settings, see Beekers 2014; DeHanas 2016).

This book shows that, even in circumstances in which direct interactions between Christians and Muslims – and the institutions they have established – are limited, their engagements with education and the learning and teaching of values have to be understood in relation to the larger societal and political-economic conditions they share (see Larkin and Meyer 2006: 286). Using a comparative framework reveals a more nuanced view of the ways in which colonial and postcolonial histories of education and interreligious encounters have shaped understandings and the quest for a good life in Dar es Salaam's Christian and Muslim schools in distinct ways. It also highlights how such notions and practices – and their corresponding institutional forms – have been configured and reconfigured through the recent politics of faith-based development and the governance of religious diversity, privatisation and transnational reforms in the education sector, and the embedding of faith-oriented schools and their practices in religiously diverse urban settings. It is only by paying systematic attention to these wider 'common grounds' (Larkin and Meyer 2006) and the adoption of a decidedly 'critical political economy' perspective (Burchardt 2017: 181) that one can grasp the multiple dynamics of similarity and difference that characterise the explicit and implicit practices of students' and teachers' moral becoming in Christian and Muslim schools in urban Tanzania. This comparative analytical perspective also helps us understand the structural locations of individual faith-oriented schools and the religious and/or denominational contexts in which they are embedded, in a hierarchical and diverse religious landscape.

I want to end this book with a call for more systematic attention to be paid to the dynamics of power, politics, class formation, and processes of institutionalisation in anthropological and interdisciplinary studies on the coexistence of Christians and Muslims, and in research on religiously diverse settings in general. The comparative study of Christian and Muslim schools (or other religious or faith-oriented institutions or organisations) in urban Africa within a joint analytical frame not only requires thorough attention to the political economies and power relations that structure the formation of diverse religious urban environments under the influence of globalisation and capitalist market expansion (see Meyer 2004: 459; Stambach 2010b: 372). It also means, following Soares (2016: 679), that 'power and politics must be understood in broader terms, from the level of micro-politics and everyday politics in specific social settings to formal institutional politics … and state policies in a variety of areas, which can have an enormous impact on how Muslims and Christians interact with each other over time'.

The comparative study of moral becoming and of the educational and professional trajectories of students and teachers in Christian and Muslim schools in urban Tanzania offers an example par excellence for 'unmasking the relations of power' (Monnot 2018) in the social constitution of religiously diverse fields – with regard to both the becoming of individual bodies and particular institutions and the position of specific religious groups and actors in an interconnected world. Situating the emergence of these schools since the 1990s within the histories of interreligious relations and education from colonial times onwards highlights their highly divergent social positions in Tanzania's educational market today. A focus on individual experiences and practices of learning values – as well as on the micro-institutional histories and materialities of the schools in which these values are embodied – allows for an understanding of the mutual entanglement of all these phenomena with dynamics of socio-religious difference, market mobilities, and urban transformation.

This book is only a starting point for the in-depth exploration of these processes, which extend far beyond the micro-social environments that anthropologists usually study. This kind of research requires attention to a variety of ethnographic approaches, which should also include quantitative methods, critical readings of statistics, and a thorough engagement with archival and historical sources in order to take account of the short- and long-term shifts and transformations in our study sites (Nolte et al. 2016). Furthermore, such an approach demands a stronger focus on long-term processes of institutionalisation, which were especially important for some of the comparative studies of the Manchester School in the mid-twentieth century (Scudder and Colson 1979) and which have recently regained importance in anthropological investigations into the development of institutions.[3] Just as students' and teachers' quests for a good life continue to be shaped by long-standing histories of power and socio-religious difference, it remains to be seen how the resulting practices – and the actors that embody them – will continue to shape Tanzania's religiously and culturally pluralist society in the years to come.

---

[3] See, for instance, Schnegg and Bollig (2016) on long-term fieldwork on community-based water management in Namibia.

References

Abdulaziz, Mohamed H. 1991. 'East Africa (Tanzania and Kenya)' in Jenny Cheshire (ed.), *English around the World: sociolinguistic perspectives*. Cambridge: Cambridge University Press.

Ahmed, Chanfi. 2008. 'The Wahubiri wa Kislamu (Preachers of Islam) in East Africa', *Africa Today* 54 (4): 3–18 [special issue: 'Performing Islamic revival in Africa'].

2009. 'Networks of Islamic NGOs in sub-Saharan Africa: Bilal Muslim Mission, African Muslim Agency (Direct Aid), and al-Haramayn', *Journal of Eastern African Studies* 3 (3): 426–37.

Altglas, Véronique and Matthew Wood. 2018. 'Introduction: an epistemology for the sociology of religion' in Véronique Altglas and Matthew Wood (eds), *Bringing Back the Social into the Sociology of Religion: critical approaches*. Leiden: Brill.

Ammah, Rabiatu. 2007. 'Christian–Muslim relations in contemporary sub-Saharan Africa', *Islam and Christian–Muslim Relations* 18 (2): 139–53.

Anderson-Levitt, Kathryn M. 2003. 'A world culture of schooling?' in Kathryn M. Anderson-Levitt (ed.), *Local Meanings, Global Schooling: anthropology and world culture theory*. New York NY and Basingstoke: Palgrave Macmillan.

Ashforth, Adam. 1998. 'Reflections on spiritual insecurity in a modern African city (Soweto)', *African Studies Review* 41 (3): 39–67.

Bader, Veit. 2009. 'Governance of religious diversity: research problems and policy problems' in P. Bramadat and M. Koenig (eds), *International Migration and the Governance of Religious Diversity*. Montreal and Kingston: McGill-Queen's University Press.

Bakewell, Oliver and Naluwembe Binaisa. 2016. 'Tracing diasporic identifications in Africa's urban landscapes: evidence from Lusaka and Kampala', *Ethnic and Racial Studies* 39 (2): 280–300.

Barker, John and Fiona Smith. 2001. 'Power, positionality and practicality: carrying out fieldwork with children', *Ethics, Place and Environment* 4 (2): 142–7.

Baumann, Gerd. 2004. 'Introduction: nation-state, schools and civil enculturation' in Werner Schiffauer, Gerd Baumann, Riva Kastoryano, and Steven Vertovec (eds), *Civil Enculturation: nation-state, school and ethnic difference in the Netherlands, Britain, Germany and France*. New York NY and Oxford: Berghahn Books.

Baumann, Gerd and Thijl Sunier. 2004. 'The school as a place in its social space' in Werner Schiffauer, Gerd Baumann, Riva Kastoryano, and Steven

Vertovec (eds), *Civil Enculturation: nation-state, school and ethnic difference in the Netherlands, Britain, Germany and France*. New York NY and Oxford: Berghahn Books.

Becker, Felicitas. 2004. 'Traders, "big men" and prophets: political continuity and crisis in the Maji Maji rebellion in southeast Tanzania', *Journal of African History* 45 (1): 1–22.

2006. 'Rural Islamism during the "War on Terror": a Tanzanian case study', *African Affairs* 105 (421): 583–603.

2008. *Becoming Muslim in Mainland Tanzania 1890–2000*. Oxford: Oxford University Press.

2014. 'Fashioning selves and fashioning styles: negotiating the personal and the rhetorical in the experiences of African recipients of ARV treatment' in Rijk van Dijk, Hansjörg Dilger, Marian Burchardt, and Thera Rasing (eds), *Religion and AIDS Treatment in Africa: saving souls, prolonging lives*. Farnham: Ashgate.

2015. 'Obscuring and revealing: Muslim engagement with volunteering and the aid sector in Tanzania', *African Studies Review* 58 (2): 111–33.

2016. 'Patriarchal masculinity in recent Swahili-language Muslim sermons', *Journal of Religion in Africa* 46 (2–3): 158–86.

2018. 'The history of Islam in East Africa', *Oxford Research Encyclopedias* [online], http://oxfordre.com/africanhistory/view/10.1093/acrefore/9780190277734.001.0001/acrefore-9780190277734-e-151 (accessed 23 April 2019).

Beckmann, Nadine. 2010. 'Pleasure and danger: Muslim views on sex and gender in Zanzibar', *Culture, Health and Sexuality* 12 (6): 619–32.

Beekers, Daan. 2014. 'Pedagogies of piety: comparing young observant Muslims and Christians in the Netherlands', *Culture and Religion* 15 (1): 72–99.

Berliner, David C. 2005. 'The abuses of memory: reflections on the memory boom in anthropology', *Anthropological Quarterly* 78 (1): 197–211.

Bettie, Julie. 2003. *Women without Class: girls, race, and identity*. Berkeley CA: University of California Press.

Bilal Muslim Mission. 2007. *Annual Report*. Dar es Salaam: Bilal Muslim Mission of Tanzania.

2008. *Annual Report*. Dar es Salaam: Bilal Muslim Mission of Tanzania.

Blanes, Ruy Llera. 2006. 'The atheist anthropologist: believers and non-believers in anthropological fieldwork', *Social Anthropology* 14 (2): 223–34.

Blum, Denise F. 2011. *Cuban Youth and Revolutionary Values: educating the new socialist citizen*. Austin TX: University of Texas Press.

Bochow, Astrid. 2020. 'Longing for connection: Christian education and emerging urban lifestyles in Botswana' in Hansjörg Dilger, Astrid Bochow, Marian Burchardt, and Matthew Wilhelm-Solomon (eds), *Affective Trajectories: religion and emotion in African cityscapes*. Durham NC: Duke University Press.

Bochow, Astrid and Rijk van Dijk. 2012. 'Christian creations of new spaces of sexuality, reproduction, and relationships in Africa: exploring faith and religious heterotopia', *Journal of Religion in Africa* 42 (4): 325–44 [special issue].

Bochow, Astrid, Thomas G. Kirsch, and Rijk van Dijk. 2017. 'Introduction: new ethical fields and the implicitness/explicitness of ethics in Africa', *Africa* 87 (3): 447–61.

Bornstein, Erica. 2001. 'Child sponsorship, evangelism, and belonging in the work of World Vision Zimbabwe', *American Ethnologist* 28 (3): 595–622.
   2005. *The Spirit of Development: Protestant NGOs, morality, and economics in Zimbabwe*. Stanford CA: Stanford University Press.
Bourdieu, Pierre. 1974. 'The school as a conservative force: scholastic and cultural inequalities' in John Eggleston (ed.), *Contemporary Research in the Sociology of Education*. London: Methuen.
   1986. 'The forms of capital' in John G. Richardson (ed.), *Handbook of Theory and Research for the Sociology of Education*. Westport CT: Greenwood.
   1996 [1984]. *Distinction: a social critique of the judgment of taste*. Translated by Richard Nice. Cambridge MA: Harvard University Press.
   2006 [1996]. 'Die Logik der Felder' in Pierre Bourdieu and Loïc Wacquant (eds), *Reflexive Anthropologie*. Frankfurt: Suhrkamp.
Bowles, Samuel and Herbert Gintis. 2002. 'Schooling in capitalist America revisited', *Sociology of Education* 75 (1): 1–18.
Boyle, Helen. 2004. *Quranic Schools: agents of preservation and change*. New York NY and London: Routledge Falmer.
Brennan, James R., Andrew Burton, and Yusuf Lawi (eds). 2007. *Dar es Salaam: histories from an emerging African metropolis*. Dar es Salaam: Mkuki na Nyota Publishers.
Brenner, Louis. 2001. *Controlling Knowledge: religion, power, and schooling in a West African society*. Bloomington IN: Indiana University Press.
Brocco, Giorgio. 2016. 'Albinism, stigma, subjectivity and global–local discourses in Tanzania', *Anthropology and Medicine* 23 (3): 229–43.
Brock-Utne, Birgit. 2002. *Language, Democracy and Education in Africa*. Discussion Paper 15. Uppsala: Nordiska Afrikainstitutet.
Brock-Utne, Birgit and Halla B. Holmarsdottir. 2004. 'Language policies and practices in Tanzania and South Africa: problems and challenges', *International Journal of Educational Development* 24 (1): 67–83.
Brown, Hannah and Ruth J. Prince. 2015. 'Introduction: volunteer labor – pasts and futures of work, development, and citizenship in East Africa', *African Studies Review* 58 (2): 29–42.
Buchert, Lene. 1994. *Education in the Development of Tanzania 1919–90*. London: James Currey.
Bunyi, Grace. 1997. 'Language in education in Kenyan schools' in Jim Cummins and David Corson (eds), *Bilingual Education: encyclopedia of language and education. Volume 5*. Dordrecht: Kluwer Academic Publishers.
Burchardt, Marian. 2017. 'Diversity as neoliberal governmentality: towards a new sociological genealogy of religion', *Social Compass* 64 (2): 180–93.
Buyandelger, Manduhai. 2018. 'Asocial memories, "poisonous knowledge", and haunting in Mongolia', *Journal of the Royal Anthropological Institute* 25 (3): 66–82.
Caplan, Pat. 1999. 'Anthropology, history and personal narratives: reflections on writing "African voices, African lives"', *Transactions of the Royal Historical Society* 9: 283–90.
Casanova, José. 1992. 'Private and public religion', *Social Research* 59 (1): 17–57.
   1994. *Public Religions in the Modern World*. Chicago IL: University of Chicago Press.

Chande, Abdin N. 1998. *Islam, Ulamaa and Community Development in Tanzania: a case study of religious currents in East Africa*. San Francisco CA: Austin and Winfield.

2008. 'Muslim–state relations in East Africa under conditions of military and civilian or one-party dictatorships', *Historia Actual Online* 17: 97–111.

Chicharro-Saito, Gladys. 2008. 'Physical education and moral embodiment in primary schools of the People's Republic of China', *China Perspectives* 2008 (1): 29–39.

Clough, Paul. 2006. '"Knowledge in passing": reflexive anthropology and religious awareness', *Anthropological Quarterly* 79 (2): 261–83.

Coe, Cati. 2005. *Dilemmas of Culture in African Schools: youth, nationalism, and the transformation of knowledge*. Chicago IL: University of Chicago Press.

Cole, Jennifer. 1998. 'The work of memory in Madagascar', *American Ethnologist* 25 (4): 610–33.

Collins, James. 2009. 'Social reproduction in classrooms and schools', *Annual Review of Anthropology* 38: 33–48.

Comaroff, Jean and John Comaroff. 1986. 'Christianity and colonialism in South Africa', *American Ethnologist* 13 (1): 1–22.

1991. *Of Revelation and Revolution. Volume 1: Christianity, colonialism and consciousness in South Africa*. Chicago IL: University of Chicago Press.

1997. *Of Revelation and Revolution. Volume 2: The dialectics of modernity on a South African frontier*. Chicago IL: University of Chicago Press.

2000. 'Millennial capitalism: first thoughts on a second coming', *Public Culture* 12 (2): 291–343.

Comaroff, John and Jean Comaroff. 1992. *Ethnography and the Historical Imagination*. Boulder CO: Westview Press.

Connell, Martin T. 2016. 'The challenge to educate: an account of inaugurating a Catholic school in Tanzania', *Journal of Catholic Education* 19: 20–48.

Cooksey, Brian and Tim Kelsall. 2011. *The Political Economy of the Investment Climate in Tanzania: research report*. London: Africa Power and Politics Programme, Overseas Development Institute.

Cooksey, Brian, David Court, and Ben Makau. 1994. 'Education for self-reliance and *harambee*' in Joel D. Barkan (ed.), *Beyond Capitalism vs. Socialism in Kenya and Tanzania*. Boulder CO: Lynne Reinner Publishers.

Csordas, Thomas. 2008. 'Intersubjectivity and intercorporeality', *Subjectivity* 22: 110–21.

CSSC. 2001. *Joint Churches and Government Programme for Sustainable Development in Social Services. Self-assessment: ten years of Education Department*. CSSC Document 16. Dar es Salaam: Christian Social Services Commission (CSSC).

2005a. *Annual Report 2005*. Dar es Salaam: Christian Social Services Commission (CSSC).

2005b. *Laboratory Organisation, Management and Techniques: a laboratory manual for science teachers*. Dar es Salaam: Christian Social Services Commission (CSSC).

Dahl, Bianca. 2009. 'The "failure of culture": Christianity, kinship, and moral discourse about orphans during Botswana's AIDS crisis', *Africa Today* 56 (1): 22–43 [special issue: 'Christianity and HIV/AIDS in East and Southern Africa'].

Darbon, Dominique. 2019. 'The political role of the African middle class: the over-politicization of an elusive category', *Oxford Research Encyclopedias: politics* [online], https://oxfordre.com/politics/view/10.1093/acrefore/9780190228637.001.0001/acrefore-9780190228637-e-739 (accessed 22 December 2020).

Dar es Salaam University Muslim Trusteeship. 2004. *Tusikubali Kubaguliwa Kielimu: Nasaha za Shaykh Hasan bin Ameir (1880–1979)*. Dar es Salaam: Dar es Salaam University Muslim Trusteeship.

De Boeck, Filip. 2012. 'Infrastructure: commentary by Filip de Boeck', *Cultural Anthropology* [online], https://journal.culanth.org/index.php/ca/infrastructure-filip-de-boeck (accessed 1 September 2020).

DeHanas, Daniel Nilsson. 2016. *London Youth, Religion, and Politics: engagement and activism from Brixton to Brick Lane*. Oxford: Oxford University Press.

De Saxe, Jennifer. 2015. 'A neoliberal critique: conceptualizing the purpose of school', *Catalyst: A Social Justice Forum* 5 (1): article 7.

DiCarlo, Lisa. 2013. 'I'm just a soul whose intentions are good: observations from the back pew' in Hillary K. Crane and Deana L. Weibel (eds), *Missionary Impositions: conversion, resistance, and other challenges to objectivity in religious ethnography*. Lanham MD: Lexington.

Dilger, Hansjörg. 2000. '"Aids ist ein Unfall": Metaphern und Bildlichkeit in AIDS-Diskursen Tansanias', *Africa Spectrum* 35 (2): 165–82.

2005. *Leben mit Aids: Krankheit, Tod und soziale Beziehungen in Afrika. Eine Ethnographie*. Frankfurt and New York NY: Campus.

2007. 'Healing the wounds of modernity: salvation, community and care in a neo-Pentecostal church in Dar es Salaam, Tanzania', *Journal of Religion in Africa* 37 (1): 59–83.

2009. 'Doing better? Religion, the virtue-ethics of development, and the fragmentation of health politics in Tanzania', *Africa Today* 56 (1): 89–110.

2013a. 'Religion and the formation of "unequal subjects" in an urban educational market: transnational reform processes and intertwined histories of Christian and Muslim schooling in Dar es Salaam, Tanzania', *Journal of Religion in Africa* 43 (4): 451–79.

2013b. 'Securing wealth, ordering social relations: kinship, morality, and the configuration of subjectivity and belonging across the rural–urban divide' in Abdoulaye Kane and Todd Leedy (eds), *African Migrations Today: patterns and perspectives*. Bloomington IN: Indiana University Press.

2014a. 'Claiming territory: medical mission, interreligious revivalism, and the spatialization of health interventions in urban Tanzania', *Medical Anthropology* 33 (1): 52–67 [special issue: 'Turning therapies: placing medical diversity', edited by David Parkin, Kristine Krause, and Gabi Alex].

2014b. 'No public? Class dynamics, the politics of extraversion, and the non-formation of political publics and (religious) AIDS activism in urban Tanzania' in Caroline Schmitt and Asta Vonderau (eds), *Transnationalität und Öffentlichkeit: Interdisziplinäre Perspektiven*. Bielefeld: Transcript.

2017. 'Embodying values and socio-religious difference: new markets of moral learning in Christian and Muslim schools in urban Tanzania', *Africa* 87 (3): 513–36.

2020. 'Governing religious multiplicity: the ambivalence of Christian–Muslim public presences in postcolonial Tanzania', *Social Analysis* 64 (1): 125–32 [special issue: 'Toward a comparative anthropology of Muslim and Christian lived religion', edited by Daan Beekers].

Dilger, Hansjörg and Dorothea Schulz. 2013. 'Introduction', *Journal of Religion in Africa* 43 (4): 365–78 [special issue: 'Politics of religious schooling: Christian and Muslim engagements with education in Africa', edited by Dorothea Schulz and Hansjörg Dilger].

Dilger, Hansjörg and Kai Malmus. 2002. 'Mission completed – democracy safe? The Tanzanian Union, international election monitoring and the general elections 2000', *Sociologus* 52 (2): 191–214.

Dilger, Hansjörg and Marloes Janson. (forthcoming 2022). 'Religiously-motivated schools and universities as "moral enclaves": reforming urban youths in Tanzania and Nigeria' in David Garbin, Simon Coleman, and Gareth Millington (eds), *Religious Urbanization and the Moral Economies of Development in Africa*. London: Bloomsbury Academic.

Dilger, Hansjörg, Marian Burchardt, Matthew Wilhelm-Solomon, and Astrid Bochow. 2020. 'Introduction: affective trajectories in religious African cityscapes' in Hansjörg Dilger, Astrid Bochow, Marian Burchardt, and Matthew Wilhelm-Solomon (eds), *Affective Trajectories: religion and emotion in African cityscapes*. Durham NC: Duke University Press.

Dohrn, Kristina. 2014. 'Translocal ethics: Hizmet teachers and the formation of Gülen-inspired schools in urban Tanzania', *Sociology of Islam* 1 (3–4): 233–56.

2017. 'A "golden generation"? Framing the future among senior students at Gülen-inspired schools in urban Tanzania' in Amy Stambach and Kathleen D. Hall (eds), *Anthropological Perspectives on Student Futures: youth and the politics of possibility*. New York NY: Palgrave Macmillan.

Eckert, Andreas. 2007. *Herrschen und Verwalten: Afrikanische Bürokraten, staatliche Ordnung und Politik in Tanzania, 1920–1970*. Munich: Oldenbourg Wissenschaftsverlag.

EDIMASHUTA (Umoja wa Elimu ya Dini na Maadili Shuleni Tanzania). 2005. 'Report of the Uganda study tour on teaching of religion and ethics in schools (primary, secondary, and teachers' colleges)'. Prepared by Clemence Lori and Sr Claudia Mashambo, June 2005. Dar es Salaam: Tanzania Episcopal Conference.

Eickelman, Dale F. and James Piscatori. 2004. *Muslim Politics*. Princeton NJ: Princeton University Press.

Engelke, Matthew. 2004. 'Discontinuity and the discourse of conversion', *Journal of Religion in Africa* 34 (1–2): 82–109.

Ewald, Jonas. 2011. *Challenges for the Democratisation Process in Tanzania: moving towards consolidation 50 years after independence?* Dar es Salaam: Mkuki na Nyota Publishers.

Fabian, Johannes. 1999. 'Remembering the other: knowledge and recognition in the exploration of Central Africa', *Critical Enquiry* 26 (1): 49–69.

Fair, Laura. 1998. 'Dressing up: clothing, class and gender in post-abolition Zanzibar', *Journal of African History* 39 (1): 63–94.

Fassin, Didier. 2013. 'On resentment and *ressentiment*: the politics and ethics of moral emotions', *Current Anthropology* 54 (3): 249–67.
    2015. 'Lecture 4: Troubled waters. At the confluence of ethics and politics' in Michael Lambek, Veena Das, Didier Fassin, and Webb Keane (eds), *Four Lectures on Ethics: anthropological perspectives*. Chicago IL: Hau Books.
Faubion, James. 2011. *An Anthropology of Ethics*. Cambridge: Cambridge University Press.
Fay, Franziska. 2019. 'Decolonizing the child protection apparatus: revisiting child rights governance in Zanzibar', *Childhood* 26 (3): 321–36.
Ferguson, James. 2002. 'Of mimicry and membership: Africans and the "new world society"', *Cultural Anthropology* 17 (4): 551–69.
    2006. *Global Shadows: Africa in the neoliberal world order*. Durham NC: Duke University Press.
Fichtner, Sarah. 2012. *The NGOisation of Education: case studies from Benin*. Mainzer Beiträge zur Afrikaforschung 31. Cologne: Rüdiger Köppe Verlag.
Fischer, Edward F. 2014. *The Good Life: aspiration, dignity, and the anthropology of wellbeing*. Stanford CA: Stanford University Press.
Fitzgerald, Anne. 2017. 'Wearing an amulet: land titling and tenure (in)security in Tanzania'. PhD thesis, Department of Anthropology, Maynooth University.
Foley, Douglas. 2010. 'The rise of class culture theory in educational anthropology', *Anthropology and Education Quarterly* 41 (3): 215–27.
Foucault, Michel. 1994. 'Technologies of the self' in Paul Rabinow (ed.), *Ethics: subjectivity and truth*. New York NY: The New Press.
Frederiks, Martha T. 2010. 'Let us understand our differences: current trends in Christian–Muslim relations in sub-Saharan Africa', *Transformation: An International Journal of Holistic Mission Studies* 27 (4): 261–74.
Freire, Paulo. 2005 [1970]. *Pedagogy of the Oppressed*. Translated by Myra Bergman Ramos. New York NY: Continuum.
Frueh, Jamie. 2020. 'Pedagogy of the privileged: globalization, identity, belonging, and empowerment', *APSA Preprints*, doi: 10.33774/apsa-2020-zl4qd.
Fumanti, Mattia. 2006. 'Nation building and the battle for consciousness: discourses on education in post-apartheid Namibia', *Social Analysis* 50 (3): 84–108.
Fung, Heidi and Eva Chian-Hui Chen. 2001. 'Across time and beyond skin: self and transgression in the everyday socialization of shame among Taiwanese preschool children', *Social Development* 10 (3): 419–37.
Fung, Heidi and Benjamin Smith. 2010. 'Learning morality' in David F. Lancy, John C. Bock, and Suzanne Gaskins (eds), *The Anthropology of Learning in Childhood*. Walnut Creek CA: Altamira Press.
Funk, Leberecht, Birgitt Röttger-Rössler, and Gabriel Scheidecker. 2012. 'Fühlen(d) lernen. Zur Sozialisation und Entwicklung von Emotionen im Kulturvergleich', *Zeitschrift für Erziehungswissenschaft* 15 (1): 217–38.
Geschiere, Peter and Josef Gugler. 1998. 'Introduction: the rural–urban connection – changing issues of belonging and identification', *Africa* 68 (3): 309–19 [special issue: 'The politics of primary patriotism'].

References

Gifford, Paul. 1998. *African Christianity: its public role*. Bloomington IN: Indiana University Press.
  2004. *Ghana's New Christianity: Pentecostalism in a globalising African economy*. London: C. Hurst and Co.
Giles, Linda. 1999. 'Spirit possession and the symbolic construction of Swahili society' in Heike Behrend and Ute Luig (eds), *Spirit Possession, Modernity and Power in Africa*. Madison WI: University of Wisconsin Press.
Gille, Zsuzsa and Seán Ó Riain. 2002. 'Global ethnography', *Annual Review of Sociology* 28: 271–95.
Godda, Henry. 2018. 'Free secondary education and the changing roles of the heads of public schools in Tanzania: are they ready for new responsibilities?', *Open Journal of Social Sciences* 6 (5): 1–23.
Grace, Gerald. 2003. '"First and foremost the church offers its educational service to the poor": class, inequality and Catholic schooling in contemporary contexts', *International Studies in Sociology of Education* 13 (1): 35–54.
Gran, Line Kjølstad. 2007. 'Language of instruction in Tanzanian higher education: a particular focus on the University of Dar es Salaam'. Master's thesis, Faculty of Education, Institute for Educational Research, University of Oslo.
Grant, Barbara. 1997. 'Disciplining students: the construction of student subjectivities', *British Journal of Sociology of Education* 18 (1): 101–14.
Hansen, Holger Bernt and Michael Twaddle (eds). 1995. *Religion and Politics in East Africa: the period since independence*. London: James Currey.
Hartmann, Sarah. 2008. 'The informal market of education in Egypt: private tutoring and its implications'. Working Paper 88. Mainz: Department of Anthropology and African Studies, Johannes Gutenberg University.
Hasu, Päivi. 2006. 'World Bank and heavenly bank in poverty and prosperity: the case of Tanzanian Faith Gospel', *Review of African Political Economy* 33 (110): 679–92.
  2007. 'Neo-Pentecostalism in Tanzania: Godly miracles, satanic interventions or human development?' in Jeremy Gould and Lauri Siitonen (eds), *Anomalies of Aid: a festschrift for Juhani Koponen*. Helsinki: Interkont Books.
  2009. 'The witch, the zombie and the power of Jesus: a trinity of spiritual warfare in Tanzanian Pentecostalism', *Suomen Antropologi* 34 (1): 70–83.
Haustein, Jörg. 2017. 'Strategic tangles: slavery, colonial policy, and religion in German East Africa, 1885–1918', *Atlantic Studies* 14 (4): 497–518.
Hearn, Julie. 2002. 'The "invisible" NGO: US Evangelical missions in Kenya', *Journal of Religion in Africa* 32 (1): 32–60.
Heilman, Bruce and Paul J. Kaiser. 2002. 'Religion, identity and politics in Tanzania', *Third World Quarterly* 23 (4): 691–709.
Hirschfeld, Lawrence A. 2002. 'Why don't anthropologists like children?', *American Anthropologist* 104 (2): 611–27.
HMSO. 1961. *Tanganyika Report for the Year 1960. Part II*. London: Her Majesty's Stationery Office (HMSO) for the Colonial Office.
Hoechner, Hannah. 2018. *Quranic Schools in Northern Nigeria: everyday experiences of youth, faith, and poverty*. Cambridge: International African Institute and Cambridge University Press.
Hölzl, Richard. 2016. 'Educating Missions: teachers and catechists in southern Tanganyika, 1890s and 1940s', *Itinerario* 40 (3): 405–28.

Horton, Mark and John Middleton. 2000. *The Swahili: the social landscape of a mercantile society*. Malden MA: Wiley-Blackwell.

Höschele, Stefan. 2007. *Christian Remnant – African Folk Church: Seventh-Day Adventism in Tanzania, 1903–1980*. Leiden: Brill.

Hunt, Nancy Rose. 1999. *A Colonial Lexicon: of birth ritual, medicalization, and mobility in the Congo*. Durham NC: Duke University Press.

Hunter, Mark. 2019. *Race for Education: gender, white tone, and schooling in South Africa*. Cambridge: International African Institute and Cambridge University Press.

Ibn Baṭūṭa. 1829. *The Travels of Ibn Baṭūṭa*. Translated by Revd Samuel Lee, BD. London: John Murray.

Ibrahim, Murtala. 2020. 'The sites of divine encounter: affective religious spaces and sensational practices in Christ Embassy and NASFAT in the city of Abuja' in Hansjörg Dilger, Astrid Bochow, Marian Burchardt, and Matthew Wilhelm-Solomon (eds), *Affective Trajectories: religion and emotion in African cityscapes*. Durham NC: Duke University Press.

Iliffe, John. 1979. *A Modern History of Tanganyika*. Cambridge: Cambridge University Press.

Ishumi, Abel G. M. 2006. 'Access to and equity in education in Tanzania' in Rwekaza Mukandala et al. (eds), *Justice, Rights and Worship: religion and politics in Tanzania*. Dar es Salaam: E&D Limited.

Islamic Education Panel. nd. *Elimu ya Dini ya Kiislamu. Shule za Sekondari. Kitabu cha 2*. Dar es Salaam: Afroplus Industries for Islamic Education Panel (chini ya usimamizi ya Bakwata na Wizara ya Elimu Zanzibar / under the supervision of BAKWATA and the Ministry of Education Zanzibar).

Ivaska, Andrew. 2011. *Cultured States: youth, gender, and modern style in 1960s Dar es Salaam*. Durham NC: Duke University Press.

Jackson, Philip W. 1968. *Life in Classrooms*. New York NY: Holt, Rinehart and Winston.

James, Deborah. 2019. 'New subjectivities: aspiration, prosperity and the new middle class', *African Studies* 78 (1): 33–50.

Jamestown Foundation. 2003. 'Tanzania: Al Qaeda's East African beachhead?', *Terrorism Monitor* 1 (5), www.jamestown.org/programs/tm/single/?tx_ttnews [tt_news]=18969&tx_ttnews[backPid]=178&no_cache=1#.VcHa9flUzIU (accessed 14 May 2019).

Janson, Marloes. 2014. *Islam, Youth and Modernity in the Gambia: the Tablighi Jama'at*. Cambridge: International African Institute and Cambridge University Press.

—— 2015. '"How, for God's sake, can I be a good Muslim?": Gambian youth in search of a moral lifestyle', *Ethnography* 17 (1): 22–46.

—— 2016. 'Unity through diversity: a case study of Chrislam in Lagos', *Africa* 86 (4): 646–72.

Janson, Marloes and Birgit Meyer. 2016. 'Introduction: towards a framework for the study of Christian–Muslim encounters in Africa', *Africa* 86 (4): 615–19.

Jennings, Michael. 2008. *Surrogates of the State: NGOs, development and Ujamaa in Tanzania*. Bloomfield CT: Kumarian Press.

Jones, Thomas Jesse. 1924. *Education in East Africa: a study of the East, Central and South Africa by the second African Education Commission under the auspices*

of the Phelps-Stoke Fund, in cooperation with the International Education Board. London: Edinburgh House Press.
Jumbe, Aboud. 1994. *The Partner-Ship: Tanganyika–Zanzibar union: 30 turbulent years*. Dar es Salaam: Amana.
Kaag, Mayke. 2013. 'Africa Muslims Agency' in Kate Fleet, Gudrun Krämer, Denis Matringe, John Nawas, and Everett Rowson (eds), *Encyclopaedia of Islam, THREE*. Leiden: Brill, http://dx.doi.org/10.1163/1573-3912_ei3_COM_27261 (accessed 21 August 2020).
  2018. 'Linking-in through education? Exploring the educational question in Africa from the perspective of flows and (dis)connections', *Sustainability* 10 (2): 496.
Kaag, Mayke and Soumaya Sahla. 2020. 'Reflections on trust and trust making in the work of Islamic charities from the Gulf Region in Africa' in Holger Weiss (ed.), *Muslim Faith-Based Organizations and Social Welfare in Africa*. Cham: Palgrave Macmillan.
Kaiser, Paul J. 1996. *Culture, Transnationalism, and Civil Society: Aga Khan social service initiatives in Tanzania*. Westport CT: Praeger.
Kaniki, M. 1974. 'TANU: the party of independence and national consolidation' in Gabriel Ruhumbika (ed.), *Toward Ujamaa: twenty years of TANU leadership*. Dar es Salaam: East African Literature Bureau.
Keane, Webb. 2007. *Christian Moderns: freedom and fetish in the mission encounter*. Berkeley CA: University of California Press.
Kempf, Wolfgang, Toon van Meijl, and Elfriede Hermann. 2014. 'Movement, place-making and cultural identification: multiplicities of belonging' in Wolfgang Kempf, Toon van Meijl, and Elfriede Hermann (eds), *Belonging in Oceania: movement, place-making and multiple identifications*. New York NY: Berghahn Books.
King, Kenneth. 1971. *Pan-Africanism and Education: a study of race philanthropy and education in the southern states of America and East Africa*. Oxford: Clarendon Press.
Kirby, Benjamin James. 2017. 'Muslim mobilisation, urban informality, and the politics of development in Tanzania: an ethnography of the Kariakoo Market district'. PhD thesis, University of Leeds.
Kironde, J. M. Lusugga. 2007. Race, class, and housing in Dar es Salaam: the colonial impact on land use structure' in James Brennan, Andrew Burton, and Yusuf Lawi (eds), *Dar es Salaam: histories from an emerging African metropolis*. East Lansing MI and Dar es Salaam: Michigan State University Press and Mkuki na Nyota Publishers, in association with the British Institute in Eastern Africa.
Kirsch, Thomas G. 2008. *Spirits and Letters: reading, writing and charisma in Africa Christianity*. Oxford and New York NY: Berghahn Books.
Kresse, Kai. 2009. 'Muslim politics in postcolonial Kenya: negotiating knowledge on the double-periphery', *Journal of the Royal Anthropological Institute* 15: 76–94.
  2018. *Swahili Muslim Publics and Postcolonial Experience in Coastal Kenya*. Bloomington IN: Indiana University Press.
Lambek, Michael. 2010. 'Introduction' in Michael Lambek (ed.), *Ordinary Ethics: anthropology, language, and action*. New York NY: Fordham University Press.

2015. *The Ethical Condition: essays on action, person, and value*. Chicago IL: University of Chicago Press.
Langewiesche, Katrin. 2007. 'Religiöse Identitäten in Bewegung: Zeitgenössische Konversionsgeschichten aus Burkina Faso', *Historische Anthropologie* 15 (1): 65–81.
Larkin, Brian. 2013. 'The politics and poetics of infrastructure', *Annual Review of Anthropology* 42: 327–43.
Larkin, Brian and Birgit Meyer. 2006. 'Pentecostalism, Islam, and culture: new religious movements in West Africa' in Emmanuel Akyeampong (ed.), *Themes in West Africa's History*. Oxford: James Currey.
Lassibille, Gérard and Jee-Peng Tan. 2001. 'Are private schools more efficient than public schools? Evidence from Tanzania', *Education Economics* 9 (2): 145–72.
Last, Murray. 2000. 'Children and the experience of violence: contrasting cultures of punishment in northern Nigeria', *Africa* 70 (3): 359–93.
Launay, Robert. 2016. 'Introduction: writing boards and blackboards' in Robert Launay (ed.), *Islamic Education in Africa: writing boards and blackboards*. Bloomington IN: Indiana University Press.
Lauterbach, Karen. 2016. 'Religious entrepreneurs in Ghana' in Ute Röschenthaler and Dorothea Schulz (eds), *Cultural Entrepreneurship in Africa*. London and New York NY: Routledge.
Leichtman, Mara. 2015. *Shi'i cosmopolitanisms in Africa: Lebanese migration and religious conversion in Senegal*. Bloomington IN: Indiana University Press.
  2020. 'Transnational networks and global Shi'i Islamic NGOs in Tanzania' in Holger Weiss (ed.), *Muslim Faith-Based Organizations and Social Welfare in Africa*. Cham: Palgrave Macmillan.
Lentz, Carola. 2015. 'Elites or middle classes? Lessons from transnational research for the study of social stratification in Africa'. Arbeitspapiere des Instituts für Ethnologie und Afrikastudien der Johannes Gutenberg-Universität Mainz 161. Mainz: Johannes Gutenberg University.
Leurs, Robert, Peter Tumaini-Mungu, and Abu Mvungi. 2011. 'Mapping the development activities of faith-based organizations in Tanzania'. Working Paper 58. Birmingham: International Development Department, University of Birmingham.
Levtzion, Nehemia and Randall L. Pouwels (eds). 2000. *The History of Islam in Africa*. Athens OH: Ohio University Press.
Lindhardt, Martin. 2009. 'More than just money: the Faith Gospel and occult economy in contemporary Tanzania', *Nova Religio* 13 (1): 41–67.
Linke, Uli. 2015. 'Anthropology of collective memory' in James D. Wright (ed.), *International Encyclopedia of the Social and Behavioral Sciences. Volume 4*. 2nd edition. Oxford: Elsevier.
Lodhi, Abdulaziz Y. 1994. 'Muslims in Eastern Africa: their past and present', *Nordic Journal of African Studies* 3 (1): 88–98.
Loimeier, Roman. 1997. *Islamic Reform and Political Change in Northern Nigeria*. Evanston IL: Northwestern University Press.
  2007. 'Perceptions of marginalization: Muslims in contemporary Tanzania' in Benjamin F. Soares and René Otayek (eds), *Islam and Muslim Politics in Africa*. New York NY: Palgrave Macmillan.

2009. *Between Social Skills and Marketable Skills: the politics of Islamic education in Zanzibar in the 20th century*. Leiden: Brill.

2010. 'Traditions of reform, reformers of tradition: case studies from Senegal and Zanzibar/Tanzania' in Zulfiqa Hirji (ed.), *Diversity and Pluralism in Islam: historical and contemporary discourses among Muslims*. London and New York NY: I. B. Tauris in association with the Institute of Ismaili Studies.

2013. *Muslim Societies in Africa: a historical anthropology*. Bloomington IN: Indiana University Press.

Louw, Antoinette, Rory Robertshaw, and Anna Mtani. 2001. 'Dar es Salaam: victim surveys as a basis for city safety strategies', *African Security Review* 10 (1): 60–74.

Ludwig, Frieder. 1996. 'After Ujamaa: is religious revivalism a threat to Tanzania's stability?' in David Westerlund (ed.), *Questioning the Secular State: the world-wide resurgence of religion in politics*. London: C. Hurst and Co.

1997. *Das Modell Tanzania: Zum Verhältnis zwischen Kirche und Staat während der Ära Nyerere*. Berlin: Dietrich Reimer Verlag.

1999. *Church and State in Tanzania: aspects of a changing relationship, 1961–1994*. Leiden: Brill.

Magesa, Laurenti. 2007. 'Contemporary Catholic perspectives on Christian–Muslim relations in sub-Saharan Africa: the case of Tanzania', *Islam and Christian–Muslim Relations* 18 (2): 165–73.

Maghimbi, Sam. 2014. 'Secularization and the rise of religious fundamentalism in Tanzania' in Thomas Ndaluka and Frans Wijsen (ed.), *Religion and State in Tanzania Revisited: reflections from 50 years of independence*. Münster: Lit Verlag.

Mahmood, Saba. 2001. 'Feminist theory, embodiment, and the docile agent: some reflections on the Egyptian Islamic revival', *Cultural Anthropology* 16 (2): 202–36.

2006. 'Feminist theory, agency, and the liberatory subject: some reflections on the Islamic revival in Egypt', *Temenos* 42 (1): 31–71.

Maoulidi, Salma. nd. *Censoring Religious Hate Speech*. Unpublished manuscript.

2002. 'The predicament of Muslim women in Tanzania', *ISIM Newsletter* 10 (02): 25.

Marshall, Ruth. 2009. *Political Spiritualities: the Pentecostal revolution in Nigeria*. Chicago IL: University of Chicago Press.

Martin, Anastasia. nd. *Report of Form Four Examination Results: analysis of the year 2004/05. Results released March 2005 and February 2006*. Dar es Salaam: Christian Social Services Commission (CSSC).

Masebo, Oswald. 2014. 'An overview of the historiography of religion and state in post-colonial Tanzania, 1960s to the present' in Thomas Ndaluka and Frans Wijsen (ed.), *Religion and State in Tanzania Revisited: reflections from 50 years of independence*. Münster: Lit Verlag.

Masquelier, Adeline. 1999. 'Debating Muslims, disputed practices: struggles for the realization of an alternative moral order in Niger' in John L. Comaroff and Jean Comaroff (eds), *Civil Society and the Political Imagination in Africa: critical perspectives*. Chicago IL: University of Chicago Press.

2018. 'Schooling, spirit possession, and the "modern girl" in Niger' in Muriel Gomez-Perez (ed.), *Femmes d'Afrique et émancipation: entre norms sociales contraignantes et nouvaux possibles*. Paris: Karthala.

Matson, A. T. 1966. 'Sewa Haji: a note', *Tanzania Notes and Records* 65: 91–4.

Mattes, Dominik. 2020. 'Politicizing elsewhere(s): negotiating representations of neo-Pentecostal aesthetic practice in Berlin', *Religion and Society: Advances in Research* 11: 163–75.

Mattes, Dominik, Omar Kasmani, and Hansjörg Dilger. 2019a. '"All eyes closed": dis/sensing in comparative fieldwork on affective-religious experiences' in Antje Kahl (ed.), *Analyzing Affective Societies: methods and methodologies*. Studies in Affective Societies 2. London and New York NY: Routledge.

Mattes, Dominik, Omar Kasmani, Marion Acker, and Edda Heyken. 2019b. 'Belonging' in Christian von Scheve and Jan Slaby (eds), *Affective Societies: key concepts*. Studies in Affective Societies 3. London and New York NY: Routledge.

Mattingly, Cheryl. 2012. 'Two virtue ethics and the anthropology of morality', *Anthropological Theory* 12 (2): 161–84.

2013. 'Moral selves and moral scenes: narrative experiments in everyday life', *Ethnos* 78 (3): 301–27.

2014. *Moral Laboratories: family peril and the struggle for a good life*. Berkeley CA: University of California Press.

Maxwell, David. 2006. *African Gifts of the Spirit: Pentecostalism and the rise of a Zimbabwean transnational religious movement*. Oxford: James Currey.

Mazrui, Alamin M. 2004a. *English in Africa after the Cold War*. Clevedon: Multilingual Matters.

2004b. 'Media of instruction in African education: the continuing paradox of dependency', *NORRAG News* 34 (September), www.norrag.org/fileadmin/Full%20Versions/NN34.pdf (accessed 8 January 2015).

2017. 'The Arabic stimulus to the Swahili language: a post-colonial balance sheet', *JULACE: Journal of University of Namibia Language Centre* 2 (2): 51–67.

Mazrui, Alamin M. and Michael Tidy. 1984. *Nationalism and New States in Africa from about 1935 to the Present*. Nairobi: Heinemann.

Mbembe, Achille. 2001. *On the Postcolony*. Berkeley CA: University of California Press.

Mbilinyi, Marjorie. 1980. 'African education during the British colonial period, 1919–1961' in Martin H. Y. Kaniki (ed.), *Tanzania under Colonial Rule*. London: Longman Group.

Mbogoni, Lawrence E. Y. 2005. *The Cross versus the Crecent: religion and politics in Tanzania from the 1980s to the 1990s*. Dar es Salaam: Mkuki na Nyota Publishers.

McClutcheon, Russel T. 2006. '"It's a lie. There's no truth in it! It's a Sin!" On the limits of the humanistic study of religion and the costs of saving others from themselves', *Journal of the American Academy of Religion* 74 (3): 720–50.

Meyer, Birgit. 1998a. '"Make a complete break with the past": memory and postcolonial modernity in Ghanaian Pentecostal discourse' in Richard

Werbner (ed.), *Memory and the Postcolony: African anthropology and the critique of power*. London: Zed Books.

1998b. 'Commodities and the power of prayer: Pentecostalist attitudes towards consumption in contemporary Ghana', *Development and Change* 29 (4): 751–76.

1999. *Translating the Devil: religion and modernity among the Ewe in Ghana*. Edinburgh: Edinburgh University Press.

2004. 'Christianity in Africa: from African Independent to Pentecostal-Charismatic churches', *Annual Review of Anthropology* 33: 447–74.

Moffett, J. P. (ed.). 1958. *The Handbook of Tanganyika*. 2nd edition. Dar es Salaam: Government Printer.

Monnot, Christophe. 2018. 'Unmasking the relations of power within the religious field' in Véronique Altglas and Matthew Wood (ed.), *Bringing Back the Social into the Sociology of Religion: critical approaches*. Leiden: Brill.

Morrell, Robert. 2001. 'Corporal punishment in South African schools: a neglected explanation for its existence', *South African Journal of Education* 21 (4): 292–9.

Mostowlansky, Till. 2020. 'Humanitarian affect: Islam, aid and emotional impulse in northern Pakistan', *History and Anthropology* 31 (2): 236–56.

Mukandala, Rwekaza, Saida-Othman Yahya, Samwel S. Mushi, and Laurian Ndumbaro (eds). 2006. *Justice, Rights and Worship: religion and politics in Tanzania*. Dar es Salaam: E&D Limited.

Mundy, Karen, Andy Green, Bob Lingard, and Antoni Verger. 2016. 'Introduction: the globalization of education policy – key approaches and debates' in Karen Mundy, Andy Green, Bob Lingard, and Antoni Verger (eds), *Handbook of Global Education Policy*. Chichester: John Wiley and Sons.

Munn, Nancy D. 1992. 'The cultural anthropology of time: a critical essay', *Annual Review of Anthropology* 21: 93–123.

Mushi, Philemon A. K. 2009. *History and Development of Education in Tanzania*. Dar es Salaam: Dar es Salaam University Press.

Musoke, Issa K. 2006. 'The relationship between religion and employment in Tanzania' in Rwekaza Mukandala et al. (eds), *Justice, Rights and Worship: religion and politics in Tanzania*. Dar es Salaam: E&D Limited.

Mwakimako, Hassan. 2007. 'Christian–Muslim relations in Kenya: a catalogue of events and meanings', *Islam and Christian–Muslim Relations* 18 (2): 287–307.

Ndaluka, Thomas. 2014a. '"We are ill-treated": a critical discourse analysis of Muslims' social differentiation claims in Tanzania' in Thomas Ndaluka and Frans Wijsen (eds), *Religion and State in Tanzania Revisited: reflections from 50 years of independence*. Münster: Lit Verlag.

2014b. 'Society and Religion Research Centre (SORRECE)' in Thomas Ndaluka and Frans Wijsen (eds), *Religion and State in Tanzania Revisited: reflections from 50 years of independence*. Münster: Lit Verlag.

2014c. 'How Christians speak about Muslims' in Thomas Ndaluka and Frans Wijsen (eds), *Religion and State in Tanzania Revisited: reflections from 50 years of independence*. Münster: Lit Verlag.

2014d. 'General introduction: "The world is too fragile, handle it with prayer!" (Mwalimu Julius K. Nyerere)' in Thomas Ndaluka and Frans Wijsen (eds),

Religion and State in Tanzania Revisited: reflections from 50 years of independence. Münster: Lit Verlag.
Ndaluka, Thomas and Frans Wijsen (eds). 2014. *Religion and State in Tanzania Revisited: reflections from 50 years of independence*. Münster: Lit Verlag.
Ndaluka, Thomas, Salvatory Nyanto, and Frans Wijsen. 2014. '"Things are getting out of control": an analysis of Muslim revivalism discourses in Tanzania' in Thomas Ndaluka and Frans Wijsen (eds), *Religion and State in Tanzania Revisited: reflections from 50 years of independence*. Münster: Lit Verlag.
NECTA. 2005. *Taarifa Ya Ziara Ya Mafunzo Nchini Uganda, Tarehe 29/05/2005–05/06/2005*. Dar es Salaam: National Examination Council of Tanzania / Baraza la Mitihani la Tanzania (NECTA).
2012. *Certificate of Secondary Education Examination Centers Ranking (Category 1: Examination centers with 40 and more registered candidates)*. Dar es Salaam: National Examination Council of Tanzania / Baraza la Mitihani la Tanzania (NECTA).
2013. *Certificate of Secondary Education Examination Centers Ranking (Category 1: Examination centers with 40 and more registered candidates)*. Dar es Salaam: National Examination Council of Tanzania / Baraza la Mitihani la Tanzania (NECTA).
Ng'atigwa, Francis Xavier. 2013. 'The media in society: religious radio stations, socio-religious discourse and national cohesion in Tanzania'. PhD thesis, University of Bayreuth.
Nimtz, August H., Jr. 1980. *Islam and Politics in East Africa: the Sufi order in Tanzania*. Minneapolis MN: University of Minnesota Press.
Njozi, Hamza M. 2002. *Mwembechai Killings, and the Political Future of Tanzania*. Ottawa: Globalink Communications.
Nolte, Insa, Rebecca Jones, Khadijeh Taiyari, and Giovanni Occhiali. 2016. 'Exploring survey data for historical and anthropological research: Muslim–Christian relations in southwest Nigeria', *African Affairs* 115 (460): 541–61.
Nolte, Insa, Olukoya Ogen, and Rebecca Jones (eds). 2017. *Beyond Religious Tolerance: Muslim, Christian and traditionalist encounters in an African town*. Rochester NY: James Currey and Boydell and Brewer.
Nora, Pierre. 1989. 'Between memory and history: les lieux de mémoire', *Representations* 26 (Spring): 7–24 [special issue: 'Memory and counter-memory'].
Nóvoa, António. 2002. 'Ways of Thinking about Education in Europe' in Nóvoa António and Martin Lawn (eds), *Fabricating Europe*. Dordrecht: Springer.
Obadare, Ebenezer. 2006. 'Pentecostal presidency? The Lagos–Ibadan "theocratic class" and the Muslim "other"', *Review of African Political Economy* 33 (110): 665–78.
2007. 'Religious NGOs, civil society and the quest for a public sphere in Nigeria', *African Identities* 5 (1): 135–53.
2018. *Pentecostal Republic: religion and the struggle for state power in Nigeria*. London: Zed Books.

Ojo, Matthews. 2007. 'Pentecostal movements, Islam and the contest for public space in northern Nigeria', *Islam and Christian–Muslim Relations* 18 (2): 175–88.
Ojong, Vivian Besem. 2008. 'Religion and Ghanaian women entrepreneurship in South Africa', *Journal for the Study of Religion* 21 (2): 63–84.
Oliver, Roland. 1952. *The Missionary Factor in East Africa*. London: Longmans, Green and Co.
Olupona, Jacob. 2011. *City of 201 Gods: Ilé-Ifè in time, space, and the imagination*. Berkeley CA: University of California Press.
Omari, C. K. 1984. 'Christian–Muslim relations in Tanzania: the socio-political dimension', *Institute of Muslim Minority Affairs. Journal* 5 (2): 373–90.
Ong, Aihwa and Stephen Collier (eds). 2004. *Gobal Assemblages: technology, politics and ethics as anthropological problems*. Malden MA: Wiley-Blackwell.
Osella, Filippo and Caroline Osella. 2010. 'Muslim entrepreneurs in public life between India and the Gulf: making good and doing good' in Filippo Osella and Benjamin Soares (eds), *Islam, Politics, Anthropology*. Oxford: Blackwell.
Palmer, Gary B. and William R. Jankowiak. 1996. 'Performance and imagination: toward an anthropology of the spectacular and mundane', *Cultural Anthropology* 11 (2): 225–58.
Pauli, Julia. 2018. 'Pathways into the middle: rites of passage and emerging middle classes in Namibia' in Lena Kroeker, David O'Kane, and Tabea Scharrer (eds), *Middle Classes in Africa: changing lives and conceptual challenges*. Cham: Palgrave Macmillan.
PCT. 2008. *Tamko la Maaskofu na Wachungaji wa PCT. Mkoa wa Dar es Salaam Kuhusu Ukiukwaji wa Katiba ya Jamhuri ya Muungano wa Tanzania Katika Kuingiza Mahakama ya Kadhi Ndani ya Katiba na Nchi ya Tanzania kuwa Mwanachama wa OIC*. Dar es Salaam: Pentecostal Churches of Tanzania (PCT).
Peel, John D. Y. 2015. *Christianity, Islam, and Orisa-Religion: three traditions in comparison and interaction*. Berkeley CA: University of California Press.
Pels, Peter. 2013 [1999]. *A Politics of Presence: contacts between missionaries and Walugru in late colonial Tanganyika*. London and New York NY: Routledge.
PEPFAR. 2019. *Tanzania Country Operational Plan COP 2019: strategic direction summary May 10, 2019*. Washington DC: President's Emergency Plan For AIDS Relief (PEPFAR), www.state.gov/wp-content/uploads/2019/09/Tanzania_COP19-Strategic-directional-Summary_public.pdf (accessed 5 August 2021).
Pfeiffer, Constanze, Collins K. Ahorlu, Sandra Alba, and Brigit Obrist. 2017. 'Understanding resilience of female adolescents towards teenage pregnancy: a cross-sectional survey in Dar es Salaam, Tanzania', *Reproductive Health* 14 (1): 1–12.
Phillips, Kristin. 2011. 'Educational policymaking in the Tanzanian postcolony: authenticity, accountability, and the politics of culture', *Critical Studies in Education* 52 (3): 235–50.
Phillips, Kristin and Amy Stambach. 2008. 'Cultivating choice: the invisible hands of educational opportunity in Tanzania' in Martin Forsey, Scott

Davies, and Geoffrey Walford (eds), *The Globalisation of School Choice?* Oxford: Symposium Books.

Pontzen, Benedikt. 2020. '"Those who pray together": religious practice, affect, and dissent among Muslims in Asante (Ghana)' in Hansjörg Dilger, Astrid Bochow, Marian Burchardt, and Matthew Wilhelm-Solomon (eds), *Affective Trajectories: religion and emotion in African cityscapes*. Durham NC: Duke University Press.

Possi, Mwajabu and Balla Maselle. 2006. 'Provision of education: infrastructure and resources' in Rwekaza Mukandala et al. (eds), *Justice, Rights and Worship: religion and politics in Tanzania*. Dar es Salaam: E&D Limited.

Punch, Samantha. 2002. 'Research with children: the same or different from research with adults?', *Childhood* 9 (3): 321–41.

Qorro, Martha. 2006. *Does Language of Instruction Affect Quality of Education?* Working Paper 8. Dar es Salaam: HakiElimu.

Quarles van Ufford, Philip and Matthew Schoffeleers (eds). 1988. *Religion and Development: towards an integrated approach*. Amsterdam: Free University Press.

Rasmussen, Lissi. 1993. *Christian–Muslim Relations in Africa: the cases of northern Nigeria and Tanzania compared*. London: British Academic Press.

Reihling, Hanspeter. 2013. 'Vulnerable men: gender and sentiment at the margins of Cape Town'. PhD thesis, Institute of Social and Cultural Anthropology, Freie Universität Berlin.

Robbins, Joel. 2013. 'Beyond the suffering subject: toward an anthropology of the good', *Journal of the Royal Anthropological Institute* 19 (3): 447–62.

Robertson, Roland and JoAnn Chirico. 1985. 'Humanity, globalization, and worldwide religious resurgence: a theoretical exploration', *Sociology of Religion* 46 (3): 219–42.

Röttger-Rössler, Birgitt. 2018. 'Multiple belongings: on the affective dimensions of migration', *Zeitschrift für Ethnologie* 143 (2): 237–61.

Rowe, Emma E. 2017. 'Politics, religion and morals: the symbolism of public schooling for the urban middle-class identity', *International Studies in Sociology of Education* 26 (1): 36–50.

Roy-Campbell, Zaline Makini. 1992. *Power or Pedagogy: choosing the medium of instruction in Tanzania*. Madison WI: University of Wisconsin.

Rukyaa, Julian Joseph. 2007. 'Muslim–Christian relations in Tanzania with particular focus on the relationship between religious instruction and prejudice', *Islam and Christian–Muslim Relations* 18 (2): 189–204.

Rydstrøm, Helle. 2001. 'Like a white piece of paper: embodiment and the moral upbringing of Vietnamese children', *Ethnos* 66 (3): 394–413.

2003. *Embodying Morality: growing up in rural northern Vietnam*. Honolulu: University of Hawai'i Press.

Sahlberg, Carl-Erik. 1986. *From Krapf to Rugambwa: a church history of Tanzania*. Nairobi: Evangel Publishing House.

Said, Mohamed. nd[a]. 'Islam and politics in Tanzania' [online], www.islamtanzania.org/nyaraka/islam_and_politics_in_tz.html (accessed 21 August 2019).

nd[b] 'Intricacies and intrigues in Tanzania: the question of Muslim stagnation in education' [online], www.islamtanzania.org/nyaraka/Elimu2.html (accessed 8 May 2019).

1998. *The Life and Times of Abdulwahid Sykes (1924–1968): the untold story of the Muslim struggle against British colonialism in Tanganyika*. London: Minerva Press.
  2014. 'In memory of Ally Kleist Sykes (1926–2013)' [online], www.mohammedsaid.com/2014/05/in-memory-of-ally-kleist-sykes-1926-2013.html (accessed 8 August 2015).
Salzbrunn, Monika. 2014. *Vielfalt/Diversität*. Bielefeld: Transcript.
Sanders, Ethan R. 2011. 'Missionaries and Muslims in East Africa before the Great War'. Henry Martyn Seminar, Westminster College, Cambridge.
Saurer, Michael. 2018. 'Konversionsprozesse in Ankole, Uganda. Initiation, Segregation und Aushandlung'. PhD thesis, Fachbereich Politik- und Sozialwissenschaften, Freie Universität Berlin.
Scharrer, Tabea. 2007. 'Konversion in Ostafrika im Spannungsfeld zwischen islamischer und christlicher Mission', *Historische Anthropologie* 15 (1): 118–25.
  2013. *Narrative islamischer Konversion. Biographische Erzählungen konvertierter Muslime in Ostafrika*. Bielefeld: Transcript.
Scharrer, Tabea, David O'Kane, and Lena Kroeker. 2018. 'Introduction: Africa's middle classes in critical perspective' in Lena Kroeker, David O'Kane, and Tabea Scharrer (eds), *Middle Classes in Africa: changing lives and conceptual challenges*. Cham: Palgrave Macmillan.
Schielke, Samuli. 2009. 'Ambivalent commitments: troubles of morality, religiosity and aspiration among young Egyptians', *Journal of Religion in Africa* 39 (2): 158–85.
Schnegg, Michael and Michael Bollig. 2016. 'Institutions put to the test: community-based water management in Namibia during a drought', *Journal of Arid Environments* 124: 62–71.
Schulz, Dorothea E. 2006. 'Promises of (im)mediate salvation: Islam, broadcast media, and the remaking of religious experience in Mali', *American Ethnologist* 33 (2): 210–29.
  2011. *Muslims and New Media in West Africa: pathways to God*. Bloomington IN: Indiana University Press.
  2013. '(En)gendering Muslim self-assertiveness: Muslim schooling and female elite formation in Uganda', *Journal of Religion in Africa* 43 (4): 396–425.
Schulz, Dorothea and Hansjörg Dilger (eds). 2013. 'Politics of religious schooling: Christian and Muslim engagements with education in Africa', *Journal of Religion in Africa* 43 (4) [special issue].
Schulz, Dorothea and Souleymane Diallo. 2016. 'Competing assertions of Muslim masculinity in contemporary Mali', *Journal of Religion in Africa* 46 (2–3): 219–50.
Scudder, Thayer and Elizabeth Colson. 1979. 'Long-term research in Gwembe Valley, Zambia' in George M. Foster, Thayer Scudder, Elizabeth Colson, and Robert V. Kemper (eds), *Long-Term Field Research in Anthropology*. New York NY: Academic Press.
Seabright, Paul. 2016. 'Religion and entrepreneurship: a match made in heaven?', *Archives de Sciences Sociales des Religions* 175 (3): 201–19.
Setel, Philip W. 1999. *A Plague of Paradoxes: AIDS, culture, and demography in northern Tanzania*. Chicago IL: University of Chicago Press.

Settler, Federico and Maria Haugaa Engh. 2018. 'Religion and migration in Africa and the African diaspora', *Alternation Journal* 22: 1–10, https://journals.ukzn.ac.za/index.php/soa/article/view/1217 (accessed 22 December 2020).

Shavit, Uriya and Frederic Wiesenbach. 2012. 'An "integrating enclave": the case of Al-Hayat, Germany's first Islamic fitness center for women in Cologne', *Journal of Muslim Minority Affairs* 32 (1): 47–61.

Sheriff, Abdul. 1987. *Slaves, Spices and Ivory in Zanzibar*. London: James Currey.

Shore, Chris and Susan Wright. 2015. 'Governing by numbers: audit culture, rankings and the new world order', *Social Anthropology* 23 (1): 22–8.

Shura ya Maimamu Tanzania, Kamati Kuu ya Siasa. 2009. *Kuelekea Uchaguzi Mkuu 2010: Muongozo kwa Waislamu*. Dar es Salaam: Rajab 1430.

Simpson, Anthony. 1998. 'Memory and becoming chosen other: fundamentalist elite-making in a Zambian Catholic mission school' in Richard Werbner (ed.), *Memory and the Postcolony*. London: Zed Books.

  2003. *'Half-London in Zambia': contested identities in a Catholic mission school*. Edinburgh: Edinburgh University Press.

Simpson, Edward and Kai Kresse (eds). 2008. *Struggling with History: Islam and cosmopolitanism in the western Indian Ocean*. New York NY: Columbia University Press.

Singleton, Michael. 1977. 'Muslims, missionaries and the millennium in upcountry Tanzania', *Cultures et Développement* IX (2): 247–314.

Sivalon, John C. 1995. 'The Catholic church and Tanzania state in the provision of social services' in Joseph Semboja and Ole Therkilsden (eds), *Service Provision under Stress in East Africa*. Copenhagen: Villiers Publications.

Smith McKinnon, Allan. 2017. 'On being Charismatic brethren: roots and shoots of Pentecostal Evangelism in Tanzania'. PhD thesis, Department of Theology and Religion, University of Birmingham.

Soares, Benjamin. 2006. 'Introduction' in Benjamin F. Soares (ed.), *Muslim–Christian Encounters in Africa*. Leiden: Brill.

  2016. 'Reflections on Muslim–Christian encounters in West Africa', *Africa* 86 (4): 673–97.

Sommers, Marc. 2001. *Fear in Bongoland: Burundi refugees in urban Tanzania*. New York NY and Oxford: Berghahn Books.

Spear, Thomas and Isaria N. Kimambo (eds). 1999. *East African Expressions of Christianity*. Athens OH: Ohio University Press.

Spronk, Rachel. 2012. *Ambiguous Pleasures: sexuality and middle class self-perceptions in Nairobi*. New York NY: Berghahn Books.

  2018. 'Afterword. The (idea of) African middle classes: theorizing *from* Africa' in Lena Kroeker, David O'Kane, and Tabea Scharrer (eds), *Middle Classes in Africa: changing lives and conceptual challenges*. Cham: Palgrave Macmillan.

Stambach, Amy. 2000. *Lessons from Mount Kilimanjaro: schooling, community, and gender in East Africa*. New York NY: Routledge.

  2004. 'Faith in schools: toward an ethnography of education, religion, and the state', *Social Analysis: The International Journal of Anthropology* 48 (3): 90–107.

  2006. 'Revising a four-square model of a complicated whole: on the cultural politics of religion and education', *Social Analysis* 50 (3): 1–18.

References 255

    2010a. *Faith in Schools: religion, education, and American Evangelicals in East Africa*. Stanford CA: Stanford University Press.

    2010b. 'Education, religion and anthropology in Africa', *Annual Review of Anthropology* 39: 361–79.

    2014. *Confucius and Crisis in American Universities: culture, capital, and diplomacy in US public higher education*. London: Routledge.

    2017. 'Introduction' in Amy Stambach and Kathleen D. Hall (eds), *Anthropological Perspectives on Student Futures: youth and the politics of possibility*. New York NY: Palgrave Macmillan.

Stambach, Amy and Zolani Ngwane. 2011. 'Development, post-colonialism, and global networks as frameworks for the study of education in Africa and beyond' in Bradely A. U. Levinson and Mica Pollock (eds), *A Companion to the Anthropology of Education*. Malden MA: Wiley-Blackwell.

Stites, Regie and Ladislaus Semali. 1991. 'Adult literacy for social equality or economic growth? Changing agendas for mass literacy in China and Tanzania', *Comparative Education Review* 35 (1): 44–75.

Strayer, Robert W. 1973. 'The making of mission schools in Kenya: a microcosmic perspective', *Comparative Education Review* 17 (3): 313–30.

Strong, Thomas. 2017. 'Becoming witches: sight, sin, and social change in the Eastern Highlands of Papua New Guinea' in Knut Rio, Michelle MacCarthy, and Ruy Blanes (eds), *Pentecostalism and Witchcraft: spiritual warfare in Africa and Melanesia*. Cham: Palgrave Macmillan.

Sumra, Suleman and Joviter K. Kataboro. 2014. *Decling Quality of Education: suggestions for arresting and reversing the trend*. Discussion Paper 63. Dar es Salaam: Economic and Social Research Foundation.

Swain, Jon. 2003. 'How young schoolboys become somebody: the role of the body in the construction of masculinity', *British Journal of Sociology of Education* 24 (3): 299–314.

Swinkels, Michiel and Anouk de Koning. 2016. 'Introduction: humour and anthropology', *Etnofoor* 28 (1): 7–10.

Tamim, Faraj Abdallah and Malinda Smith. 2010. 'Human rights and insecurities: Muslims in post-9/11 East Africa' in Malinda Smith (ed.), *Securing Africa: post 9/11 discourses on terrorism*. Farnham: Ashgate.

Tanzania. nd. *Requirements for Registration of Societies*. Dar es Salaam: Ministry of Home Affairs, United Republic of Tanzania.

    1977. *The Constitution of the United Republic of Tanzania of 1977*. Dar es Salaam: United Republic of Tanzania.

    1995. *Education and Training Policy*. Dar es Salaam: Ministry of Education and Culture.

    2002. *The Societies Act*. Dar es Salaam: Parliament of the United Republic of Tanzania.

    2004. *Secondary Education Development Plan (2004–2009)*. Dar es Salaam: Education Sector Development Programme, Ministry of Education and Culture, United Republic of Tanzania.

    2010. *Secondary Education Development Programm II (July 2010–June 2015)*. Dar es Salaam: Education Sector Development Programme, Ministry of Education and Vocational Training, United Republic of Tanzania.

Tayob, Abdulkader. 2017. 'The national policy on religion and education, and religious dress observances in South African schools' in M. Christian Green, Rosalind I. J. Hackett, Len Hansen, and Francois Venter (eds), *Religious Pluralism, Heritage and Social Development in Africa*. Stellenbosch: Sun Media Bloemfontein.

——— 2018. 'The representation of religion in religion education: notes from the South African periphery', *Education Sciences* 8 (3): 146.

ter Haar, Gerrie. 2011. 'Religion and development: introducing a new debate' in Gerrie ter Haar (ed.), *Religion and Development: ways of transforming the world*. London: C. Hurst and Co.

Throop, C. Jason. 2012. 'Moral sentiments' in Didier Fassin (ed.), *A Companion to Moral Anthropology*. Hoboken NJ: Wiley-Blackwell.

TIE. 2008a. *Mwongozo wa Uandishi wa Mihtasari ya Masomo ya Elimu ya Dini ya Kiislamu*. Dar es Salaam: Tanzania Institute of Education (TIE).

——— 2008b. *Mwongozo wa Uandishi wa Mihtasari ya Masomo ya Elimu ya Dini ya Kikristo*. Dar es Salaam: Tanzania Institute of Education (TIE).

Tolmacheva, Marina. 1976. 'The origin of the name Swahili', *Tanzania Notes and Records* 77–8: 27–37.

Towse, Peter, David Kent, Funja Osaki, and Noah Kiruac. 2002. 'Non-graduate teacher recruitment and retention: some factors affecting teacher effectiveness in Tanzania', *Teaching and Teacher Education* 18 (6): 637–52.

Trimingham, John Spencer. 1964. *Islam in East Africa*. Oxford: Oxford University Press.

Tripp, Aili Maria. 1997. *Changing the Rules: the politics of liberalization and the urban informal economy in Tanzania*. Berkeley CA: University of California Press.

——— 1999. 'The political mediation of ethnic and religious diversity in Tanzania' in Crawford Young (ed.), *The Accommodation of Cultural Diversity*. London: Palgrave Macmillan.

Turner, Jane. 2015. 'The disentchantment of Western performance training, and the search for an embodied experience: toward a methodology of the ineffable' in M. Perry and C. L. Medina (ed.), *Methodologies of Embodiment: inscribing bodies in qualitative research*. London: Routledge.

UMAKA. 2004. *Kumbukumbu za Kikao cha Viongozi wa Serikali na Madhehebu ya Dini Kuhusu Uboreshaji wa Kufundisha Somo la Dini Katika Shule za Msingi na Sekondari Tanzania. Kilichofanyika Chuo Cha Ualimu Dar es Salaam, Tarehe 5 Julai 2004*. Dar es Salaam: Umoja wa Madhehebu wa Mkoa wa Kagera (UMAKA).

US Department of State. 2007. *International Religious Freedom Report: Tanzania*. Washington DC: Bureau of Democracy, Human Rights and Labor, US Department of State, https://2009-2017.state.gov/j/drl/rls/irf/2007/90124.htm (accessed 18 August 2019).

——— 2014. *2013 International Religious Freedom Report: Tanzania*. Washington DC: Bureau of Democracy, Human Rights and Labor, US Department of State, www.state.gov/j/drl/rls/irf/religiousfreedom/index.htm?year=2013&dlid=222105#wrapper (accessed 8 May 2019).

van de Bruinhorst, Gerard C. 2007. *'Raise Your Voice and Kill Your Animals': Islamic discourses on the Idd El-Hajj and sacrifices in Tanga (Tanzania)*.

Authoritative texts, ritual practices and social identities. Leiden: International Institute for the Study of Islam (ISIM) and Amsterdam University Press.
van der Geest, Sjaak. 1990. 'Anthropologists and missionaries: brothers under the skin', *Man* 25 (4): 588–601.
van Dijk. 2010. 'Social catapulting and the spirit of entrepreneurialism' in Gertrud Hüwelmeier and Kristine Krause (eds), *Traveling Spirits: migrants, markets and mobilities.* New York NY and Abingdon: Routledge.
Van Klinken, Adriaan. 2019. *Kenyan, Christian, Queer: religion, LGBT activism and arts of resistance in Africa.* University Park PA: Pennsylvania State University Press.
Von Sicard, Sigvard. 1978. 'Christian and Muslim in East Africa', *Africa Theological Journal* 7 (2): 53–67.
Ware, Rudolph. 2014. *The Walking Qur'an: Islamic education, embodied knowledge, and history in West Africa.* Chapel Hill NC: University of North Carolina Press.
Weiss, Brad. 2004. 'Street Dreams: inhabiting masculine fantasy in neoliberal Tanzania' in Brad Weiss (ed.), *Producing African Futures: ritual and reproduction in a neoliberal age.* Leiden: Brill.
Westerlund, David. 1980a. *Ujamaa na Dini: a study of some aspects of society and religion in Tanzania, 1961–1977.* Stockholm: Almqvist and Wiksell International.
  1980b. 'Christianity and socialism in Tanzania, 1967–1977', *Journal of Religion in Africa* 11 (1): 30–55.
  1982. 'Freedom of religion under socialist rule in Tanzania, 1961–1977', *Journal of Church and State* 24 (1): 87–103.
Wiegele, Katherine L. 2013. 'On being a participant and an observer in religious ethnography: silence betrayal and becoming' in Hillary K. Crane and Deana L. Weibel (eds), *Missionary Impositions: conversion, resistance, and other challenges to objectivity in religious ethnography.* Lanham MD: Lexington.
Wijsen, Frans. 2014. '"Keep the conversation going": regulating Islamic revivalism in Tanzania' in Thomas Ndaluka and Frans Wijsen (eds), *Religion and State in Tanzania Revisited: reflections from 50 years of independence.* Münster: Lit Verlag.
Wijsen, Frans and Bernardin Mfumbusa. 2004. *Seeds of Conflict: religious tensions in Tanzania.* Nairobi: Paulines Publications Africa.
Wilkens, Katharina. 2009. *Holy Water and Evil Spirits: religious healing in the Marian faith healing ministry in Tanzania.* Münster: Lit. Verlag.
Willis, Paul E. 1977. *Learning to Labor: how working class kids get working class jobs.* Farnborough: Saxon House.
Winchester, Daniel. 2008. 'Embodying the faith: religious practice and the making of a Muslim moral habitus', *Social Forces* 86 (4): 1753–80.
Woods, Ruth. 2013. *Children's Moral Lives: an ethnographic and psychological approach.* Malden MA: Wiley-Blackwell.
World Bank. 2004. 'International Development Association. Program document for a proposed adjustment credit in the amount of SDR 82.7 million (US $123.6 million) and a grant in the amount of SDR 17.7 million (US$26.4 million) to the United Republic of Tanzania for a secondary education

development program'. Dar es Salaam: Country Department 4, World Bank Africa Regional Office, www-wds.worldbank.org/external/default/WDSContentServer/WDSP/IB/2004/05/18/000160016_20040518092331/Rendered/PDF/276310TA.pdf (accessed 8 May 2019).

Wortham, Stanton. 2006. *Learning Identity: the mediation of social identity through academic learning*. New York NY: Cambridge University Press.

2008. 'Linguistic anthropology of education', *Annual Review of Anthropology* 37: 37–51.

Wulf, Christoph. 2008. 'Mimetic learning', *Designs for Learning* 1 (1): 56–67.

2012. 'Towards a historical cultural anthropology of education: the Berlin ritual study' in Kathryn M. Anderson-Levitt (ed.), *Anthropologies of Education: a global guide to ethnographic studies of learning and schooling*. New York NY and Oxford: Berghahn Books.

Xu, Jing. 2014. 'Becoming a moral child amidst China's moral crisis: preschool discourse and practices of sharing in Shanghai', *Ethos* 42 (2): 222–42.

Yonemura, Akemi. 2010. 'IICBA, international migration of teachers: supply, quality, and ethical recruitment', *IICBA Newsletter* 12 (2): 2–3, https://unesdoc.unesco.org/ark:/48223/pf0000231310 (accessed 1 September 2020).

Index

Note: Page numbers with the suffix n indicate a footnote and those in bold indicate figures.

Africa Muslims Agency (AMA)
  aims, 139
  Dar es Salaam premises, 140
  finances, 139–41
  see also Al-Farouq Islamic Seminary for Boys
Aga Khan IV, 49, 78–89
Al-Farouq Islamic Seminary for Boys
  caning, 159–61, 198, 201, 225
  funding, 140–1
  local and translocal networking, 142–3, 174
  location, 101–2
  management, 140, 144
  marginal status, 148–9, 175, 221, 227–8
  mosque, 140, 156
  overseas donations, 140–1, 148–9
  parental expectations, 141, 146
  poor facilities, 149, 222
  role of faith downplayed, 145–6
  school fees, 140–1
  structural dependency, 148–9, 228
Al-Farouq Islamic Seminary for Boys pupils, 139–61
  declining academic performance, 141–3
  dress, 147
  exam preparation, 158
  family background, 148, 152–3
  future expectations, 148
  interest in Islam and politics, 27
  Islamic identity, 230
  Islamic Knowledge lessons, 153–4, 154n16
  Islamic religious and moral values, 146–7
  language concerns, 61n41
  lessons on un/ethical behavior, 151–2, **153**
  patriarchal masculinity, 154–7
  pupil transport concerns, 149–50
  student questionnaires, 27–8
Al-Farouq Islamic Seminary for Boys teachers
  encouraging and disciplining students, 157–61
  longevity of service, 144–5
  poor English language, 149
  salary dissatisfaction, 142, 144
  socioeconomic background, 143–4
  spirit of work, 143
  teaching style, 157–8, 223
  training, 143
Ali, Tahir, 83–7n25, 86–7
Ansaar Sunna, 138, 163
Ansar as-Sunna, 71
anthropology
  of education, 16
  morality and ethics, 15–16
  of religion, 232–3
  researcher positionality, 24–8
Arabic language, 57–9n38, 153, 162, 230
aspirations
  Christian pupils, 11
  Kenton High School, 107
  Kipata Girls' Islamic Seminary, 166, 228
  St. Joseph's schools, 190
  St. Mary's, 105–6

BAKWATA (National Muslim Council of Tanzania)
  criticisms, 137–8
  establishment, 70, 75
  study tour, 77
  successor to EAMWS, 75–86, 90
  training, 70
Baldegger Schwestern, 181
Baraza Kuu la Waislamu Tanzania *see* BAKWATA
Benedictine order, 181
Bible Knowledge, 23–30, 76

259

Index

Bongo Flava, 64
bridewealth, 155
British colonial rule, 45–50, 177

caning, 159–61, 198, 201, 225
Catholic Church
  and divisions in society, 189, 191–2
  letter on civic education, 65n3
  social welfare, 178–9, **180**
  Way of the Cross service, 213–15
Catholic schools
  ethical values, 178
  low status of teachers, 178
  privileged status, 175–8, 196–217
  relations with postcolonial state, 216
  summary, 30–1
  see also mission schools; missionaries; St. Joseph's schools
Christian church
  educational initiatives, 18
  services, 26–30
  social service provision, 72
  values and social class, 189
Christian organisations, 79, 81–2
Christian schools
  background, 23
  improved performance, 55
  international links, 19–29, 55
  privileged status, 19, 40, 221, 226
  religious knowledge, 23–30
  student governments, 202–3, 202n11, 222
  see also Catholic schools; St. Joseph's schools; St. Mary's schools
Christian Social Services Commission (CSSC), 8–9, 11, 72, 75, 179–84
Christian-Muslim relations
  changes of affiliation, 36
  Christian cultural reservations, 28n27
  claims and counterclaims, 94
  common but unequal ground, 29–30
  conversion, 19
  friction, 29–30, 37–40, 64–5, 219
  interreligious competition, 65–6, 73–4
  origins of conflict, 94
  pluralism, 232–3
  political power balance, 36–7
  social relations, 35
Christians, population numbers, 23n22, 37n5, 73–4
colonialism, 150–1
  see also British colonial rule; German colonial rule
community schools, 51–3

corporal punishment, 159–61, 198, 201, 225
Council of Imams (Shura la Maimamu), 70
Council of Pentecostal Churches of Tanzania (PCT), 67
cultural capital, 13–23n13, 38, 143

Dar es Salaam
  dangers of everyday life, 151–2
  diverse educational landscape, 2–3
  Islamic healing market, 70–1
  perceived moral dangers, 103n3, 103, 212
Dar es Salaam Pentecostal Church (DPC), 68
development aid, 71–2, 75
  Tanzania Muslim Welfare Network, 72–3
Dhala, Count Fatehali, 87
dhikr (ritual prayer), 69–70
discipline
  Al-Farouq Seminary, 157–61
  Kipata Girls' Islamic Seminary, 171–2
  St. Joseph's schools, 197–200, 217
  St. Mary's schools, 100, 109–12
divorce, 155
Dowdall, D.J.A., 83–7n25, 86–9
dress
  Al-Farouq Islamic Seminary, 147
  Full Gospel Bible Fellowship Church, 124–5
  Kenton High School, 125
  Kipata Girls' Islamic Seminary, 164–5, 168, 170–1
  St. Mary's schools, 120–5
  terminology, 170
  women, 156–7

East African Muslim Welfare Society (EAMWS), 85–93
  Certificate of Incorporation, 87
  challenges to conventional accounts, 90–3
  Muslim activists' accounts, 85–7
  Muslim schools, 137
  replaced by BAKWATA, 75–86, 90
  RITA files, 86–90, **91**, 94–5
  support for East African Muslims, 49, 87
EDIMASHUTA, 77
English language
  administrative language, 58
  educational shortcomings, 57–61
  faith-oriented schools, 23, 218
  Kenton High School concerns, 107–8
  language gap, 29, 38, 40, 61n41, 61–2
  neo-Pentecostal church, 68

Index

St. Mary's International Primary School, 99–100
in secondary education, 23, 55–6, 58
and social class, 58
students' coping mechanisms, 61–3
ethical values
Al-Farouq Islamic Seminary, 146–7, 151–2, **153**
Catholic schools, 178
Christian church, 189
compassion, 194–6
economic and political dimensions, 15–17, 22
embodied learning, 14–15
explicit aspects, 3
explicit and implicit aspects, 12–14, 223–4
faith-oriented schools, 2, 2n4, 126–7, 220
historical forces, 3–4
Islamic seminaries, 230
Kenton High School, 126
Kipata Girls' Islamic Seminary, 161, 164–5, 173–4
Lutheran seminary, 4–7
moral self-formation, 11–15
partial and pragmatic acceptance, 224–5
in quest for a good life, 3–4, 189, 218–19
in religious knowledge curriculum, 76–7
ritualised events, 222
St. Joseph's schools, 192, 197–200, 217
St. Mary's schools, 100–1, 118–26, 135
uncertainty and humour, 225–6

faith-oriented schools
admission policies, 229
advertisements, 3, 35–6
compared with government schools, 5–6, 12, 113
ethical values *see* ethical values
foundation for good life, 1–4, 218–19
and labor market prospects, 7
local and international networks, 220–2
political-economic dimensions, 3–4, 6–7, 16
post-privatisation, 1–3
processes of social differentiation, 228–9
realignment after deregulation, 2
religious diversity and cultural plurality, 229–32
statistics, 8n10
see also private schools
fees *see* school fees
Feza schools, 6–8n8, 138n2, 185

finance
Africa Muslims Agency (AMA), 139–41
Al-Farouq Seminary, 140–1
colonial era, 45–7
Kipata Girls' Islamic Seminary, 162–3
St. Joseph's schools, 183, 191–209
see also school fees
Full Gospel Bible Fellowship Church, 75, 124–5
fundamentalist religiosity, 29–30
Fundikira, Abdallah Said, 83–7n25, 87, 90, **91**, 93

German colonial rule, 43–5
government schools
compared with faith-oriented schools, 5–6, 12, 113
compared with Kipata Girls' Seminary, 164–5, 167–71
competition from private sector, 54–5
criticisms, 182–3
fixed budgets, 11
pupils, 189–90
under British rule, 47
see also community schools

hate speech, 64, 70
health services
colonial era, 46n21
funding, 45–6
HIV/AIDS projects, 73
Islamic healing market, 70–1
Ismaili medical centers, 48–9
history
British colonial rule, 45–50
coastal trading centers, 41
German colonial rule, 43–5
Islamic seminaries, 137–8
limited sources, 39–40
and memory, 38–9
Omani Sultanate, 42
postcolonial era, 50–2
St. Joseph's schools, 179–81
humour, 225–6

Ibn Batuta, 41
illiteracy, 51
inequalities
education reforms, 50–1
socioeconomic, 4–22
sociopolitical, 38, 71–2
socioreligious, 15, 29, 38
international links
Christian schools, 19–29, 55
Evangelical spectrum, 3

international links (cont.)
  faith-oriented schools, 220–2
  Muslim revivalists, 65, 70–1, 73
  Muslim schools, 19–29, 55n33
  neo-Pentecostalists, 65
  St. Joseph's, 190
  St. Mary's, 120
Islamic "infrastructures", 138
Islamic Knowledge, 23–30, 76, 153–4, 154n16, 162, 230
Islamic Propagation Centre, 70
Islamic revivalism, 19–29, 23n23, 227
Islamic rituals, 69–70
Islamic seminaries, 137–9, 174–5
  historical background, 137–8
  marginal status, 148–9, 175, 221, 227–8
  morality and Muslim identity, 230
  summary, 30
  see also Al-Farouq Islamic Seminary for Boys; Kipata Girls' Islamic Seminary
Ismaili schools, 48–9, 55n33

Kadhi court, 35
Kakobe, Bishop, 64, 75, 124–5
Karimjee, Alibhai Mohamedali, 87
Karimjee, Anver Ali, 88
Kenton High School
  advertisements, 3
  English language concerns, 107–8
  location, 104–6n8
  pupil aspirations, 107
  pupil transport, 104n5, 104–5, 107
  pupils from poor families, 106–7, 135, 228
  school fees, 107
  students' home kinship ties, 119
  teaching style, 112
  uniform, 125
  values lessons in English classes, 126
Khaki, Aziz, 88–9
Kikwete, Jakaya, 36–7, 37n4
Kinondoni Secondary School, 137
Kipata Girls' Islamic Seminary, 162–74
  curriculum, 162
  ethical and moral values, 161, 164–5, 173–4
  finances, 162–3
  Islamic network, 163
  location, 162
  (male) researcher's interview room, 168, **169**
  modernist orientation, 163–4
  objectives, 163
  parental aspirations, 166
  quality of facilities, 222
  school fees, 162, 166

Kipata Girls' Islamic Seminary pupils
  aspirations, 228
  benefits of single-sex education, 163, 167, 175
  dress, 164–5, 168, 170–1
  family background, 166–7
  moral agency, 168–71, 230
Kipata Girls' Islamic Seminary teachers
  discipline, 171–2
  headmistress, 162, 164–5
  male teachers, 167–8
  teaching style, 172–4
  training, 164
Kiswahili
  educational shortcomings, 57–61
  German era administrative language, 43
  lessons on un/ethical behavior, 151–2, **153**
  national language, 51n29
  postcolonial language of education, 50–1
  in primary school, 58–9
  students' coping mechanisms, 61–3
  teaching values and virtues, 125–6
Kurasini National Children's Home, 192–6

Lakha, Hassen Kassim, 87
languages
  language gap, 29, 38, 40, 61n41, 61–2
  see also Arabic language; English language; Kiswahili
league tables, 7–9
Life Bible Church, **79**

Maji Maji rebellion (1905-07), 44
marginalisation of Muslims, 29, 71–2, 148–51, 227
  Al-Farouq pupils, 148–9, 175, 221, 227–8
  historical marginalisation, 9, 27, 49–50
  Muslim schools, 227
marriage
  Al-Farouq pupils, 156–7, 226
  Islamic sermons, 156
  St. Joseph's discussion, 208–10, 225
  St. Joseph's rules, 200n10
Masasi, Saleh, 88
Mawlid celebration, 69–70
Mikocheni B Assemblies of God Church, 68–9, 102, 106n12, 124–5
Ministry of Education and Culture (MoEC), 76–7
Ministry of Home Affairs (MoHA), 78–82
mission schools
  growth under German rule, 43–5
  importance under British rule, 46–7

Index

Muslim students, 45n18, 47–8
nationalisation, 177
statistics, 43–7
missionaries
 British colonial rule, 177
 German colonial rule, 44–5
 as historical source, 39
 Omani Sultanate, 42–3
 Portuguese, 41–2
Mohammed, Bibi Titi, 86
moral sentiments, 15
 see also ethical values
Muslim Association of Tanganyika, 49
Muslim organisations
 educational initiatives, 18, 70
 nationalist movements, 49
 registrations, 82–3, **83**
 state surveillance, 71
Muslim pupils
 in Christian schools, 121, 125, 128–30, 185, 215–16
 in mission schools, 45n18, 47–8
 secondary level concerns, 51–2
Muslim revivalists
 criticism of religious instruction curriculum, 77
 diversity, 69, 69n7
 early reformers, 69–70
 government restrictions, 75
 interreligious competition, 64–5
 political reform organisations, 70
 proselytisation, 36
 public rallies, 72
 and sociopolitical inequalities, 38, 71–2
 Tanzania as a Christian state, 37, 72
 transnational links, 65, 70, 73
Muslim schools
 background, 23
 Feza schools, 6–8n8, 138n2, 185
 international links, 19–29, 55n33
 Ismaili schools, 48–9
 marginalisation, 227
 mistrust of fieldwork researcher, 26–7
 religious knowledge, 23–30
 socioreligious inequalities, 15
 terminology, 1n2
 transnational ties, 55n33
 weakness position, 19
Muslim Writers' Workshop (Warsha ya Waandishi wa Kiislam), 70
Muslims
 coastal trading centers, 41
 German colonial rule, 43, 45
 historical marginalisation, 9, 27, 49–50
 as "hostile" and "violent", 27–8
 institutional discrimination, 35, 71
 marginalisation, 29, 71–2, 148–51, 227
 marriage law, 75
 population numbers, 23n22, 37n5, 73–4

Nasibu, Adam, 86, 90
nation-building, 16, 40, 120, 217
National Muslim Council of Tanzania
 see BAKWATA (National Muslim Council of Tanzania)
Nazerally, V.M., 83–7n25, 88–9
NECTA (National Examination Council of Tanzania), 6–8n8, 77–8
neo-Pentecostal schools
 capitalist logics, 134–5
 entrepreneurial founders, 3, 100–1
 symbolism, **127**, 127–8
 see also St. Mary's schools
neo-Pentecostalists
 charity days, 68
 corruption allegations, 81–2
 diversity, 66–7, 67n5
 government restrictions, 75
 interreligious competition, 38n8, 64–5
 proselytisation, 36
 transnational ties, 65
 upper middle-class followers, 68–9
 urban and lower-middle class followers, 67–8
networks
 Al-Farouq Islamic Seminary, 142–3, 174
 faith-oriented schools, 220–2
 Kipata Girls' Islamic Seminary, 163
 St. Mary's schools, 101–2, 114–15
 St. Mary's teachers, 135–6
nongovernmental actors, 16, 18
Nyerere, Julius, 40, 50, 70, 75, 93–4, 178, 181

Omani Sultanate, 42
Organization of Islamic Conference (OIC), 35, 37, 72n10, 72
orphanage trip, St. Joseph's school, 192–6

Parliament (*mbunge*)
 Christianity issues, 69–77
 language problems debate, 59–61, 60n39
pedagogy *see* teaching style
Pentecostalists
 early missions, 66 *see also* neo-Pentecostalists
Phelps Stokes Commission, 45–6
population, religious affiliation, 23n22, 37n5, 73–4
Portuguese rule, 41–2

Primary Education Development Program (PEDP), 53n31
primary schools
  pupil playfulness, 23
  teaching styles, 172–4, 203–5
  see also Kipata Girls' Islamic Seminary; St. Joseph's Primary school; St. Mary's International Primary School
private schools
  early concerns over quality, 52–3
  increased numbers and performance, 54–6
  marginal locations, 101
  see also faith-oriented schools

Qur'anic schools (*madrasa*), 43n14, 43

reformist churches, 19–29, 23n23
Registration Insolvency and Trusteeship Agency (RITA), 82–3, **83**, 86–90
religious affiliation
  exclusion from post 1967 censuses, 74
  population, 23n22, 37n5, 73–4
  Tanzanian presidents, 36, 74
religious diversity, 35–6, 232
religious festivals, 35–7, 37n4
religious freedom, 73–4
religious hate speech, 64, 70
religious instruction, 18–30, 76–8
  PPI (pastoral program instruction), 129–32
  see also Islamic Knowledge
religious organisations
  increased registrations, 78, **78**
  open registrations, 78–9, **79**
  registration process, 74–8n15, 83
  rejected registrations, 77–84n20, **79**, 83–4
  see also Muslim organisations
religious schools see faith-oriented schools
research framework, 22–4
researcher positionality, 24–8, 226
RITA (Registration Insolvency and Trusteeship Agency), 82–3, **83**, 86–90, 139
Roman Catholic Church see Catholic Church
rural areas, 51, 177
Rwakatare, Gertrude
  on the English language, 59–61
  Mikocheni B Assemblies of God Church, 68–9, 102, 106n12, 124–5
  orphanage, 101–2
  parliamentary activities, 69–77
  rumours of *majini* (spirits), 102–3, 133

St. Mary's school network, 99, 101–2, 106–7, 113–15
  on social differentiation, 105
  support networks, 102

St. Joseph's primary school
  family backgrounds, 185
  group work, 204–5
  morning assemblies, 198, **199**
  orphanage trip, 192–6, **194**, 227
  Religion lessons, 207–8
  social differentiation, 190–1
St. Joseph's pupils
  ambitions, 190
  awareness of privilege, 190–1
  church services, 213–16
  close relations between male and female students, 201–12
  compassion, 194–6
  continuity across school levels, 185n6
  family backgrounds, 184–215
  international links, 190
  lack of connection to real life, 182, 189–92
  leisure pursuits, 190
  Muslim students, 185, 215–16
  non-Catholic pupils, 185, 214–17
  privilege and social distinctions, 190–2, 196, 227
  reasons for school choice, 185–6
  Secondary School, 184
  sponsorships, 191–2, 227
  student government, 202–3, 202n11
  study trips, 188, 190
St. Joseph's schools
  assemblies and prayers, 197–200
  Catholic affiliation, 231
  funding, 183, 191–209
  historical background, 179–81
  location, 179–81
  mission statements, 196–7
  moral disciplining, 197–200, 217
  moral responsibilities, 192
  punishments, 201
  Religion lessons, 207–10
  religious entrepreneurship, 183
  return to Archdiocese, 182
  visible Christian faith, 206–7
St. Joseph's Secondary (High) School
  assemblies, 198–200
  Divinity Studies, 201–10
  fees, 184
  kneeling as punishment, 201
  marriage and sexual relations, 200n10, 208–10, 225

Index

philosophical discussion on angels, 205–6, 226
refurbishment, 183
Religion lesson (love and marriage), 208–10
top-performing school, 6–8n8, 183–5, 184n4
uniform, 200
St. Joseph's teachers
  engagement with pupils, 194–200
  family responsibilities, 187
  headmistress, 182–3
  non-Catholic denominations, 214–17
  primary school, 186–7
  St. Joseph's preference over St. Mary's, 186–7
  school as social community, 187–8
  Secondary School, 187
  sense of inferior social status, 188–90, 216–17
  separation from pupils and respect, 201
  teaching style, 203–6, 222–3
  top school environment, 221
St. Mary's International Primary School
  Bible School, 120–1
  English language, 99–100
  fees, 105
  internal evaluation system, 114, 116–18
  location, 101–2
  quality of facilities, 109, 222
  values lessons in Kiswahili classes, 125–6
St. Mary's pupils
  aspirations, 105–6
  awareness of transitory social circumstances, 109–30, 135, 228
  boarding arrangements, 103
  dress codes, 120–5
  family background, 105–7
  home kinship ties, 115–19
  middle and upper class pupils, 105
  Muslim students, 121, 125, 128–30
  spirit (*majini*) healings, 101, 103, 132–4, 230–1
  study trips, 119–20
  transport, 104–5, 104n4, **109**
St. Mary's schools
  academic and moral belonging, 114–16, 135
  ambiguous experiences of faith, 127–9, 135
  assemblies, 124
  business-oriented approach, 100, 136
  compared unfavorably with St. Josephs, 186–7
  establishment, 99

moral education and guidance, 100–1, 103, **103**, 122–6
neo-Pentecostal symbolism, **127**, 127–8
PPI (pastoral program instruction), 129–32
privilege, 228
religious plurality, 127–9, 230–1
reputation, 100
school rituals, 120, 124
summary, 29–30
see also Kenton High School
St. Mary's teachers
  busyness, 111–13, 221
  caring discipline, 100, 109–12
  fellowshipping, 122–3, 230
  from abroad, 114–16, 118–23, 125–7
  insecure employment conditions, 100, 113–14, 228
  internal evaluations, 114, 116–18
  national and ethnic favoritism, 100, 115–16
  networks of belonging, 135–6
  salaries and work ethos, 112–13
  social interactions, 122
  teaching style, 110–12, 125–6
  see also Rwakatare, Gertrude
salaries
  Al-Farouq Islamic Seminary, 142, 144
  government sector, 113
  St. Mary's International Primary School, 112–13
school fees
  Al-Farouq Islamic Seminary, 140–1
  Christian schools, 5
  effect of transitory social circumstances, 109–30, 135
  Kenton High School, 107
  Kipata Girls' Islamic Seminary, 162, 166
  Muslim family struggles, 10
  St. Joseph's Secondary School, 184
  state rules, 5n7
Secondary Education Development Program (SEDP I), 53–4, 57
Secondary Education Development Program (SEDP II), 53–7n34, 54, 57
secondary schools
  background, 23
  English language, 55–6
  enrollment, 53–4
  quality concerns, 53–4
  quota system, 50, 52
  transition rates, 53–4
  young people's prospects, 55
sexual relations
  Al-Farouq pupils, 156–7, 226
  St. Joseph's discussion, 208–10, 225

Sharia law, 37, 72n10, 72
social class
  Al-Farouq Islamic Seminary, 148
  and English language, 58
  St. Mary's schools, 105–7, 133–5
socioeconomic inequalities, 4–22
sociopolitical inequalities, 38, 71–2
socioreligious inequalities, 15, 29, 38
spirit (*majini*) possession, 101, 103, 132–4, 230–1
statistics
  faith-oriented schools, 8n10
  mission schools, 43–7
  religious affiliation, 23n22, 37n5, 73–4
Sufism, 69–70, 70–1n8
Supreme Council of Islamic Organizations and Institutions in Tanzania (Baraza Kuu la Jumuyia na Taasisi za Kiislamu), 70

Tanganyika African Association, 35–49
Tanzania Muslim Professionals Organization (TAMPRO), 70
teacher training, 53–7n34, 143

teaching style
  Al-Farouq Islamic Seminary, 157–8, 223
  faith-oriented schools, 222–3
  Kenton High School, 112
  Kipata Girls' Islamic Seminary, 172–4
  primary schools, 172–4, 203–5
  St. Joseph's schools, 203–6, 222–3
  St. Mary's schools, 111–12
  schools, 203–5
terrorism
  effects of 9/11 and East African embassy attacks, 3, 139, 227
  government preventive measures, 19, 75
Tewa, Said Tewa, 86–8
transport
  Al-Farouq Islamic Seminary for Boys, 149–50
  St. Mary's schools, 104–5, 104n4, 109

Uamsho (The Awakening), 71

wazazi schools, 52–3n32, 53
World Bank, 53, 67, 226
World War I, 45

Titles in the Series

65. HANSJÖRG DILGER, *Learning Morality, Inequalities, and Faith: Christian and Muslim Schools in Tanzania*
64. MARLOES JANSON, *Crossing Religious Boundaries: Islam, Christianity, and 'Yoruba Religion' in Lagos, Nigeria*
63. DANELLE VAN ZYL-HERMANN *Privileged Precariat: White Workers and South Africa's Long Transition to Majority Rule*
62. BENEDIKT PONTZEN *Islam in a Zongo: Muslim Lifeworlds in Asante, Ghana*
61. LOUISA LOMBARD *Hunting Game: Raiding Politics in the Central African Republic*
60. MARK HUNTER *Race for Education: Gender, White Tone, and Schooling in South Africa*
59. LIZ GUNNER *Radio Soundings: South Africa and the Black Modern*
58. JESSICA JOHNSON *In Search of Gender Justice: Rights and Relationships in Matrilineal Malawi*
57. JASON SUMICH *The Middle Class in Mozambique: The State and the Politics of Transformation in Southern Africa*
56. JOSÉ-MARÍA MUÑOZ *Doing Business in Cameroon: An Anatomy of Economic Governance*
55. JENNIFER DIGGINS *Coastal Sierra Leone: Materiality and the Unseen in Maritime West Africa*
54. HANNAH HOECHNER *Quranic Schools in Northern Nigeria: Everyday Experiences of Youth, Faith, and Poverty*
53. HOLLY PORTER *After Rape: Violence, Justice, and Social Harmony in Uganda*
52. ALEXANDER THURSTON *Salafism in Nigeria: Islam, Preaching, and Politics*
51. ANDREW BANK *Pioneers of the Field: South Africa's Women Anthropologists*
50. MAXIM BOLT *Zimbabwe's Migrants and South Africa's Border Farms: The Roots of Impermanence*
49. MEERA VENKATACHALAM *Slavery, Memory and Religion in Southeastern Ghana, c.1850–Present*
48. DEREK PETERSON, KODZO GAVUA, and CIRAJ RASSOOL (eds) *The Politics of Heritage in Africa: Economies, Histories, and Infrastructures*
47. ILANA VAN WYK *The Universal Church of the Kingdom of God in South Africa: A Church of Strangers*
46. JOEL CABRITA *Text and Authority in the South African Nazaretha Church*
45. MARLOES JANSON *Islam, Youth, and Modernity in the Gambia: The Tablighi Jama'at*
44. ANDREW BANK and LESLIE J. BANK (eds) *Inside African Anthropology: Monica Wilson and Her Interpreters*
43. ISAK NIEHAUS *Witchcraft and a Life in the New South Africa*
42. FRASER G. MCNEILL *AIDS, Politics, and Music in South Africa*
41. KRIJN PETERS *War and the Crisis of Youth in Sierra Leone*
40. INSA NOLTE *Obafemi Awolowo and the Making of Remo: The Local Politics of a Nigerian Nationalist*

39. BEN JONES *Beyond the State in Rural Uganda*
38. RAMON SARRÓ *The Politics of Religious Change on the Upper Guinea Coast: Iconoclasm Done and Undone*
37. CHARLES GORE *Art, Performance and Ritual in Benin City*
36. FERDINAND DE JONG *Masquerades of Modernity: Power and Secrecy in Casamance, Senegal*
35. KAI KRESSE *Philosophising in Mombasa: Knowledge, Islam and Intellectual Practice on the Swahili Coast*
34. DAVID PRATTEN *The Man-Leopard Murders: History and Society in Colonial Nigeria*
33. CAROLA LENTZ *Ethnicity and the Making of History in Northern Ghana*
32. BENJAMIN F. SOARES *Islam and the Prayer Economy: History and Authority in a Malian Town*
31. COLIN MURRAY and PETER SANDERS *Medicine Murder in Colonial Lesotho: The Anatomy of a Moral Crisis*
30. R. M. DILLEY *Islamic and Caste Knowledge Practices among Haalpulaar'en in Senegal: Between Mosque and Termite Mound*
29. BELINDA BOZZOLI *Theatres of Struggle and the End of Apartheid*
28. ELISHA RENNE *Population and Progress in a Yoruba Town*
27. ANTHONY SIMPSON *'Half-London' in Zambia: Contested Identities in a Catholic Mission School*
26. HARRI ENGLUND *From War to Peace on the Mozambique–Malawi Borderland*
25. T. C. MCCASKIE *Asante Identities: History and Modernity in an African Village 1850–1950*
24. JANET BUJRA *Serving Class: Masculinity and the Feminisation of Domestic Service in Tanzania*
23. CHRISTOPHER O. DAVIS *Death in Abeyance: Illness and Therapy among the Tabwa of Central Africa*
22. DEBORAH JAMES *Songs of the Women Migrants: Performance and Identity in South Africa*
21. BIRGIT MEYER *Translating the Devil: Religion and Modernity among the Ewe in Ghana*
20. DAVID MAXWELL *Christians and Chiefs in Zimbabwe: A Social History of the Hwesa People c.1870s–1990s*
19. FIONA D. MACKENZIE *Land, Ecology and Resistance in Kenya, 1880–1952*
18. JANE I. GUYER *An African Niche Economy: Farming to Feed Ibadan, 1968–88*
17. PHILIP BURNHAM *The Politics of Cultural Difference in Northern Cameroon*
16. GRAHAM FURNISS *Poetry, Prose and Popular Culture in Hausa*
15. C. BAWA YAMBA *Permanent Pilgrims: The Role of Pilgrimage in the Lives of West African Muslims in Sudan*
14. TOM FORREST *The Advance of African Capital: The Growth of Nigerian Private Enterprise*
13. MELISSA LEACH *Rainforest Relations: Gender and Resource Use among the Mende of Gola, Sierra Leone*

12. ISAAC NCUBE MAZONDE *Ranching and Enterprise in Eastern Botswana: A Case Study of Black and White Farmers*
11. G. S. EADES *Strangers and Traders: Yoruba Migrants, Markets and the State in Northern Ghana*
10. COLIN MURRAY *Black Mountain: Land, Class and Power in the Eastern Orange Free State, 1880s to 1980s*
9. RICHARD WERBNER *Tears of the Dead: The Social Biography of an African Family*
8. RICHARD FARDON *Between God, the Dead and the Wild: Chamba Interpretations of Religion and Ritual*
7. KARIN BARBER *I Could Speak Until Tomorrow:* Oriki, *Women and the Past in a Yoruba Town*
6. SUZETTE HEALD *Controlling Anger: The Sociology of Gisu Violence*
5. GÜNTHER SCHLEE *Identities on the Move: Clanship and Pastoralism in Northern Kenya*
4. JOHAN POTTIER *Migrants No More: Settlement and Survival in Mambwe Villages, Zambia*
3. PAUL SPENCER *The Maasai of Matapato: A Study of Rituals of Rebellion*
2. JANE I. GUYER (ed.) *Feeding African Cities: Essays in Social History*
1. SANDRA T. BARNES *Patrons and Power: Creating a Political Community in Metropolitan Lagos*

Lightning Source UK Ltd.
Milton Keynes UK
UKHW022348111221
395473UK00003B/24

9 781316 514221